Transport Planning for Third World Cities

Transport Planning for Third World Cities

Edited by Harry T. Dimitriou
Assisted by
George A. Banjo

Routledge
London and New York

First published 1990
by Routledge
11 New Fetter Lane, London EC4P 4EE

Simultaneously published in the USA and Canada
by Routledge
a division of Routledge, Chapman and Hall, Inc.
29 West 35th Street, New York, NY 10001

Printed and bound in Great Britain by
Biddles Ltd, Guildford and King's Lynn

British Library Cataloguing in Publication Data

Transport planning for third world cities.
1. Developing countries. Transport services
I. Dimitriou, Harry T. II. Banjo, G. Adegboyega
380.5'09172'4

ISBN 0-415-00448-9

Library of Congress Cataloging in Publication Data has been applied for

Contents

Contents

Figures

Tables

Tables

Foreword

The need for the systematic planning of urban transport arose first in the USA. The dramatic increase in the number of private cars in the first half of the twentieth century combined with the generous layouts of American cities created problems for which the experience of the much slower introduction of mechanised transport in Europe did not provide adequate guidance.

Several engineering and research centres in the States took up the quest for a systematic approach to the solution of urban transport problems. These attempts ended up in an approach which, by the mid-1970s, was sufficiently standardised to allow the World Bank to incorporate it into guidelines to its staff on a worldwide basis. This approach became known as the *Urban Transport Planning Process* (usually known as the *UTP Process*) and after wide application in the States, was exported to Europe and Latin America and eventually, also to a number of the major Third World cities.

This volume contains an impressive list of the cities which, either directly or through international aid agencies, have employed well-known consultants to apply the UTP Process to their transportation problems. It is not surprising that many consultants have welcomed such opportunities of helping poor countries to benefit from the American research and experience. What should surprise us is that so few have asked the question 'Are demographic, social, economic, climatic and political conditions in such Third World cities sufficiently similar to those of the US cities to justify such a transfer?' The authors of this book are clearly among the few who have asked such questions. They are well qualified to do so, because they are not only transport planning experts, but have lived and worked long enough in developing countries to know what can – and cannot – be done in cities so different from those of the West. What is important is that the right questions are asked and investigated. Armed with this knowledge and personal experience, they have produced a book that will be of inestimable value to those concerned with the problems of the fast-growing Third World cities.

Otto Koenigsberger

Preface

In writing this book, the editors had two aims. The first was to provide a publication which assists the development of urban transport planning paradigms appropriate to Third World countries. The second objective was to produce a text for students of urban transport planning for that part of the world which has had to rely largely on literature based on the experience of industrialised nations.

The need to address these aims is manifestly clear from the rapidly increasing interest among professionals concerned with transport problems of Third World cities. It is also apparent from the growing investments made in the field and in the many failures of transport planning in such cities over the last two to three decades - many of which have been associated with the application of inappropriate policies, concepts and techniques.

The book provides not only a contextual account of Third World city transport problems and a review of the state of the art of urban transport planning, but also directions and techniques for future action based upon the experiences of a number of leading professionals and academics in the field.

At present, there is a dearth of books of this kind. Furthermore, many of the available publications tend to offer token transport chapters in some standard text on Third World city development and merely explain the transport 'situation' of such countries as a special variant of those found in industrialised countries. This outlook is challenged by the editors of this book, whose contention is that urban transport in the Third World requires study and understanding on its own terms.

Harry T. Dimitriou

Hong Kong

Acknowledgements

In producing this book, I am especially indebted to George Banjo with whom the idea of the publication was first conceived and who assisted in the editing of seven of the twelve chapters (Chapters 3, 4, 7, 8, 9, 10 and 11) and contributed to writing to the preface and introduction.

I am also indepted to a large number of other persons, too many to mention individually, who include academic and professional colleagues, students and clients. Through my experience of teaching and consultancy practice these people have over the years, helped me to further develop the book's framework by greatly influencing my thoughts.

In terms of book production, I am especially grateful to the following without whom this publication would have remained a set of manuscripts piled on desks in Lagos, London, Jakarta and Hong Kong - the various places where the book was edited. These are my wife, Vicky Dimitriou, who heroically typed what seemed to be endless drafts of the text; Diana Martin, who copy-edited the manuscript; Lau Kwan Wai, Tsang Ping Fai together with Dilys Lui, and her staff at the University of Hong Kong's Centre for Media Studies, who tolerated the many changes, and completed the graphic work for the book; and Ralph Gakenheimer of MIT, who encouraged me to complete the book at a time when all odds of this happening seemed rather slim.

I am indepted financially to Training and Development Consultants (TDC S.A.), Lausanne - a Swiss consultancy firm specialising in planning and training aspects of Third World urban transport - which met the costs of preparing the book.

The vast range of international material drawn on during the long period of preparation of this publication may mean that acknowledgements to some sources have unwittingly been overlooked. If and where this is so, authors are encouraged to inform the editors of this, so that due acknowledgement can be made.

Finally, I am grateful to the authors and publishers for permission to reproduce in a revised or redrawn form the following copyright of materials:

Redrawn Book Cover Design from Independent Commission on International Development Issues (1981): North-South: A Program for Survival, Pan Books with copyright of permission given by Dr. Arno Peters of the University of Bremen (reproduced here as **Figure 1.1**).

Figure 4.3 from World Bank (1984): World Development Report, Oxford University Press (reproduced here as **Figure 1.3**).

Tables 1, 27 and 32 from World Bank (1988): World Development Report, Oxford University Press, (reproduced here as **Appendix Tables 1.1, 1.2 and 1.3** respectively).

Table 2.3 from World Bank (1984): World Development Report, Oxford University Press (reproduced here as **Appendix Table 1.4**).

Figures 4 and 2 from World Bank (1986): Urban Transport: A World Bank Policy Paper (reproduced here as **Figures 2.2 and 2.3** respectively).

Figure 4 from Banjo, G.A. and Dimitriou, H.T. (1983): Urban Transport Problems of Third World Cities: The Third Generation, Habitat International (reproduced here as **Figure 2.6**).

Figure from Proudlove, J.A. (1968): Some Comments on the West Midlands Transport Study, Traffic Engineering and Control (reproduced here as **Figure 5.1**).

Figure 11.1 from Institution of Highways and Transportation, and Department of Transport (1987); Roads and Traffic in Urban Areas, HMSO (reproduced here as **Figure 5.3**).

Figure 1.1 from Hutchinson B.G. (1974): Principles of Urban Transport Systems Planning, Hemisphere Publishing Corporation, USA (reproduced here as **Figure 5.4**).

Figures 4.1, 4.6, 3.7 and 3.12 from TDC S.A. (1988): IUIDP Policy, Planning and Design Guidelines for Urban Road Transport (reproduced here as **Figures 12.3, 12.4, 12.5 and 12.6**, respectively).

Table 9 from Hamer et al (1986): Indonesia, World Bank (reproduced here as **Table 12.1**).

Figure of Transport Gaps from Bouladon (1967b): The Transport Gaps, Science Journal (reproduced here as **Figure 12.1**).

Introduction

Harry T. Dimitriou

This publication contains twelve chapters and is divided into three parts.

Part One is devoted to an examination of the key problems and issues of transport in the fast growing cities of the Third World. These issues are investigated within the wider context of the urban development process, since an underlying premise of the book, emphasised in Part One, is that urban transport problems cannot be viewed in isolation from the wider development experience.

Part Two provides a review of key concepts and methodologies currently employed in transport planning for Third World cities, giving special attention to project appraisal and institutional development. The various contributions examine the relevance of developments in the field for the Third World. Particular attention is paid to the appropriateness of transferring transport planning principles and techniques formulated in the industrialised countries to totally different development contexts.

The third and final part of the book examines some emerging approaches to urban transport planning for the Third World. Whilst the approaches vary, all tackle aspects of the urban transport problem within a framework and set of policies responsive to wider development circumstances of Third World settlements.

Chapter 1 provides an overview of the relationship between transport, city development and Third World development. It commences by outlining the problems of defining the Third World, and classifying the countries included. Common characteristics of Third World city development are described, including the transport features, and the implications of these on the pursuance of transport and urban development goals are traced.

Chapter 2 argues, among other things, that many aspects of what is conventionally called 'the urban transport problem' are in fact manifestations of other problems. The chapter investigates the extent to which various analyses of this problem are products of particular professional or disciplinary perceptions and in terests, and dwells on the complex issue of technology-transfer in efforts at problem resolution in urban transport planning.

A review follows in Chapter 3 of typical inade quacies of urban public transport, referring to both formal and informal systems. It is stressed that the principal cause of these in-adequacies is the low level of capital investment in transport infrastructure and public transport vehicles, as well as lack of maintenance and systems control. It is explained that under these circumstances, Third World city public transport systems have great difficulty in simply meeting existing (and future) travel demand, let alone contributing to wider development goals.

Chapter 4 gives an account of the role of non-motorised travel in Third World cities and emphasises its need for a better planning approach. The discussion is based primarily on the situation in India and covers both informal and formal sector systems. An explanation is given of the demand and supply characteristics of non-motorised travel, the relationship between non-motorised movement and urban form, and the benefits and costs of such modes to both the community at large and its users.

Apart from serving as an introduction to the detailed discussions which follow in Part Two, Chapter 5 both outlines the framework and assesses basic elements and assumptions of the conventional urban transport planning process and its derivatives. The discussion reviews the evolution of the process, and its application to the Third World, through five discrete stages of development, each displaying distinctly different levels of professional confidence and impact on Third World practice. Following a discussion of different issues of technology-transfer, the chapter concludes by advancing certain considerations believed to lead to more appropriate approaches to Third World urban transport planning.

Chapter 6 continues partially in the same vein and reviews the principles, steps and techniques employed in urban transport project appraisal, paying particular attention to the evaluation stage. It is shown how developments in the field have shifted the focus of analysis from purely economic matters to wider considerations. The chapter describes key issues revelant to Third World urban transport projects, different project situations, and the implications of new developments on the practice of transport planning for Third World settlements.

An assessment of the role of institutional development in the implementation of transport plans for Third World cities follows in Chapter 7. Recognising that many urban transport proposals are made in apparent isolation of the institutional capacity to implement them, this chapter provides an examination of the determinants of this capacity. It also outlines the types of technical, management and administrative expertise involved in translating plans into action. The chapter, which argues for greater agency co-operation in urban transport, draws heavily in its conclusions on the case study of the Sao Paulo Metropolitan Area in Brazil.

Chapter 8 offers an overview of relatively recent developments in urban transport planning, while assessing their relevance to Third World practice. The chapter focuses on the role of transport analysis in urban transport planning, and the range of analytical choices available. It shows how these have been enhanced by developments in computer technology and theoretical advancements, the chapter also comments on the training requirements and techniques of responsive analysis.

Chapter 9 presents a method of modelling urban traffic movements with limited data which is considered most appropriate for Third World cities. The discussion examines principles of modelling urban traffic, and high lights the errors and complexities involved. A case is then made for the use of less complex transport models. In this regard, the chapter provides an overview and illustration of network models based on traffic counts, explicit travel demand model approaches, and models based on network data alone. The chapter concludes with a review of simplified models and planning styles associated with urban traffic modelling.

The evolution and practice of Urban Transport Systems Management (TSM), with particular reference to Urban Transport Corridor Planning is examined in Chapter 10. This now well-established approach is discussed as it relates to land-use policies and urban management, with the intention of investigating the legislative and regulative support required. Its application to Third World cities is investigated, and the problems discussed. A critical review of Urban Transport Corridor Planning proposals for both Cairo, Egypt, and Guadalajara, Mexico, is presented to illustrate several issues in the chapter.

Chapter 11 outlines the concept, practice and problems of street management, with illustrations of its application to Madras, India, and Teheran, Iran. Street management is presented as the management of all human activities in street space, of which traffic activities are only a part. Third World settlements, with their congested, mixed and (often) conflicting street activities, are particularly suited to this approach which relies greatly for its success on street design, traffic enforcement and education in the use of streets.

The final chapter, Chapter 12, draws from the different ideas and discussion throughout the book, with a view to establishing guidelines for more appropriate transport planning approaches. The chapter gives a detailed account of the Integrated Urban Infrastructure Development Programme (IUIDP) approach to planning urban transport recently developed for Indonesia, and emphasises the need for a transport hierarchy which matches different transport technologies to settlements and communities of varied sizes. The development approach to urban transport planning advocated seeks to incorporate the above concepts and positively integrate goals of city planning, traffic engineering, and relevant aspects of development economics and planning.

Chapter 1

Transport and Third World City Development

Harry T. Dimitriou

INTRODUCTION

This book is concerned with the planning of transport in Third World cities within an overall environment of rapid change and development. The principal purpose of this chapter is twofold. First, it is to provide the reader with a Third World contextual framework for the contributions which follow. Second, it is to trace the role of urban transport in Third World cities (especially those of 500,000 inhabitants and above), in circumstances of changing ideas and expectations about urban development and the function of the transport sector.

DEFINING THE THIRD WORLD

Problems of Definition

Although the 'Third World' is now a widely used term, it is employed in so many different ways that one cannot assume a universal definition. As Worsley points out (1980), this is not merely due to a lack of intellectual rigour but is also the result of various historical conceptions of the term that evolved at different times in response to different situations. According to the same source, the term was first used by the French demographer, Alfred Sauvey, who in the title of an article written in 1952, applied it to those countries which were outside the two international power blocs, and also, at the time, outside the communist world. In this

1

paradigm, the 'First World' refers to the capitalist industrialised countries; the 'Second World' is made up of the centrally planned economies; and the 'Third World' represents the remaining 'developing' countries'.

The initial use of 'Third World' as a term was therefore, closely associated with the 'Third Force' concept, coined by French scholars in the late 1940s and early 1950s, to denote a non-aligned force. In the late 1960s, newly established African countries employed a similar non-aligned intepretation. When East-West tensions declined, and more colonies emerged as new countries, the connotations of 'Third Force' with non-alignment altered. The term re-emerged in the 1970s, to connote development with common characteristics. The notion of confrontation however, was transferred to the North-South dialogue (or rather, lack of dialogue), as summarised by the Brandt Report (Independent Commission on International Development Issues, 1981). This later paradigm presents the 'North' as containing all the capitalist countries of the Western world (the majority of which, apart from Australia and New Zealand are located in the Northern hemisphere), as well as the centrally directed economies of the Comecon Countries (excluding Cuba and China); and the 'South' as including the majority of the poor nations, also referred to as the 'Third World' or the 'developing nations' (see Figure 1.1).

If the three world paradigm is too simple, then there are obvious objections to an even more simplified view of the world as two broad camps. This is particularly so since the 'South' includes affluent newly industrialising countries ('the Nics') such as Korea and Taiwan, at one end of the scale, and poor nations such as Bangladesh and Chad at the other. The division becomes even more misleading if one focuses on per capita GNP figures. Some countries in the 'South' (mostly oil-exporting nations such as Saudi Arabia and Kuwait) have higher per capita GNP figures than many countries of the industrialised 'Northern World' (Table 1.1 - see Appendix 1).

Despite these limitations of definition so well articulated by Harris (1986) in his book 'The End of the Third World', the editors of the present book are of the view that as a term 'Third World' still has a substantial degree of conceptual validity in its representation of countries with a common past or present set of development experiences. For this reason this term rather than 'Developing Country' is used by the editors. Since to use the latter would erroneously imply that only so-called 'Developing Countries' are

Figure 1.1 The North-South Divide

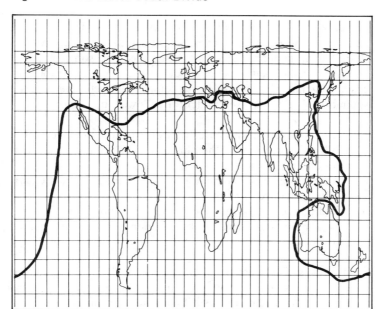

Source: Redrawn from book cover, Independent Commission on International
Development Issues, 1981.

making 'progress', and that there is a universally known and accepted form of 'development' to progress to.

The latter presumption is seen by Bauer (1971) to encourage
the imposition as international standards of the development indices of the industrialised world. Countries that do not meet or
share these standards are then by implication considered
'backward'. Bauer goes on to argue that the use of either of the
terms - 'underdeveloped' or 'developing' countries - suggests that
their conditions are not only abnormal but rectifiable. Whereas,
in fact, the real chances of improving the situation of many Third
World countries are small, since the industrialised capitalist and
Eastern European countries enjoy more than four-fifths of the
world's income. On this basis, Bauer concludes that in reality, it
is the 'Northern Nations' that are 'abnormal' in as much as they
are exceptional.

Third World Characteristics

The case for referring to a bloc of countries as the 'Third World', despite all the dangers of over-simplification, arises from their shared socio-economic features (some past and some present), and the international sense of solidarity their common experiences have generated. Third World country characteristics can be summarised and discussed under the following headings:

1. dependence on the industrialised world, combined with a shared perception of their historical development experiences;
2. rapid growth phenomena in major socio-economic trends affecting development;
3. a dual economy with widespread inequalities; and
4. a dominant role played by the public sector in national development.

Dependency. The sense of solidarity among Third World nations is reinforced by the common colonial past of many of them, during which the colonised countries became the main providers of raw materials to the then industrialising nations. It is argued by some (see later discussion on structural-internationalists) that this dependency is currently being perpetuated through:

1. international trade, foreign investment and the activities of multi-national enterprises;
2. international monetary arrangements, foreign aid and related activities;
3. international consulting organisations;
4. Western university education, training and literature; and
5. the research and development activities associated with all the above.

These activities and interests, pursued in close collaboration with a small indigenous elite, are also claimed to reinforce further the dominant position of the industrialised countries over the Third World.

Shared Perception of Historical Development Experiences. An increased sense of common purpose in the Third World has, according to Mabogunje (1980), arisen out of the realisation (substantiated by development planning failures) that the aid and loan policies of capitalist countries with their associated development strategies are not necessarily the effective 'medicine' they were thought to be. In certain instances, this realisation has led to a search for new and more appropriate development strategies. Some of these strategies relating to the urban transport sector are discussed in this book.

Rapid Growth Phenomena. None of the numerous indicators representing the common plight of Third World countries is perhaps more striking than their high population growth rates (Table 1.2 - see Appendix 1). Associated population characteristics include (World Bank, 1985):

1. a high participation of the total labour force in agriculture, generally between 30 per cent (for middle income economies) and 59 per cent (for low income economies), compared with an average of 6 per cent in the industrialised countries);
2. a significant proportion of the total population residing in rural areas, averaging between 36 per cent (for middle income economies) and 78 per cent (for low income economies), compared with an average of 23 per cent in the industrialised countries); and
3. relatively low per capita GNP, ranging from an average of US$1,300 (for middle income economies) to US$260 (for low income countries), compared with an average US$11,060 for the industrialised nations.

A feature of Third World rural populations is that their social and cultural values are in direct contrast to (if not in conflict with) urban values. The life-styles of Third World city-dwellers, on the other hand, are greatly influenced by industrialisation and modernisation, both of which are commonly associated with trends of rapid urbanisation (discussed at greater length later in this chapter).

Rapid urbanisation in many Third World countries has reached critical levels (Table 1.3 - see Appendix 1). In middle and low-income economies, respectively, urbanisation has increased by an average of 3.5 per cent and 3.7 per cent per annum. In the high-income oil exporting nations, it has even risen by an average of 6 per cent per annum, compared with an average of 1.5 per cent per annum in the industrialised countries. The increase in urban population has taken place largely because of the fast growing population movements from rural to urban areas, and an over-concentration of new employment opportunities in the cities. In addition, natural population growth rates are rapid within many such settlements.

Together, these growth phenomena have created a lethal combination of interrelated and self-generating urban problems of enormous proportions. Problems of urban transport associated with the rapid growth in vehicles (see later discussion and Chapter 2), are but one integral component of the wider urban development situation of Third World cities.

The backcloth to these circumstances in most of these countries consists of (World Bank, 1985):

1. widespread under-employment;
2. a lack of skilled manpower especially at managerial levels;
3. occasional high rates of inflation (a 29.3 per cent per annum average for middle-income economies, compared with 8 per cent per annum for industrialised countries);
4. high birth and death rates of (for example) 48.8 and 17.7 per thousand average, respectively, for Sub-Saharan Africa, as against comparable figures of 13.9 and 9.1 per thousand in the industrialised countries;
5. relatively low life expectancy between 59 and 61 years for low-income and middle-income economies, respectively, compared with an equivalent figure of 76 years for the indistrialised countries; and
6. high illiteracy levels, with an average 30 per cent of the population's relevant age group attending school and 4 per cent attending further education in the low-income countries; 42 and 12 per cent respectively, in middle-income nations, as against comparable figures of 87 and 37 per cent in industrialised countries.

Dual Economy. Third World countries are also characterised by an internal dual economy; a domestic economy in which a 'superior' (advantaged) and 'inferior' (disadvantaged) economic system co-exist. A dual economy manifests itself in the co-existence of: modern and traditional methods of production; 'formal' (registered and taxable) and 'informal' (unregistered and illegal) economic activies; and extreme poverty and affluence. Although these inequalities exist in various parts of the world, they are particularly widespread and indeed on the increase in many Third World countries.

Dominant Role of Public Sector. A final key feature of Third World nations is the dominant and critical role played by the public sector in the guidance and motivation of overall national development. This role is typically controlled by a small elite who have an influence out of proportion to their numbers.

Typologies of Third World Countries

The taxonomy of Third World countries varies according to the principal development interest of those drawing up the classification. The categories employed here to cite illustrative development characteristics have as a matter of convenience been based upon the classification employed by the World Bank as this has provided the source statistics.

The World Bank classification discriminates among Third World nations on the basis of their Gross National Product per capita, and according to whether they are importers or exporters of oil. On this basis, the four major categories of Third World nations are those (see Tables 1.1 - 1.3 in Appendix) with:

1. a Gross National Product per capita less than US$405 (referred to as 'low-income economies', estimated at 42);
2. a Gross National Product per capita in excess of US$405 and which also import oil (referred to as 'medium-income oil importers', estimated at 83);
3. a Gross National Product per capita in excess of US$405 but below US$6,000, and which also export oil (referred to as 'medium-income oil exporters', estimated at 17); and
4. a Gross National Product per capita in excess of US$6,000 which are also principal exporters of oil (referred to as 'high-income oil exporters', estimated at eight).

Recent estimates indicate that 150 countries (excluding China) make up the Third World. This compares with 21 nations in the industrialised world and eight East European non-market economies.

A review of the literature, however, suggests that there are at least four typologies of Third World countries, namely:

1. economic and resource-based categories, e.g.,those based on some measure of GNP or GDP, or estimates of national export and import levels of natural resources, particularly oil;
2. politically defined categories which differentiate among centralised economies, mixed economies and market economies;
3. historical development categories, e.g., those based upon Rostow's stages of growth (Rostow, 1961), concepts of colonial and neo-colonial models of development, and some measure of industrialisation; and
4. international development agency categories employed by agencies such as: the International Labour Office (ILO), United Nations (especially UNDP), World Bank (IBRD), and the Organisation for Economic Co-operation and Development (OECD). These are drawn up for the agency's own purposes, and therefore often constitute a mix of the above categories.

Definition and Measurement of Development

Before effective action can be taken to redress or alleviate development problems one must first be clear about how to assess progress so as to formulate useful measurements of development. One way is employing development goals, targets and indicators which governments and/or international development agencies adopt and which facilitate the measure of change and progress arising from development efforts. This in turn, requires that those in a position of power who formulate the policies in the light of their own values, have a clear understanding of 'development'. Much ambiguity, however, sorrounds the term.

The concept implies an 'advance' on the past or 'progress', usually through progressive growth in the various factors that con- tribute to the improvement. 'Development' signifies movement towards a pre-defined set of ends considered to be 'modern' and economically healthy, promoted by - as a rule - government and/or international agencies. However, development has been per- ceived by too many and for too long as synonymous with economic growth alone. In part, it is because politicans have found economic indicators, such as national income measures, politically useful; especially as Seers (1969) points out, when these indices are out of date.

Whilst economic progress is clearly an essential component of development, it is not the only one. Development is a phenomenon comprising many interrelated and inseparable components. Those who now subscribe to this school of thought have, however, had the benefit of reviewing ideas and debates contained in the literature of development economics and planning over the last thirty years. This literature, according to Todaro (1981), has, by and large, focused upon 'economic growth' theories - first articulated by Rostow (1961), and later 'structural-internationalist' models of development, including the work of Seers (1969 and 1977). In the former, the process of development is regarded as a series of inevitable stages whereby the correct combination of economic ingredients such as: savings, investments and foreign aid, ultimately enables Third World countries to progress along the economic growth path of the more 'developed' nations.

Among academics (but not international bankers), support for this perception has now largely been replaced by an increasingly widespread subscription to structural-internationalist views on development, in which the predicament of the Third World is increasingly seen as a product of dual economies and dual societies - both within nations and among them. In this school of thought the response to the plight of the Third World is within a context of economic growth and emphasises the eradication of poverty and inequalities, the re-distribution of wealth, and the meeting of basic needs.

Todaro (1981), differentiates between two groups of structural-internationalists, namely, between those who subscribe to:

1. the 'neo-colonial dependence' model where the existence and perpetuation of the Third World's circumstances is a consequence of the unequal relationships formed between rich and poor countries during the development of international capitalism; and

2. the 'false paradigm model' - where the Third World's current predicament is largely attributed, on the one hand, to the well-meant provision of sophisticated, but innapropriate kinds of expertise by international development agency advisors, and on the other hand to the overseas training of

Third World public officials. Both these kinds of assistance merely support the existing interests of the domestic and international powers, which in many cases, perpetuate the current inequitable system.

Although both schools of thought are to varying degrees subscribed to by contributors to this volume, the editors tend toward the 'false paradigm model' (see particularly Chapter 5) in their analysis of urban transport planning practice for Third World countries.

FEATURES OF THIRD WORLD CITY DEVELOPMENT

Urbanisation and City Population Growth

Urbanisation is the process whereby a settlement's land use, and the activity patterns of the inhabitants shift from dependence on a rural-based economy to a predominantly urban one. Its population characteristics are measured (Table 1.3 - see Appendix 1) in terms of:

1. the number of urban inhabitants as a percentage of total population;
2. the growth of urban populations; and
3. the percentage of the total population in cities of given sizes.

The phenomenon is associated with population transfers from rural areas to cities and the inter-sectoral re-allocation of resources from subsistence agriculture to the production of non-agricultural goods in urban areas (Richardson, 1977). The trends of urbanisation are therefore, directly correlated with a nation's economic development as many of the changes have led directly to increases in GNP, and are closely associated with the development of urban-based industrialisation.

World trends in urbanisation have been increasing at an extremely rapid rate. In the Third World, urbanisation has doubled since the Second World War; since the 1950s it has reached levels at least equal to those in the industrialised world. Third World city populations are currently increasing at almost twice the rate of overall populations (Table 1.4 - see Appendix 1). According to the World Bank (1984) in the past half of this increase is attributed to the balance of births over deaths within urban areas, and the remainder both to migration from rural areas and the re-classification of rural areas to urban status.

Latin America contains the largest and highest number of urbanised areas in the Third World. Two-thirds of its population is urban, cities such as Sao Paulo and its Metropolitan Area and Mexico City (see Chapters 7 and 10 respectively) are likely to attain sizes in excess of 20 million by the end of the century. In contrast, Asia and Africa are still predominantly rural with approximately 25 per cent of their population living in urban areas. Nevertheless, in Asia it is anticipated that jumbo cities such as Tokyo, Shanghai and Beijing, will join the league of cities of over 20 million inhabitants by the year 2000. As these trends show, it is forecast that the largest cities will belong to Third World countries. Indeed, of the 24 cities which will have populations in excess of 11 million by the year 2000, only four will be in the industrialised world (see Figure 1.2). Nevertheless, it should be emphasised that the *proportion* of urban to rural inhabitants in the Third World has not dramatically risen, because rural populations are also increasing.

Cities, particularly those in the Third World, have been classified in a variety of ways. Stretton (1978), for instance, distinguishes among poor capitalist, poor communist, rich capitalist and rich communist cities. Mabogunjie (1980) differentiates among colonial, traditional, and (pre - and post colonial) industrial cities; and Galbraith (1974) coins the terms political household, merchant, industrial and polyglot city. Since cities, however, are made up of many parts, those in the Third World (especially the largest) do not fit neatly into any one category. Even the type of city currently having the most visible impact on development - the post-colonial industrial city - is quite different from its contemporary counterpart in the industrialised world.

Urbanisation and Industrialisation

Urban-based industrialisation as a vehicle for national development, particularly the kind based on 'import-substitution' policies, has become an increasingly dominant economic force in many Third World countries and especially Latin America. The relationship between 'industrialisation' (i.e., the building up of a country's capacity to 'process' raw materials and to 'manufacture' goods for consumption or further production [Todaro, 1983]) and

11

Figure 1.2: Urban Agglomerations with More Than 10 Million Inhabitants: 1950, 1975 and 2000

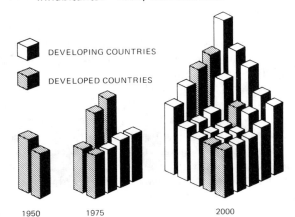

1950	(millions)		(millions)
New York, northeast New Jersey	12.2	London	10.4

1975			
New York, northeast New Jersey	19.8	London	10.4
Mexico City	11.9	Tokyo, Yokohama	17.7
Los Angeles, Long Beach	10.8	Shanghai	11.6
		Sao Paulo	10.7

2000			
Mexico City	31.0	Sao Paulo	25.8
Tokyo, Yokohama	24.2	New York, northeast New Jersey	22.8
Shanghai	22.7	Rio de Janeiro	19.0
Beijing	19.9	Calcutta	16.7
Greater Bombay	17.7	Seoul	14.2
Jakarta	16.6	Cairo, Giza, Imbaba	13.1
Los Angeles, Long Beach	14.2	Bangkok, Thonburi	11.9
Madras	12.9	Delhi	11.7
Greater Buenos Aires	12.1	Paris	11.3
Karachi	11.8	Istanbul	11.2
Bogota	11.7	Osaka, Kobe	11.1
Tehran	11.3		
Baghdad	11.1		

Source: Redrawn from Figure 4.3, World Bank, 1984.

the city is a long-standing one. It was first forged in the nineteenth century in the UK, during the Industrial Revolution. Later, 'urbanisation' was used by some as a surrogate measure of industrialisation, and cities were viewed merely as part of the capital base of industrial production (Harris, 1984).

The relationship, according to Roberts (1978), has today released two sets of sub-forces. One is the tendency for the semi-industrialised and industrialising Third World city to accentuate its dependence on the industrialised countries by becoming an increasingly major consumer of imported technologies and luxury goods. The other is the introduction of new political and social influences (and conflicts) associated with capital-intensive industrial activities, and the resultant changes in the economic structure of such cities.

It is generally thought that industrialisation encourages (World Bank, 1972):

1. increased technological innovation (and transfer);
2. the development of managerial and entrepreneurial talent;
3. the improvement of technical skills;
4. increased standardisation in production;
5. a rise in consumerism; and
6. additional demands for urban infrastructure.

Urban industrialisation also contributes among other things, to:

1. dramatic changes in urban structure, land prices, and the predominant patterns of land use and tenure;
2. extremely high rates of unemployment and under-employment;
3. increased migration of persons from rural to urban areas; and
4. widespread technology dualism, especially in the sectors of transport and industry.

Characteristics of technology dualism are particularly spectacular in the transport sector of many Asian cities and are well written about by Rimmer (1986). Here, traditional and modern modes of transport operate side-by-side (see Chapter 4) sometimes complimentarily but in many instances in conflict (see Chapter 2). Similar features of technology dualism may be noted in the manufacturing sector of these cities. The technology of motorised transport has had an immense impact on the Third World city. Planners and politicians alike have had great difficulty in coping with the complex ramifications affecting almost all spheres of urban development associated with this kind of movement as explained by Thomson (1977) in his book 'Great Cities and their Traffic'.

Equally, if not more complex implications for Third World urban development have long been foretold by planners, as a result of the anticipated speed-up of communications and information systems (Meier, 1962). A likely scenario is that technological advances in these areas will encourage urban decentralisation, and aggravate social inequalities, since the already privileged will have further access to new opportunities generated by these technological developments.

Urbanisation, Modernisation and Social Change

Just as the hallmark of urban industrialisation in the Third World is the increased economic specialisation and interdependence of productive activities so, the features of modernisation are rapid (often institutionalised) changes in patterns of traditional behaviour. Social and economic norms change profoundly and start to resemble those of urban inhabitants. Counsumer-oriented values - similar to those in the Western industrialised world - take on a greater importance. Myrdal (1971) summarises the ideals of modernisation as incorporating:

1. the emergence and pursuance of a new (modern) form of rationality;
2. the promotion of the concept of equity; and
3. the encouragement of effective competition, individual enterprise and social and economic mobility.

The old influences of 'Europeanisation' and 'Westernisation' are thus replaced by 'modernisation' which has become a more potent and widespread force for development. Its ideas and values are now disseminated more rapidly and efficiently (usually from urban centres), by cheaper and more comprehensive means of communication including mass media, more widespread access to education and improved marketing techniques. The enhanced performance of the Third World city in most parts of the globe as a receiver, synthesiser and disseminator of international information and ideas (of the kind the very survival of the city often depends on), has increasingly made modernisation a key force in the development of Third World cities.

Urbanisation, Land Use and Transport Interaction

The city has been depicted by many urban analysts in their writings (Mitchell and Rapkin, 1954; Meier, 1962; Webber, 1969; and Needham, 1977), as a kind of dynamic interface machine of movement (transport) channels and communication (information) links, serving activities accommodated by the settlement. Such links provide for the needs of industrialisation and commerce, encourage further economic and urban growth, and generally increase the pace of modernisation. The rapid growth phenomena associated with Third World urbanisation i.e., population increases, rising vehicle ownership and traffic, rising land-use densities and expanding areas, together have the effect of speeding-up urban land use and transport interaction (see Figure 1.3). In many cases, traffic overload on transport and communication links is the result. These phenomena have made the management of the Third World city complex, difficult and expensive, as the demand for additional urban space for new activities (and the traffic they generate) introduces severe competition for the use of land. Typically such cities have a total land area of below 10 per cent, and rarely above 15 per cent allocated to roads. By comparison in cities in industrialised countries, land allocated to roads is generally 15 to 25 per cent of total land areas; and even up to 30 per cent in newer lower density North American cities (World Bank, 1975).

Problems are often aggravated by newly constructed transport infrastructure intended to improve accessibility but which leads to the displacement to the periphery of traditional means of transport, and economic and commercial activities (especially of the informal sector). In this way many of the everyday requirements of low-income urban inhabitants are pushed out of the central areas. Within a short period of time, the speed-up of the interaction of land use and transport/communication brought about by the implementation of such projects have drastically altered the proportions of land-use types within central areas, so that housing land has been reduced, and land for pur-

15

Figure 1.3: The Urban Land Use Transport System

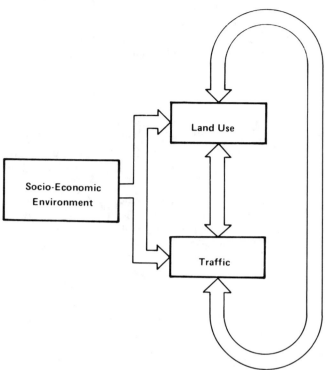

poses of new transport infrastructure, commerce and industry has been increased.

Such developments have also been associated with the dramatic increase in cost of land and rents in central areas and the construction of high-rise buildings epitomised by developments in Hong Kong. These buildings in turn, both generate and attract high-density traffic into urban roads with inadequate capacity. There is furthermore, far more intra-urban travel as people and institutions are unable or unwilling to meet the costs of central area locations and decentralise their activities. Such decentralisation inevitably gives rise to longer average trip lengths.

THIRD WORLD CITY TRANSPORT CHARACTERISTICS

Urban Transport Characteristics and Trends

Reports of urban transport problems from Third World (especially large) cities have mushroomed over the last two decades (see Chapter 2). The severity of the problems encountered is in part explained by the rise in the number of automobiles which has outstripped the growth in urban population. In the coming decades, these problems are expected to become even more serious - particularly in fast-growing cities currently hovering just below the one million mark. These trends are already apparent in some of the largest and most heavily populated Third World countries namely: Brazil, China, Indonesia, India and Nigeria.

Many of the past trends in urban traffic growth (in some cases well exceeding 5 per cent per annum), may be attributed to economic growth. Higher incomes, especially during the 1970s, have led to increased vehicle ownership, rising consumption of transport goods, and the construction of new infrastructure (which in turn, encouraged the generation of additional traffic). It is, however, now believed that as the effects of international recession are feared to have spread, Third World urban transport problems in the coming decades in the poorer countries, are more likely to be associated with declining economic growth and stagnation. In these circumstances, the initial transport problems (generated by increased vehicle ownership and the construction of new transport facilities) are likely to be superseded by issues related to the inadequacy of resources to provide for the maintenance and management of transport services and infrastructure in the face of further urbanisation.

These problems already especially prevalent in low-income cities, are expected to become increasingly common in cities in the oil exporting Third World countries, whose economies have experienced a dramatic decline due to the international fall in oil prices. The difference between the more affluent and poorer Third World countries is that in the former's case, the burden of urban transport maintenance has been considerably increased by investments in urban infrastructure of earlier more prosperous years.

Whilst the economic performance of a country obviously influences city development, the demand for urban transport is also affected by city size and population density (Linn, 1983). Large

17

settlements with lower peripheral population densities tend to increase trip lengths and encourage efforts to raise travel speeds. Transport fuel costs are thus increased. Poorly enforced (or non-existent) land-use control regulations have furthermore permitted 'unplanned' development in areas with inadequate urban transport facilities, thus causing locational traffic congestion.

The provision and pricing of urban public transport services also play an important role in urban development. The level of government subsidy, the capacity of the public transport system *vis-a-vis* the demand for its services, and the role of the informal transport sector, all have a great bearing on the performance of a city's overall transport system. The level of motorisation and cost of its accommodation are directly correlated with trends in per capita income. Thus, rising incomes share a positive correlation with other features, such as rises in fuel consumption, increased pollution, more road accidents and environmental disruption. Conversely, low incomes are related to larger proportions of non-motorised movement, increased pressures for public transport facilities, and a greater likelihood of a reduction of motorisation costs.

Urban Transport Related Costs

The cost of urban movement varies according to the mode of transport used, each of which has its own associated capital, operating, maintenance and foreign exchange costs. All costs are rising, in some cases considerably (Linn, 1983).

Low-income urban communities throughout the Third World inevitably rely most heavily on the cheapest form of transport (see Chapter 4), namely, non-motorised movement and particularly walking. Since such communities are expected to grow, so non-motorised travel - especially walking (and cycle-driven modes in Asia) will increase in importance for the urban poor. This is inevitable if alternative cheaper motorised public transport is not provided, and despite efforts to restrict the movements of rickshaws in cities such as Jakarta and Calcutta, as well as the actions of more affluent Third World settlements such as Singapore and Hong Kong which have already, for all intents and purposes, cleared rickshaws from the road.

After the cycle rickshaw, motor-cycle/scooter-driven para-transit modes, such as the *bajaj* in Indonesia, are the cheapest mode of transport in terms of operating costs. According to World Bank estimates, the next most economic mode is buses. Minibuses are somewhat more costly than buses, but the reverse often prevails where efficiently run private minibuses run side by side with inefficiently operated public bus companies. Taxis are more costly yet. However, for cars there appears to be a quantum leap to almost four times the costs of a taxi, some eight times the cost of a bus, and fifty-seven times the cost of a bicycle trip (Linn, 1983). Research conducted by Soegijoko (1986) in Indonesia indicates that revenue per passenger kilometre is lowest for the bus and highest for the *bajaj*. Comparing revenue to costs, rickshaws give the highest ratio followed by the bus and the minibus. The lowest ratio of revenue to cost is offered by the *bajaj*.

Not only do statistics on private vehicle operational costs show that it is by far the most expensive means of transport, but it is expected to become more so in the future. The private car, furthermore, consumes approximately nine times more road space per passenger than does a bus (Linn, 1983) and requires proportionately much heavier investment in the maintenance of roads than do buses. The considerable flexibility provided by the mode to its user is thus furnished at a very high premium and at considerable opportunity cost, particularly if one includes associated foreign exchange costs.

Urban rail transport systems which are usually confined to main traffic corridors and are not suitable for distributing passengers throughout secondary and tertiary transport networks are of varied kinds. At one extreme there are the light rail transit systems, such as trams, which share the roadway with other users, and at the other extreme are the highest capacity exclusive right of way urban rail and metro systems. Exclusive right of way light rail systems can cope with peak hour volumes of 36,000 passengers per hour, whilst metro systems have been reported to achieve 60,000 passengers an hour in each direction (World Bank, 1986). According to the same source, light rail systems with exclusive rights of way cost in the region of US$0.10 to US$0.15 per passenger kilometre to operate, and between US$6 million and US$10 million per kilometre to construct for ground level systems. Elevated systems cost between US$25 million and US$40 million and underground networks can cost up to US$40 million per kilometre. This compares to between US$30 million and US$40 million per kilometre for underground or elevated urban rail and metro structures; and even US$65 million to US$100 million per kilometre where 'cut and cover' methods of construction are required.

Clearly, the above costs (especially their foreign exchange costs) can only be warranted along high density corridors and in cities of particular sizes with significant proportions of populations who find the services offered affordable. Rapid transit proposals for Madras and Calcutta have both been questioned on this basis. The on-going debate between planners and rail transit hardware manufacturers as to the minimum settlement sizes for different rail systems has also raised issues of contention. This was perhaps most graphically illustrated by the case of the rapid transit system proposal for Penang. With a population of 720,000 there was a clear conflict of views between the consultants proposing the system and the city planners who believed the population size did not warrant such a system.

Urban Transport Systems

To talk of urban transport 'systems' in many Third World cities may seem to imply a greater degree of integration and co-ordination of transport modes than in reality exists. Nevertheless, co-ordination among traditional and modern, as well as informal and formal transport operations, does take place, although with varying degrees of efficiency. The structure, mix and organisation of such working relationships are however, more a product of the evolution of the city in question, and often less an outcome of the city's management and investment programmes. They instead generally reflect the transport needs (over time) of those who extensively use the systems.

In any urban transport system the different modes both complement each other and compete with each other. They have different associated costs and benefits for the user and non-user, and are often associated with a variety of operators. The complementary characteristics are those which facilitate the inter-change of modes, so that a combination of transport means provides coverage of a given area and accommodates the needs of different markets. Whereas competition exhibits the contest between modes for patronage of the same routes and/or geographical area.

Many Third World cities contain a rich mixture of traditional and modern modes of transport (see Chapters 3 and 4). In some places they share the same routes and, although competing for road space, cater for different market segments of the public. However, where the market can stand it, there is keen competition among most motorised modes of transport, especially between formally and informally operated systems. This commonly occurs where the capacity of the former is unable to meet the demands made upon it, or where it is too costly for the majority of would-be passengers to patronise it. One might conclude from this that the wider the range of transport modes offered and the greater the spectrum of income brackets accommodated, the more effective the transport system, and that diversity reflects the response to changing transport demands of different urban areas and groups. Many Third World city officials, however, do not consider such diversity an asset. Instead, given the city's limited capacity to accommodate growing motorised traffic volumes, traditional and informal transport modes are often considered 'obstacles' to the modernisation (read 'motorisation') of the transport system.

In an increasing number of cities such as Mexico City, Cairo and Hong Kong, the range of transport systems has been enhanced by the construction of relatively new metro schemes to relieve the traffic pressure on city road systems. Solutions of this kind are however, far beyond the available resources of many other urban areas of the Third World, particularly intermediate-sized settlements.

Functions of Urban Transport Systems

The significance of urban transport systems lies in their provision of linkages between points of residence and employment, their contribution to the economies of scale and specialisation of urban-based activities (particularly industrial and commercial activities), the employment opportunities they offer to the inhabitants of settlements, and their impact on geographical growth and urban form. Acknowledgement of the importance of urban transport to development has been a relatively recent affair. It was not until 1972, for example, that the World Bank became involved in urban transport projects. However, with rising levels of urbanisation in the Third World and with cities performing an increasingly recognised productive function in the development of this part of the globe, the influential role of urban transport is expected to grow.

The expectation is reflected in the recent international development agency lending programme for urban transport. In the case of the World Bank, for example, from 1972 to 1985, 17 urban transport projects were approved, and another 32 urban projects had significant transport components. The total investment in the first set of projects amounted to US$1,900 million (of which the Bank financed US$800 million). Transport components in the second type of projects cost US$520 million (of which US$240 million was Bank financed). Together, approval for the total financial participation of the agency over the 13 year period amounted to US$1,040 million (World Bank, 1986), with an average annual investment of US$148.6 million per annum. This compares with earlier calculated average annual investments of US$29.6 million between 1970 and 1974.

With World Bank estimates of rates of return on such projects having substantially increased over the years, and with urban areas of Third World countries contributing between 50 and 70 per cent of gross national product (GNP) to the economies of these nations, the agency has been encouraged to invest further in urban transport. The World Bank has thus embarked upon numerous additional projects, among which the most recent is the Regional Cities Urban Transport Project for Indonesia and the Jakarta Urban Transport Project (1987), costing in the region of US$82 million and US$210 million respectively.

Because this growing priority assigned to urban transport has been accompanied (in real terms) by declining available funds - aspects of transport systems operations, management, finance (especially cost recovery) and improvement, are at present receiving more attention than new road construction. These circumstances call for a clearer appreciation of the diverse tasks of urban transport (and their relative costs) before decisions are taken concerning the allocation of scarce resources to the sector. Two particular aspects of urban transport systems development need to be considered. One is the relative importance of current urban development activities serviced by transport, the other is the compatibility of urban development goals and policies with those assigned to the transport system.

TRANSPORT AND URBAN DEVELOPMENT GOALS

Urban Transport Efficiency

Urban activities serviced by transport systems are those of internal importance to the settlement, and those of significance to the city's function as a national and/or regional transport/communication centre. Whilst this chapter focuses on the latter, it must be appreciated that the two functions are closely interrelated and often inseparable.

To enhance the efficiency of urban transport systems, there is therefore an obligation in urban transport planning not only to respond to locally generated movement requirements, but also to relate to the country's national urban development strategy where one exists. Such a strategy should indicate the phasing of transport investments with the rest of a national urban policy, the preferred transport inter-modal mix, the use of transport as a tool of spatial development policy, and the role of urban transport in national urban policy making (Gakenheimer, 1986). In so doing it would offer guidelines as to how better to ensure that urban transport investments are developmentally effective, economically and operationally efficient, as well as justified in relation to opportunity costs to other sector investments (see Chapter 12).

The evolution of urban transport systems can be said both to respond to, as well as (belatedly) to adapt to, changing basic needs (and aspirations) of urban activities - namely households, firms and institutions - as they attempt to maximise their accessibility to other activities they rely on. The operation and development of a city's transport systems are also influenced by the organisational structure and geographical distribution of a settlement's major activities, and institutionalised and cultural norms and routines associated with their development. It is these latter considerations which especially make Third World city transport characteristics so different from those of the industrialised world.

The provision of urban transport facilities to meet the most basic of needs, however, is a major problem in many Third World cities - especially in the low-income countries (see Chapters 2 and 3). This is particularly so, as the same transport system has other tasks to perform which are often considered to be of greater economic importance. It is obliged, for example, to provide commerce and industry with opportunities for transporting raw materials to points of urban production. It must also distribute the services and goods of commerce and industry to markets within and outside the city, as well as to points of transport interchange for locations further afield.

In seeking to provide for these varied needs, Third World cities are faced with a conflict between catering for increased productivity of the urban economy (with the rising costs of expanding urban transport sufficiently to ensure continued economic growth), and catering for the under-privileged who depend on cheap means of travel to expand their opportunities. Additional influential factors which have a detrimental effect on the efficient use of transport systems (see Chapters 2 to 5) include:

1. the rapid geographical spread of urban areas which encourages both longer trip making and the generation of additional demands for ill affordable peripheral transport facilities;
2. inadequate traffic restraint and management efforts pursued by governments which fail to contain trends of the increased indiscriminate use of motorised (especially private car) transport in urban areas; and
3. the employment of ineffective development control measures and urban transport planning efforts by municipal agencies which allow major traffic generators and land-use developments to take place at locations which are incompatible with transport facility provision.

It is in this context, and against an economic background of limited resources, that low cost efforts at urban traffic management and transport planning (see Chapters 9 to 12) become significant. For they are attempts at managing and planning urban movement with a view to fulfilling better both the needs of inhabitants and of the city's economy.

Changing Urban Development Policies

Any assessment of Third World city transport systems must ultimately be made against some measure of performance that can realistically be expected of it, rather than aspired to standards taken from the industrialised world. The degree of multi-purposeness of an urban transport system, and the level of integration offered to its component parts, are far more important to Third

World city development than any degree of technological modernisation it may appear to offer.

In the 1970s, in response to the agenda of Third World city
development problems, more enlightened approaches to urban
development planning sought to (Safier, 1981):

1.   sustain per capita growth of income in real terms;
2.   eradicate poverty;
3.   decrease inequalities of income distributions;
4.   provide additional urban capacity to absorb rural migrants;
      and
5.   lessen inequalities in urban services provision.

In addition to the above, to ensure that basic needs were
met some later efforts sought not only to utilise resources more efficiently but simultaneously to mobilise local authority resources
and power (see Chapter 12).

Changes of thought on urban development planning have,
according to Safier, thus (slowly) reflected the shifting emphasis
of ideas among national and regional development planners, and
(some) economists. Whereas thirty years ago they saw development as synonymous with economic growth, today, there is a
greater awareness of the inadequacies of the economic growth
concept without some consideration of equity, and the consolidation of local (especially informal sector) resources.

The emphasis by international agencies such as the International Labour Office (ILO) and other United Nations agencies on
meeting basic needs (see UN Secretariat, 1977), together with the
stated increased concern for the urban poor by the World Bank,
led in the early 1980s to an apparent change in direction of goals
and policies to be pursued for Third World urban development.
The extent to which the practice of urban and transport planning
has been able (and willing) to adopt the same spirit however, is
open to debate. For professionals in these fields have been obliged
to come to terms with the constraints of everyday local political
trade-offs and influential industrial and commercial pressures,
many of which are contrary to the above espoused spirit of urban
development planning. Recent moves by the World Bank and
many Third World governments to improve project cost recovery
and enhance urban management efforts have furthermore added
to these constraints.

Changing Expectations of the Role of Urban Transport

Development planners and economists have long had consi derable difficulties in translating their macro-economic ideas and policies into spatial and urban development terms, and thus into meaningful terms to the city and transport planner. If however, development planners and economists have had difficulties in coming to terms with the spatial and urban dimensions of Third World development, transport planners and traffic engineers have found it even more difficult to accommodate themselves to the changing schools of thought on development and how they affect transport (see Figure 1.4).

The contributions of urban transport to economic growth in opening up new economically productive opportunities and reducing the cost of travel is a concept well understood since the 1950s by transport planners and traffic engineers alike. Indeed the enhancement of this contribution has become to a large extent the *raison d'etre* of the role of these professions. But an equivalent appreciation of the function of transport in urban development spheres other than those associated with the generation of economic growth has been less well marked, both in the industrialised countries and the Third World.

In Third World city circumstances, where the achievement of 'development' goals is seen to be so critical, and where transport is universally acknowledged to be the servant of development, one can argue (see Chapter 12) that an understanding of the dynamics and issues of urban development is as much a prerequisite for urban transport planning and traffic engineering practice, as sound professional engineering competence.

In conclusion, to accommodate changing expectations of the role of transport in Third World city development, therefore, it is important for transport plans, programmes and projects to incorporate not only economic goals and aims of equity fulfillment, but also objectives which attempt efficiently to utilise local resources and facilities prior to investing in new ones. Among other things, this would involve placing more emphasis in urban transport planning on (Dimitriou and Safier, 1982):

1.　the mobilisation of new resources - through, for example, improved city staff administrative and technical manpower training efforts, and greater utilisation of private sector resources;

Figure 1.4:   Changing Concepts of Development in Urban
Transport Planning

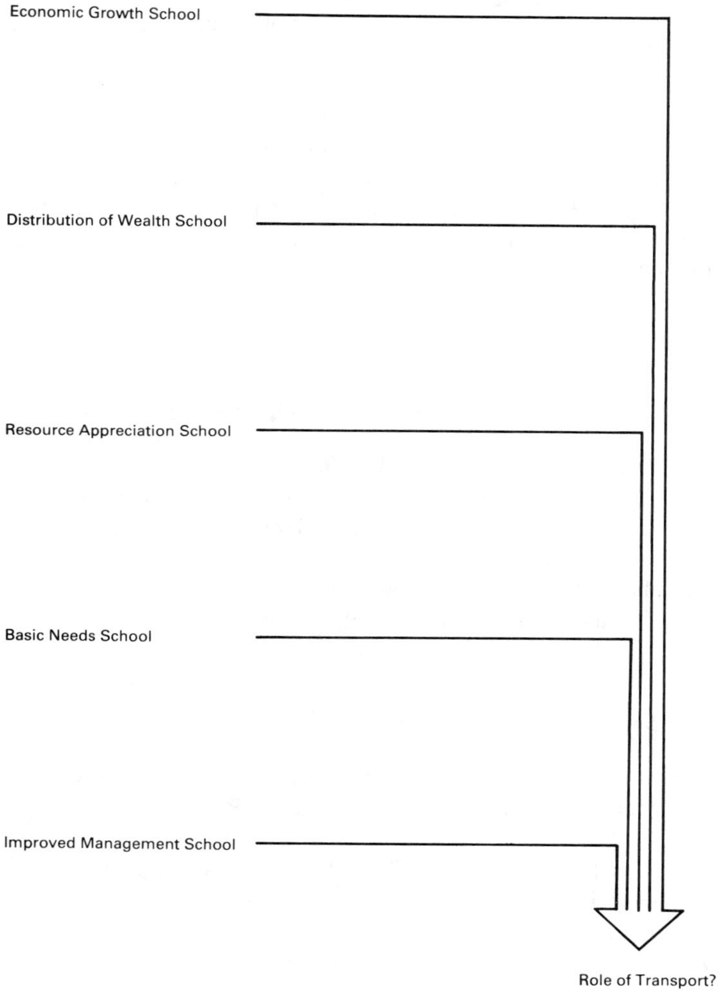

Economic Growth School

Distribution of Wealth School

Resource Appreciation School

Basic Needs School

Improved Management School

Role of Transport?

Source: Modified from Figure 1.5: Dimitriou H.T. and Safier M., 1982.

2.   the incorporation (and thereby recognition) of the roles of
the informal and traditional sectors of transport - in a manner whereby both contribute positively to an integrated and
financially more viable urban transport system; and

27

3.   the measurement and monitoring of costs and benefits of
     transport proposals - against cost recovery requirements
     and the needs of the full spectrum of income groups they are
     expected to serve.

In so doing, the conventional wisdom of urban transport
planning may thus be reorientated toward the planning of
transport specifically for Third World urban development rather
than the planning of urban transport systems per se. The chapters
that follow offer some insights and ideas on how such a reorienta-
tion may be achieved.

REFERENCE

Bauer, P.T. (1980) **Dissent on Development**, Weidenfeld and
    Nicholson, London.
Dimitriou, H.T. and Safier, M. (1982) 'A Developmental Ap-
    proach to Urban Transport Planning', **Proceedings of
    Universities Transport Study Group Seminar, University
    College**, London.
Gakenheimer, R. (1986) 'Transportation as a Component of Na-
    tional Urban Strategy', **Habitat International**, vol. 10, no. 12,
    1/2, Pergamon Press, Oxford.
Galbraith, J.K. (1974) 'On the Modern City - or History as the
    Future', **Royal Institute of British Architects Journal**, Oc-
    tober, London.
Harris, N. (1984) 'Some Trends in the Evolution of Big Cities',
    Habitat International, vol. 8, no. 1, Pergamon Press, Ox-
    ford.
_____ (1986) **The End of the Third World: Newly Industrializing
    Countries and the Decline of an Ideology**, Penguin Books,
    Harmondsworth, Middlesex.
Independent Commission on International Development Issues,
    under the Chairmanship of Willy Brandt (1981) **North-
    South: A Program for Survival**, Pan Books, London.
Linn, J.F. (1983) **Cities in Developing Countries**, World Bank
    Research Publication, Oxford University Press, Oxford.
Mabogunje, A.L. (1980) **The Development Process**, Hutchinson
    Uiversity Library, London.
Meier, R. (1962) **A Communications Theory of Urban Growth**,
    Publication of the Joint Center for Urban Studies of the

Massachusetts Institute of Technology and Harvard University, Massachusetts, Cambridge.

Mitchell, R.B. and Rapkin, C. (1954) **Urban Traffic: A Function of Land Use**, Columbia University Press, New York.

Myrdal, G. (1971) **Asian Drama**, Pantheon Press, New York.

Needham, B. (1977) **How Cities Work**, Pergamon Press, Oxford.

Renaud, B. (1979) **National Urbanization Policy in Developing Countries**, World Bank and Oxford University Press, New York.

Richardson, H. (1977) 'City Size and National Spatial Strategies in Developing Countries', **World Bank Staff Working Paper**, no. 252, World Bank, Washington DC.

Rimmer, P.J. (1986) **Rikisha to Rapid Transit: Urban Public Transport Systems and Policy in Southeast Asia**, Pergamon Press, Oxford.

Roberts, B. (1978) **Cities of Peasants**, Edward Arnold, London.

Rostow, W.W. (1961) **The Stages of Economic Growth**, Cambridge University Press, Cambridge.

Safier, M. (1981) 'Urban Development and Cities in a Global Context', unpublished Lecture given at DPU Special Programme on 'National Planning and Urban Development', University College, London.

Seers, D. (1969) 'The Meaning of Development', **International Development Review**, vol.11, no. 4, University of Sussex, Brighton.

Soegijoko, B.T. (1986) 'The Becaks of Java', **Habitat International**, vol. 10, no. 1/2, Pergamon Press, Oxford.

Stretton, H. (1978) **Urban Planning In Rich and Poor Countries**, Oxford University Press, Oxford.

Thomson, J.M. (1977) **Great Cities and Their Traffic**, Victor Gollancz, London.

Todara, M.P. (1981) **Economic Development in the Third World**, Longman, New York and London.

UN Secretariat (1977) 'Measurement of Basic Minimum Needs', **Asian Development Review**, nos. 5 and 6, United Nations, New York.

Webber, M.M. (1969) **On Strategies for Transport Planning**, OECD, Paris.

World Bank (1972) 'Industry', **World Bank Sector Working Paper**, Washington DC.

____(1984) **World Development Report**, Oxford University Press, Oxford.

____ (1985) **World Development Report**, Oxford University Press, Oxford.

____ (1986) **Urban Transport: A World Bank Policy Paper**, Washington.

_____(1988) **World Development Report**, Oxford University Press, Oxford.

Worsley, P. (1980) 'How Many Worlds', in Why the Third World?, by Wolf-Phillips, **Third World Foundation, Monograph**, no. 7, London.

Appendix 1

Table 1.1   Basic Development Indicators

	Population (millions) mid-1986	Area (thousands of square kilometers)	GNP per capita[a] Dollars 1986	GNP per capita[a] Average annual growth rate (percent) 1965-86	Average annual rate of inflation[a] (percent) 1965-80	Average annual rate of inflation[a] (percent) 1980-86	Life expectancy at birth (years) 1986
Low-income economies	**2,493.0 t**	**33,608 t**	**270 w**	**3.1 w**	**4.6 w**	**8.1 w**	**61 w**
China and India	**1,835.4 t**	**12,849 t**	**300 w**	**3.7 w**	**2.9 w**	**5.3 w**	**64 w**
Other low-income	**657.6 t**	**20,759 t**	**200 w**	**0.5 w**	**11.3 w**	**19.1 w**	**52 w**
1 Ethiopia	43.5	1,222	120	0.0	3.4	3.4	46
2 Bhutan	1.3	47	150	..	..	..	45
3 Burkina Faso	8.1	274	150	1.3	6.2	6.3	47
4 Nepal	17.0	141	150	1.9	7.7	8.8	47
5 Bangladesh	103.2	144	160	0.4	14.9	11.2	50
6 Malawi	7.4	119	160	1.5	7.0	12.4	45
7 Zaire	31.7	2,345	160	-2.2	24.5	54.1	52
8 Mali	7.6	1,240	180	1.1		7.4	47
9 Burma	38.0	677	200	2.3	8.7	2.1	59
10 Mozambique	14.2	802	210	..	..	28.1	48
11 Madagascar	10.6	587	230	-1.7	7.9	17.8	53
12 Uganda	15.2	236	230	-2.6	21.5	74.9	48
13 Burundi	4.8	28	240	1.8	8.4	6.4	48
14 Tanzania	23.0	945	250	-0.3	9.9	21.5	53
15 Togo	3.1	57	250	0.2	6.9	6.7	53
16 Niger	6.6	1,267	260	-2.2	7.5	6.6	44
17 Benin	4.2	113	270	0.2	7.4	8.6	50
18 Somalia	5.5	638	280	-0.3	10.3	45.4	47
19 Central African Rep.	2.7	623	290	-0.6	8.5	11.5	50
20 India	781.4	3,288	290	1.8	7.6	7.8	57

Table 1.1   Basic Development Indicators (Cont.)

21 Rwanda	6.2	26	290	1.5	12.4	5.6	48
22 China	1054.0	9,561	300	5.1	0.0	3.8	69
23 Kenya	21.2	583	300	1.9	7.3	9.9	57
24 Zambia	6.9	753	300	-1.7	6.4	23.3	53
25 Sierra Leone	3.8	72	310	0.2	8.0	33.5	41
26 Sudan	22.6	2,506	320	-0.2	11.5	32.6	49
27 Haiti	6.1	28	330	0.6	7.3	7.7	54
28 Pakistan	99.2	804	350	2.4	10.3	7.5	52
29 Lesotho	1.6	30	370	5.6	8.0	13.1	55
30 Ghana	13.2	239	390	-1.7	22.8	50.8	54
31 Sri Lanka	16.1	66	400	2.9	9.6	13.5	70
32 Mauritania	1.8	1,031	420	-0.3	7.7	9.9	47
33 Senegal	6.8	196	420	-0.6	6.5	9.5	47
34 *Afghanistan*	..	648	..	..	4.9	..	..
35 *Chad*	5.1	1,284	..	..	6.3	..	45
36 *Guinea*	6.3	246	..	..	2.9	..	42
37 *Kampuchea, Dem.*	..	181	..	..	..	..	..
38 *Lao PDR*	3.7	237	..	..	..	..	50
39 *Viet Nam*	63.3	330	..	..	..	..	65
Middle-income economies	**1,268.4 t**	**37,278 t**	**1,270 w**	**2.6 w**	**21.0 w**	**56.8 w**	**63 w**
Lower middle-income	**691.2 t**	**15,029 t**	**750 w**	**2.5 w**	**22.3 w**	**22.9 w**	**59 w**
40 Liberia	2.3	111	460	-1.4	6.3	1.1	54
41 Yemen, PDR	2.2	333	470	..	..	4.8	50
42 Indonesia	166.4	1,919	490	4.6	34.3	8.9	57
43 Yemen Arab Rep.	8.2	195	550	4.7	..	13.1	46
44 Philippines	57.3	300	560	1.9	11.7	18.2	63

Table 1.1 Basic Development Indicators (Cont.)

45 Morocco	22.5	447	590	1.9	6.1	7.7	60
46 Bolivia	6.6	1,099	600	-0.4	15.7	683.7	53
47 Zimbabwe	8.7	391	620	1.2	6.3	13.0	58
48 Nigeria	103.1	924	640	1.9	14.4	10.5	51
49 Dominican Rep.	6.6	49	710	2.5	6.8	15.9	66
50 Papua New Guinea	3.4	462	720	0.5	8.1	5.1	52
51 Côte d'Ivoire	10.7	323	730	1.2	9.3	8.3	52
52 Honduras	4.5	112	740	0.3	6.3	5.2	64
53 Egypt, Arab Rep.	49.7	1,001	760	3.1	7.5	12.4	61
54 Nicaragua	3.4	130	790	-2.2	8.9	56.5	61
55 Thailand	52.6	514	810	4.0	6.8	3.0	64
56 El Salvador	4.9	21	820	-0.3	7.0	14.9	61
57 Botswana	1.1	600	840	8.8	8.0	7.6	59
58 Jamaica	2.4	11	840	-1.4	12.8	19.8	73
59 Cameroon	10.5	475	910	3.9	9.0	11.0	56
60 Guatemala	8.2	109	930	1.4	7.1	11.3	61
61 Congo, People's Rep.	2.0	342	990	3.6	7.1	7.5	58
62 Paraguay	3.8	407	1,000	3.6	9.4	19.0	67
63 Peru	19.8	1,285	1,090	0.1	20.5	100.1	60
64 Turkey	51.5	781	1,110	2.7	20.7	37.3	65
65 Tunisia	7.3	164	1,140	3.8	6.7	8.9	63
66 Ecuador	9.6	284	1,160	3.5	10.9	29.5	66
67 Mauritius	1.0	2	1,200	3.0	11.4	8.1	66
68 Colombia	29.0	1,139	1,230	2.8	17.4	22.6	65
69 Chile	12.2	757	1,320	-0.2	129.9	20.2	71
70 Costa Rica	2.6	51	1,480	1.6	11.3	32.3	74
71 Jordan	3.6	98	1,540	5.5		3.2	65
72 Syrian Arab Rep.	10.8	185	1,570	3.7	8.4	6.2	64
73 *Lebanon*	:	10	:	:	9.3	:	:

Table 1.1 Basic Development Indicators (Cont.)

Upper middle-income	577.2 t	22,248 t	1,890 w	2.8 w	20.5 w	72.0 w	67 w
74 Brazil	138.4	8,512	1,810	4.3	31.3	157.1	65
75 Malaysia	16.1	330	1,830	4.3	4.9	1.4	69
76 South Africa	32.3	1,221	1,850	0.4	9.9	13.6	61
77 Mexico	80.2	1,973	1,860	2.6	13.1	63.7	68
78 Uruguay	3.0	176	1,900	1.4	57.8	50.4	71
79 Hungary	10.6	93	2,020	3.9	2.6	5.4	71
80 Poland	37.5	313	2,070	:	:	31.2	72
81 Portugal	10.2	92	2,250	3.2	11.5	22.0	73
82 Yugoslavia	23.3	256	2,300	3.9	15.3	51.8	71
83 Panama	2.2	77	2,330	2.4	5.4	3.3	72
84 Argentina	31.0	2,767	2,350	0.2	78.3	326.2	70
85 Korea, Rep. of	41.5	98	2,370	6.7	18.8	5.4	69
86 Algeria	22.4	2,382	2,590	3.5	9.9	6.1	62
87 Venezuela	17.8	912	2,920	0.4	8.7	8.7	70
88 Gabon	1.0	268	3,080	1.9	12.7	4.8	52
89 Greece	10.0	132	3,680	3.3	10.5	20.3	76
90 Oman	1.3	300	4,980	5.0	20.5	3.6	54
91 Trinidad and Tobago	1.2	5	5,360	1.6	14.0	8.6	70
92 Israel	4.3	21	6,210	2.6	25.2	182.9	75
93 Hong Kong	5.4	1	6,910	6.2	8.1	6.9	76
94 Singapore	2.6	1	7,410	7.6	4.7	1.9	73
95 Iran, Islamic Rep.	45.6	1,648	:	:	15.6	:	59
96 Iraq	16.5	435	:	:	:	:	63
97 Romania	22.9	238	:	:	:	:	71
Developing economies	3,761.4 t	70,922 t	610 w	2.9 w	16.7 w	44.3 w	61 w
Oil exporters	538.3 t	13,053 t	930 w	2.5 w	15.3 w	26.0 w	59 w
Exporters of manufactures	2,132.4 t	22,472 t	540 w	4.0 w	13.0 w	51.0 w	64 w
Highly indebted countries	569.5 t	21,213 t	1,400 w	2.3 w	26.5 w	91.6 w	63 w
Sub-Saharan Africa	424.1 t	20,895 t	370 w	0.9 w	12.5 w	16.1 w	50 w

Table 1.1 Basic Development Indicators (Cont.)

High-income oil exporters	19.1 t	4,011 t	6,740 w	1.8 w	16.4 w	-1.3 w	64 w
98 Saudi Arabia	12.0	2,150	6,950	4.0	17.2	-1.3	63
99 Kuwait	1.8	18	13,890	-0.6	14.1	..	73
100 United Arab Emirates	1.4	84	14,680	..	..	-1.4	69
101 Libya	3.9	1,760	..	..	..	..	61
Industrial market economies	741.6 t	30,935 t	12,960 w	2.3 w	7.6 w	5.3 w	76 w
102 Spain	38.7	505	4,860	2.9	11.8	11.3	76
103 Ireland	3.6	70	5,070	1.7	12.2	10.7	74
104 New Zealand	3.3	269	7,460	1.5	9.6	11.0	74
105 Italy	57.2	301	8,550	2.6	11.2	13.2	77
106 United Kingdom	56.7	245	8,870	1.7	11.2	6.0	75
107 Belgium	9.9	31	9,230	2.7	6.6	5.7	75
108 Austria	7.6	84	9,990	3.3	5.8	4.5	74
109 Netherlands	14.6	41	10,020	1.9	7.6	3.1	77
110 France	55.4	547	10,720	2.8	8.0	8.8	77
111 Australia	16.0	7,687	11,920	1.7	9.5	8.2	78
112 Germany, Fed. Rep.	60.9	249	12,080	2.5	5.2	3.0	75
113 Finland	4.9	337	12,160	3.2	10.4	8.1	75
114 Denmark	5.1	43	12,600	1.9	9.2	7.3	75
115 Japan	121.5	372	12,840	4.3	7.8	1.6	78
116 Sweden	8.4	450	13,160	1.6	8.3	8.2	77
117 Canada	25.6	9,976	14,120	2.6	7.2	5.5	76
118 Norway	4.2	324	15,400	3.4	7.7	7.0	77
119 United States	241.6	9,363	17,480	1.6	6.4	4.4	75
120 Switzerland	6.5	41	17,680	1.4	5.3	4.2	77

Table 1.1 Basic Development Indicators (Cont.)

Nonreporting nonmembers	367.3 t	25,825 t	..	..	..	..	..	69 w
121 Albania	3.0	29	..	..	..	..	..	71
122 Angola	9.0	1,247	..	..	..	..	..	44
123 Bulgaria	9.0	111	..	..	..	..	..	72
124 Cuba	10.2	115	..	..	..	..	..	75
125 Czechoslovakia	15.5	128	..	..	..	..	..	70
126 German Dem. Rep.	16.6	108	..	..	..	..	..	72
127 Korea, Dem. Rep.	20.9	121	..	..	..	..	..	68
128 Mongolia	2.0	1,565	..	..	..	..	..	64
129 USSR	281.1	22,402	..	..	..	..	..	70

Note: For data comparability and coverage, see the technical notes. Figures in italics are for years other than those specified.

For U.N. and World Bank member countries with populations of less than 1 million, see Box A.

a. See the technical notes in source

Source: Table 1, World Bank, 1988.

Table 1.2 Population Growth and Projections

	Average annual growth of population (percent)			Population (millions)			Hypothetical size of stationary population (millions)	Assumed year of reaching net reproduction rate of 1	Population momentum 1985
	1965-80	1980-86	1986-2000	1986	1990a	2000a			
Low-income economies	**2.3 w**	**1.9 w**	**1.9 w**	**2,493 t**	**2,700 t**	**3,246 t**			1.9
China and India	**2.2 w**	**1.6 w**	**1.6 w**	**1,835 t**	**1,963 t**	**2,281 t**			1.7
Other low-income	**2.7 w**	**2.8 w**	**2.8 w**	**658 t**	**736 t**	**966 t**			1.9
1 Ethiopia	2.7	2.4	2.9	43	49	65	205	2040	1.9
2 Bhutan	1.6	2.0	2.2	1	1	2	4	2035	1.7
3 Burkina Faso	2.0	2.5	2.9	8	9	12	42	2040	1.8
4 Nepal	2.4	2.6	2.5	17	19	24	63	2035	1.8
5 Bangladesh	2.7	2.6	2.5	103	114	145	342	2030	1.9
6 Malawi	2.9	3.2	3.3	7	8	12	42	2040	1.9
7 Zaire	2.8	3.1	3.0	32	36	48	142	2035	1.9
8 Mali	2.1	2.3	2.7	8	8	11	39	2040	1.8
9 Burma	2.3	2.0	2.3	38	42	52	102	2020	1.7
10 Mozambique	2.5	2.7	3.0	14	16	22	74	2040	1.9
11 Madagascar	2.5	3.3	3.2	11	12	16	52	2035	1.9
12 Uganda	2.9	3.1	3.2	15	17	23	82	2040	1.9
13 Burundi	1.9	2.7	3.1	5	5	7	24	2035	1.8
14 Tanzania	3.3	3.5	3.4	23	27	37	123	2035	2.0
15 Togo	3.0	3.4	3.3	3	4	5	16	2035	2.0
16 Niger	2.7	3.0	3.2	7	7	10	36	2040	1.9
17 Benin	2.7	3.2	3.4	4	5	7	22	2035	2.0
18 Somalia	2.7	2.9	3.1	6	6	8	30	2040	1.9
19 Central African Rep.	1.8	2.5	2.9	3	3	4	12	2035	1.8
20 India	2.3	2.2	1.8	781	846	1,002	1,698	2010	1.7

Table 1.2 Population Growth and Projections (Cont.)

21 Rwanda	3.3	3.3	3.7	6	7	10	40	2040	1.9
22 China	2.2	1.2	1.4	1,054	1,117	1,279	1,695	2000	1.6
23 Kenya	3.6	4.1	3.9	21	25	36	121	2030	2.1
24 Zambia	3.1	3.5	3.4	7	8	11	37	2035	2.0
25 Sierra Leone	2.0	2.4	2.6	4	4	5	18	2045	1.8
26 Sudan	3.0	2.8	2.9	23	25	34	101	2035	1.8
27 Haiti	2.0	1.8	2.0	6	7	8	17	2030	1.7
28 Pakistan	3.1	3.1	3.0	99	113	150	423	2035	1.8
29 Lesotho	2.3	2.7	2.7	2	2	2	6	2030	1.8
30 Ghana	2.2	3.5	3.1	13	15	20	58	2030	1.9
31 Sri Lanka	1.8	1.5	1.5	16	17	20	30	2005	1.7
32 Mauritania	2.3	2.6	2.8	2	2	3	9	2040	1.8
33 Senegal	2.5	2.9	3.0	7	8	10	30	2035	1.9
34 *Afghanistan*	2.4	..	..	..	..	..	..	..	..
35 *Chad*	2.0	2.3	2.5	5	6	7	22	2040	1.8
36 *Guinea*	1.9	2.4	2.4	6	7	9	26	2040	1.8
37 *Kampuchea, Dem.*	0.3	..	..	..	..	..	..	..	..
38 *Lao PDR*	1.4	2.0	2.8	4	4	5	15	2035	1.8
39 *Viet Nam*	..	2.6	2.4	63	70	88	168	2015	1.8
Middle-income economies	**2.4 w**	**2.3 w**	**2.1 w**	**1,268 t**	**1,380 t**	**1,680 t**			
Lower middle-income	**2.5 w**	**2.6 w**	**2.3 w**	**691 t**	**758 t**	**941 t**			
40 Liberia	3.0	3.3	3.2	2	3	3	11	2035	1.9
41 Yemen, PDR	2.0	3.1	2.8	2	3	3	9	2035	1.9
42 Indonesia	2.3	2.2	1.8	166	178	207	335	2005	1.8
43 Yemen Arab Rep.	2.8	2.5	3.0	8	9	12	39	2040	1.9
44 Philippines	2.9	2.5	2.3	57	62	76	137	2015	1.8

Table 1.2 Population Growth and Projections (Cont.)

45	Morocco	2.5	2.5	2.2	22	25	30	59	2020	1.8
46	Bolivia	2.5	2.7	2.6	7	7	9	24	2030	1.8
47	Zimbabwe	3.1	3.7	3.0	9	10	13	33	2025	2.0
48	Nigeria	2.5	3.3	3.3	103	118	164	529	2035	2.0
49	Dominican Rep.	2.7	2.4	2.1	7	7	9	13	2015	1.5
50	Papua New Guinea	2.3	2.1	2.2	3	4	5	10	2025	1.8
51	Côte d'Ivoire	4.2	4.2	3.6	11	12	17	51	2030	2.0
52	Honduras	3.2	3.6	3.0	5	5	7	16	2020	2.0
53	Egypt, Arab Rep.	2.4	2.7	2.2	50	55	67	132	2020	1.8
54	Nicaragua	3.1	3.4	3.0	3	4	5	13	2025	2.0
55	Thailand	2.7	2.0	1.6	53	56	65	99	2000	1.8
56	El Salvador	2.7	1.2	1.9	5	5	6	13	2015	1.8
57	Botswana	3.5	3.5	3.3	1	1	2	5	2025	2.0
58	Jamaica	1.5	1.5	1.4	2	3	3	4	2005	1.7
59	Cameroon	2.7	3.2	3.3	11	12	17	51	2030	1.9
60	Guatemala	2.8	2.9	2.7	8	9	12	29	2025	1.8
61	Congo, People's Rep.	2.7	3.3	3.5	2	2	3	10	2030	1.9
62	Paraguay	2.8	3.2	2.5	4	4	5	10	2015	1.8
63	Peru	2.8	2.3	2.1	20	22	27	48	2015	1.8
64	Turkey	2.4	2.5	1.9	51	56	67	112	2010	1.7
65	Tunisia	2.1	2.3	2.2	7	8	10	18	2015	1.8
66	Ecuador	3.1	2.9	2.4	10	11	13	26	2015	1.9
67	Mauritius	1.6	1.0	1.2	1	1	1	2	2000	1.7
68	Colombia	2.2	1.9	1.8	29	31	37	59	2010	1.7
69	Chile	1.8	1.7	1.2	12	13	14	20	2000	1.6
70	Costa Rica	2.6	2.4	2.1	3	3	3	5	2005	1.8
71	Jordan	2.6	3.7	3.1	4	4	6	13	2020	1.8
72	Syrian Arab Rep.	3.4	3.5	3.3	11	13	17	42	2020	1.9
73	*Lebanon*	1.6	:	:	:	:	:	:	:	1.9

Table 1.2 Population Growth and Projections (Cont.)

Upper middle-income	2.2 w	1.9 w	1.8 w	577 t	622 t	739 t			
74 Brazil	2.4	2.2	1.9	138	150	180	306	2015	1.8
75 Malaysia	2.5	2.7	1.9	16	18	21	33	2005	1.8
76 South Africa	2.4	2.2	2.3	32	36	45	90	2020	1.8
77 Mexico	3.1	2.2	2.1	80	87	107	187	2010	1.9
78 Uruguay	0.4	0.4	0.7	3	3	3	4	2000	1.3
79 Hungary	0.4	−0.1	−0.1	11	11	11	10	2030	1.1
80 Poland	0.8	0.9	0.6	38	39	41	48	2020	1.3
81 Portugal	0.6	0.5	0.3	10	10	11	11	2030	1.3
82 Yugoslavia	0.9	0.7	0.5	23	24	25	27	2030	1.3
83 Panama	2.6	2.2	1.8	2	2	3	4	2005	1.8
84 Argentina	1.6	1.6	1.1	31	33	36	52	2005	1.5
85 Korea, Rep. of	1.9	1.4	1.2	41	44	49	65	1985	1.6
86 Algeria	3.1	3.1	2.9	22	25	33	81	2025	1.9
87 Venezuela	3.5	2.9	2.2	18	20	24	40	2005	1.8
88 Gabon	3.5	4.4	2.8	1	1	1	4	2035	1.7
89 Greece	0.7	0.5	0.3	10	10	10	10	2030	1.2
90 Oman	3.6	4.7	3.2	1	2	2	5	2030	1.9
91 Trinidad and Tobago	1.3	1.5	1.3	1	1	1	2	2010	1.6
92 Israel	2.8	1.7	1.4	4	5	5	7	2005	1.6
93 Hong Kong	2.1	1.2	1.0	5	6	6	7	2030	1.4
94 Singapore	1.6	1.1	0.8	3	3	3	3	2030	1.4
95 Iran, Islamic Rep.	3.2	2.8	3.0	46	52	69	169	2025	1.9
96 Iraq	3.4	3.6	3.6	16	19	27	75	2025	1.9
97 Romania	1.1	0.5	0.5	23	23	24	28	2030	1.3

Table 1.2 Population Growth and Projections (Cont.)

Developing economies	2.3 w	2.0 w	2.0 w	3,761 t	4,079 t	4,926 t			1.8
Oil exporters	2.7 w	2.7 w	2.5 w	538 t	595 t	754 t			1.8
Exporters of manufactures	2.2 w	1.6 w	1.5 w	2,132 t	2,277 t	2,635 t			1.4
Highly indebted countries	2.5 w	2.4 w	2.2 w	570 t	625 t	773 t			1.9
Sub-Saharan Africa	2.7 w	3.1 w	3.2 w	424 t	482 t	659 t			1.9
High-income oil exporters	5.3 w	4.2 w	3.6 w	19 t	22 t	31 t			
98 Saudi Arabia	4.6	4.1	3.8	12	14	20	54	2025	1.8
99 Kuwait	7.0	4.4	2.9	2	2	3	5	2015	1.8
100 United Arab Emirates	16.1	5.6	2.8	1	2	2	4	2020	1.4
101 *Libya*	4.6	3.9	3.6	4	5	6	17	2025	1.9
Industrial market economies	0.8 w	0.6 w	0.4 w	742 t	756 t	782 t			
102 Spain	1.0	0.6	0.4	39	39	41	41	2030	1.3
103 Ireland	1.2	0.8	1.0	4	4	4	6	2020	1.4
104 New Zealand	1.3	0.9	0.6	3	3	4	4	2030	1.3
105 Italy	0.6	0.3	0.1	57	58	58	46	2030	1.1
106 United Kingdom	0.2	0.1	0.1	57	57	58	56	2030	1.1
107 Belgium	0.3	0.0	-0.1	10	10	10	8	2030	1.1
108 Austria	0.3	0.0	-0.1	8	8	7	6	2030	1.1
109 Netherlands	0.9	0.5	0.3	15	15	15	13	2030	1.2
110 France	0.7	0.5	0.4	55	56	58	58	2030	1.2
111 Australia	1.8	1.4	1.0	16	17	18	20	2030	1.4
112 Germany, Fed. Rep.	0.3	-0.2	-0.3	61	60	59	40	2030	1.0
113 Finland	0.3	0.5	0.2	5	5	5	4	2030	1.1
114 Denmark	0.5	0.0	-0.1	5	5	5	4	2030	1.1
115 Japan	1.2	0.7	0.5	121	124	129	119	2030	1.1
116 Sweden	0.5	0.1	0.0	8	8	8	7	2030	1.0

Table 1.2 Population Growth and Projections (Cont.)

117 Canada	1.3	1.1	0.7	26	27	28	28	2030	1.3
118 Norway	0.6	0.3	0.2	4	4	4	4	2030	1.2
119 United States	1.0	1.0	0.6	242	249	263	279	2030	1.3
120 Switzerland	0.5	0.3	0.0	7	6	6	5	2030	1.1
Nonreporting nonmembers	1.0 w	1.0 w	0.8 w	367 t	381 t	414 t			
121 *Albania*	2.5	2.1	1.8	3	3	4	6	2005	1.7
122 *Angola*	2.8	2.6	2.8	9	10	13	43	2040	1.9
123 *Bulgaria*	0.5	0.2	0.2	9	9	9	10	2030	1.1
124 *Cuba*	1.5	0.9	0.8	10	11	11	12	2030	1.5
125 *Czechoslovakia*	0.5	0.3	0.3	16	16	16	19	2030	1.2
126 *German Dem. Rep.*	-0.2	-0.1	0.0	17	17	17	15	2030	1.1
127 *Korea, Dem. Rep.*	2.7	2.5	2.1	21	23	28	49	2015	1.8
128 *Mongolia*	3.0	2.8	2.4	2	2	3	6	2020	1.8
129 *USSR*	0.9	1.0	0.7	281	291	312	398	2020	1.3

Note: For data comparability and coverage, see the technical notes. Figures in italics are for years other than those specified.

a. For the assumptions used in the projections, see the technical notes in source

Source: Table 27, World Bank, 1988.

Table 1.3 Urbanisation Levels

	Urban population				Percentage of urban population				Number of cities of over 500,000 persons	
	As percentage of total population		Average annual growth rate (percent)		In largest city		In cities of over 500,000 persons			
	1965	1985	1965-80	1980-85	1960	1980	1960	1980	1960	1980
Low-income economies	17 w	22 w	3.6 w	4.0 w	10 w	16 w	31 w	55 w	54 t	148 t
China and India	18 w	23 w	3.0 w	3.6 w	7 w	6 w	33 w	59 w	49 t	114 t
Other low-income	13 w	20 w	4.9 w	5.4 w	26 w	30 w	19 w	40 w	5 t	34 t
1 Ethiopia	8	15	6.6	3.7	30	37	0	37	0	1
2 Bhutan	3	4	3.7	5.2	..	..	0	0	0	0
3 Burkina Faso	6	8	3.4	5.3	..	41	0	0	0	0
4 Nepal	4	7	5.1	5.6	41	27	0	0	0	0
5 Bangladesh	6	18	8.0	7.9	20	30	20	51	1	3
6 Malawi	5	..	7.8	..	14	19	0	0	0	0
7 Zaire	19	39	7.2	8.4	32	28	14	38	1	2
8 Mali	13	20	4.9	4.5	23	24	0	0	0	0
9 Burma	21	24	2.8	2.8	23	23	23	23	1	2
10 Mozambique	5	19	11.8	5.3	75	83	0	83	0	1
11 Madagascar	12	21	5.7	5.3	44	36	0	36	0	1
12 Uganda	6	7	4.1	3.0	38	52	0	52	0	1
13 Burundi	2	2	1.8	2.7	..	..	0	0	0	0
14 Tanzania	6	14	8.7	8.3	34	50	0	50	0	0
15 Togo	11	23	7.2	6.4	..	60	0	0	0	0
16 Niger	7	15	6.9	7.0	..	31	0	0	0	0
17 Benin	11	35	10.2	4.4	..	63	0	63	0	1
18 Somalia	20	34	6.1	5.4	..	34	0	0	0	0
19 Central African Rep.	27	45	4.8	3.9	40	36	0	0	0	0
20 India	19	25	3.6	3.9	7	6	26	39	11	36

Table 1.3 Urbanisation Levels (Cont.)

21 Rwanda	3	5	6.3	6.7	..	..	0	0	0	0
22 China	18	22	2.6	3.3	6	6	42	45	38	78
23 Kenya	9	20	9.0	6.3	40	57	0	57	0	1
24 Zambia	24	48	7.1	5.5	..	35	0	35	0	1
25 Sierra Leone	15	25	4.3	5.1	37	47	0	0	0	0
26 Sudan	13	21	5.1	4.8	30	31	0	31	0	1
27 Haiti	18	27	4.0	4.1	42	56	0	56	0	1
28 Pakistan	24	29	4.3	4.8	20	21	33	51	2	7
29 Lesotho	2	17	14.6	5.3	..	..	0	0	0	0
30 Ghana	26	32	3.4	3.9	25	35	0	48	0	2
31 Sri Lanka	20	21	2.3	8.4	28	16	0	16	0	1
32 Mauritania	7	31	12.4	3.4	..	39	0	0	0	0
33 Senegal	27	36	4.1	4.0	53	65	0	65	0	1
34 *Afghanistan*	9	..	6.0	..	33	17	0	17	0	1
35 *Chad*	9	27	9.2	3.9	..	39	0	0	0	0
36 *Guinea*	12	22	6.6	4.3	37	80	0	80	0	1
37 *Kampuchea, Dem.*	11	..	1.9	..	..	..	..	..	..	..
38 *Lao PDR*	8	15	4.8	5.6	69	48	..	..	..	0
39 *Viet Nam*	..	20	..	3.4	..	21	..	50	..	4
Middle-income economies	37 w	48 w	4.4 w	3.5 w	28 w	27 w	37 w	49 w	59 t	131 t
Lower middle-income	27 w	36 w	4.5 w	3.7 w	29 w	31 w	31 w	46 w	22 t	55 t
40 Liberia	23	37	6.2	4.3	..	..	0	0	0	0
41 Yemen, PDR	30	37	3.2	4.9	61	49	0	0	0	0
42 Indonesia	16	25	4.7	2.3	20	23	34	50	3	9
43 Yemen Arab Rep.	5	19	10.7	7.3	..	25	0	0	0	0
44 Philippines	32	39	4.0	3.2	27	30	27	34	1	2
45 Morocco	32	44	4.2	4.2	16	26	16	50	1	4
46 Bolivia	40	44	2.9	5.6	47	44	0	44	0	1
47 Zimbabwe	14	27	7.5	5.0	40	50	0	50	0	1
48 Nigeria	15	30	4.8	5.2	13	17	22	58	2	9
49 Dominican Rep.	35	56	5.3	4.2	50	54	0	54	0	1

Table 1.3 Urbanisation Levels (Cont.)

50 Papua New Guinea	5	14	8.4	4.9	:	25	0	0	0	0
51 Côte d'Ivoire	23	45	8.7	6.9	27	34	0	34	0	1
52 Honduras	26	39	5.5	5.2	31	33	0	0	0	0
53 Egypt, Arab Rep.	41	46	2.9	3.4	38	39	53	53	2	2
54 Nicaragua	43	56	4.6	4.5	41	47	0	47	2	1
55 Thailand	13	18	4.6	3.2	65	69	65	69	1	1
56 El Salvador	39	43	3.5	4.0	26	22	0	0	0	0
57 Botswana	4	20	15.4	4.5	:	:	:	:	:	:
58 Jamaica	38	53	3.4	3.2	77	66	0	66	0	1
59 Cameroon	16	42	8.1	7.0	26	21	0	21	0	1
60 Guatemaia	34	41	3.6	4.2	41	36	41	36	1	1
61 Congo, People's Rep.	35	40	3.5	3.6	77	56	0	0	0	0
62 Paraguay	36	41	3.2	3.7	44	44	0	44	0	1
63 Peru	52	68	4.1	3.8	38	39	38	44	1	3
64 Turkey	32	46	4.3	4.4	18	24	32	42	3	4
65 Tunisia	40	56	4.2	3.7	40	30	40	30	1	1
66 Ecuador	37	52	5.1	3.7	31	29	0	51	0	2
67 Mauritius	37	54	4.0	2.1	:	:	:	:	:	:
68 Colombia	54	67	3.5	2.8	17	26	28	51	3	4
69 Chile	72	83	2.6	2.1	38	44	38	44	1	1
70 Costa Rica	38	45	3.7	3.8	67	64	0	64	0	1
71 Jordan	47	69	5.3	4.0	31	37	0	37	0	1
72 Syrian Arab Rep.	40	49	4.5	5.5	35	33	35	55	1	2
73 *Lebanon*	49	:	4.6	:	64	79	64	79	1	1
Upper middle-income	49 w	65 w	3.8 w	3.2 w	27 w	26 w	39 w	50 w	37 t	76 t
74 Brazil	50	73	4.5	4.0	14	15	35	52	6	14
75 Malaysia	26	38	4.5	4.0	19	27	0	27	0	1
76 South Africa	47	56	2.6	3.3	16	13	44	53	4	7
77 Mexico	55	69	4.5	3.6	28	32	36	48	3	7
78 Uruguay	81	85	0.7	0.9	56	52	56	52	1	1

Table 1.3 Urbanisation Levels (Cont.)

79 Hungary	43	55	1.8	1.3	45	37	45	37	1	1
80 Poland	50	60	1.8	1.6	17	15	41	47	5	8
81 Portugal	24	31	2.0	3.3	47	44	47	44	1	1
82 Yugoslavia	31	45	3.0	2.5	11	10	11	23	1	3
83 Panama	44	50	3.4	2.6	61	66	0	66	0	1
84 Argentina	76	84	2.2	1.9	46	45	54	60	3	5
85 Korea, Rep. of	32	64	5.7	2.5	35	41	61	77	3	7
86 Algeria	38	43	3.8	3.7	27	12	27	12	1	1
87 Venezuela	72	85	4.5	3.5	26	26	26	44	1	4
88 Gabon	8	12	4.2	4.6	:	:	:	:	:	:
89 Greece	48	65	2.5	1.9	51	57	51	70	1	2
90 Oman	4	9	8.1	7.3	:	:	:	:	:	0
91 Trinidad and Tobago	30	64	5.0	3.3	:	:	0	0	0	0
92 Israel	81	90	3.5	2.4	46	35	46	35	1	1
93 Hong Kong	89	93	2.3	1.3	100	100	100	100	:	1
94 Singapore	100	100	1.6	1.2	100	100	100	100	1	1
95 *Iran, Islamic Rep.*	37	54	5.5	4.6	26	28	26	47	1	6
96 *Iraq*	51	70	5.3	6.3	35	55	35	70	:	3
97 *Romania*	34	51	3.4	1.0	22	17	22	17	1	1
Developing economies	24 w	31 w	3.9 w	3.8 w	19 w	21 w	34 w	46 w	113 t	279 t
Oil exporters	29 w	41 w	4.3 w	3.5 w	24 w	24 w	34 w	48 w	17 t	47 t
Exporters of manufactures	23 w	29 w	3.2 w	3.5 w	12 w	12 w	37 w	46 w	70 t	154 t
Highly indebted countries	44 w	57 w	3.5 w	3.5 w	23 w	23 w	35 w	50 w	29 t	67 t
Sub-Saharan Africa	13 w	25 w	6.2 w	5.7 w	22 w	32 w	8 w	42 w	2 t	14 t
High-income oil exporters	40 w	73 w	9.5 w	6.0 w	29 w	28 w	0 w	34 w	0 t	3 t
98 Saudi Arabia	39	72	8.5	6.1	15	18	0	33	0	2
99 Kuwait	78	92	8.2	5.1	75	30	0	0	0	0
100 United Arab Emirates	56	79	18.9	5.5	:	:	:	:	:	:
101 *Libya*	29	60	9.7	6.7	57	64	0	64	0	1

Table 1.3 Urbanisation Levels (Cont.)

Industrial market economies	70 w	75 w	1.4 w	1.5 w	18 w	18 w	1.8 w	48 w	55 w	104 t	152 t
102 Spain	61	77	2.4	1.6	13	17		37	44	5	6
103 Ireland	49	57	2.2	2.7	51	48		51	48	1	1
104 New Zealand	79	83	1.5	0.9	25	30		0	30	0	1
105 Italy	62	67	1.0	0.9	13	17		46	52	7	9
106 United Kingdom	87	92	0.5	0.3	24	20		61	55	15	17
107 Belgium	93	96	0.5	0.4	17	14		28	24	2	2
108 Austria	51	56	0.1	0.7	51	39		51	39	1	1
109 Netherlands	86	88	1.5	0.9	9	9		27	24	3	3
110 France	67	73	2.7	1.0	25	23		34	34	4	6
111 Australia	83	86	0.2	1.4	26	24		62	68	4	5
112 Germany, Fed. Rep.	79	86	0.8	0.1	20	18		48	45	11	11
113 Finland	44	60	2.5	2.9	28	27		0	27	0	1
114 Denmark	77	86	1.1	0.3	40	32		40	32	1	1
115 Japan	67	76	2.1	1.8	18	22		35	42	5	9
116 Sweden	77	86	1.0	1.2	15	15		15	35	1	3
117 Canada	73	77	1.5	1.7	50	32		50	32	1	1
118 Norway	37	73	5.0	0.9	14	18		31	62	2	9
119 United States	72	74	1.2	2.3	13	12		61	77	40	65
120 Switzerland	53	60	1.2	0.9	19	22		19	22	1	1
Nonreporting nonmembers	52 w	65 w	2.4 w	1.8 w	9 w	8 w		23 w	32 w	31 t	59 t
121 *Albania*	32	34	3.4	3.3	27	25		0	0	0	0
122 *Angola*	13	25	6.4	5.8	44	64		0	64	0	1
123 *Bulgaria*	46	68	2.8	1.7	23	18		23	18	1	1
124 *Cuba*	58	71	2.7	0.8	32	38		32	38	1	1
125 *Czechoslovakia*	51	66	1.9	1.4	17	12		17	12	1	1
126 *German Dem. Rep.*	73	76	0.1	0.6	9	9		14	17	2	3
127 *Korea, Dem. Rep.*	45	63	4.6	3.8	15	12		15	19	1	2
128 *Mongolia*	42	55	4.5	3.3	53	52		0	0	0	0
129 *USSR*	52	66	2.2	1.6	6	4		21	33	25	50

Note: For data comparability and coverage, see the technical notes. Figures in italics are for years other than those specified

Source: **Table 32, World Bank, 1988.**

Table 1.4 Rural and Urban Population Growth, 1950-2000

Country group	Percentage urban population			Average annual percentage growth			
				1950-80		1980-2000	
	1950	1980	2000	Urban	Rural	Urban	Rural
All developing countries	18.9	28.7	-	3.4	1.7	-	1.1
Excluding China	22.2	35.4	43.3	3.8	1.7	3.5	1.1
Low-income							
Asia	10.7	19.5	31.3	4.4	2.0	4.2	0.9
China	11.2	13.2a	-	2.5	1.8	-	-
India	16.8	23.3	35.5	3.2	1.8	4.2	1.1
Africa	5.7	19.2	34.9	7.0	2.5	5.8	1.5
Middle-income							
East Asia and Pacific	19.6	31.9	41.9	4.1	1.8	3.1	0.9
Middle East and North Africa	27.7	46.8	59.9	4.4	1.6	4.3	1.6
Sub-Saharan Africa	33.7	49.4	55.2	3.1	1.0	2.9	1.7
Latin America and Caribbean	41.4	65.3	75.4	4.1	0.8	2.9	0.4
Southern Europe	24.7	47.1	62.3	3.8	0.5	2.9	-0.2
Industrial countriesb	61.3	77.0	83.7	1.8	-0.7	1.0	-1.1

Notes:

– Not available.

a. Government estimate for 1979.

b. Excludes East European nonmarket economies.

Source: Table 4.3, World Bank, 1984.

Chapter 2

Transport Problems of Third World Cities

Harry T. Dimitriou

INTRODUCTION

Conditions of Rapid Urban Change

Although rapid motorisation growth rates have been most commonly associated with the deteriorating conditions of urban transport systems in the Third World, high rates of urbanisation and related changes to the economic base of settlements in this part of the globe are in fact (as indicated in the previous chapter) the more influential contributing factors. What is especially important about these trends is that they have taken place in settlements which are foci, in their respective countries, of forces of modernisation, industrialisation and technology-transfer, and thus constitute very important centres of local, national and regional development.

Between 1970 and 1980, populations of Third World urban areas increased by an average of 50 per cent and are expected by the year 2000 to accommodate approximately 2.2 billion of the globe's population (World Bank, 1986). Such developments are fuelled by rising natural population growth, as well as rapid migration increases to the city, especially of persons in search of employment from rural areas. Urbanisation is further encouraged by the concentration of wealth, the enhancement of development opportunities in urban locations, and the resultant physical expansion of city land areas and infrastructure. Together, these conditions have brought about a widespread rise in urban land values and new ways of life, very different from those of the traditional indigeneous cultures, and with values more akin to those of the West. The accompanying changes in the economic base of many Third World cities - brought about by a transition of a settlement's economic base from one previously geared toward serving a colonial nation, to one increasingly integrated into today's world market - have been encouraged by more aggressive international sales practices and by vastly improved transport, telecommunication and information systems.

Typology of Urban Transport Problems

Against a backcloth of the above, this chapter discusses two sets of Third World urban transport problems: those traditionally included on the agenda of national and city governments, such as traffic congestion and related environmental impacts, inefficient public transport operations, high road accident rates, weak institutional support, limited management and enforcement cabability etc.; and those associated with the planning and management response to urban movement needs, involving issues of perception in problem identification, differing technology-transfer priorities in problem resolution, and varied approaches to urban transport decision-making. The two sets of problems are often inseparable, particularly in the long run, when some existing traffic problems become aggravated by, or are in part attributable to, misconceived planning and management responses.

An additional method of differentiating among various kinds of urban transport problems (see Figure 2.1) is to distinguish between those which may be considered 'root problems' such as, rising incomes and car ownership levels, and 'manifestation problems' which include widespread traffic congestion and rising traffic accidents. Poor planning or management responses to transport problems may in fact be regarded as a particular kind of 'root problem'; an aspect discussed in greater depth in the last part of this chapter.

TRADITIONAL AGENDA OF URBAN TRANSPORT PROBLEMS

Transport problems of Third World cities inevitably take on a variety of forms, depending upon their location, wealth and levels

51

Figure 2.1: Urban Transort Manifestation and Root Problems

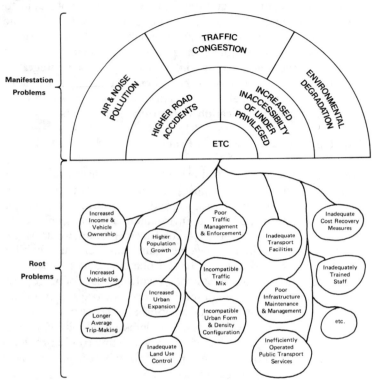

of motorisation. For most such problems are also a product of differing broader Third World national and urban development characteristics of the kind outlined in the preceding chapter. Notwithstanding this, it is common for Third World city governments to present a common agenda of transport problems of the kind discussed below.

Rapid Traffic Growth

Whilst motorisation in most Third World settlements is at relatively low levels in comparison to many cities of the industrialised world (1) its availability has sharply increased in recent decades. The number of vehicles per 1,000 population between 1970 and 1981 for example, increased twofold in Brazil, threefold in Indonesia, fivefold in Nigeria and seven to tenfold in Korea (World Bank, 1986). These trends received a particular impetus in the early 1980s during the downturn of the motor industry in the industrialised world, when international vehicle manufacturers marketed their products more aggressively and entered into many more agreements to build motor vehicle assembly plants in the Third World.

The most notable growth in traffic in many Third World cities has been of motorcycle vehicles. Statistics in Southeast Asia for example, show that in 1980 more than 60 per cent of the registered vehicles in Jakarta and Kuala Lumpur were motorcycles. Between 1980 and 1982 alone, cities such as Bangkok and Jakarta had their motorcycle modal split share increased by 29 and 15 per cent respectively, to 62 and 81 per cent. Comparable 1983 estimates for Kuala Lumpur indicate a 7 per cent rise since 1980 and a 1987 modal split share of 73 per cent (Spencer, 1988).

Rapid traffic growth in the Third World (especially of motorised movement) is concentrated primarily in the larger cities (see Table 2.1). It has been largely stimulated both by increased incomes (see Figure 2.2) and an overall expansion in related urban economic activities. Many Third World settlements have furthermore generated additional use of transport by virtue of their physical growth which has encouraged longer trip distances, rising in the case of Bogota by an average of 13 per cent between 1972 and 1978 (World Bank, 1986). Interesting work on this aspect of transport development has been conducted by Zahavi (1976 and 1980).

As a result of their population increase, Third World cities have also generated a growth in transport demand which is roughly proportional to their urban population increase (see Figure 2.3). Additional transport demand has been further created through (where this has taken place) improved transport infrastructure and service provision.

Shortage of Adequately Maintained Transport Facilities

The traffic growth described above has taken place at a pace far in excess of the rate of investment in suitably constructed and maintained urban transport infrastructure. This in turn has contributed to both widespread and location-specific congestion problems. Circumstances of this kind are typically a result of insufficient funds allocated to the urban transport sector and the absence of appropriate fund-raising mechanisms by which public

Table 2.1 Urban Transport Data: Selected Cities

City	Population 1980 (1,000)	Population Annual growth rate 1970-80 (per cent)	Metro area 1980 (square km)	GNP per capita[a] 1980 (US$)	Cars Total number 1980 (1,000)	Cars Per 1,000 pop. 1980	Cars Annual growth rate 1970-80 (per cent)	Buses Total number 1980	Buses Per 1,000 pop. 1980[b]	Commercial vehicles 1980 (number)
Abidjan	1,715	11.0	261	1,150	85	50	10.0	2,410	1.41	–
Accra	1,447	6.7	1,390	420	27	19	–	709	0.49*	7,411
Amman	1,125	4.1	36	1,420	81	72	–	433	0.38*	32,000
Ankara	1,900	4.4	237	1,470	65	34	14.2	781	0.41*	–
Bangkok	5,154	9.1	1,569	670	367	71	7.9	6,300	1.22	34,155
Bogota	4,254	7.1	–	1,180	180	42	7.8	9,081	2.13	–
Bombay	8,500	3.7	438	240	180	21	6.1	3,066	0.36*	38,447
Buenos Aires	10,100	1.7	210	2,390	537	53	10.0	12,089	1.20	97,245
Cairo	7,464	3.1	233	580	239	32	17.0	8,177	1.10*	42,000
Calcutta	9,400	3.0	1,414	240	95	10	5.6	3,160	0.33*	28,500
Harare	670	5.2	–	630	107	160	3.0	504	0.75	5,300
Hong Kong	5,067	2.5	1,060	4,240	200	39	7.4	9,278	1.83	58,801
Jakarta	6,700	4.0	650	430	222	33	9.8	4,798	0.72	77,781
Karachi	5,200	5.2	1,346	300	184	35	8.4	12,064	2.32	17,628
Kuala Lumpur	977	3.5	244	1,620	37	38	–	1,148	1.18	7,923
Lagos	1,321	8.1	665	1,010	62	47	–	–	–	58,857
Lima	4,415	4.2	–	930	333	75	7.2	8,853	2.01	1,060
Manila	5,925	5.1	636	690	266	45	8.0	31,403	5.30	100,725
Medellin	2,078	3.2	1,152	1,180	91	44	–	4,800	2.31	10,800
Mexico City	15,056	5.0	1,479	2,090	1,577	105	–	18,500	1.23	155,500
Nairobi	1,275	8.8	690	420	60	47	–	1,100	0.86	–
Rio de Janeiro	9,200	2.4	6,464	2,050	957	104	12.1	11,000	1.20	95,945

Table 2.1 Urban Transport Data: Selected Cities (Cont.)

San Jose, C.R.	637	3.5	180	1,730	—	—	—	500	0.78	—
Sao Paulo	12,800	4.5	1,493	2,050	1,935	151	7.8	16,400	1.28	240,000
Seoul	8,366	5.0	627	1,520	127	15	11.7	13,000	1.55	63,222
Singapore	2,413	1.5	618	4,430	164	68	6.8	6,512	2.70	78,038
Tunis	1,230	6.4	115	1,310	38	31	—	642	0.52	—

Note:
— Not available.
a. National data.
b. Figures with asterisk indicate levels of bus provision considered by the World Bank to be below satisfactory levels.

Source: Modified from Table A.1, World Bank, 1986.

Figure 2.2: Income and Car Ownership

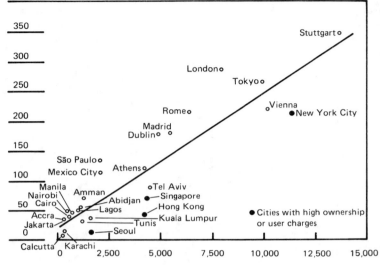

Source: Redrawn from Figure 4, World Bank, 1986

authorities are able to raise adequate finance from those who benefit most from the provided transport facilities.

It is not uncommon for urban public authorities to spend between 15 and 20 per cent of their annual budgets on transport related investments and operations. In some instances, the proportion is even higher, as in Calcutta, where it is reported that between 1972 and 1978, the equivalent of 48 per cent of the city's total planned investment was spent on transport (World Bank, 1986) (2). In Indonesia, the issue of cost recovery and public sector income generation to service urban transport became a major issue during the formulation of its Fifth Five Year National Plan (1989-94).

Figure 2.3: Population and Total Daily Trips

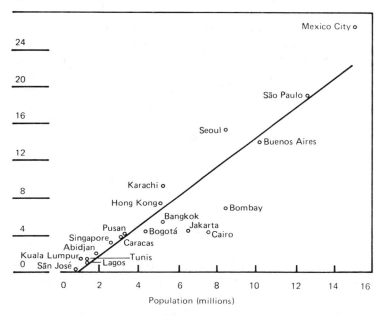

Trips per day
(millions)

Source: Redrawn from Figure 2, World Bank, 1986

Transport Systems Efficiency and Settlement Structures

The efficiency of an urban transport system is greatly influenced by its management, its capacity, the conditions under which the system operates and the demands made upon it as a result of the settlements' geographical location, its population size and urban form. The predominance of a single high density central area in most Third World cities for example, and the lack of developed secondary centres with adequate transport networks, not only encourages longer average trip-making but presents grave circulation problems - both for the central area in question and its immediate environs. Many Third World cities, furthermore, such as Cairo, Caracas, and Delhi, encompass within their central area an 'old city', typically made up of narrow street systems pre-dating the motor vehicle. These historic parts of settlement are usually best supported by non-motorised transport modes (see Chapter 4) and contain land uses (often mixed) which are serviced by poor road access and inadequate parking areas. Attempts to use motorised vehicles in these parts of the city not only create localised traffic congestion but often also affect the overall traffic circulation of the settlement.

Equally important are considerations of the environmental impact of traffic movement, particularly in areas of significant architectural heritage (often these same 'old city areas') and where residential populations are adversely affected by traffic (air and noise) pollution, visual intrusion, structural vibration and community disruption. Unfortunately, these negative environmental impacts of transport in Third World cities typically receive too little attention, as may be observed in Lagos, Jakarta and Mexico City. However, newly established of environmental protection agencies in more affluent Third World settlements, such as Hong Kong and Singapore, are now begining to play a more positive and active role.

Transport Technology Mix and Mis-use

The mix of (especially old and new) transport technologies, highlighted by the shared use of road space by fast moving motorised vehicles with slow-moving human-powered and animal-drawn vehicles (such as rickshaws, hand drawn carts and animal drawn vehicles), typifies many street scenes of the Third World (see Chapter 4). In addition to the traffic conflict, road congestion and road safety problems commonly ascribed to these conditions, there is evidence of widespread technological abuse of the use of transport modes. For some vehicles (particularly the motorcar) are used for trip distances and purposes for which they are not operationally the most efficient. The findings of research into the operational efficiency of various transport modes carried out by the Battelle Institute in Geneva (Bouladon, 1967) presented the mis-use of transport technology as a significant contributor to transport problems in cities of the industrialised countries. The research identified two 'transport gaps', one of which was associated with the misuse of the car for inappropriate distances and the shortage of suitable transport modes to service trip distances of between 0.3 and three miles (see Chapter 12).

A similar abuse of the use of the motorcar in the Third World was observed by a study of the use of different transport modes in various Indonesian cities (TDC S.A., 1988). The study recommended policy and design guidelines to encourage the most appriopriate and efficient use of transport technologies in accordance with (among other things) trip distance, trip purpose and city size considerations. Unlike the Battelle Institute research, the Indonesian study noted a considerable choice of local transport modes efficiently serving trip distances of between 0.3 and three miles. However, many such modes are currently increasingly in danger of being marginalised by traffic enforcement efforts on the one hand, and by the sheer growth of motorised traffic on the other.

Ineffective Traffic Management and Enforcement

Given the rapid growth rates of traffic and problems caused by such factors as: widespread poor driver behaviour, inadequately maintained vehicles and infrastructure, the general lack of regard for traffic regulations, a common absence of adequate road signs and markings, and a growth of uncontrolled street hawker activities, more has been expected from traffic enforcement in Third World cities today than ever before. The need to make city transport systems more efficient through selected traffic management and control measures (see Chapters 10 and 11), including the installation and maintenance of traffic control signals, the rerouting of traffic, the designation of one-way street systems, and the banning of conflicting turns, have placed a great deal of pressure on traffic enforcement agencies, in excess of the resources they have at their disposal (World Bank, 1986).

The burden on such institutions has been further aggravated in some instances by the introduction of sophisticated measures and traffic control technologies for which they have been inadequately prepared. In Bangkok for example, a computerised Area Traffic Control (ATC) scheme was introduced in the late 1970s by the City's Traffic Engineering Unit. By virtue of a whole series of pre-installation oversights in the dissemination of the function and workings of this scheme, it has been claimed that the operational relationship between the Traffic Police and Municipality deteriorated, because members of the former agency felt their on-street enforcement powers had been undermined by the introduction of the scheme. As result, it has been said that Traffic Police personnel regularly override the computerised system on more occasions than necessary, thereby defeating the very purpose of the installation of the traffic control system.

Insufficient Public Transport Services

Deficiencies of urban public transport in the Third World can be largely attributed both to the pace of urbanisation outstripping that of public sector investment in passenger transport services, and the poor co-ordination among constituent parts of the public transport system. This in turn has contributed to the poor maintenance of vehicles, insufficient supply of buses, and inadequate provision of public transport service frequencies and routes. Table 2.1 shows transport data for selected cities of the Third World and highlights those which in accordance with World Bank guidelines (Armstrong-Wright, 1986) are deemed to have inadequate public transport facilities. The cities were chosen on the basis that they have less than one bus per 2000 persons and include Accra, Ankara, Amman, Bombay, and Calcutta.

Another indicator of the adequacy or otherwise of urban public transport systems is the proportion of the vehicle fleet available for service. It has been suggested (Armstrong-Wright, 1986) that anything less than 70 per cent during peak periods is unsatisfactory (see Table 2.2). In reality, however, the availability of buses can range from as low as 24 per cent of the total fleet (as in Accra), to a more usual 63 per cent (as in Jakarta), and even as high as 95 per cent (as in Guatemala City). A more in-depth coverage of the inadequacies of public transport operations in Third World cities is given in Chapters 3 and 4, focusing on motorised and non-motorised transport systems respectively.

Transport Problems of the Urban Poor

Access to transport facilities in Third World cities is particularly important to the poor. These are persons earning an income which is insufficient to provide them with basic shelter and nutrition and who typically earn less than US$250 per annum. They are thus at the margin of subsistence which as Linn (1983) points out, makes them very sensitive to disruptions in their earnings brought about by inadequate transport policies. Transport related problems among urban low income groups are exacerbated by rising transport costs and the subsequent growing need for the poor to

Table 2.2   Bus Services: City Comparisons, 1983

City	Owner-ship	Number of buses (1)	Avail-ability (%) (2)	km per operating bus per day	Staff per operating bus	Passengers per operating bus per day	Annual operating cost (US $ mill) (3)	Total cost per passenger kilometer (4)	Annual operating revenue (US $ mill) (5)	Fare (typical, 5 km) (US $)	Ratio operating revenue /total costs (6)
1 Abidjan	Mixed	1,044	85*	183	7.1	829	91.29	0.07	69.40	0.26	0.67
2 Accra	Public	44	24*	292	28.1	2,092	1.03	0.03	0.63	0.13	0.51
3 Accra	Private	665	73*	223	5.5	676	10.43	0.04	17.72	0.18	1.37
4 Addis Ababa	Public	164	58*	205	13.1	2,467	7.96	0.02	6.59	0.07	0.67
5 Ankara	Public	899	67*	210	5.8	1,273	25.62	0.01	15.31	0.14	0.48
6 Bombay	Public	2,325	92	216	14.0	2,093	81.95	0.01	72.97	0.05	0.77
7 Cairo	Public	2,454	69*	246	14.6	2,417	60.41	0.01	36.19	0.07	0.50
8 Calcutta	Public	981	64*	133	18.0	1,641	23.05	0.01	13.09	0.04	0.45
9 Dakar	Mixed	439	70	287	9.6	1,193	22.97	0.04	20.41	0.26	0.76
10 Guatemala City	Private	1,600	95	304	–	1,037	29.00	0.02	54.60	0.10	1.55
11 Hong Kong	Private	2,392	85*	243	4.7	1,610	117.96	0.03	136.10	0.13	1.00
12 Karachi	Public	646	65*	267	9.9	1,135	11.73	0.01	6.73	0.04	0.43
13 Kuala Lumpur	Private	358	80	250	4.3	753	12.03	0.02	12.38	0.17	1.00
14 Mombasa	Mixed	89	90	315	7.5	1,640	3.93	0.03	4.48	0.11	0.96
15 Nairobi	Mixed	295	84	330	9.7	1,762	16.31	0.03	17.98	0.15	1.08
16 Porto Alegre	Private	1,492	95	218	4.3	669	46.68	0.05	65.35	0.23	1.17
17 San Jose	Mixed	621	80	128	–	2,013	19.39	0.02	24.24	0.07	1.04
18 Sao Paulo	Public	2,631	83	284	7.4	795	159.51	0.03	75.64	0.26	0.41
19 Sao Paulo	Private	6,590	83	280	5.1	765	–	–	–	0.26	1.00(5)
20 Seoul	Private	8,310	95	340	3.9	1,326	398.18	0.03	443.43	0.16	1.04
21 Singapore	Private	2,859	91	269	3.9	374	110.23	0.10	147.75	0.24	1.32

Table 2.2   Bus Services: City Comparisons, 1983 (Cont.)

Notes:

1. Number of buses belonging to the principal corporation or group of private operators covered by the survey. The total number of buses operated in the city as a whole is given in Table 2.1.

2. Figures with asterisk are availability percentages (at peak period) considered by the World Bank to be below satisfactory levels.

3. Operating costs excluding depreciation and interest charges.

4. Total costs including operating costs, depreciation and interest charges. For comparative purposes a uniform method to determine depreciation and interest charges has been used to obtain total costs. Passenger kilometers are imputed using an average trip length of five kilometers.

5. Operating revenue including fare box and advertising revenue but excluding subsidies.

6. Cost and revenue data for Sao Paulo private operators are not available; however, private operators receive no subsidy from the government and are known to at least break even.

Source: Modified from Table II.2, World Bank, 1986b.

travel longer distances in search of employment (often due to their residential displacement to the periphery). Such circumstances hamper their opportunities to engage in and contribute to economic activities of the city.

Issues of social justice in the provision of urban transport are not exclusive to Third World cities. They have also been highlighted in the industrialised world (see Hillman, 1975). The scale and severity of the problem in the Third World however, is much greater and more widespread. For the urban poor in this part of the globe can constitute more than 50 per cent of a city's population, as in Calcutta and Madras. Estimates in Latin America suggest that between 20 and 30 per cent of its urban populations have incomes that are insufficient for the adequate provision of their food and shelter, and if one takes into account households with fluctuating incomes on the fringes of poverty, this percentage increases to 40 per cent (Roberts, 1978). Household expenditure surveys indicate that the urban poor tend to devote on average between 1 and 10 per cent of their income to transport (Linn, 1983). For the poorest, who often can only afford to walk, most traditional efforts at urban transport systems improvement are therefore of marginal help, unless focused on facilities such as pedestrian infrastructure and low-cost public transport facilities servicing basic needs (see Chapter 12).

Four principal kinds of access problems which require a policy and management response are experienced by the poor of Third World cities (see Figure 2.4). These include (Dimitriou, 1982):

1. problems of physical proximity to transport facilities;
2. problems of the ease of access onto public transport vehicles;
3. problems of economic accessibility (i.e., affordability) of public transport services; and
4. problems of city-wide access provided by the transport system.

High Road Accident Rates

Rapid traffic growth in association with a number of other factors such as: increased numbers of pedestrians, widespread undisciplined road user behaviour, mixed traffic conditions and inade-

Figure 2.4: Typology of Accessibility Problems

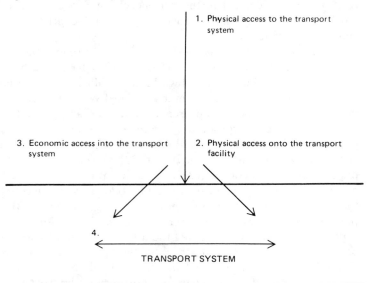

1. Physical access to the transport system

3. Economic access into the transport system

2. Physical access onto the transport facility

4.

TRANSPORT SYSTEM

4. Citywide access provided by the transport system, this being a function of:

    i)   service characteristics (including congestion encountered)

    ii)   network spread

    iii) location of transport systems discharge and collection points (i.e. terminals)

Source: Figure 2, Dimitriou H.T., 1982

quate vehicle maintenance, poor road conditions and insufficient road markings have all contributed significantly to the rise in traffic accidents in Third World cities. Cities such as Metro Manila, Kuala Lumpur and Bangkok have reported accident death rates per 10,000 vehicles of 11.23, 22.7 and 10.3 respectively, against Tokyo's figure of 1.21 (Ichihara, 1983).

Determining which of the above factors are most responsible for road accidents however is, as Spencer (1988) points out, notoriously difficult. Nevertheless, there is widespread evidence to show that motorcyclists are especially accident prone. In Surabaya for example, they have constituted 57 per cent of the vehicles involved in accidents (Jacobs and Sayer, 1977).

Pedestrians who are recent arrivals from rural areas are suspected to be especially vulnerable to accidents.

Measurable costs of traffic accidents have been estimated at about 1 per cent of GNP for Third World countries (3) (World Bank, 1986). The same source indicates that road safety measures with associated education and enforcement programmes in Brazil during the first five years of its road safety agency campaign managed to reduce traffic accident deaths from 4.5 to 1 per million vehicle-kilometres travelled.

Weak Institutional Support

The considerable burden placed on Third World city transport in-stitutions as a result of the above agenda of problems is exacer-bated by inadequate co-ordination among the various authorities involved and insufficient trained manpower resources.

There is also widespread evidence in Third World cities of the duplication of responsibilities in urban transport planning and traffic management which has led to a general lack of clarity as to who does what. Such circumstances are often aggravated by an absence at the national level of a single overall co-ordinating policy unit ready to provide guidelines for urban transport. Among public transport operators, this has proven especially problematic where it concerns co-ordinating the services of the informal sector (4) with those of the formal. Such problems have led to the increasing incorporation of institutional studies into urban traffic and transport projects.

The absence of adequately trained staff constitutes a root cause of many urban transport problems in the Third World (see Chapters 6 and 7). This lack critically handicaps efforts at most levels of action - from policy investment decisions, to management and construction matters. In Indonesia, the shortage of adequately experienced technical and management staff in urban transport was found by a World Bank study to endanger the success and viability of a proposed US$83 million urban transport project (Dimitriou, 1988). There have, however, been problems in explaining the importance of manpower development training programmes to many public agencies and some international development agencies. For as Dickey and Miller (1984) point out, many such programmes are frequently sponsored out of a sense of duty rather than commitment; partially because training is often viewed by management as detracting from the work programme. This attitude is however increasingly giving way to more enlightened views on training as more and more governments and international development agencies are now actively investing in training.

From 1972 to 1985, US$13.1 million of World Bank funds were made available to Third World governments for training in the urban transport field (see Table 2.3). This represented 0.6 per cent of the total sector loan for the same period (World Bank, 1986) and is expected to increase significantly over the next few years. Many Third World governments including those of Nigeria, Egypt, Tunisia, Indonesia and China have recently embarked (or are about to embark) upon significant manpower development and training programmes in urban transport; notwithstanding the fact that problems of measuring the benefits of training still remain a difficulty in project appraisal.

PROBLEMS OF PLANNING RESPONSE: PERCEPTION ISSUES

Perceptions Employed

In any kind of problem-solving exercise, the choice of method is greatly influenced by how the problem is perceived and defined at the outset for this determines both the scope and character of analysis which follows. In the field of urban transport, it is common knowledge that problems are perceived and presented in a variety of ways by different people and agencies (see Figure 2.5). Such perceptions vary with among other things, the analysts' interests, institutional allegiances, political ideologies, and educational and training backgrounds. The lack of compatibility and agreement among many of these perceptions, as well as the partial coverage of the field that some of them provide, have contributed considerably to problems of urban transport planning and transport facility provision.

In the case of Third World city transport problems, the difference of perception in their identification and analysis seems to be particularly marked. For whilst there are common characteristics of the sector widely recognised to present important obstacles to urban development, there are numerous interpretations as to which of these are the most critical. In some

Table 2.3   World Bank Urban Transport Lending for
Technical Assistance and Training, 1972-85

Country and project name	Technical assistance		Training	
	Cost	Per cent	Cost	Per cent
Malaysia: Kuala Lumpur Urban Transport	2.9	9.2	...	...
Turkey: Istanbul Urban Program	0.6	100.0	...	...
Iran: Teheran Urban Transport	10.2	15.5	...	...
Tunisia: Tunis Urban Transport	2.9	10.1	...	...
India: Calcutta Urban Dev.	...	...	...	...
Korea: Secondary Cities	...	...	...	...
Malaysia: Second Kuala Lumpur Urban Transport	6.9	11.1	...	...
Philippines: Manila Urban Dev.	5.9	21.7	...	...
India: Bombay Urban Transport	1.0	2.0	...	...
Ivory Coast: Urban Dev.	1.0	1.9	...	...
India: Madras Urban Dev.	...	...	...	...
Costa Rica: San Jose Urban Transport	1.3	4.0	1.0	3.2
India: Second Calcutta Urban Dev.	...	...	...	...
Kenya: Second Urban	0.3	100.0	...	...
Brazil: Urban Transport	4.3	1.7	0.3	0.1
Thailand: Bangkok Urban Transport	3.2	9.4	0.3	0.9
Tunisia: Second Urban Dev.	0.1	10.0	...	...
Korea: Second Gwangji	...	...	...	...
Philippines: Urban Dev.	...	...	...	...
Brazil: Second Urban Transport (Porto Alegre)	3.9	1.2	...	...
India: Calcutta Urban Transport	10.6	8.8	0.6	0.5
Mauritius: Urban Rehab. and Dev.	0.5	20.8	...	...
India: Second Madras Urban Dev.	0.1	0.5	...	...
Brazil: Third Urban Transport	21.9	8.5	...	...
Ivory Coast: Second Urban	11.3	13.1	...	...
India: Kanpur Urban Dev.	0.1	4.8	...	...
Philippines: Urban Engineering	...	...	0.7	100.0
Brazil: Recife Metro Region Dev.	...	...	...	...
Egypt: Greater Cairo Urban Dev.	...	...	2.2	2.4
Mexico: Mexico City Deconcentration	2.0	100.0	...	...
Ethiopia: Urban Dev.	0.4	19.0	0.7	35.1
Tunisia: Third Urban	1.8	100.0	...	...
Cameroon: Urban Dev.	0.8	100.0	...	...
Philippines: Regional Dev.	2.6	8.6	...	...
Brazil: Parana Market Towns	...	...	...	...
India: Third Calcutta Urban Dev.	0.7	1.6	...	...
Dominican Republic: Technical Assistance	0.1	16.3	...	...
Jordan: Amman Urban Transport	1.1	2.0	...	...
India: Madhya Pradesh Urban Dev.	...	...	...	...
Korea: Jeonju Regional Dev.	...	...	...	...
Jamaica: Kingston Urban Transport	4.3	14.4	1.1	3.7
Zimbabwe: Urban Dev.	0.7	46.7	0.8	53.3
Tunisia: Urban Transport II	2.4	2.9	4.5	5.5
Peru: Lima Urban Transport	4.7	6.0	0.8	1.0
Madagascar: Urban Dev.	0.3	42.9	...	...
Senegal: Technical Assistance	0.8	53.3	...	...
Thailand: Regional Cities	...	...	...	...
Paraguay: Asuncion Municipal Dev.	0.1	1.1	0.03	0.3
Korea: Seoul Urban Transport	1.3	0.6	...	...
Total	113.1	4.9	13.1	0.6

Source: Adapted from Table A.7, World Bank, 1986.

Figure 2.5: Multiple Perceptions and Dimensions of the Urban Transport Problem

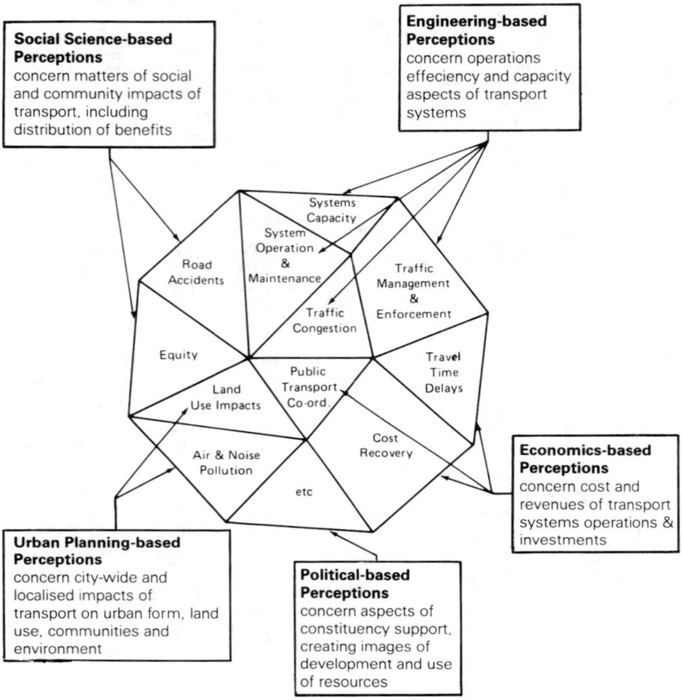

cases, there is no agreement as to whether certain characteristics are problematic at all. Given these circumstances, it is important that the 'problem-solver' (or 'problem-alleviator' for one could argue that many urban transport problems are 'insoluble') possesses a clear conceptual understanding of what constitutes a problem in the first place (5).

Preceptions of the Engineer

Of all professionals involved in urban transport the most numerous are engineers, mainly civil engineers. The large majority of these adopt, in their professional practice, aims which emphasise the operational aspects of transport systems rather than the system's.

The evolution of this perception has its origins in the highway and traffic engineering professions - the two most influential groups in the road transport sector. Their influence is especially strong in Third World countries where they constitute an elitist, influential and scarce group of trained technocrats, without whom governments are unable to plan, design, implement or maintain transport and other infrastructure projects. The pre-occupation of many highway and traffic engineers with issues of road space optimisation has led to problems of traffic congestion being seen as a main obstacle to efforts at reducing travel time and cost, and thus the overall efficient use of transport systems capacity. To assist the engineer in his efforts at allieviating these problems, he relies extensively on theories and techniques of road capacity optimisation, and measures of traffic flow efficiency first developed in the industrialised world.

Perceptions of the Economist

Another influential group of technocrats extensively involved in urban transport matters of the Third World are economists. One of their principal concerns is to match transport supply with demand. In these terms, urban transport problems are usually perceived as shortfalls in the supply and demand of transport facilities. Economists involved in the transport sector, some of whom have particularly trained to specialise in the field (i.e., transport economists), concentrate upon efforts to minimise simultaneously the costs of the sector and maximise its benefits. This is done in the belief that some kind of economic optimisation of transport resources can be achieved. It is believed that this can be best measured by comparing transport user costs against benefits.

Perceptions and views of economists are important to the transport sector, since their advice is frequently sought by governments and international development agencies to help assess the basis upon which to invest in, and price, transport improvements and proposals. Unlike engineers, who by and large possess standardised criteria to assist them in making judgements and recommendations about the efficient use of transport systems, economists differ considerably among themselves as to the optimum use of urban road systems and associated transport services. For although they are concerned with the need to match transport supply and demand in the most economically efficient manner - differences of intepretation can arise in deciding what constitute costs and benefits. Even where agreement is reached, differences of professional opinion also emerge as to the relative importance (i.e., weighting) assigned to these costs and benefits, and in the significance of equity in their distribution. So that whilst economists share a common use of monetary values in the methods and tools of analysis they employ, the advice they offer can vary a great deal. Their underlying assumption is to presume most transport costs and benefits are somehow convertible and measurable in monetary terms.

Perceptions of Other Social Scientists

Those who often do not share the perceptions and views of (especially the more orthodox) economists in urban transport problem resolution are other social scientists, including sociologists, political scientists, anthropologists and development planners. Many of these take issue with traditional economic thought (particularly in Third World contexts), on the grounds that it often conflicts with concepts of equity, political reality and appropriate development. Formalised concepts of optimisation, standardised assumptions and set evaluation criteria akin to those used by the engineer and economist do not feature strongly in the problem analysis of these social scientists.

Social science disciplines by their very nature, tend to view problems of urban transport from a much wider standpoint than either the economist or engineer. They are, for example, more likely to be concerned with social and community impacts of transport on the poor and other underprivileged groups, the use of transport in serving basic needs, and the impact of transport as an agent of urban development. In institutional areas of concern, the attention of social scientists in urban transport is increasingly directed toward the role of government and other organisations in guiding and encouraging change, and in the extent of decentralisation in the decision-making that is generated. Their interest would extend to investigating and proposing the institutional response to urban transport problems with special concern, for instance, for the lack of effective government agency co-ordination.

Perceptions of the Physical Planner

Architect-planners, city planners and transport planners (often collectively referred to as physical planners) tend to view urban transport problems more in spatial and physical terms than social scientists, and on a more macro scale than engineers. Physical planners pride themselves on their multi-disciplinary approach to the areas they plan, and believe that not only are physical structural developments of the city addressed by their profession but also the welfare of the communities and people that inhabit them.

This broad-brush approach almost inevitably places the planner in a position of conflict with those economists and engineers who tackle local urban transport problems outside of any pre-agreed city-wide planning framework or set of policies. Given the physical planner's broader perspective, he views many of the urban transport problems, particularly problems of traffic congestion, as mere symptoms of wider urban developments warranting a more comprehensive approach to problem reso lution than conventionally advocated by the engineer. Physical planners have however been criticised by many in the development field for adopting a deterministic approach resolving to urban problems. It is widely argued, for example, that too many city and transport planning approaches assume physical plans can improve the quality of life and provide better opportunities for urban development ultimately through the mere re-organisation of space and its infrastructure, and by creating a new physical order over time. Such an approach has been particularly evident in the planning and building of new towns, where different road patterns and transport policies have been employed, each assumed to provide specific community, environmental, economic and development advantages (see Potter, 1976). Physical determinism may also be detected in the assumptions adopted by the conventional wisdom of the Urban Transport Planning Process (UTP) and its derivatives, used in the preparation of many urban land use/transport plans and discussed at great length in Chapter 5.

Perceptions of the Politician

One of the principal problems of the inter-face of professionals with politicians in the business of resource allocation in urban development is the difference in time scales each employs and the priorities they uphold. This is well displayed in the transport sector of Third World cities where ribbon-cutting of highly visible infrastructure projects, especially at key times prior to elections, is often of more importance to the politician than policy measures advocated by the professional. This is particularly true where longer gestation periods are required before benefits (often less tangible) emerge.

Associated with this phenomena is the strong preference of many politicians for projects which present an image of 'modern development' through the construction of sophisticated transport systems, such as elevated high capacity urban freeways (as in Lagos and Delhi) and urban rapid transit systems (as proposed for Bangkok and Calcutta). This is not to say that Third World cities do not require high capacity road and/or rapid transport systems. The rapid transit system of Mexico City, for example, has proved essential to its development, if not survival. What is more in question is the affordability of such projects, and their opportunity costs. Too often the nature and scale of urban transport investments have been a product of political influence, rather than fiscal and professional judgement.

An additional facet of the often difficult relationship between the politician and the professional (especially the planner), concerns the latter's common inability to articulate in politically acceptable terms the justification of comprehensive and integrated planning efforts, and the uncertainties such an approach includes. This has reinforced the political importance of projects over plans (6).

Multiple Dimensions of the Urban Transport Problem

In spite of the differing perceptions discussed above, since urban transport problems are a joint product of the dynamics of their component parts and complex interaction, they cannot be effectively tackled by any one profession or interest group. What is required instead, is the use of several perspectives, simultaneously considered and weighted in accordance with (ideally) a pre-set framework of priorities and resource constraints. A framework of this kind however, needs to be capable of accommodating prevailing economic and policial considerations for it not to be too easily discarded for more pragmatic and less directed decision making.

The interdependent nature and multiple dimensions of what is commonly called 'the urban transport problem' (see Figure 2.5) is most apparent when actions taken to tackle one of its aspects aggravates another. On some occasions, actions of this kind even create new problems. In the traffic management field for example, whilst traffic re-routing may improve flows and reduce travel times, they have frequently led to increased trip lengths, higher energy consumption, and more widespread adverse environmental impacts. Similarly, although the construction of major transport projects such as rapid transit systems and urban toll roads may offer higher capacity line-haul routes for city-wide travel, when planned with little regard to their environments they dramatically alter adjacent land uses and values, as well as related traffic patterns, in a manner that does not always benefit local needs.

PROBLEMS OF PLANNING RESPONSE: TECHNOLOGY-TRANSFER ISSUES

Questions for Technology-Transfer

Planning and management responses to transport problems of Third World cities employing one or more of the perceptions discussed above inevitably involve some aspect of cross-cultural technology-transfer (7). This is particularly the case where consultants are involved in project work in countries other than their own, even though the full impact of the transfer is not always clear to them. An analysis of issues of technology-transfer is especially important for urban transport planning practice because many of the dominant professional perceptions used in the Third World have their origins in the industrialised countries (see Chapter 5). Some issues that warrant examination are discussed below (Dimitriou, 1989).

Urban Development Goals and Traditional Transport Planning Practices. These practices need to be further investigated to establish whether they are compatible with Third World city conditions? How fundamentally different for example, are the development objectives of capitalist governed New York to those of Hong Kong's newly industrialising society? And how different are the development goals of communist administered Calcutta to those of Moscow? Above all, what implications do these differences have for the planning and management of urban transport systems?

The Conventional Urban Transport Planning and Free Market Land Use Forces. The principal issue requiring clarification here is whether the North American heritage of transport planning practice predetermines the treatment of the relationship between transport and urban land use? And if so, what are the implications of this on various kinds of cities in the Third World? This matter is particularly important for those settlements which aspire to strong land use development controls. It raises specific questions as to how well North American consultancy transport proposals for master plans in the Third World, can be adapted to local development policies? It would be interesting, for example, to investigate how this was tackled by the Canadian consultants who drew up transport proposals for Dadoma, the capital of socialist Tanzania.

The Influence of Urban Planning Approaches and Transport Planning. The fundamental issue requiring enquiry here is whether urban transport planning practice ought significantly to vary according to the different concepts of urban planning pursued? If, for example, an 'integrated urban development programming' (IUIDP) approach is adopted, as for Dacca and selected cities in Indonesia, does this warrant a particular kind of urban transport planning approach which significantly differs from conventional transport planning (see Chapter 12)? If so, what are the implications for transport planning of other urban development planning efforts?

Issues of Technology-Transfer

An excellent analysis of various aspects of technology-transfer in Third World development of relevance to the above questions has been conducted by Streeten (1974). In this work he levels five main charges against those involved in this kind of transfer, all of which may be applied to the field of urban transport planning. These are charges of: 'academic imperialism' (which for the purpose of this chapter may be said to include 'professional imperialism'); 'irrelevance'; 'inappropriateness' and 'bias of trans-ferred concepts, models and theories'; 'research in the service of exploitation'; 'domination through superior and self-reinforcing exploitation'; and 'illegitimacy' of standpoints employed. Each are discussed below as they relate to transport planning for Third World cities.

Academic and Professional Imperialism. Evidence of the first of Streeten's charges in the urban transport field may be found in the nature of the one-way communication of planning expertise that commonly takes place between some international consulting firms and their Third World clients. The latter are often made to feel excessively dependent upon consultants (through the use of specialist techniques, jargon, sophisticated software, modelling exercises, technical standards and technological hardware) in their efforts to resolve transport problems.

Similar dependency relationships (unintentional or otherwise) are created through the training and education of Third World government personnel in transport courses offered by universities and other educational establishments in the industrialised world. Many such programmes until relatively recently, have almost exclusively focused upon industrialised country situations and made little effort to address problems of Third World conditions; except where they are treated as special kinds of more general urban transport problems found world-wide.

Irrelevance and Inappropriateness. Streeten's view that adopted Western concepts, models, and paradigms are frequently inap-propriate, is particularly relevant to the field of transport planning for Third World cities. This aspect of concern has been the theme of several papers and articles since the mid 1970s (see Kumar and Rao, 1975; Viola, 1976; McNeill, 1977; Dimitriou, 1977, Ziv, 1978, and Banjo and Dimitriou, 1983). What is of special interest, is that not only are some conventional transport planning concepts, paradigms and techniques now more readily considered to be of questionable value for Third World cities, their validity in cities in the industrialised world is also open to question. A more detailed discussion of this aspect is presented in Chapter 5.

Research in the Service of Exploitation. Particular international research consultancies, foreign investment interests, aid donors and universities of the industrialised world have (wittingly or unwittingly), with the enlisted support of a small class of privileged (often Western educated) persons of the Third World, successfully pushed research and development projects in urban transport, in a manner that reflects the interests of the industrialised nations more than the countries they are intended to serve. This kind of technology-transfer is described by Streeten as 'opportunistic' and sometimes 'irrelevant'. It is perhaps most evident in the encouragement of the indiscriminate use of the motorcar. What is very important about the success of this kind of technology-transfer is its tendency to reinforce the dominant position and perceptions of professionals of the industrialised countries in a way that encourages the further reliance on their views and know-how.

Streeten argues that some presumptions made by governments of industrialised countries in assessments of foreign aid needs, further provide examples of technology-transfer in the service of Third World exploitation. This is especially true where the donor's perception of what is needed coincide with the economic interests of the donor countries, whether it be air-conditioned rear-engine double-decker buses, monorails or urban rapid transit systems (8).

Self-Reinforcing Exploitation. Streeten's further charge that the Third World is exploited by virtue of the industrialised countries' privileged position vis-a-vis its location to international funds and accumulated skills, is also pertinent to the urban transport field. For the concentration of financial and technical manpower resources in the industrialised world are such that they provide an inevitable superiority of Western expertise and interests over those of the Third World in major urban transport project developments. This was for the most true up until the entrance of Arab oil producing countries into the business of international banking. Because so much of the resources made available to the Third World are both financially and politically supported by international institutions with attitudes and personnel derived from the same source, some observers claim that as in the examples of 're-search in the service of exploitation', these developments have tended to reinforce conventional views and dampen innovative research.

Illegitimacy of Stand. Streeten's final charge of technology-transfer, 'illegitimacy', refers to situations when research and consultancy studies conducted by persons and organisations from the industrialised world (the costs of which are borne by people of a different country to the consultants) make recommendations which advocate drastic, painful and often politically unacceptable measures. Streeten sees many such recommendations as 'illegitimate and distasteful'. For example, persons far removed from the scene, such as overseas universities and professional consultancy firms, are able to recommend actions which are not only sometimes impossible to implement, but in some instances have been rejected in the consultants' own country. The responsibility to supervise the implementation of such proposals generally lies with others rather than the professionals who conducted the study. This criticism could apply especially to the advocates of road pricing schemes in Third World cities proposed (and rejected) for Kuala Lumpur and Hong Kong.

New Generation of Urban Transport Problems

An article 'Urban Transport Problems of Third World Cities: The Third Generation' (1983) by the editors of the present book made reference to several of the above technology-transfer issues. The principal argument in this paper was one that partly attributed the unresolved (and more complex) nature of many current Third World city movement problems to an excessive reliance upon inappropriate transport planning approaches (also see Chapter 5). More specifically, the argument depicts transport problems of post-colonial Third World cities (typically those of Africa and the Indian sub-continent) as evolving not only from the characteristics of the settlements themselves, and their inhabitants' travel demands, but also from the planning responses to which they have been subjected.

The new generation of transport problems of these cities was presented in the article as a historical culmination (see Figure 2.6) of:

1.   the inheritance of an urban transport system predominantly designed to service colonial economic, administrative and residential needs, developed and operated separately from

Figure 2.6: The Genesis of Urban Transport Problems in Ex-Colonial Cities

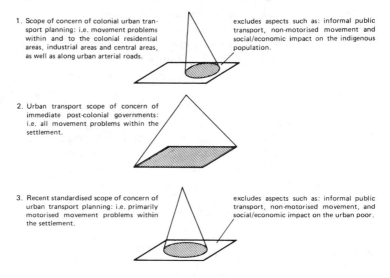

1. Scope of concern of colonial urban transport planning: i.e. movement problems within and to the colonial residential areas, industrial areas and central areas, as well as along urban arterial roads.

excludes aspects such as: informal public transport, non-motorised movement and social/economic impact on the indigenous population.

2. Urban transport scope of concern of immediate post-colonial governments: i.e. all movement problems within the settlement.

3. Recent standardised scope of concern of urban transport planning: i.e. primarily motorised movement problems within the settlement.

excludes aspects such as: informal public transport, non-motorised movement, and social/economic impact on the urban poor.

Source: Redrawn from figure 4, Banjo G.A. and Dimitriou H.T., 1983

    the local transport system predominantly utilised by indigenous populations;

2.   the subsequent abandonment of separate development after independence, thus making the whole city more accessible to the indigenous population, in turn dramatically changing demands made upon the city's transport systems overnight; and

3.   the reliance upon foreign technical assistance to tackle the resultant transport problems, involving too restrictive a scope of analyses and often a poor understanding of local conditions.

    Although the particular characteristics of the new generation of urban transport problems differ from city to city, features most closely associated with it include: the destruction of existing (especially old) urban form structures; the penalising of the non-motorised community; a failure to incorporate the informal transport sector into urban transport plans; the dominance of transport user considerations; and the use of past trends as a basis for 'blueprint' planning.

GOAL FORMULATION PROBLEMS

Problems of Goal Setting

What much of the preceding discussion implies is that perhaps one of the most common sources of transport problems has been unclear and unrealistic goal-setting in urban transport planning, both during plan-making and in project implementation. For transport planning goals not only formalise the direction(s) and purpose(s) toward which transport investments may be orientated, but also help to reveal more clearly over time (with the assistance of monitoring), the degree to which these investments are compatible with grass-root needs. Good goal-setting, furthermore, offers a sounder basis for making judgements concerning the desirability of different kinds of technology-transfer on offer.

The often observed mismatch between adopted urban transport planning goals and Third World city grass-root needs is most notably reflected in the pre-occupation of many urban transport studies with meeting private motorised transport needs and tackling related problems of traffic congestion, rather than addressing wider issues affecting a larger proportion of society. As a result, there has been an under-emphasis of the importance of pedestrian, cycle and animal movement; on matters of social justice; and on the productive role of the informal transport sector (see Chapter 4).

Although, in Third World cities such as Sao Paulo and Mexico city, which have more motorised vehicles than Philadelphia or Dallas respectively, the emphasis on motorised traffic is understandable (though not laudable), in other cities this approach blatantly ignores the needs of the majority of trip-makers. These cities include: Dacca, with a population of 2.1 million and a mere 12,000 motorised vehicles (Bangladesh Bureau of Statistics, 1979); Madras, with 44 per cent of all daily trips undertaken by non-motorised means (Madras Metropolitan Development Authority, 1977); and Calcutta, where in 1980 less than 0.1 per cent of the population possessed a private car (World Bank, 1986). In this approach, problems of urban transport, particularly those associated with the poor, have not only been perpetuated but accentuated with little recourse, for public participation is uncommon in most such cities.

Goals and the Availability of Resources

Many aspects of incompatability between urban transport planning goals and the resources available to meet them may be traced to an underlying presumption that there is some kind of 'obligation' to accommodate traffic growth (see Chapter 5). Associated with this view, is the inherent belief that increased traffic speeds are desirable, even though related overall costs and benefits are often less clear than presented. Levels of resource scarcity in many Third World cities are in reality so considerable that to accommodate the traffic and motorisation growth rates experienced (often higher than those observed in the industrialised countries), is to expect more (from less resources) than has been feasible in the industrialised world.

Another aspect that requires scrutiny with regard to its resource implications, is the premise that it is better to plan for a wide choice of 'modern transport modes', even where this leads to the displacement of traditional vehicles performing important functions. This has led to the erosion of a previous rich spectrum of local transport modes in many Southeast Asian cities and its replacement by newer (often less flexible) modes, unable to meet travel needs previously served.

A final matter warranting consideration is the fact that many urban highway and traffic engineering schemes associated with transport planning efforts seem to rely upon the misconception that problems of traffic congestion and car parking can be successfully tackled by engineering measures, independent of meaningful land use control. In a Third World context, this can be said to reflect in part the weak enforcement capability of planning agencies. In more general terms, however, it is also indicative of the unrealistic expectations frequently associated with much of urban highway and traffic engineering practice.

This raises in conclusion, two final issues. The first has to do with the appreciation of the level of complexity of the problem at hand. If the complexity of a transport problem is not reflected in the approach employed to resolve it, there is the danger that the mere simplicity of approach will ultimately lead to more costly solutions, after several attempts at 'getting it right'. The other issue concerns the resources needed to implement projects. Many central highway and traffic engineering agency schemes tend to arrive at higher cost solutions beyond the means of many local municipalities. Whilst, this in part may be explained by the kind of analysis adopted, it is also attributable to the reliance upon international (often inappropriate) standards and the lack of adequately formulated indigenous ones; an aspect addressed in greater depth in Chapter 12 of this book.

NOTES

(1)   It should be noted that some Third World cities, such as Sao Paulo and Mexico City, possess motorisation rates in excess of those of many cities of the industrialised world.

(2)   It is unclear however, whether this figure is unsually high as a result of the construction of the city's metro system during these years.

(3)   The source of this statistic does not make it clear whether the percentage quoted refers to all traffic accidents or those of urban areas alone.

(4)   The informal transport sector may be defined as that part of the transport sector provided by bodies and private companies which are neither government nor quasi-government starts. The provision of such transport services is often illegal in that the vehicles used are unlicensed and/or operate along unauthorised routes (see Chapters 3 and 4).

(5)   Problems may be defined as obstacles to, and a departure from, the desired end.

(6)   For further discussion with regard to this particular aspect, the reader is encouraged to refer to the early writings of Altshuler on 'Opportunism vs. Professionalism in Planning' (1965) and Benveniste on 'The Prince and the Pundit', (1972).

(7)   Technology-transfer as defined by Streeten (1974) is 'the transfer of skills, knowledge and procedures for making, using and doing useful things' - for the purpose of this discussion, 'things' relate to efforts to tackle and resolve urban transport problems of Third World cities.

(8)   Concern for such aspects has led the Japanese government to commission a study of technology-transfer considera-

tions in the Third World transport field (International Development Centre of Japan, 1987).

(9)   Goals may be defined (after Barlow, 1978) as 'idealised end-states of the total environment (in this case, of the urban transport sector) toward which planners strive'.

REFERENCES

Altshuler, A. (1965) **The City Planning Process: A Political Analysis**, Cornell University Press, Ithaca.

Armstrong-Wright, A. (1986) 'Urban Transit Systems: Guidelines for Examining Options', **World Bank Technical Paper**, no. 52, IBRD Washington DC.

Bangladesh Bureau of Statistics (1979), 'Statistical Year Book', Mininstry of Planning, Dacca.

Banjo, G.A. and Dimitriou, H.T. (1983) 'Urban Transport Problems of Third World Cities: The Third Generation', **Habitat International**, vol. 7, no. 3/4, Pergamon Press, Oxford.

Barlow, P. (1978) 'Developing Goals and Objectives', **Transport Planning Research Reports**, no. TPRR 1-10, National Institute for Transport and Road Research, Pretoria.

Benveniste, G. (1972) **The Politics of Expertise**, Croom Helm, London.

Bouladon, G. (1967), 'The Transport Gaps', **Science Journal** April, Associated Iliffe Press, London.

Dickey, J.W., and Miller, L.H. (1984) **Road Project Appraisal for Developing Countries**, John Wiley and Sons, Chichester.

Dimitriou, H.T. (1977) 'A Call for the Effective Integration of Urban and Transport Planning for Developing Countries', **Proceedings of PTRC Summer Annual Meeting**, University of Warwick, PTRC Education and Research Services Ltd., London.

_____ (1982) 'Transport and the Urban Poor in the Third World', Paper presented to Habitat International Council (NGO Committee on Human Settlements) at Town and Country Planning Association, London.

_____ (1988) 'Urban Transport and Manpower Development and Training Needs of Four Asian Cities', **Habitat International**, vol. 12, no. 3, Pergamon Press, Oxford.

_____ (1989) 'The Transport Planning Process and its Derivatives: An Assessment of their Contribution to the Formulation of Appropriate Guidelines for Third World Cities', Unpublished PhD Thesis, Department of Town Planning, University of Wales, Cardiff.

Hillman, M. (1975) 'Social Goals for Transport Policy', **Proceedings of Transport for Society Conference**, Institution of Civil Engineers, London.

Ichihara, K. (1983) 'Survey on Road Safety Conditions in Major Southeast Asian Cities', volume 3, **Proceedings of SEATAC Workshop**, SEATAC, Bangkok.

International Development Centre of Japan, (1987) 'Technology Transfer for Better Transport Systems in Developing Countries', IDC, Tokyo.

Jacobs, G.D. and Sayer I.A. (1977) 'A Study of Road Accidents in Selected Urban Areas in Developing Countries', **Transport and Road Research Laboratory**, Report, no. LR 775. TRRL, Crowthorne.

Kuamar, R.K. and Rao, S.V. (1975) 'An Appraisal of Transportation Planning and Travel Forecasting Techniques', **Indian Highways Journal**, vol. 3, no. 9, New Delhi.

Linn, J.F. (1983) **Cities in the Developing World**, World Bank Research Publications, Oxford University Press, Oxford.

Madras Metropolitan Development Authority (1977) 'Madras; A Few Facts', MMDA, Madras.

McNeill, D. (1977) 'Urban Transport in Developing Countries', **Development Planning Unit**, Working Paper, no. 1, University College, London.

Potter, S. (1976) 'Transport and New Towns: Transport Assumptions Underlying the Design of New Towns 1946-1976', New Towns Study Unit, The Open University, Milton Keynes.

Roberts, B. (1978) **Cities of Peasants**, Edward Arnold, London.

Spencer, A.H. (1988) 'Urban Transport' in **South East Asian Transport: Issues in Development** by Leinbach, T.R. and Chia L.S. (eds), Oxford University Press, Kuala Lumpur.

Streeten, P. (1974) 'Some Problems in the Use and Transfer of An Intellectual Technology in The Social Sciences and Development, **Proceedings of Conference in Bellagio,** Italy, World Bank, Washington DC.

Training and Development Consultants S.A. (1988) **IUIDP Policy, Planning and Design Guidelines for Urban Transport,**

Final Report to Department of Public Works, Government of Indonesia and UNDP/UNCHS, Jakarta and Nairobi.

Viola, P. (1976) 'Large Scale Land-Use Transport Studies: How Relevant to Asian Cities?', **Proceedings of PTRC Annual Meeting**, University of Warwick, PTRC Education and Research Services Ltd., London.

World Bank, (1975) 'Urban Transport', **World Bank Sector Policy Paper**, IBRD, Washington DC.

_____ (1986) **Urban Transport**, A World Bank Policy Study, IBRD Washington DC.

Zahavi, Y. (1976) 'Travel Characteristics of Developing Countries', **World Bank Staff Working Paper**, no. 20, IBRD, Washington DC.

_____ (1980) 'Urban Travel Patterns', **Economic Development Institute Report**, World Bank, Washington DC.

Ziv, J. (1977) 'La Genese des Modeles de Trafic aux Etats-Unis', Unpublished PhD Thesis, Cornell University, Ithaca.

Chapter 3

Inadequacies of Urban Public Transport Systems

Peter R. White

INTRODUCTION

This chapter provides a review of the present inadequacies of urban public transport systems in Third World cities, and the measures which could be taken to resolve (or at least alleviate) such problems (1) (2). These inadequacies rest essentially on the low level of capital investment, resulting in very limited capacity, both in terms of vehicles and of infrastructure. Allied to this are problems of maintenance and system control. Urban public transport systems thus experience considerable difficulty in meeting existing demand levels, let alone contributing to any wider objectives.

In addition to the formal public transport modes of rail and full-size buses, the informal sector plays a major role with a wide variety of smaller vehicles. However, present functions of the formal and informal public transport sectors are not necessarily complementary, for inconsistent forms of regulation are often applied. A co-ordinated approach to the activities of the two sectors is thus required (see Chapter 2), in which transport modes are encouraged to adopt the most suitable roles so that they may contribute to wider development objectives. Such co-ordination should also link public transport with the management of the urban highway network and land use planning.

Objectives of the Operator

Whatever broader goals may be set in Third World cities the major objectives and constraints for public transport operators are usually financial. The private operator will expect to obtain some level of profit after covering costs, together with a wage element; although in the case of some informal sector operators the latter may be very low. Public sector transport operators, on the other hand, are typically required to break even, possibly with a substantial interest charge burden in addition to covering operating costs. Within this overall constraint, cross-subsidy may be encouraged, with lossmaking routes covered by profits elsewhere. However, the desirability of such practices is open to question, both on grounds of economic efficiency and the effect of informal sector competition.

Losses are usually met on an *ad hoc* basis, rather than pre-budgeted as in Western Europe and North America. Public finance and overseas aid, in the form of outright grants and low-interest loans, are generally used to provide investment rather than to meet operating deficits. Support for concessionary fares for the elderly for example, is much less common in Third World cities; concessionary fare losses being met by cross-subsidy. The public sector operator may experience additional constraints in the form of requirements to pay minimum wage levels and observe certain working conditions which are not enforced or applicable in the case of the informal, private sector operators. Given these circumstances, most operators will attempt to meet peak demand, although limited capital investment in public transport fleets often prevents this. The desirability of aiming fully to meet the peak is discussed later in this chapter.

Public Transport User Requirements

Within the constraints of the available time and money, the public transport user will generally try to maximise access to facilities he/she desires to reach - employment opportunities, education facilities, medical services, places of entertainment, etc. Given the rapid growth of cities, and the frequent location of low-income areas on the fringes of such settlements, low-income trip makers may have to travel much greater distances than they would wish (see Chapter 2). Minimising costs thus becomes the main consideration. For those with higher incomes a mix of higher cost/higher quality modes offering greater comfort and privacy is often available, with the 'informal' sector also providing facilities. One example is the air-conditioned buses in Manila.

The mix of transport modes used in Third World cities therefore reflects a wide range of travel demands, incomes and lifestyles, rather than a single 'public transport market'. Whereas in Western Europe and North America, public transport users benefit from the substantial central or local government aid given to public transport operators - up to 50 per cent or more of total costs - such aid is generally absent in Third World cities where the full cost of provision (or the greater part of it) is usually reflected in the fare.

PROBLEMS OF MATCHING DEMAND AND SUPPLY

Vehicle Ownership

The demand for public transport in most Third World cities far outstrips supply (see Bayliss, 1981). This contrasts with Western cities where such a problem rarely arises except at the height of peak periods. The high demand is associated with low car owner-ship levels, but is also constrained by several factors other than supply. Indeed, as is shown later, the absolute level (in trips per head of population per annum) is not necessarily higher than in Western cities, but is high *vis-a-vis* the capacity available.

In Third World countries, car ownership levels typically average 1 to 5 per 100 residents. In cities a somewhat higher rate may be found resulting from the concentration of higher-income groups. In more prosperous Third World countries, such as Malaysia, there may be about 10 cars per 100 residents, a level similar to that in older parts of industrial cities in the industrialised world. However, few cities approach the Western average of 20 to 40 cars per 100 population. In many Third World settlements, private vehicle ownership typically means ownership of pedal cycles (especially in China and India), motor scooters and motorcycles, whose numbers often exceed those of cars (see Chapter 4).

In addition to low car ownership, public transport demand is also stimulated by other factors, such as the low level of television ownership and consequent desire for mass entertainment. This may have the effect of producing a high demand level throughout the day and not only at peak periods.

Public Transport Capacity

One simple means of illustrating the low capacity of public transport services available is to look at the number of buses owned for public service per 1,000 head of population (also see Chapter 2). In India and many lower-income countries, it is in the region of 0.3 rising to about 0.6 in Third World countries as a whole. As Table 3.1 shows, in the more prosperous Kuala Lumpur region an average of approximately 0.7 has been attained. In Britain, by comparison, the average is in the region of 0.9, and Singapore (where there is a high level of investment in public transport), it is about 1.1. At these higher levels, urban public transport peak demand may be fully satisfied, but at levels such as in India, gross overcrowding and/or inability to travel in peak hours becomes evident. The estimate of available capacity may be refined, as in Table 3.1, by estimating authorised passenger spaces per 1,000 population (seated and standing), thus allowing for bus size. In the case of Pune, India, for example, the need for small vehicles in order to gain access to narrow streets in the city centre further reduces available capacity.

In addition to the limited size of bus fleet, low investment results in few Third World cities having any appreciable rail network, and even very large cities being almost totally dependent upon buses to handle peak demand. Bombay benefits from a high-density rail corridor but cities as large as Karachi and Kuala Lumpur, possess only very limited rail networks. Low investment levels are also evident in the limited road space available, and inadequate depot and workshop facilities. Together with a tendency to prolong bus life, due to difficulties in funding replacements, the already low number of buses per 1,000 population in urban areas is further reduced (in terms of those actually available for service) by maintenance problems. The best availability that can be attained is about 90 per cent, as in Bombay, but for many operators elsewhere it is much lower, 50 per cent or even less.

The size of bus fleets per head of population is gradually rising. To take a large sample of state road transport undertakings in India (serving rural as well as urban areas), buses per 1,000

Table 3.1 Comparative Indices of Public Transport Provision and Performance

*Indicator	Country/Operator						
	India		Malaysia		Singapore (SBS)	Third World cities (a)	British urban systems average
	Bombay	Pune	KL:stage	mini			
GDP per head, (US $)	150	150	1,500		3,000	NA	4,500
Buses per 1,000 population	0.25	0.3	0.4 (0.7)	0.3	1.1	0.63	0.9
Authorised bus pax. spaces/1,000 pop.	20	17	30 (35)	5	75	NA	55
Km. run per bus p.a. (thousands)	72	70	96 (98)	100	70	52	40
Staff per bus owned	10	11	4.5 (4.4)	4.3	4.3	7.4	3.6
Bus trips per head	150 (300)*	140	117 (161)	44	300	150	150+
Bus operating cost structure (%). Staff Fuel Taxes etc.	44 15 7	40 20 8	40 13 NA	45 15 3	49 NA 8	NA NA NA	70 6 1

Table 3.1 Comparative Indices of Public Transport Provision and Performance (Cont.)

*Indicator	Country/Operator						
Peak output as % of bus fleet	90	85	c85	c95	c82	NA	75
Persons per car	50	70	(10)		15	NA	4
Bus fare for work trip of 5 km each way, as % of GDP/head	(15)		(7)		(7)	NA	4
Bus industry employees per 1,000 population	2.5	3.3	(3.1)		4.7	NA	3.25

*Notes

Data describes the typical situation in the late 1970's, being based on 1977/8 or 1978/9 for the developing countries, and 1979/80 for British systems. The proportion of cost comprising of fuel may be understated, in view of sharp price rises from 1979 onward. All figures shown should be regarded as approximate.

Sources of data include annual reports of the operators in question, the sample of 55 British operators held as a database by PCL Transport Studies Group, and the following references cited at the end of this chapter – Fouracre, Maunder et al 1981 (especially tables 10 and 30); Jamieson Mackay and Partners 1981 (especially table 7); Jacobs et al 1979.

(a) Average for sample quoted by Jacobs et al 1979.

*If suburban rail included, **trips per head of population are approximately doubled, from 150 to 300.**

Where Kuala Lumpur data is shown in brackets, e.g. (0.7) buses per 1,000 population, this is a combined figure for the stage and minibuses operations.

population rose from 0.12 in 1961 to 0.19 in 1981 (El-Mezawie, 1981). More Third World cities are now getting urban rail networks. Nonetheless, this process is very slow and several decades may be needed before capacity meets demand. The amount of foreign aid naturally plays a role, but most investment will have to come from within the countries themselves (especially for vehicles), thus it is important to ensure that savings within the country are directed toward productive investment. An interesting example of encouraging this trend may be found in Singapore (White, 1981a) where citizens may purchase shares in the bus company up to a certain limit, by using money saved compulsorily as part of a national savings scheme. Mixed private and public ventures may also be more successful in attracting capital than those exclusively in the public sector, which have to compete with other public sector demands for scarce loan capital.

Having mentioned some of the problems faced by Third World cities due to low investment, it is also fair to point out that vehicles often achieve much higher utilisation rates than in Britain or Western Europe. As Table 3.1 shows, up to 70,000 km or more per annum may be attained by urban buses in some Third World cities, compared with about 45,000 km in Britain. This high figure results from vehicles being in service for much of the day, rather than for limited peak periods only, and with maintenance being carried out overnight. In expanding fleets, it is desirable to try and retain a good spread of work throughout the day; aiming to meet the entire potential peak demand is not necessarily desirable.

Lack of peak capacity in some cases forces adaptation by spreading the working hours. For example, it was evident from discussions with transport and planning officials in Bombay in 1979 that the peak concentration on flows to the Fort area (Figure 3.1) forced a spread of working hours, with the morning peak extending from about 07:30 to 10:30. Under high peak demand, travellers making short journeys may often be forced to use non-motorised modes, as public transport vehicles fill up near the outer terminals and intermediate passengers are unable to gain access. This is evident in Pune, for example.

As prosperity and investment levels rise, rail capacity may be provided in the form of suburban or metro systems. This may permit some 'peaking' of demand, where a greater spread was previously evident. The opening of the Hong Kong Metro (MTR) appears to have had such an effect, with surprisingly peaked demand at traditional journey-to-work times in a city where a very

Figure 3.1: Bombay Area Transportation System

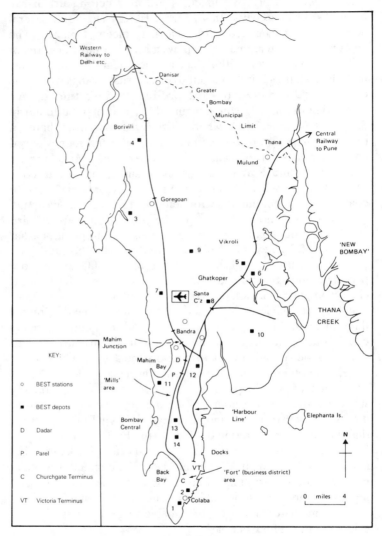

good spread of traffic through the day was previously evident. Of course, from the users' point of view, this is a benefit, since more convenient working hours to match childrens' hours at school etc. may be adopted. But for the transport operator diseconomies of peak-only provision are increased. In bus operations, more 'split shift' working of crews becomes necessary, as in Singapore.

Economic Activities Rates

In addition to the constraints imposed by lack of capacity, peak journey-to-work demand in many Third World cities is affected by lower economic activity rates (i.e., the proportion of the population employed in regular paid activity) than found in similar-sized Western cities. In Western cities, ecomomic activity rates may be as high as 45 per cent to 50 per cent, but even in a major industrial Third World city such as Sao Paulo, it was no higher than 38 per cent in 1975 (CET, 1978), and in Tanzanian urban areas it ranges from about 15 per cent to 25 per cent (Hussain, 1980). One should acknowledge that the formal employment level is only part of the picture, with extensive 'informal sector' activity, including part of the transport sector itself. However, many of those in the informal sector may work largely at home, or as itinerant street traders and thus have little demand for motorised home-to-work trips. The formal activity rate is also reduced by the high proportion of school-age children within the population, and a lower proportion of women in employment.

Cost of Public Transport

Potential demand for public transport is also reduced by relatively high fares. Although fares in countries such as India may appear low to Western visitors, they are much higher relative to incomes, as Table 3.1 shows. The cost of a 5 km journey from home to work and back on 20 days per month is shown as a percentage of GDP per head. In Britain this was about 4 per cent, and elsewhere in Western Europe (with higher real incomes, and lower fares) fell to about 2 per cent during the same period. Conversely, in India it reached about 15 per cent, and in Malaysia and Singapore, about 6 to 8 per cent respectively. Many poorer people thus cannot afford to use motorised public transport regularly. Unpaid trips, (either through deliberate evasion or because overcrowding prevents conductors collecting fares) form a significant proportion, partly offsetting this effect for the user.

A very useful indication of the impact of high transport costs on low income earners is given in the study of two areas in Delhi - Nand Nagri and Janakpuri - in 1979 (Maunder et al, 1981). Few optional journeys were made, most being for work and education. About 10 per cent of all household expenditure was on transport, mostly bus fares. As a proportion of the lowest income household expenditure it was considerably higher, about 15 per cent or more, and as a proportion of disposable income (after housing, fuel and food) it ranged from 18 per cent to 36 per cent. Even in those households with motor vehicles, their use was low, since high fuel prices often made it cheaper to use bus services. It should be noted that the overall average of 10 per cent of household income spent on transport is somewhat lower than the figure shown in Table 3.1. The latter, however, was estimated in relation to GDP per head for India as a whole (this being the only satisfactory means of comparison with other countries), which is influenced by the much lower per capita incomes in rural areas.

Putting all these factors together, we can show that the use of public transport (measured in trips per head of population per annum) is not as high in many Third World countries as one might imagine - around 140 in Pune, 160 in Kuala Lumpur for example. These are rates akin to those now found in British cities of similar size, despite the much higher car ownership and decline in use of public transport that has occured in Britain since the early 1950s. The image of grossly overcrowded buses and trains owes more to their lack of numbers *vis-a-vis* the population, than high use per capita.

It can be argued that the high fares and limited capacity provided do themselves serve to bring supply and demand into some crude equilibrium. Indeed, by raising fares, overcrowding could be reduced, and higher standards offered for remaining passengers. For example, in Bombay, rail season tickets are priced very cheaply (a monthly season ticket being equal to the cost of only about 13 singles). This enables low-income users to find housing further from the city, and commute inward. The deficit is made up by cross-subsidy from profitable inter-city and freight traffic. The low fares encourage this commuting pattern, with its diseconomies of operation. To raise fares to a realistic level however, would result in severe hardship, and also generate strong political opposition if not unrest.

The pattern is mitigated by some reverse commuting to the office district at Bandra, but this is small in comparison with flows to the Fort area. An increase in peak period fares to a realistic level would encourage some decentralisation from the Fort area, aiding the New Bombay development on the eastern shore of the Thana Creek (Figure 3.1). Growth here has been modest to date. Increased public transport accessibility would also be a necessary condition of encouraging its growth.

Labour and Materials

The final aspect of demand and supply to be considered is that of the supply of labour and materials to the operator. Although the low capital investment manifests itself most clearly in the small fleet size and limited infrastructure, the ability to make the best use of this is affected by supply of fuel, spares and skilled labour.

Although labour is generally cheap and plentiful, there are not always sufficient skilled staff available, especially for maintenance. Education in many Third World countries places too much stress on academic skills, with little emphasis on technical qualifications (this is particularly evident in former British colonies such as Sri Lanka). A welcome attempt to provide training geared to practical requirements is now being made in a number of countries (Hussain, 1980) as indicated in Chapters 5, 6 and 8. Political interference and nepotism however can still result in unqualified people being appointed to supervisory and skilled posts. Where operators do not have sufficient skilled staff, more breakdowns occur in service and vehicle availability is reduced.

Supply of spares is affected by reliance on imports and lack of sufficient foreign exchange, resulting in shortages. Bus fleet standardisation is furthermore often difficult to achieve, as tied - aid causes the supply of vehicles to switch from one donor to another, according to who is providing aid at the time. The Dar-es-Salaam urban bus (UDA) fleet in 1981, for example, included vehicles from Leyland, Fiat, Mercedes, Isuzu and Ikarus, each requiring different sets of spares, and the familiarisation of the maintenance staff. In many ways, permanently tied - aid - with a guaranteed supply of future spares - would be preferable, or else completely untied aid, with the recipient country able to decide on which makes to standardise.

Fuel costs have risen sharply, as experienced in 1979, with severe problems resulting for non-oil-producing countries. Availability may also be erratic due to problems in supply countries, and inadequate internal distribution in the recipient country. It is therefore all the more important to encourage the use of non- motorised modes (see Chapter 4), and within the motorised sector, to concentrate on public transport and the use of large vehicles.

THE FORMAL PUBLIC TRANSPORT RESPONSE

Public Transport Agencies

The term 'formal' in this section is taken to cover public transport systems generally using large vehicles and operating scheduled services at fixed fare scales. It includes those in both public ownership (almost all railways and some urban bus systems) and in private hands (for example, conventional buses in Kuala Lumpur and many South American cities).

As Hibbs has shown (1981), in almost all countries some form of regulatory system exists in the formal public transport sector, even where other sectors of the economy (including the informal transport sector) are largely uncontrolled. This situation arises from a wish to ensure stability in service provision and provide some protection for investments (whether foreign or domestic). Prices are controlled to ensure 'fair' levels are maintained. The regulatory system may operate on a franchise basis, rights to operate profitable routes being conditional upon also operating unprofitable services and offering an agreed fare scale. Problems caused by regulation, especially the inconsistencies between the formal and informal public transport sectors, are considered later in this chapter.

Where bus services are in public ownership, the municipal authority is generally responsible, with the elected council determining policy. This is the case in Bombay and Penang, for example. The degree of coverage of the municipal operation will be affected first by the boundaries of the authority (which may often be less extensive than the built-up area as a whole) and second, by whether it aims to provide all public transport services within the area (as in Bombay), or a limited network additional to that of the private operators (as in Caracas). The pattern is generally determined by historical accident.

Suburban rail services are usually provided by the operator of the national rail systems, under central government control (as in Sao Paulo). Self-contained urban metro systems, however, are almost always under the city authority itself. The degree of co-ordination between the various public transport authorities (see Chapter 7) is often poor - Buenos Aires being a striking example with separate policies for the metro, suburban railways, and bus services - and between public transport and other related functions (traffic management, land-use planning, etc.). Such problems are not unique to Third World countries, but often have more severe effects since waste is more harmful where resources are scarce.

Another form of organisation is that where an expatriate company operates a city network on a contract basis (for example, within an agreed cost budget, or at an agreed profit margin). This is how many Third World city undertakings were initially established, but ownership of assets and overall control now rests within the country concerned, with only (in some instances) the managerial expertise coming from outside. In some cases, the same company operates the same system it used to operate prior to transfer to local public ownership. One example is the public transport operation in Lagos by United Transport Overseas (Lefevre, 1981). This form of operation can permit the provisions of greater management expertise, and by working as a team, offer greater resistance to political pressure than could one or two expatriates working as individuals. The contract form of management can also be used to set up entirely new operations, as in Saudi Arabia in 1979-81, with expertise provided by the American company ATE.

Operational Characteristics of Bus Systems

The first aspect to be considered is the bus itself. Table 3.2 gives common examples of bus types. Legal limits normally determine maximum dimensions, and may be more severe in Third World cities. For example, Malaysia imposes an axle-load limit of 8 tons, compared with 10 tons in Britain. This limit restricts the scope for double-deckers (see Figure 3.2), and length limits may likewise restrict the use of articulated single-deckers or artics (see Figure 3.3). Nonetheless, both types are now appearing in areas where previously only short, conventional single-deckers were found - artics in Dar-es-Salaam, and Leyland double-deckers in Singapore and the Philippines - their extra capacity clearly being most useful in view of the constraints discussed earlier.

Table 3.2 Example of Urban Bus Types

Layout	Manufacturers/Models	Seating Capacity
Front-engined, Forward contrcl Single-decker	Leyland Victory J, CD23; Tata; Mercedes 1617, Ford R1014	30 to 60, dependent on length
Minibus/midibus	Mercedes 0309; Ford Transit; Isuzu	12 to 18
Articulated single-decker	Ikarus 280, Volvo B10M	70 upward
Rear-engined double-decker	Leyland Atlantean, Olympian; MCW Metro-bus	80 upward
Front-engined double-decker	Dennis Jubilant, Volvo B55	80 upward

Figure 3.2:   Double-Decker Bus: Delhi, India

Figure 3.3: Articulated Single-Decker Bus: Dar-es-Salaam, Tanzania

The front-engined type of vehicle is generally more robust, and easily cooled, and is thus particularly suitable for Third World conditions, especially in rural and inter-urban services. More sophisticated low-floor types may be adopted in urban areas, although the experience of some rear-engined single-deckers, such as the Leyland National in South America, has not been a happy one. One-person-operation is rare in Third World cities except for minibuses.

Apart from some more recent Western designs, bus manufacture has retained a craft industry scale, with separate chassis and body manufacturers. This often suits Third World countries such as Tanzania, which can import chassis, but make bodies locally. Imports are generally from Western countries, but the Indian Tata single-decker is common throughout the Middle and Far East. South American manufacturers are also playing an increasing role. 'CKD' construction, in which both chassis and body components are imported then assembled locally, also permits a substantial local input, reducing foreign exchange costs, as in the M type single-decker built from British parts in Jamaica.

Although some minibuses (see Figure 3.4) may be petrol-engined, diesel is the norm for larger vehicles, giving about 8 mpg on urban routes. Although minibuses may attain better performance, (around 20 mpg or more), the much lower capacity generally results in higher energy consumption per passenger/kilometre for minibuses and small passenger vehicles.

Figure 3.4:   Minibus: Kuala Lumpur, Malaysia

Cost Structure of Bus Operation

Some characteristics of a range of public transport systems are displayed in Table 3.1 in which per capita GDP ranges from US$150 (India) to that of US$4,500 (Britain). Labour costs increase from about 40 per cent of total costs (in the public sector operations) to about 70 per cent or more in Britain and Western Europe. Private operators, with less strict conditions of employment and wages to meet, may incur labour costs of only about 25 per cent to 30 per cent of total costs. An intermediate position is occupied by Singapore at about 50 per cent of total cost.

The low proportion of labour cost in India occurs despite the high number of staff per bus (around ten in urban services). It will be evident that as labour costs rise in real terms with economic development, there is a substantial reduction to about four staff per bus (or less if kilometres per bus fall, due to more peak-only working etc). This does not necessarily imply unemployment, since as Table 3.1 shows, bus industry employees are fairly stable at about 3 per 1,000 population. In effect, more capital is added to a similar proportion of labour as fleet size rises. Given the operating methods used elsewhere, India could of course run its existing fleet with substantially fewer staff. However, the short-run effect could be to reduce employment significantly, conflicting with other development objectives.

After labour, fuel and materials constitute a major cost, especially where they are imported. Fuel ranges from about 15 per cent to 20 per cent or more of total costs in Third World operations, compared with about 6 per cent in Britain. Continuity of supply may also be critical, especially where a country (Tanzania in 1981 for instance) has limited foreign exchange reserves. In some cases, the cost of fuel to an operator within a country may not reflect the full scarcity so far as the country as a whole is concerned. Over half the foreign exchange earnings of India and Tanzania go on oil imports, for example. A form of shadow pricing in such circumstances may thus be desirable in the evaluation of internal projects (Pathak, 1981). Given that buses are already among the most fuel-efficient vehicles, little further improvement within this sector can be expected, apart from increasing vehicle size. At a broader level however, it is clearly vital to ensure that transport fuel oil demands are minimised through encouragement to non-motorised modes, discouragement of the private car, rail electrification, and as far as practicable the use of large vehicles within the road public transport sector.

Other cost elements include materials, depreciation and interest on loans. As with fuel, cost of materials (tyres, spares, etc.) may occupy a higher proportion of the total costs in the Third World than in Western countries, due to the high import element. In India, fuel and materials jointly accounted for about 34 per cent in 1979-80 (El-Mezawie, 1981).

The importance of depreciation depends on how it is assessed. If full-cost replacement depreciation (as distinct from historic cost) is taken, then this may be about 10 per cent of total costs; if historic, about 5 per cent or less. As fleets expand, even replacement depreciation is not sufficient to fund all purchases. Additional vehicles may be financed through profits (if any), fixed-interest borrowings, and raising equity capital. Many public undertakings suffer from the cost of fixed-interest borrowing which can take up to about 10 per cent of all costs. Raising equity capital, as in the extended shareholdings in Singapore Bus

101

Services (White, 1980), is much to be preferred, since the dividend can be varied year-to-year according to profitability and does not represent a high fixed charge.

Whereas in Western countries the bus industry is generally a net recipient of public spending, its high utilisation in Third World countries may enable it to be profitable, even to make a net contribution through taxes - for example, on fuel, vehicle purchase, number of passengers carried, etc. In India, up to 15 per cent and more of costs may comprise taxes (El-Mezawie, 1981). Indeed, high taxation is largely responsible for the deficits incurred by operators. Where it is alleviated, operations that break even become practicable, and borrowing to cover deficits not so necessary. In Malaysia, taxes on bus use have been reduced, following the effects on profitability of higher car ownership and minibus competition (White, 1980).

Suburban Railways, Metro Systems and Tramways

The scarcity of capital investment reflected in the low ratio of buses to population shows up even more in the relative paucity of urban rail systems. Whereas most cities in Western Europe of one million or above have intensive light rapid transit, suburban rail services, and/or metro systems, very few cities in the Third World have such facilities. The rail schemes listed above are electrically operated; some diesel-operated suburban services can also be found on lower-density networks, such as Karachi.

Relatively new metro systems are found in Sao Paulo, Caracas, Hong Kong, Mexico City and several other very large cities, and many more are now being built in the rapidly-growing Third World cities (Vuchic, 1982). However they only meet a small part of the total growth in urban transport demand. Intensive suburban rail services are found in a number of cities, including Bombay, Calcutta, Madras, and Buenos Aires, but given the thinly-developed nature of many national rail systems, there is often no substantial base on which to build the networks. Light rapid transit lines - generally built from scratch rather than upgraded from tramways as in Europe - can be found in some Third World cities, including Rio de Janeiro, Cairo, Hong Kong, Tunis and Manila.

In some cases, change has followed the European, and in particular, British pattern, of abandoning rail services in favour of competing buses - as in the case of the street tramways in Manila and Singapore. Only in large cities where there are very dense flows do rail services remain (such as the Calcutta tramways). As in Europe, urban railway revenue rarely covers all costs. Capital costs are often subsidised through grants and low-interest loans; operating costs are sometimes cross-subsidised from profitable inter-city passenger and freight services as in Bombay.

In a fully segregated, self-contained metro system such as that of Hong Kong, very high passenger flows can be accommodated, with train headways at about two minutes or less, and around 2,000 passengers per train (giving an hourly flow per track of 60,000). Parts of the Bombay and Hong Kong networks approach this figure at peak periods. A general review of factors affecting urban rail capacity has been provided by the author elsewhere (White, 1986). The figure of 60,000 compares with an upper figure of about 25,000 attained in Western Europe with higher comfort levels.

Given the low capital available in Third World countries, urban rail investment only occurs on the heaviest corridor flows. For example, the Hong Kong Metro Modified Initial System (essentially a single route) carries about 360 million passengers per year, compared with 550 million per year on the entire London Transport underground network. The Bombay suburban lines carry about 1,000 million per year (see Figure 3.5), almost twice the London total, and there are only two main termini. Somewhat lower capacities per hour are found on light rapid transit systems (up to about 10,000 or more) in view of flows attained on the Manila system for London Docklands in UK and some suburban lines, where tracks are shared with other services, thus limiting the frequency.

Urban railways are electrified by two principal means:

1. by third rail direct current, at about 700 volts. This is typical of largely underground metro systems as in Hong Kong, where substations are needed due to the low voltage, but less on-train equipment; and

2. by overhead source, either at 1,500 or 300 volts direct current, or 25,000 volts alternating current. This is typical of suburban lines sharing track with inter-city routes, as in Bombay and Madras. The 25,000 volt system is common in entirely new systems, such as the electrification of the

Figure 3.5:   Suburban Railway: Bombay, India

Kowloon - Canton line in Hong Kong. Direct current is also found on older networks.

Street tramways are suited to passenger volumes of about 6,000 to 10,000 per hour, with higher figures attainable where reserved track and articulated vehicles are operated (as in Cairo), combining the benefits of electrification with modest capital investment. It must be stressed that conventional buses can, on the other hand, carry very heavy flows (up to about 25,000 passengers per hour on a single corridor), especially where suitable priority measures are provided as in Sao Paulo (CET, 1978). New busways offer further scope with the benefits of segregation from other traffic as already enjoyed by railways, but at lower capital cost. A particular attraction is that such a development can be incremental, with successive sections of route transferred to busway as it is built. Following the example of Runcorn in Britain, the new capital (Dodoma) of Tanzania has been built around a segregated busway. Elsewhere, more extensive bus priority measures and busway construction are also proposed.

As oil costs fluctuate, interest in alternative fuels increases. Urban rail and light rapid transit systems already offer scope for using electric traction with its alternative primary sources. This can be applied with lower investment to road public transport in the form of trolley buses. Brazil expanded its trolleybus fleet very rapidly to a total of about 4,000 (Gevert, 1980). Battery electric vehicles however, are not worthwhile due to their high weight, high capital cost and limited range. Energy savings may also be obtained within the diesel-powered sector by using larger vehicles, such as articulated single-deckers or double-deckers, requiring less energy per passenger-space-km.

Network Planning and Structure

Most urban public transport networks evolved in simple radial form with spokes extending outward from the central area as cities grew. Bus services in many cities of the industrialised world typically enable most of the population to be within about 500 to 750 metres of a route, although some areas may not enable access by fullsize vehicles. Additional branch services from earlier trunk routes thus become necessary in order to maintain satisfactory access as cities grow outward. Public transport stops are usually placed at intervals of up to 400 metres.

Within city centres, separate feeder/distributor services are sometimes operated, as with Singapore's City Centre Shuttle. However, these generally incur high unit operating costs. It is thus preferable to minimise the need for them by giving the best practicable access to radial routes, if necessary by traffic priority measures. Central bus stations are sometimes favoured by planners but are usually inconvenient for bus passengers and impose extra costs on operators. In general, picking up and setting down passengers in the street is more efficient, enabling operators to run radial routes linked across city centres and eliminating dead terminal time in the city centre. Where routes do terminate in the central area, then simple turning points and parking areas are desirable. Only for rural and longer-distance services are separate stations with luggage facilities, etc. necessary.

Requiring conventional bus services to run to and from bus stations may place them at a disadvantage to the informal sector whose services may not be so regulated. This situation occured in Kuala Lumpur, where minibuses operated in streets within the central area that were quite able to take larger vehicles, while conventional services terminated at less accessible bus stations

(White, 1981a). Fortunately, this has been corrected to some extent in route revisions.

Where there is high public transport demand and no rail or rapid transit links, demand on some radial corridors may be such as to justify additional limited-stop services, calling only at selected points. Where overcrowding occurs, this may happen naturally inasmuch as the bus will run non-stop once it is full, but this is clearly unsatisfactory for intermediate traffic. Singapore offers a good example of planned limited-stop public transport services operating from new housing developments to the city centre.

As city size grows to above 200,000, demand for direct inter-suburban services becomes sufficient to justify their provision (although this will be lacking where operators fail to perceive the need, or where resources are so limited that only trunk routes can be served). Patronage on such routes arises from visits to friends and relatives, dispersed workplaces, and so forth. Harare, Zimbabwe, with a population of about one million possessed virtually no services between the surrounding townships in 1979.

Peripheral and other specialised services are also often provided for, or on behalf of, employers for the exclusive use of their own staff. This provision is necessary if a factory is not served by the conventional network, or if the workers' residential area is isolated. In addition, the unreliability of the scheduled network may make it difficult to ensure that workers reach their place of employment on time. However, the result can often be wasteful, with vehicles performing only two loaded trips per day, while public fleets are over stretched. An equity issue also arises, in that employees of those organisations able to provide their own transport benefit from free travel, while those using the public network pay fares which are high in relation to earnings. In some cases, government organisations providing transport for their own workers may be able to obtain capital more readily than public transport operators themselves. This can be seen in Nigeria and Tanzania for example.

Another illustration of the inefficient use of transport resources can be seen in Malaysia, where buses for works contracts *(bas kilang)* and school service *(bas sekolah)* cannot be used in ordinary public transport - even where the same operator provides them. A more positive approach exists in Singapore, where school buses supplement the public network at other times of day. This approach could be followed elsewhere, especially where the total bus fleet is very limited.

Pricing Policy

In a typical situation in which an operator is expected to break even or make a profit, prices should be related closely to costs. Given the approaches already described, a distance-based fare may be most appropriate if costs are allocated largely on a time or mileage-based system. However, flat fares may be more appropriate for small networks, and those where cost is determined mainly by the number of buses and trains required simultaneously to meet peak demand. The relationship between costs and appropriate pricing policy with examples from Third World countries is reviewed in greater depth elsewhere (White, 1981b).

The extent to which graduated or flat fares have been adopted is often a consequence of former colonial links. Many British-influenced countries, for example, tend toward graduated fares (as in most Indian cities), with others preferring flat or zonal fares. There is generally no need to simplify fares in many such countries in order to facilitate Western European-style one-person-operation, due to much lower labour costs; apart from in Singapore and Hong Kong which have a higher staff turnover on account of the availability of competitive employment. However, some simplification is desirable where through bus/rail ticketing is introduced, as on the Sao Paulo metro.

THE INFORMAL PUBLIC TRANSPORT RESPONSE

Composition

In view of the coverage given elsewhere in this book on the informal public transport sector (see Chapter 4), only a brief outline is given here, indicating its present relationship with the formal sector and discussing possible future developments.

As already indicated, the limited capacity of the formal public transport system is due to, among other things, inadequate investment, poor availability of vehicles and limited networks. An unsatisfied potential demand thus exists, especially in those areas where the formal system is unable to serve the demands made upon it due to roads being unable to accommodate large vehicles, as in many shanty town areas of Third World cities.

Added to this demand is the ready supply of certain resources to the transport sector. Large numbers of unemployed may be willing to work for very low sums, and long hours. Simple forms of labour-intensive vehicle construction, which largely use local materials (or remanufacture imported equipment), may thus enable vehicles to be provided without the effect of foreign exchange constraints, as well as generate a cash flow which is fed back into the local economy. The informal sector may furthermore, offer benefits to the user, in being able to offer different types of services which are often more demand-oriented (at higher fares) for:

1. areas which the formal sector does not serve (such as new housing on the steep hillsides of Caracas);
2. unmade roads (as in parts of Kinshasa) (Poletti, 1977); and
3. the same roads as are served by the formal sector but at different speed, frequency, etc.

Types of Modes

A wide variety of names is given to modes within the informal sector, which are often grouped under the term paratransit (see Case, 1980; Rimmer, 1979 and Silcock, 1981). They range from the man-powered rickshaw still found in India (see Unnayan and Thomas, 1981) and Indonesia (see Soegijoko, 1986), to small motor vehicles derived from motorcycle technology, such as the two-seater autorickshaws, and small minibuses and shared taxis (see Chapter 4). Larger vehicles may also be included in this sector which carry loads of 16 or so persons, similar to those of formal sector public transport vehicles. The largest vehicles are generally based on modified full-size four-wheel goods chassis with a capacity for about 60 passengers, (mostly standees), such as the *fula-fulas* of Kinshasa (Poletti, 1977).

Operations

The term informal implies that the organisation of such systems tends to be small-scale, almost invariably private, and in practice largely unregulated. Fares may be determined by a crudely-enforced consensus among the operators themselves and not be formally advertised. Fixed stopping points are not usually followed.

The total scale of these operations is considerable, and may often exceed that of formal public transport. For example, Table 3.3 shows the proportions of all motorised travel by informal and formal modes for several major cities. In some cities, such as Manila, the informal mode clearly predominates. The importance of the informal sector therefore must be clearly acknowledged.

Table 3.3 Proportion of Trips by Car, Bus and Informal Sector Public Transport in Selected Cities

City and Survey Date	Percentage of Trips by		
(a) Motorised modes	Car	Bus	Informal sector & other
Bangkok (1970)	29	59	12
Hong Kong (1977)	30	39	31
Jakarta (1972)	29	49	22
Karachi (1971)	16	63	21
Kingston (1978)	36	49	15
Manila (1974)	29	22	49
(b) Bus and informal/other			
Delhi (1979)	–	78	22
Hyderabad (1979)	–	49	51
Bangalore (1979)	–	48	52
Kampur (1980)	–	6	94
Jaipur (1979)	–	18	82
Agra (1979)	–	13	87
Baroda (1979)	–	45	55
Chieng Mai (1976)	–	7	93
(c) All modes	Car & motorcycle	Bus	Minibus	Other
Kuala Lumpur (1978)	50	19	11	20

Notes and Sources:

(a) Silcock, 1981

(b) For Indian cities, in which car proportion is very small in any case, Maunder et al 1981.

For Chieng Mai, Maunder, D.A.C. and Fouracre, P.R., Public transport in Chieng Mai, Thailand, Transport & Research Laboratory Supplementary Report SR285, 1979.

(c) Jamieson Mackay, 1981. Data refers to inbound morning peak period traffic crossing survey cordon around central area.

This is not, however, to accept uncritically that role or the desirability of its future expansion. Much research and planning in recent years seems to have gone from one extreme to another in their response to such operations, firstly ignoring the existence of informal modes, and then combining a sudden awareness of their importance with an implicit assumption that they are to be supported and expanded.

In many respects, the informal sector can be regarded as an *intermediate* form of public transport which may disappear or be greatly reduced in scope, when an adequate formal system becomes available (Vuchic, 1981). These are some of its disadvantages:

1. The small size of vehicles tends to result in high unit costs, especially of labour and fuel. In some cases, large public operators may also have high costs (due to organisational diseconomies of scale), but given similarly efficient methods of operation, a large vehicle will normally have substantially lower unit costs.

2. Long-run capital costs may be higher. Where new vehicles are used in the formal sector - as with the minibuses in Kuala Lumpur - their lighter construction often results in a much shorter vehicle life under similar operating conditions, and lower safety standards than is the case for more robust, larger vehicles. A life of four to five years rather than ten to twelve years may be expected, with greater annual depreciation per passenger place, if replacements are to be provided when required. Where the vehicle is largely remanufactured from second-hand components this may not apply.

3. Traffic congestion may be aggravated, especially, where very small vehicles make frequent stops to pick up passengers. This is certainly true of manually-propelled vehicles when they share the same road space as larger motor vehicles. The most harmful effect is undoubtedly that from shared taxis or small minibuses operating along fixed routes, with frequent intermediate stops in the nearside lane. The delay at a stop caused to other traffic is similar to that created by conventional buses, but the number of passengers per vehicle is far smaller. Studies of the Turkish *dolmus* (shared-taxis), which can take five passengers (Orer et al, 1978), suggest that a single nearside lane of road occupied largely by such vehicles has a capacity equal to only about 1,800 pas-

sengers per hour. This is little more than the capacity attained by private cars each carrying one driver and one passenger. Conventional buses in such a lane could take over 5,000 passengers per hour.

4. A tendency to concentrate on the more attractive routes is evident in some cases, taking traffic from the formal sector on routes which it finds profitable, rather than providing a complementary network. Given the high unit cost of much of the informal sector, it becomes necessary to get very high load factors if fares are not to reach very high levels. In order to have a good chance of picking up casual traffic, concentration on the busiest streets becomes usual (the same is true of individual hire taxis).

The informal public transport sector thus tends to take traffic which might otherwise be picked up by conventional modes or to provide an alternative price/quality of service mix generally for those on higher incomes. The lower-income user may thus lose out, as the reduced potential traffic for the formal sector operators means that they then have to cut back frequencies, and therefore possibly increase fares as is evident in Kuala Lumpur, for example (Jamieson McKay, 1981 and White, 1981b). The problem is aggravated when a restrictive system of regulation applies only to the formal sector. The formal sector operator may thus be compelled to operate at tightly-controlled fares, under stricter working and wage conditions, and to cross-subsidise less renumerative routes. The natural advantages of the larger vehicle are thus artificially offset. A consistent degree of regulation, whether strict or liberal, would produce a more rational allocation of traffic between the two sectors.

NEED FOR CO-ORDINATION

The need for co-ordination in public transport operations can be viewed in two ways:

1. In the day-to-day, operational sense - i.e., through the introduction of common route-numbering systems, stopping points, etc. for various operators, and possibly through a common fare structure; improvement of interchanges,

especially between feeder and trunk routes and (where rail plays a significant role), through bus/rail co-ordination.

2. In the policy sense - i.e., to make the best overall use of resources, and co-ordinate transport policy with land-use planning, housing, national investment, foreign exchange purchase priorities, policing of traffic regulations, etc.

In general, the degree of co-ordination of either of the above kind is a good deal less in Third World countries than in Western Europe despite the greater need.

Whereas public transport systems in Western Europe have to meet a high degree of competition from the private car, and thus must maximise the quality of service to attract users, most Third World public transport systems (with some exceptions, such as those in Malaysia), generally operate against a background of low car ownership. Within the public transport sector, however, competition with informal systems, private operators, etc. may be more important than in Western Europe. Western Europe also differs in the nature of co-ordination, in that high investment levels (mostly in railways) create a greater need to provide good bus feeder interchange and through ticketing. Apart from a few cities, such as Sao Paulo, urban railways play a less significant role in Third World urban development. Where railways are significant, situations such as those in Bombay are more typical, with suburban rail and bus services running parallel within a north-south axis (see Figure 3.1). The buses also act as suburban feeders and city centre distributors for the railways, but without any formal co-ordination or through ticketing.

There is a common misconception that operational co-ordination entails common ownership, usually under a single public body. This is not the case. Indeed, any economies of scale in bus operation (of fleet size) are hard to establish. Such organisations are likely to have higher unit costs, and over-centralised management, as the experience of the Bangkok Mass Transit Authority, which took over most of the city's independent companies, indicates (Mundy, 1982). According to the system of regulation, a wide diveristy of operators and vehicle types can successfully form a co-ordinated network, as recent European experience indicates. For example, a city authority can establish a clear system of route numbers and stopping places for bus services, and run an urban rail system, but simultaneously permit small independent bus operators to provide most of the bus services, especially in the suburban areas. To some extent this has been attained in Kuala Lumpur, albeit within each network (minibus and conventional bus), with overlap between the two networks.

The concept of co-ordinating complementary modes is most applicable to the Third World in respect of the formal and informal systems as advocated by Soegijoko (1986) on the basis of research findings in Indonesia. Informal systems, especially when using very small vehicles, are best suited to serving those areas which larger vehicles cannot reach, providing a facility for short-distance trips, and for those in which some special facility is required (for example, luggage space). The formal modes are best suited to trunk radial routes, and other relatively high-density flows. In this way better use is made of large vehicles, with their savings in capital cost and energy, and the congestion caused by small vehicles on busy main streets is reduced.

It is in policy and organisation, that the lack of the second form of co-ordination is most serious. Better use of congested road space is urgently needed (see Chapter 10) as the operation of scarce resources such as buses is impaired. The application of Transportation Systems Management concepts (see Chapter 11) must itself be dependent upon an overall framework in which road design, policing and public transport operation are assessed by the same planning team. In many countries, different government departments often take separate intiatives in policing, road construction, land use planning, etc. Even railways and other forms of public transport may be dealt with under separate ministries, as in India and Pakistan. This agency fragmentation in the urban transport sector (see Chapter 2) makes it difficult to handle urban problems as a whole, and in particular to implement proposals from recent transport studies. New urban development is all too often sited in areas difficult to serve by public transport, except with high-cost small vehicles rather than along concentrated demand corridors.

Whilst the appropriate solution for each city must suit local conditions, it is clear that a co-ordinating body covering the relevant specialisation and with executive power could contribute a great deal to ensuring that urban transport plans are implemented and related resources are used most effectively (see Chapter 7).

CONCLUSION

From the preceding discussion one may conclude that not only is the demand for public transport in Third World cities rapidly rising, but in most cases is not satisfied - particularly at peak periods. Whilst this may be attributed to limited resources and low capital investment in bus fleets, rail infrastructure and related facilities - low vehicle availability (due to lack of sufficient spares), poor maintenance and difficulties in raising adequate funding also account for such inadequacies.

Under these circumstances, the use of large conventional buses within the formal public transport sector, is the most efficient use of capital and fuel, coupled with the development and use of railways in the very largest cities, employing simple, standardised and rubust types of rolling stock. Informal public transport systems (motorised and non-motorised) on the other hand, need to be co-ordinated with that of the formal sector, and encouraged to meet travel needs where these cannot adequately be met by conventional buses.

Notwithstanding this, regulation of the two sectors need to be made consistent so as to avoid the misallocation of resources, particularly along high-demand density corridors. This in turn calls for greater and better co-ordination in policy-making, particularly among the various city, provincial, and central government agencies whose plans and policies affect public transport development. The response to meeting Third World urban public transport needs however, must reflect the range of per capita incomes and other variables affecting operations in such cities, and also be incorporated in appropriate planning practice for public transport.

NOTES

(1)   The chapter was originally prepared in 1982 for publication in 1984.
(2)   The term 'public' refers to the availability of a mode to the general public (in contrast with the private use of a car, for example), and refers to systems both in public (state or local authority) and private ownership.

REFERENCES

Bayliss, D. (1981) 'A Billion City Dwellers - How Will They Travel?'. **Transportation**, vol. 10, no. 4, Elsevier Science Publisher, Amsterdam.

Case, D. (1980) 'A Comparison of Public Transport in Cities in South East Asia' **Proceedings of PTRC Summer Annual Meeting**, University of Warwick, PTRC Education and Research Services Ltd., London.

CET (Companhia de Engenharia de Trafego) (1978) Special Issue of **Technical Bulletin**, no. 9 (in English), Sao Paulo.

El-Mezawie, A.A. et al (1981) 'State Road Transport Undertakings in India: A Study of Performance, Problems and Prospects'. ILO/UNDP Project IND/73/002, Central Institute of Road Transport, Pune.

Fouracre, P.R., Maunder, D.A.C., Pathak, M.G. and Rao, C.H. (1981) 'Public Transport Supply in Indian Cities', **Transport and Road Research Laboratory Report**, no. LR1018, TRRL, Crowthorne.

Gevert, T.A. (1980) 'Brazil Pushes Trolleybuses' **Trolleybus Magazine**, no. 111, Trolley Bus Museum Co. Ltd., West Byfleet, Surrey.

Heraty, M.J. (ed) (1987) **Developing World Land Transport**, Grosvenor Press, London.

Hibbs, J. (1981) 'A Comparative Study of the Licensing and Control of Public Road Passenger Transport in Selected Overseas Countries', University of Birmingham.

Hussain, K.A. (1980) **Bus Logistics for Developing Countries,** Published by author, Dar-es-Salaam.

Jacobs, G.D. Maunder, D.A.C., and Fouracre, P.R. (1979) 'A Comparison of Bus Operations in Cities of Developed and Developing Countries', **Traffic Engineering and Control**, Printerhall Ltd., June, London.

Jamieson Mackay and Partners (1981) 'The Minibuses and the Public Transport System of Kuala Lumpur, **Transport and Road Research Laboratory Report**, no. SR687, TRRL, Crowthorne.

Lefevre, J. (1981) 'Urban Buses: Wind of Change Blows at Home and Abroad', **Transport**, Journal of Chartered Institute of Transport, March/April, London.

Maunder, D.A.C. et al (1981) 'Household and Travel Characteristics in Two Residential Areas of Delhi, India', **Transport** and Road Research Laboratory Report, no. SR673, TRRL, Crowthorne.

Maunder, D.A.C. (1984) 'Trip Rates and Travel Patterns in Delhi', **Transport and Road Research Laboratory Report**, no. RR1, TRRL, Crowthorne.

Mundy, J. (1982) 'Private Sector Rejects Takeover of Bangkok Buses', **Transport**, Journal of the Chartered Institute of Transport, January/February, London.

Orer, M., Ozden, Y., and Ozdirim, M. (1978) 'The Dolmus'. Paper at EMCT Round Table 40 on 'Paratransit', ECMT, Paris.

Pathak, M. (1981) 'Energy Efficient Transport Systems in India', CIRT, Pune and Polytechnic of Central London.

Poletti, J.C. (1977) 'Les Transports Urbains de Kinshasa', **Transport Urbains**, no. 40, Paris.

Rimmer, P.R. (1986) **Rikisha to Rapid Transit**, Pergamon Press, Oxford.

Silcock, D.T. (1981) 'Urban Paratransit in the Developing World'. **Transport Reviews**, vol. 1, no. 2, Taylor and Francis, April-June, Philadelphia.

Soegijoko, B.T. (1986) 'The Becaks of Java', **Habitat International**, vol. 10, no. 1/2, Pergamon Press, Oxford.

Unnayan in association with Thomas. T.H. (1981) 'Rickshaws in Calcutta', Unnayan, Calcutta.

Vuchic, V.R. (1981) **Urban Public Transportation Systems and Technology**, Prentice-Hall, New Jersey.

_____ (1982) 'Designers Widen the Urban Rail Options' **Railway Gazette International**, Business Press International Ltd., January, West Sussex.

White P.R. (1980) 'Bus Operations in Developing Countries under Different Economic Conditions', **Proceedings PTRC Annual Summer Meeting**, University of Warwick, PTRC Education and Research Services Ltd., London.

_____ (1981a) 'The Benefits of Minibuses : A Comment' **Journal of Transport Economics and Policy**, January, vol. XV, no. 1, University of Bath (see also rejoinder by A.A. Walters).

_____ (1981b) 'Recent Developments in the Pricing of Local Public Transport Services' **Transport Reviews**, vol. I, no. 2, Taylor and Francis. April/June, Philadelphia.

_____ (1986) **Public Transport: Its Planning, Management and Operation**, Hutchinson, London.

Chapter 4

The Role of Non-Motorised Urban Travel

M.S.V. Rao and A.K. Sharma

INTRODUCTION

All cities are faced with transport problems of one kind or another. Whilst efforts to alleviate such problems in cities of the industrialised nations may have met with some success, efforts to ensure a satisfactory widespread level of mobility in the major urban areas of the Third World have been much less successful.

This failure of transport planning to alleviate significantly the movement problems of Third World cities can in part be attributed to urban transport planning policies and perceptions which are more concerned with motorised transport as indicated in Chapters 2 and 5. Although this approach has validity in the industrialised world, the wide variety of transport modes found in many Third World cities means that motorised movement is usually a small proportion of all traffic. The neglect of non-motorised travel, particularly in cities in the Indian sub-continent and Southeast Asia, has led to excessive focus on problems of the motorcar, and measures to restrict non-motorised movement which is seen as hindering motorised traffic flows.

In India, where there is a very high and longstanding dependence on non-motorised travel, such an approach is completely inconsistent with the realities of the urban transport situation, even in the larger metropolitan areas of Bombay and Calcutta. It is therefore disturbing to note that such forms of movement have been neglected ever since the earliest set of city-wide transport studies undertaken in the Third World, typified by the Bombay and Calcutta Transport studies (Wilbur Smith and Associates, 1955 and CMPO, 1967 respectively). The plans which came out of these studies envisaged a higher dependence upon motorised modes of transport and therefore recommended massive urban road programmes. At the same time, little if any attention was paid to the infrastructure needs of non-motorised movement.

Urban transport studies conducted in the second round of transport planning efforts in India, for cities such as Madras (Government of Tamil Nadu, 1974), shed some additional light on the characteristics of non-motorised movement and its importance to the development of Third World cities. Work undertaken by Owen (1973) also provided an insight into this area. Indeed, these studies have proved to be useful starting points for later research. However, apart from recognising the scale and intensity of non-motorised travel, such studies failed to evolve any meaningful planning guidelines for the promotion of the interests of non-motorised travel.

In part, this failure was due to an incomplete comprehension of the relationship between movement (and its various transport technologies) and its socio-economic and cultural context. With hindsight, this was especially true of traffic generated by the informal economic sector, since even today most urban transport studies of the Third World are much more concerned with the formal economic sector than the informal. However, it is the latter which depends more upon (and is involved in the provision of) non-motorised movement.

The much needed focus on non-motorised movement in the Third World was initially brought about by the global energy crisis of 1973, and the subsequent interest shown in energy-saving transport modes by the World Bank. A research programme in urban public transport in India, undertaken jointly by the Association of State Road Transport Undertakings of India and the Transport Road Research Laboratory in Britain, (Fouracre et al, 1981), further focused on the role of non-motorised transport in various Third World cities. Its findings confirmed the need for transport planners to identify and plan for alternative modes of public transport to the bus, and especially for non-motorised public transport modes which are more consistent with prevailing economic and development constraints. The joint research identified non-motorised movement as playing a vital role in the transport systems of the cities investigated.

A major benefit of such research, including the public transport study of Kingston, Jamaica (Heraty, 1980), of Surabaya, Indonesia (Fouracre and Maunder, 1978) of Southeast Asian cities (Case and Latchford, 1981), of Indian cities, (Rao and Sharma, 1980), and in different parts of the Third World (Fouracre, 1977; Ocampo, 1982 and Soegijoko, 1986), is that there are now valuable insights into the characteristics of a large variety of non-motorised public transport travel. In this chapter the role and characteristics of this form of movement in India will be discussed, illustrating its widespread need, both as a means of travel, and as a source of employment.

TRANSPORT AND URBAN DEVELOPMENT IN INDIA

Rapid urbanisation trends in India since the beginning of the century have resulted in almost one fifth of its total population of 547 million living in urban areas. Of these, approximately half live in settlements of 100,000 or more (see Table 4.1). The remaining urban population is distributed throughout the country in cities of less than 100,000. Of the eight Indian metropolitan cities, four-Delhi, Bombay, Calcutta and Madras - at present account for nearly 20 per cent of the nation's urban population.

The widely varying socio-economic characteristics and development profiles of these different sized cities, typified by their different rates of industrialisation, modernisation and urbanisation, exert a strong influence upon the use and choice of urban transport modes within them. Recent studies conducted in the metropolitan and medium sized cities (i.e., those with a population of 100,000 and more) have shown that urban transport problems are both extensive and varied, revealing the widespread use of different transport modes. These studies have also indicated that the share of non-motorised travel in all such settlements was a stable component of modal split characteristics (see Table 4.2). The principal implication of this is that non-motorised urban travel is vital to Indian cities and must be planned for.

A particular feature of medium and small sized urban areas in India (i.e., cities with a population of 100,000 and less) is the notable inadequacy of their bus public transport facilities as shown in Table 4.2. Even in metropolitan areas, where conscious efforts have been made to provide improved public transport services,

119

Table 4.1 Urbanisation Trends in India, 1901-1971

Census Year	Per cent of urban population to national-population	Per cent of Urban Population in Each Settlement Size Class						
		Class-I Greater than 100,000	Class-II 50,000 100,000	Class-III 20,000 50,000	Class-IV 10,000 20,000	Class-V 5,000 10,000	Class-VI 5,000	Total
1901	10.85	22.93	11.84	16.50	22.06	20.38	6.29	100.0
1911	10.29	24.19	10.90	17.69	20.46	19.81	6.95	100.0
1921	11.18	25.31	12.43	16.89	18.91	19.03	7.44	100.0
1931	12.00	27.37	11.95	18.76	18.97	17.32	5.63	100.0
1941	13.86	35.40	11.77	17.71	16.29	15.38	3.45	100.0
1951	17.30	41.77	11.06	16.73	14.02	13.20	3.22	100.0
1961	17.98	48.37	11.89	18.53	13.03	7.23	0.95	100.0
1971	19.87	52.41	12.15	17.56	12.04	5.24	0.80	100.0

Source: National Transport Policy Committee, 1979 (Annexure 1.)

there are far too few buses (see Table 4.3). Nor is it expected that this situation will alter greatly in the foreseeable future, since the provision of organised bus public transport services on a continuous basis for all major urban areas in India is well beyond the available resources of local, state and central government. Hence the gigantic investment in the urban public transport sector required to bring about changes is not forthcoming. This is in part due to the fact that public transport operations are incurring huge economic deficits, despite substantial subsidy support from state and central government.

Against this backcloth of insufficient bus public transport in Indian cities, there is a growing belief among professionals involved in the transport sector that non-motorised forms of public transport should be relied on far more to supplement the shortage of motorised services. This viewpoint takes on particular significance in the light of the rapid population growth Indian settlements are facing, and the subsequent increased travel demands that will be generated.

Table 4.2   Provision of Public Transport Facilities in Selected Indian Cities

City	Population (millions)	Conventional buses (per 100,000)	Auto-rickshaws (per 100,000)	Cycle-rickshaws (per 100,000)
Hyderabad	2.37	25.7	260	620
Bangalore	2.08	31.1	446	200
Ahmedabad	1.95	29.8	336	336
Kanpur	1.51	3.3	N.A.	3,000
Jaipur	0.81	9.2	217	1,050
Agra	0.73	16.8	70	2,470
Baroda	0.63	22.0	22	N.A.

Source: Urban Transport Statistics, ASRTU/TRRL Working Paper No.30
(unpublished), 1978-9 (Annexure 1, Table 3).

A further argument for encouraging non-motorised urban transport relates to their efficiency in compact old urban areas. Most Indian cities possess a rich urban development heritage which is reflected in their older quarters. These areas usually consist of high density development where non-motorised transport technologies, and particularly pedestrian and animal

Table 4.3 Main Indicators of Bus Public Transport Operational Efficiency in Indian Metropolitan Areas

Indicators	CALCUTTA–(CSTC)					BOMBAY–(BEST)				
	73-74	74-75	75-76	76-77	77-78	73-74	74-75	75-76	76-77	77-78
1. Average fleet strength (as on 31st March) year end	1363.00	1436.00	1331.00	1226.00	1178.00	1478.00	1530.00	1639.00	1667.00	1817.00
2. Av. effective fleet strength	920.00	988.00	886.00	983.00	938.00	1385.00	1453.00	1506.00	1614.00	1675.00
3. Av. number of buses on road	553.00	515.00	538.00	608.00	574.00	1257.00	1307.00	1370.00	1486.00	1541.00
4. Percentage fleet utilisation	40.60	35.90	40.40	49.60	48.73	91.00	90.00	91.00	92.00	93.00
5. Vehicle utilisation (per day [kms])	137.00	137.00	141.00	152.00	139.00	218.00	214.00	217.00	221.80	222.00
6. Average breakdown (per 10,000 kms)	25.90	28.50	23.90	15.40	20.40	3.30	N.A.	2.48	1.15	1.91
7. Accidents (per annum)	674.00	687.00	750.00	759.00	N.A.	3726.00	3498.00	4186.00	3824.00	N.A.
8. Av. number of passengers carried per (lakhs)	8.45	7.75	7.48	8.13	N.A.	29.46	29.71	30.93	33.01	35.45
9. Passengers per bus daily	1527.00	1505.00	1390.00	1338.00	N.A.	2344.00	2273.00	2258.00	2330.00	2301.00
10. Operating cost (paise per km)	436.25	539.24	569.95	561.33	N.A.	236.09	N.A.	328.68	327.56	361.86
11. Revenue earnings (paise per km)	175.74	190.83	222.38	243.65	N.A.	200.68	N.A.	286.26	311.29	320.86
12. Bus staff ration	18.81	17.92	16.84	16.40	N.A.	9.19	N.A.	11.32	14.29	14.34
13. No. of buses per 1000 pop.										

Source: National Transport Policy Comittee, 1979 (Derived from Annexure VI.)

movement, have been, and still are dominant. As a result, motorised traffic within such areas encounters acute congestion problems. In addition, the street system in these old compact areas is not conducive to the efficient operation of bus transport services thus making non-motorised modes invaluable.

Urban form and road patterns characteristic of most Indian cities accentuate the problems of transport planning for motorised movement by virtue of the fact that most such settlements have not experienced major improvements to their road network since the British colonial period - with the possible exception of Delhi and Bombay. This situation has mainly arisen from the longstanding inadequacy of resources made available to the transport sector over the years, which has typically produced low road space allocations in comparison with other land uses.

TYPES OF NON-MOTORISED URBAN TRANSPORT MODES

The wide spectrum of non-motorised modes of transport employed in Indian cities, ranging from pedestrian movement to the *tonga*, are used for both passengers and goods. The numerous modes reflect both the variety of movement needs and financial means to pay for such services.

Pedestrian Movement

Walking is one of the most dependable means of movement - certainly the cheapest. An analysis of walk trip characteristics in Indian cities of different sizes showed a close correlation between low income groups and an extensive dependence upon walking (Wakankar, 1977). The same research indicated that people in medium and small-sized cities were far more dependant upon walk trips than those in the larger metropolitan areas. In the former, 30 per cent of all trips were made on foot (see Table 4.4).

The study further pointed out that the characteristics of pedestrian movement in Indian cities are substantially different from those in urban areas of industrialised nations, particularly with regard to average walking distances per trip which are much lower in the latter kind of settlements. Studies conducted in Delhi and Madras for example, indicate that the average walk trip distances in these cities range between two to three kilometres per trip (TCPO, 1972 and Rao and Sharma, 1980) although longer distances are no doubt covered by the poorest of poor inhabitants.

Table 4.4   Model Split Characteristics of Travel in Indian Cities

	Meerut 1	Calicut 2	Gurgaon 3	Cochin 4	Agra 5*
Population (1981) (in lakhs)	5.38	5.46	1.01	6.86	7.7
Pvt. Fast	21.30	4.21	17.00	6.80	6.6
Cycle	22.60	13.10	52.00	12.80	53.6
Mass Transport	2.80	40.64	8.00	70.00	1.7
I.P.T./Hired Modes	20.20	0.55	23.00	4.50	0.9
Walk	33.00	41.50	N.A.	5.90 (work only)	37.2

Source: 1. Assessment of Travel Demand in Meerut, School of Planning and Architecture (unpublished report), 1982.

2. Work Trip Characteristics of Calicut City; Thesis by S.Sevini, 1971, School of Planning and Architecture, New Delhi.

3. Technique for Assessment of Travel Demand: Case Study Gurgaon, School of Planning and Architecture, New Delhi, 1981.

4. Report on Urban Transport Planning, Table No.9, (page 14), NATPAC Annual Report, 1980-81.

5. Mode of Travel Work Trips in Agra 1970-71 Appendix No. V/4, Master Plan of Agra, Vol.5.

*   For work trips only.

Cycle Movement

The various types of cycle are an important means of travel in most Indian cities. As in China, the bicycle, for example, represents a valuable household asset, particularly in medium and small sized settlements. In design, the bicycle in India has remained the same since its introduction by the British, despite the fact that it is now manufactured in India. With marginal modifications, the bicycle moves goods and people (see Figure 4.1).

A more innovative and substantial adaptation of the bicycle is the cycle-rickshaw (see Figure 4.2). This mode of transport, which is widespread throughout all major settlements in India (indeed throughout the Indian sub-continent and Southeast Asia), can typically carry two passengers or up to 175 kilos of goods, (Meier, 1977). There are three principal types of cycle-rickshaws in Asia, two of which have a different position (front or back) for the driver and passenger (or freight). In the Indian cycle-rickshaw the driver sits at the front. This allows for easier

Figure 4.1: Bicycle as Goods Carrier

Figure 4.2: Indian Cycle-Rickshaw

pedalling and manoeuvrability, although it has the disadvantage of a smaller carrying capacity than the other designs.

Indian cycle-rickshaws are locally manufactured and are rarely exported outside the city of their production. As a result, their detailed design characteristics tend to vary from city to city. The average speed capabilities however, are much the same, except where they have been fitted with power transmission, as in an experiment in Madras. The manually operated cycle-rickshaw has an average speed of approximately 10-15 kph, (depending upon its load) in favourable operating conditions. Improvements to the overall design of the rickshaw have not however been very popular, principally because of the additional cost involved. This factor is especially important for those rickshaw owner/drivers of limited means, although in fact the majority of rickshaw drivers rent their vehicles from proprietors, who generally own several of them.

In addition to the conventional cycle-rickshaw, adaptations of its use as a means of transport for school children have been made (see Figure 4.3). Other adaptations include goods-carrying cycle-rickshaws (see Figure 4.4) - in some cases specifically designed to transport perishable goods.

Figure 4.3: School Bus Cycle-Rickshaws in Old Delhi

Figure 4.4: Goods Carrying Cycle-Rickshaw

Man-powered Vehicular Movement

In some Indian cities, such as Calcutta, the traditional cycle-rickshaw has been banned from the central area, since the authorities maintain that they obstruct other traffic, particularly motorised movement. Instead, hand-rickshaws are used as many consider them to be far more manoeuvrable in difficult traffic conditions than the cycle-rickshaw.

More widespread than hand-rickshaws are hand carts, or *rehras* as they are more commonly known (see Figure 4.5). These are pushed or pulled by human power and used primarily for carrying freight for short distances within urban areas. A single man pulling or pushing a handcart can carry up to 5000 kilos in weight.

Animal-powered Vehicular Movement

Larger and heavier freight is usually transported in animal-drawn vehicles such as bullock carts (see Figure 4.6) especially in areas where motorised trucks are not used. These carts are extensively employed in Indian cities to distribute goods, particularly from

Figure 4.5: Hand Cart – *Rehra*

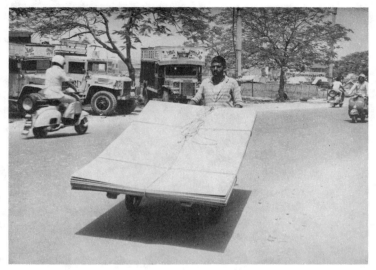

Figure 4.6: Bullock Cart

wholesale and retail market areas to other parts of the city. Given that average traffic speeds are low where these vehicles operate (because of narrow streets and mixed traffic characteristics), the slowness of these carts is no real disadvantage to their users. They do moreover, contribute significantly to the overall economy of many Indian cities.

The *Tonga*

The horse-drawn carriage (see Figure 4.7) is also widely employed in Indian cities. Very little change in their design and operating characteristics has taken place over the many decades of its use. The vehicle has a seating capacity of six to eight people, and in most versions, the seats can be easily removed or adjusted in order to carry freight. Given the large dimensions of its wooden wheels, the average running speed of the *tonga* (15-20 kph) in favourable operating conditions is greater than that of the cycle-rickshaw, although this also depends upon the relative loads carried. On the other hand, the *tonga's* large size makes it not very manoeuvrable and thus unable to operate successfully in narrow and congested streets.

Figure 4.7: Horse Carriage – *Tonga*

Tonga public transport services in Indian cities tend to operate along specific routes, handed down by operators from generation to generation. The use of this mode has however, declined in the larger cities due to the rising costs of maintaining the horse, as well as the increased problems encountered by its use in mixed traffic conditions.

SUPPLY AND DEMAND CHARACTERISTICS OF NON-MOTORISED URBAN TRANSPORT

Enforcement Restrictions

Despite the widespread importance of non-motorised urban travel in many parts of the Third World and India in particular, it is usually regarded unsympathetically by transport planners and governments alike. Invariably, sufficient road space and related amenities are not provided for this kind of travel. Indeed, in certain instances (for example in Calcutta), legislation and traffic enforcement regulations have been introduced to prohibit the operation of particular types of non-motorised vehicles along specific routes or within particular areas of the city. Decisions of this kind, (frequently directed at the cycle-rickshaw) are generally taken in the belief that non-motorised travel excessively inhibits traffic flows and generates major traffic hazards.

Nevertheless the number of non-motorised vehicles has increased significantly over the years throughout India (see Table 4.5). Data collected relatively recently suggests that the increase in non-motorised movement is in fact, considerably greater than that indicated by official vehicle registration statistics. For example, research conducted in Agra revealed that almost 6000 cycle rickshaws operate without a licence, and are thus unregistered (SPA, 1979). Lack of control of unregistered non-motorised vehicles has contributed substantially toward the complexities of transport problems in Indian cities, since the number of non-motorised vehicles operating in such settlements is unknown. Furthermore, their operational characteristics have not been widely researched, nor are details of vehicle ownership available.

This state of affairs is in part due to the fact that the use and operation of these types of transport modes in Indian settlements are governed by legislation formulated and enforced by local

Table 4.5 Growth of Non-Motorised Vehicles in Indian Cities

Vehicle Type	City	Year				
		1972	1973	1974	1975	1976
Cycle-Rickshaw	Delhi	1130	1680	7387	7345	5157
	Madras	2392	5203	5334	5351	5513
	Bangalore	221	276	39	N.A.	N.A.
	Hyderabad	12699	N.A.	N.A.	N.A.	14000
	Ahmedabad	1500	1606	1704	1884	2083
	Meerut	6993	7284	7774	8565	8717
	Faridabad	1326	1922	2527	3194	3276
	Gurgaon	N.A.	N.A.	N.A.	951	1028
Tonga	Delhi	1542	2495	2470	2273	1962
	Madras	117	138	123	100	90
	Bangalore	236	637	514	N.A.	N.A.
	Poona	169	139	105	105	117
	Meerut	400	468	482	495	584
	Aurangabad	35	77	N.A.	124	43
	Gurgaon	N.A.	N.A.	N.A.	25	30

Source: Report on Objective Assessment of the Role of Intermediate Public Transport, School of Planning and Architecture, New Delhi, 1979.

government bodies. Information about the non-motorised transport sector thus varies from city to city, depending upon the amount of local resources that can be committed to collecting and analysing transport data of this kind. Similarly, the restrictions on non-motorised movement, and the degree to which they are enforced, also differ from city to city. Since the level of enforcement is a direct function of the various local institutional capacities which are invariably limited, the general level of traffic enforcement tends to be lax. This of course greatly constrains local government efforts at supervising the maintenance and operation of non-motorised vehicles.

The situation with regard to the motorised urban transport sector, on the other hand, is quite different. Here the operation of transport is controlled by the Motor Vehicles Act. By virtue of the nationwide application of this Act by central government representative agencies, enforcement tends to be comparatively widespread and consistent. The information base of the motorised transport sector is also more detailed and reliable than that of the non-motorised sector; principally because of the more frequent, consistent and efficient data gathering efforts by central government bodies in the field.

Trip Making Characteristics

Findings of studies into non-motorised movement in Indian cities (SPA, 1979) were employed by the Planning Commission of the Government of India in its formulation of national urban transport policies (National Transport Policy Committee, 1979). It was revealed, among other things, that in several Indian cities the share of non-motorised travel represented at least 33 per cent of all travel in metropolitan cities which compares with an equivalent share of 50 per cent in medium sized cities (SPA, 1980); it is even higher in smaller settlements.

Socio-economic travel surveys conducted in Delhi, Bangalore, Agra and Jaipur (SPA, 1979 and 1980) suggest that the reasons for the extensive use of non-motorised modes lies in their affordability and the unreliability of alternative public transport services. This was found to be especially true for 'essential trips', i.e., work and education trips. This is supported by findings from Madras, where of the 42 per cent non-motorised share of all travel in the city, 51 per cent of this share were work trips and 45 per cent education trips (see Table 4.6).

Table 4.6   Percentage Share of Total Trips by Non-Motorised Travel for Major Trip Purposes in Indian Cities

City	Trip Purpose			Total
	Work (%)	Education (%)	Others (%)	
Delhi	75.00	6.00	19.00	100.00
Bangalore	39.00	30.00	31.00	100.00
Madras	51.30	45.10	32.40	100.00

Source: (1) Re-analysis of Tables on Travel Characteristics, Comprehensive Traffic and Transportation Studies for Delhi, 1969, Central Road Research Institute, New Delhi.

(2) Comprehensive Traffic and Transportation Studies for Bangalore, Table 55.0, Page 146, Distribution of Trips according to Purpose and mode of Transport. Central Road Research Institute, New Delhi, January 1973.

(3) Table 9.0, page 40. Report on Moderation of MATSU's Traffic and Transportation Studies for Madras Metropolitan Area. August, 1976, New Delhi.

Although social and recreational trips in most Indian settlements constitute a small proportion of the total daily travel, their share of non-motorised trips is appreciable, as may be seen from the *tonga* and cycle-rickshaw trip-making details shown in Table 4.7. Data gathered for the same study whose findings are featured in Table 4.7 further reveal that the bicycle in India occupies a very important position in the hierarchy of non-motorised transport modes. On the basis of surveys conducted in Delhi, Hyderabad, Bangalore, Madras and Poona, it was found that (next to walking) the bicycle was the most reliable personalised mode of transport.

Among the factors influencing bicycle usage are household income and trip distance. Thus, whilst bicycles in India are largely used by the lower income groups, the extent of their use, particularly in the larger metropolitan areas, also reflects the distances to be covered. This is confirmed in Table 4.8 which shows a much wider cross- section of income groups using the bicycle in Delhi in comparison with other Indian cities.

Statistical information pertaining to the use of cycle-rickshaws in Indian cities is difficult to obtain. The data that is

Table 4.7 Use of *Tonga* and Cycle-Rickshaw Modes by Trip Purpose in Selected Indian Cities

Mode	Name of City	Population (in millions)	Work trips (%)	Business (%)	Education (%)	Shopping (%)	Medical (%)	Social cultural & others (%)	Sight-seeing & recreation (%)	Total
Tonga	Delhi	3.60	48.36	24.43	2.78	12.00	8.06	-	4.28	100.00
	Agra	0.60	56.03	12.07	2.59	1.72	6.90	15.52	5.17	100.00
	Meerut	0.30	57.45	2.13	-	6.38	17.02	15.96	1.06	100.00
	Jaipur	0.60	——54.97——		4.10	12.27	8.19	20.47	-	100.00
Cycle Rickshaw	Delhi	3.00	28.83	24.88	6.04	20.46	4.88	-	14.91	100.00
	Agra	0.60	33.76	8.92	11.46	12.12	6.34	22.94	4.46	100.00
	Meerut	0.30	36.45	10.71	-	8.21	30.92	9.07	4.64	100.00
	Faridabad	0.12	14.97	26.84	0.28	3.11	29.10	16.38	9.32	100.00
	Jaipur	0.60	——45.65——		6.52	13.04	17.39	10.87	6.53	100.00

Source: Delhi School of Planning and Architecture, 1979 and 1980, and Maunder et al, 1981.

available however, indicates that cycle-rickshaw ownership increases with reduced city population size (see Table 4. 9). For

Table 4.8   Percentage of Total Trips by Bicycle for Different Income Groups in Selected Indian Cities

Income Level (Rupiah)	Delhi	Jaipur	Bangalore
0-200	13.6	22.90	-
201-400	56.5	38.50	35.00
401-600	28.5	21.20	-
601-800	1.0	7.80	45.00
801-1000	-	7.60	-
1000-above	0.4	2.00 ·	20.00
Total	100.00	100.00	100.00

Source: A Comparison of Cycle Usage in Delhi, Jaipur and Hyderabad, ASRTU/TRRL W.P. No.33. 1987-8 (unpublished)

Table 4.9   Cycle-Rickshaw Supply and City Size in India

City	Population	No. of Cycle-Rickshaws per 1000 Population
Faridabad	0.2	19
Meerut	0.5	18
Delhi	5.0	1

Source: School of Planning and Architecture, New Delhi, Report on Objective Assessment of the Role of Intermediate Public Transport in Delhi, 1978

every cycle-rickshaw per thousand inhabitants in metropolitan areas, the number of rickshaws increases to nineteen per thousand in the smaller and medium sized cities. This greater dependence upon rickshaws in the non-metropolitan areas may be attributed to the lower average trip lengths, as well as to the lower overall income levels. Field studies conducted in Agra, Jaipur, Meerut and Faridabad (SPA, 1979 and 1980, and Maunder et al, 1981) show a high usage of cycle rickshaws (and *tongas*) especially for social and recreational purposes.

Most cycle-rickshaw and *tonga* operations provide a taxi-type transport service for which the fare is negotiated between the operator and user prior to the commencement of the trip. Although cycle-rickshaw operators do not have a fixed preference for a particular route or part of the city (unlike *tonga* operators), they do tend to commence and complete their day's work near to their home. Furthermore, since there are no serious restrictions on rickshaw parking (with the exception of Calcutta), most cycle-rickshaw operators minimise dead mileage by parking close to their previous destination during the day.

The studies in Agra, Jaipur, Faridabad and Delhi referred to earlier indicate that a substantial proportion of all cycle-rickshaw operators in these cities are 20 to 30 years old, although tonga operators tend to be somewhat older averaging 30 to 40 years old. Most rickshaw operators are rural migrants taking up their first urban employment. They are, by and large, illiterate, belong to poor urban communities and live in sub-standard environments. It has been estimated that 25 per cent of all India's rickshaw operators are pavement dwellers (see Figure 4.8).

Figure 4.8: Cycle-Rickshaw Operators as Pavement Dwellers in Madras

Most rickshaw and *tonga* operators earn a monthly income of Rs 300-500 (US$33-55). The earnings in medium sized cities such as Faridabad, Meerut and Agra, tend to be a little higher than those in the metropolitan areas, primarily because shorter and more frequent trips are undertaken. The increased earnings can also in part be accounted for by the tougher bargaining stance of the operators because of poor alternative public transport facilities in the mon-metropolitan areas.

Whilst many non-motorised public transport services in Indian cities are available twenty-four hours a day, cycle-rickshaw operators usually work a 10 to 12 hour day in the non-metropolitan urban areas, and typically cover distances of between 20 and 24 kilometres a day. This compares with a working day of 14 to 16 hours for rickshaw operators in metropolitan areas, covering shorter average daily distances than their counterparts in smaller cities. This shorter distance coverage is largely due to the greater number of restrictions on the operation for non-motorised public transport services in the metropolitan areas. The absence of these restrictions in smaller cities means that there are now nearly twice as many rickshaws in some of the medium sized cities as in Delhi.

It has been found that the fares of non-motorised public transport services in non-metropolitan Indian cities are generally higher per kilometre than those of the conventional bus, so that they are rarely affordable to the poorest. It should be pointed out, however, that there is an acute shortage of buses in such settlements, so that the demand for non-motorised transport still remains very high, despite the fare difference.

In certain cities, a formal fare structure for rickshaw journeys between specific points is agreed upon. But as it is rarely adhered to, the result is a flexible fare structure. This, some claim, has distinct advantages, in that the system provides both rickshaw passenger and operator with equal opportunities to arrive at the most 'acceptable' fare. Others, however, point out that most patrons of non-motorised modes of public transport, are captive to such services as there is no other viable transport. This captivity was confirmed by surveys conducted in Meerut, Faridabad and Agra where 46 per cent, 75 per cent and 40 per cent respectively of non-motorised trip-makers interviewed, indicated that they had no viable alternative (SPA, 1979).

By and large, the bulk of the financial investment in the non-motorised public transport sector is provided by private entrepreneurs. Whilst such investments are welcome, particularly in resource-poor countries such as India, studies have suggested that this has often led to an undesirable exploitation of the economically weaker sections of society. Moreover, despite the provision of financial assistance to rickshaw operators by some nationalised banks in India under the 'Own Your Vehicle Scheme', the conditions attached to these loans are no better than those imposed by the private entrepreneur. Perhaps the only real advantage is that the bank permits greater freedom for the rickshaw operator to maximise the use of his vehicle, in order to facilitate the repaying of the loan. One method of accelerating the growth of the non-motorised public transport industry and simultaneously improving the lot of the urban poor involved in it, is to liberalise the financial conditions imposed on the loans.

TOWARDS BETTER PLANNING FOR NON-MOTORISED TRANSPORT

A number of general observations can be made in order to develop a more appropriate approach for planning non-motorised movement in Indian cities and in other settlements in poorer Third World countries. They may be summarised under the following headings of: traffic accidents, employment in the transport sector, traffic congestion and transport management and planning (also see Chapter 2).

Traffic Accidents

Traffic safety in urban areas is of concern to all those involved in urban transport planning in the Third World. In India, apart from some efforts in the metropolitan areas, measures designed to enhance traffic safety have been extremely limited. Given that many of the traffic safety problems arise from motorised and non-motorised traffic sharing common road space, urgent attention needs to be given to the segregation of incompatible transport modes.

It is pedestrians who are most adversely affected by mixed traffic conditions. Traffic accident statistics for Delhi (Bawa, 1979) reveal that almost 40 per cent of those killed on the roads in the metropolitan areas were pedestrians. According to Bawa, this is a direct result of the inadequate provision of infrastructure facilities for walking, the lack of respect for pedestrian rights, as well as excessive encroachments by motorists and other non-pedestrian functions on the few pavements and footpaths that do exist. Enforcement actions and specific projects therefore need to be urgently introduced.

It is common knowledge in India that the bicycle user also sustains a high proportion of injuries in road traffic accidents in urban areas. An analysis of traffic accidents in Delhi for example shows that 20 per cent of all road traffic accidents in the city involve bicycles. This figure reinforces, in many cases, the need for the provision of segregated rights of way for cycle movement.

Employment in the Transport Sector

The non-motorised transport sector provides immense opportunities for immediate gainful employment to the rural migrant in Indian cities. In Madras, for example, the findings of a survey of recent entrants to the city in 1979/80 (Operations Research Group, 1980) revealed that at least 22 per cent of those interviewed looked to the informal transport sector for their employment. Similarly, a very interesting study of rickshaws in Calcutta, showed that the income earned from the rickshaw pulling industry alone, supported 175,000 families in the city - in other words, approximately one million persons (Unnayan and Thomas, 1981).

Whilst no accurate statistics exist for all the major cities in India, it is widely believed that dependence upon the transport sector for employment in the non-metropolitan areas is greater. This in part is due to the larger proportion of non-motorised vehicles in such settlements. It is thus quite evident that any restrictions imposed on the growth of non-motorised means of movement will do more than affect traffic - it will reduce employment opportunities in circumstances where such opportunities are at a premium. This effect is one that should be taken into account whenever traffic management and transport planning projects are proposed and implemented.

Traffic Congestion

On account of the extensive inter-mixing of motorised and non-motorised modes of transport (see Figure 4.9), congestion is widespread. Indeed, congestion is often upheld as the main urban transport problem. Major roads are seen to be used well below their operational efficiency, travel times between journey points are seen to be excessive and resultant transport costs too great. Given the estimated rise in non-motorised transport in India (in medium and small size cities for example, it has been forecast that cycle-rickshaws will increase from 1.3 million to 2.2 million by the turn of the century), urban traffic congestion resulting from such conditions will inevitably increase.

Figure 4.9: Mixed Mode Traffic Congestion in Old Delhi

Much of this congestion could be reduced by traffic management measures to segregate motorised from non-motorised movement (see Chapter 11). A greater understanding of non-motorised transport operations and provision would also generate more appropriate transport planning and management responses to congestion problems.

Transport Planning and Traffic Management

Instead of introducing more enforcement measures designed to restrain the movement of non-motorised modes of transport, and thus (hopefully) reduce traffic congestion, more sensitive approaches to planning such modes are urgently required. This can be best accomplished with the assistance of data about key aspects of non-motorised transport. For example, additional information about the operational, financial and infrastructure requirements of this type of movement will inevitably provide policy makers and professionals with a greater insight into what functions these modes perform, and will lead to better planning.

Certainly, the data presented in this chapter provides ample evidence that knowledge about the non-motorised transport sector is exceedingly limited. However, whilst more appropriate approaches to planning this kind of movement is long overdue (especially in India where it plays a major role in city development), planning responses must still be decided upon. This is particularly so with regard to the often conflicting need to control non-motorised modes and at the same time promote urban employment. Indeed, it can be argued that the problem of the appropriate planning response to non-motorised modes is closely associated with that of how to deliver basic urban services to the growing number of inhabitants of Third World cities (see Chapter 12). Moreover, it raises issues of the appropriate form and structure for Third World cities. For if a greater role needs to be accorded to non-motorised travel modes, it follows that urban services and activity centres need to be distributed in conformity with the characteristics of these modes. This is an important issue that needs to be addressed both in new settlements and in the redevelopment of the older parts of existing cities and the layout of their extensions.

NOTE

This Chapter was initially prepared in 1982 for publication in 1984.

REFERENCES

Bawa, P.S. (1979) 'Basic Issues in Traffic Management: Regulation and Enforcement', Workshop on Traffic Management, New Delhi.

Calcutta Metropolitan Planning Organisation (1967) **Traffic and Transportation Plan: Calcutta Metropolitan District 1966-1986**, Government of West Bengal, CMPO Calcutta.

Case, D.J. and Latchford J.C.R. (1981) 'A Comparison of Public Transport in Cities of Southeast Asia', **Transport and Road Research Laboratory Report**, no. 659, TRRL, Crowthorne.

Delhi School of Planning and Architecture (1979) 'Objective Assessment of the Role of Intermediate Public Transport in Settlements of Different Sizes, **SPA Report**, New Delhi.

_____ (1980) 'Public Transport in Medium Sized Settlements - Case Study of Agra, **SPA Report**, New Delhi.

Directorate of Town and Country Planning (1974) **Madras Area Transportation Study: Traffic and Transportation Plan for Madras Metropolitan Area**, MMDA, Government of Tamil Nadu, Madras.

Fouracre, P.R. (1977) 'Intermediate Public Transport in Developing Countries', **Transport and Road Research Laboratory Report**, no. 772, TRRL, Crowthorne.

Fouracre, P.R. and Maunder D.A.C.(1978) 'Public Transport in Surabaya', **Transport and Road Research Laboratory Report**, no. 370, TRRL, Crowthorne.

Fouracre, P.R., Maunder D.A.C., Pathak M.G. and Rao C.H. (1981) 'Public Transport Supply in Indian Cities', **Transport and Road Research Laboratory Report**, no. 1018, TRRL, Crowthorne.

Heraty, M.J.(1980) 'Public Transport in Kingston, Jamaica and its Relation to Low Income Household', **Transport and Road Research Laboratory Report**, no. 546, TRRL, Crowthorne.

Maunder, D.A.C., Fouracre P.R., Pathak M.G. and Rao C.H. (1981) 'Characteristics of Public Transport Demand in Indian Cities', **Transport and Road Research Laboratory Report**, no. 709, TRRL, Crowthorne.

Meier, A.R. (1977) 'Becacks, Bemos, Lambros and Productive Pandemonium', **Technological Review**, Energy and Resources Group, University of California, Berkeley.

National Transport Policy Committee (1979) **Report of the Working Group on Urban Transport**, Planning Commission, Government of India, New Delhi.

Ocampo, R.B. (1982) 'Low Cost Transport in Asia: A Comparative Report on Five Cities', **International Development Research Centre Report**, no. IDRC-183e, IDRC, Ottowa.

Operations Research Group (1980) **Informal Sector Enterprises in Madras**, ORP, Madras.

Owen, W. (1973) **Automobiles and Cities: Strategies for Developing Countries**, OECD Environment Directorate, Division of Urban Affairs, Paris.

Rao, M. S. V. and Sharma, A. K. (1980) 'Transport in Medium Sized Cities' **Journal of Institute of Town Planners**, no. 106, New Delhi.

Soegijoko, B.T. (1986) 'The Becaks of Java', **Habitat International**, vol. 10, no. 1/2, Pergamon Press, Oxford.

Town and Country Planning Organisation (1972) **Rapid Transit Studies for Delhi and Madras**, TCPO, New Delhi.

Unnayan in association with Thomas T. H. (1981) **Rickshaws in Calcutta**, Unnayan, Calcutta.

Wakankar, W.R. (1977) Planning for Pedestrians; vols. 1 and 2, Unpublished Research Report, Delhi School of Planning and Architecture, New Delhi.

Wilbur Smith and Associates (1955) **Bombay Traffic and Transportation Study**, New Haven, Connecticut.

Chapter 5

The Urban Transport Planning Process: Its Evolution and Application to Third World Cities

Harry T. Dimitriou

INTRODUCTION

Of all urban issues associated with Third World city development, traffic and transport problems are high on the agenda of indigenous governments. The growing realisation that urban movement problems are intricately tied up with other development factors such as rapid population increases, urban sprawl and resource constraints, has led over the last three decades or so, to a wave of city-wide transport planning studies in the Third World. The studies have often been based on the implicit preconception that they could 'solve' urban movement problems, the aim of politician, technocrat and layman alike, being to rid their city of traffic congestion.

Because formalised urban transport planning studies have been the response to similar problems in the USA and other industrialised countries, it was believed appropriate to model Third World urban transport studies on similar assumptions and concepts, and utilise the same techniques. In this way urban traffic and transport problems world-wide came to be seen as an internationally common set of phenomena with merely local differences considered in themselves insufficient to invalidate employing a universal analysis and related set of proposals.

In the discussion which follows, this universalist perception is challenged and a much more location and development-specific approach to tackling urban movement problems is advocated (also see Chapter 12). It is argued that transferring urban transport planning technology from the industrialised countries to the Third World is suspect on three counts: in terms of relevance, conceptual validity, and empirical evidence. The usual argument for the continued use of the conventional wisdom on the grounds that it is the only comprehensive systematic approach that the transport planning profession possesses is seen to be akin to a doctor giving the same medicine to his patients irrespective of its healing power merely because there is no alternative. The use of this approach presumes that the medicine produces no adverse effects; a conclusion not substantiated in the transport field (see Banjo and Dimitriou, 1983).

The chapter commences with an overview of the functions, features, components and claimed capabilities of urban transport planning, as well as a brief historical analysis of its evolution to the stage whereby it became a standardised approach world-wide. The analysis emphasises the extent to which this kind of universalistic professional practice is a product of the time and place of its inception, and provides an assessment of its effectiveness in Third World cities.

THE URBAN TRANSPORT PLANNING PROCESS

Purpose and Functions

The conventional wisdom of transport planning practice in urban areas is closely identified with the application of the 'Urban Transport Planning (UTP) Process' and its derivatives. This Process is in effect, a formalised planning methodology designed to provide guidelines and priorities for future investment and construction of urban transport infrastructure and facilities. In some countries such as Brazil, UK and USA, the methodology has in the past been institutionalised by government and supported by legislation, obliging planning agencies to adopt particular procedures of the Process in order to qualify for central government funding.

In character, the UTP Process represents a 'scientific effort' at planning urban transport demand, particularly motorised road traffic, by:

1. observing current travel behaviour;
2. advancing certain hypotheses concerning the relationship between urban land use and movement;

3.   testing these hypotheses as a basis for making estimates of future travel demand; and

4.   ultimately recommending additional transport capacity.

Different versions and derivatives of this Process have been widely adopted over time by policy makers and technocrats throughout the world when confronted with major traffic congestion problems thought to require a city-wide planning response.

An indication of the extent of international application of the UTP Process is illustrated by the fact that in 1975 the World Bank issued guidelines to its staff based upon the Process for standard formating of its urban transport studies. The US Department of Transport furthermore, in the late 1970s similarly made available to some thirty countries (many of them in the Third World) its Urban Transport Planning guidelines. The latter (US DOT, 1977) initially intended for US Federal Government use, were also based upon the UTP Process defined as:

> ......a long range system, wherein the alternatives to be analysed are few in number but in sufficient detail to estimate land development impacts, system costs, major facility and corridor volumes, level of service, and some impacts such as energy use, major air quality effects, accidents and others.

General Framework and Features

Transport planning recommendations derived from the UTP Process are arrived at through the simulation of land use and transport relationships on a city-wide and zonal basis, employing data from household and road-side surveys, as well as planning studies. In theory, the Process and its derivatives are not supportive of any one transport mode but are concerned with the provision and distribution of *all* types of urban transport facilities - a claim challenged by many in the industrialised countries, including professionals and community groups alike.

The general framework of the Process (see Figure 5.1) has its origin in the urban transport studies of Detroit (Detroit City, 1953-6) and Chicago (Chicago City, 1959-62), as well as the seminal research conducted by Mitchell and Rapkin (1954) at Columbia University which presented numerous key hypotheses regarding the relationship of traffic and land use. The basic stages of the classical format of the Process include:

Figure 5.1: The Urban Transport Planning Process

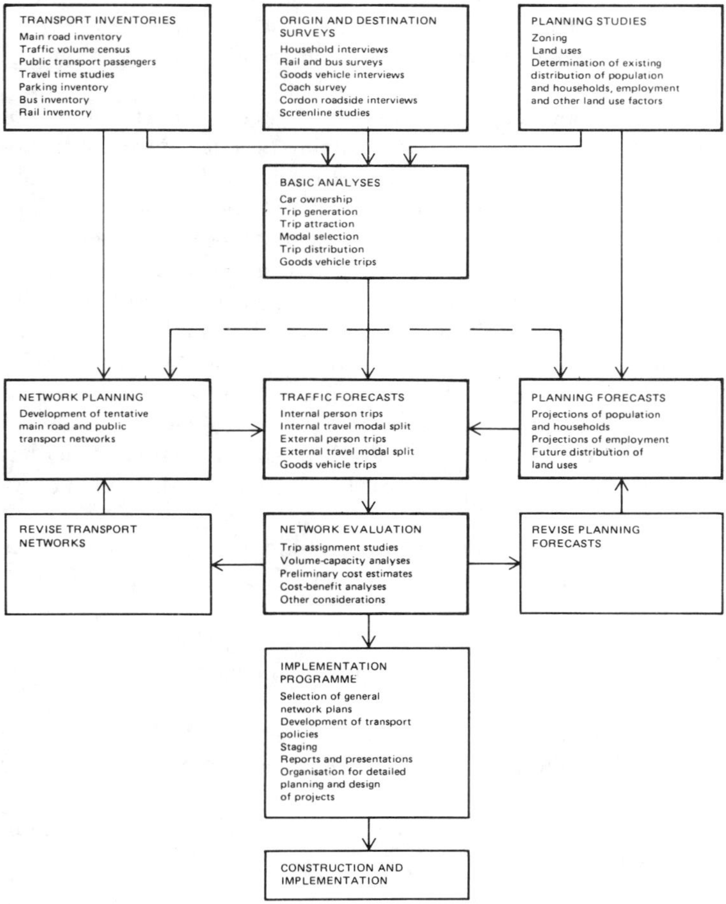

TRANSPORT INVENTORIES	ORIGIN AND DESTINATION SURVEYS	PLANNING STUDIES
Main road inventory Traffic volume census Public transport passengers Travel time studies Parking inventory Bus inventory Rail inventory	Household interviews Rail and bus surveys Goods vehicle interviews Coach survey Cordon roadside interviews Screenline studies	Zoning Land uses Determination of existing distribution of population and households, employment and other land use factors

BASIC ANALYSES
Car ownership
Trip generation
Trip attraction
Modal selection
Trip distribution
Goods vehicle trips

NETWORK PLANNING	TRAFFIC FORECASTS	PLANNING FORECASTS
Development of tentative main road and public transport networks	Internal person trips Internal travel modal split External person trips External travel modal split Goods vehicle trips	Projections of population and households Projections of employment Future distribution of land uses

REVISE TRANSPORT NETWORKS	NETWORK EVALUATION	REVISE PLANNING FORECASTS
	Trip assignment studies Volume-capacity analyses Preliminary cost estimates Cost-benefit analyses Other considerations	

IMPLEMENTATION PROGRAMME
Selection of general
network plans
Development of transport
policies
Staging
Reports and presentations
Organisation for detailed
planning and design
of projects

CONSTRUCTION AND IMPLEMENTATION

Source: Proudlove J.A., 1968. 'Some comments on the West Midlands Transport Study' **Traffic Engineering and Control**, November

1.   the preparation of land use, transport and travel inventories of the study area;
2.   the analysis of present land use and travel characteristics;
3.   the forecast of land use and travel characteristics;
4.   the setting of goals and the formulation of transport alternatives designed to accommodate the projected travel demands and land use changes; and
5.   the testing and evaluation of alternative transport plans.

The above stages have remained the major corner-stones of conventional urban transport planning practice since the inception of the Process during the 1950s in the USA. It has subsequently been applied world-wide in one form or other, to cities as diverse as London (Freeman Fox et al, 1964-6) and Athens (Wilbur Smith and Associates, 1963) in Europe; Calcutta (Wilbur Smith and Associates, 1967) and Kuala Lumpur (Wilbur Smith and Associates, 1974) in Asia; Lagos (Wilbur Smith and Associates, 1974) and Nairobi (Wilbur Smith and Associates, 1978) in Africa; and Bogota (Freeman Fox et al, 1974) and Sao Paulo (Wilbur Smith and Associates, 1975) in Latin America. In the industrialised world, the Process (or modified versions of it) has been employed in every major urban area of the UK and in every metropolitan city of the USA.

The major features of the concepts underlying this universally adopted planning process, include (after Creighton, 1970):

1.   an extensive dependence upon simulation and quantification;
2.   a semblance of comprehensiveness;
3.   a formality of approach, based on principles of systems thinking; and
4.   a set of procedures akin to a scientific approach to problem solving.

The reliance of the UTP Process and many of its constituent parts on simulation and quantification is most evident in the modelling of travel demand. This simulates the adjustment of transport demand and supply by modelling various factors believed to affect travel. The simulation exercise is represented by a set of inter-related sub-models which estimate trip generation, trip distribution, modal split and traffic assignment. The extensive dependence upon quantification arises from the ability of the transport analyst to measure vehicular flows and their speed. The early concern of urban transport planning with highway engineering and design issues such as road capacity problems underlies the 'quantification tradition'. The need to cost proposed transport facility provision to assist investment decisions, placed further emphasis on the quantitative data requirements of the Process.

The claim that the UTP Process is 'comprehensive' in its concern, is derived from its attempt at providing a city-wide coverage of all types of urban transport modes. The semblance of comprehensiveness also arises from its incorporation of land-use/transport interactions as a basis for estimating future travel demand.

The formality of the Process and its extensive reliance upon systems thinking as a pre-requisite to formulating recommendations, emerges from the methodology's need to handle complex inter-relationships and analyse large amounts of data. With the rapid growth in use of main-frame, and (more recently) micro and personal computers, as well as the reduction of computer operating costs (see Chapters 8 and 9), the format of the UTP Process and its derivatives have over the years reflected a growing reliance upon the computer in all stages of the planning process.

Principal Components and Assumptions

There is a great deal of technical literature which over the years has outlined and detailed various versions, aspects and derivatives of the UTP Process (see Martin and Whol, 1961; Creighton, 1970; Bruton, 1970; Lane et al 1971; Dickey, 1975; Morlok, 1978; Black, 1981; and Blunden and Black, 1984). The literature has been disseminated so extensively that it has done much to reinforce the conventional wisdom associated with the Process. In the light of policy and other changes of the 1980s, reflections on the scope and content of these standard texts have subsequently been written by a number of academics (see Meyer and Miller, 1984; Jansen et al, 1985; and Nijkamp and Reichman, 1987).

Whilst coverage of this literature will not be repeated here, it is important before embarking upon a critique of the UTP Process clearly to differentiate among:

1. the principal components of the Process;
2. the various modelling procedures it employs;
3. its derivatives; and
4. its context.

Much of the technical literature fails to do so, yet it is essential if one is to disentangle failures and benefits associated with developments in the field. It is also a pre-requisite to understanding how to dismantle and re-assemble valuable components and techniques of the Process for future use, in a manner which better serves differing development contexts.

For the purpose of this discussion, components of the UTP Process may together be likened to a generalised travel demand model, based upon certain broad assumptions incorporating a number of sub-models, each with their own related assumptions, (see Figure 5.2). The three principal components are:

1. traffic and transport systems analysis and forecasting;
2. land use based urban development analysis and forecasting; and
3. transport goal, policy plan formulation and evaluation.

Before examining each of the above, it is beneficial to dwell a little further on the general assumptions that underlie the Process. Although now somewhat dated, these assumptions are best expressed by Bruton (1970) as follows:

1. decisive relationships exist between all modes of transport and therefore, the role of a particular mode cannot be determined separately;
2. transport systems both influence and serve the development of an area;
3. the transport situation in areas of continuous urbanisation requires regional treatment;
4. an urban transport study is integral to the overall planning process and cannot be considered in isolation; and
5. the transport planning process is on-going and thus requires constant updating.

If however, one looks back at more than thirty years at the application of the UTP Process and its derivatives, it is apparent that these generalised assumptions are more reflective of norma-

Figure 5.2 Principal Components of Urban Transport Planning Process

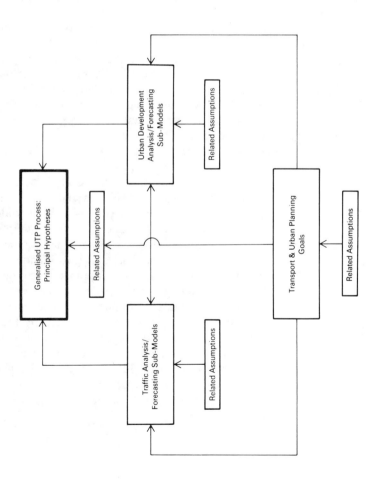

tive (sometimes wishful) thinking and (even convenient) hypothesis-setting, rather than well understood empirical evidence and practice. This and other criticisms, especially as they relate to Third World circumstances, were voiced by a number of academics and practitioners in the 1970s (see Viola, 1976; Mc-Neill, 1977; Dimitriou, 1977 and Darbera, 1978). Unfortunately many of the criticisms are still valid today with regard to several newer developments, particularly in the transport modelling field. The employment of generalised assumptions by these modelling efforts ignores major limitations of the Process. Their use in urban transport planning is akin to an architect continuing to elaborate upon the interior designs of a building, even though he knows its foundations are suspect.

Reservations about the conceptual validity and empirical evidence supporting generalised assumptions of the UTP Process have received renewed interest (see Atkins, 1986; and Supernak and Stevens, 1987). The questionable of generalised assumptions however, is merely one aspect of concern pre-occupying Third World planners when examining the transfer of this planning approach to non-industrialised countries. Another important dimension warranting serious investigation is the compatability of the assumptions to the *development context* and the related goals of Third World settlements (see Chapters 1 and 2).

The analysis of the evolution of the UTP Process (see following section) shows that the hypotheses and techniques it employs are primarily taken from experiences of industrialised countries. This is especially evident if one examines assumptions concerning the relationship of transport to urban development in land use/transport integration models, and those made about travel behaviour and the value of travel time in discrete choice modelling. Assumptions about desired paths of urban development however, cannot have universal application, since the notion of what is desirable varies from place to place. Similarly, the use of assumptions about travel behaviour based on traditional market economics of industrialised nations can only be applied with caution to the Third World given the different cultural dimensions and economic priorities (Banjo, 1982).

Traffic and Transport Systems Analysis

Within the general framework of the UTP Process, a number of more specific concepts and assumptions are employed. These are usually tied to a set of sub-models used to analyse, simulate and forecast traffic movements - movements which are seen to be a function of land use and socio-economic changes of an urban area. This set of sub-models is commonly referred to as the 'Four Stage Process' or the 'Urban Transport Planning Modelling Process' (see Figure 5.3). It is considered by many to be the most well-developed part of the UTP Process. Indeed, this set of sub-models is often confused with the overall UTP Process itself. The 'Four Stage Process' is intended to correspond to the decision-making stages of the trip-maker (Wilson et al, 1969), namely:

1.   whether to make a trip (trip generation);
2.   where to go (trip distribution);
3.   which mode of transport to use (modal split); and
4.   which route to use (traffic assignment)?

Sub-models representing these decisions constitute the heart of the conventional wisdom of urban transport planning. The models are however, exlusively concerned with the trip-maker and with trip-making characteristics, and do not include wider considerations of planning for urban movement. On the basis of observed and measured current travel patterns, future trip movements in the UTP Process are forecast by the 'Four Stage Process', by assuming a not very different future for:

1.   travel behaviour;
2.   transport technology;
3.   land use; and
4.   land use/traffic interaction.

The sub-models are usually calibrated in sequence during the analytical, forecasting and testing phases of urban transport planning. Their format and output are based upon variations of the relationships considered to have been established during the analysis of existing transport and land use data. Such relationships are seen in terms comparable to the Newtonian Laws of Gravitational Attraction, in which trip attraction and distribution patterns

Figure 5.3:   Urban Transport Planning Modelling Process
(also known as 'four-step' model)

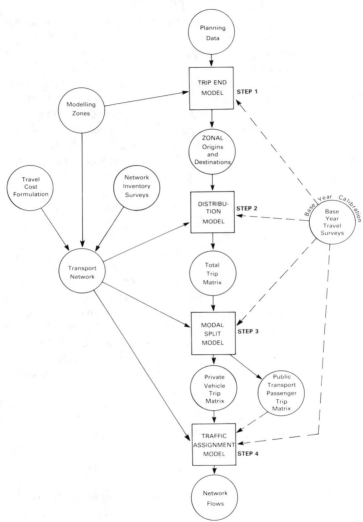

Source: Redrawn from Figure 11.1, Institution of Highways and Transportation and
Department of Transport 1987, Roads and Traffic in Urban Areas, HMSO,
London.

can be explained by some measure of 'push and pull' forces on trip origins and destinations.

Land Use Based Urban Analysis and Forecasting

Sub-models of urban development analysis and forecasting associated with the UTP Process are much less clearly defined - some would say less well-developed than sub-models of the 'Four Stage Process'. The models relate to land use changes, population growth characteristics and trends, as well as economic and employment features and forecasts. The purpose of these models in the overall context of the Process, is to provide inputs to the traffic sub-models, (see Figure 5.4) as functions of:

1. proportions, densities and levels of availability of different types of urban land uses (in case of land use models);
2. population growth rate and distribution characteristics, being in turn a product of changes in natural growth-rates, and in-out migration movements (in case of population models); and
3. employment and income level, as well as measures of the performance of the urban economy (in the case of economic models).

The forecasts are based upon data collected from secondary sources such as census data, and in the inventory stage of the UTP Process from household surveys - all projected to selected target years.

In all land use based modelling exercises, certain assumptions about public and private sector policies need to be made before any realistic outputs can be arrived at. Similarly, assumptions concerning human behaviour and the decision-making logic of the householder and trip-maker also need to be adopted. Many such assumptions, however, became more tenuous as the horizon dates employed become more distant. There are in fact, two alternative kinds of assumptions used in such efforts, namely:

1. trend assumptions - i.e., assumptions based upon the premise that future developments will be largely determined by past trends; and

155

Figure 5.4: Stages, Inputs and Sub-Models of the Urban
Transport Planning Process

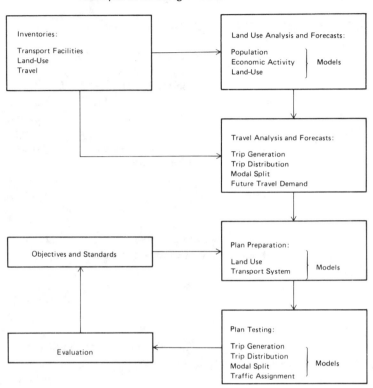

Source: Hutchinson B.G. 1974, **Principles of Urban Transport Systems Planning**
McGraw-Hill, adapted from Figure 1.1

2. scenario assumptions - i.e., assumptions reliant upon the
premise that a family of events will take place as a result of
the emergence of a group of correlated factors influencing
change in a particular direction.

On the basis of the above, projections dependent upon past trends
may be seen as merely one of numerous possible scenarios. To be
consistent with the common use of trend assumptions in traffic
sub- models, most land use inputs to the Process have traditionally relied based upon trend analysis, rather than scenario building
exercises.

Many of the earliest, as well as subsequent models, owe their origin to (Echenique, 1975):

1. the emergence of large scale urban land use transport planning studies;
2. the advent of and later developments in computer technology; and
3. the success of modelling in other important fields, especially in management, industry and military areas.

Several of the underlying concepts and features of these modelling efforts mirror those of the UTP Process in general, and those of its traffic sub-models in particular. These include the use of systems thinking, the employment of laws of Newtonian physics and the general concern for quantification. For a more in-depth review of these modelling concepts and features, the reader is referred to the works of Echenique (1975), Mohan (1979), Foot (1981), Putman, (1983), and Hutchinson and Batty (1986).

Transport Goal, Policy, Plan Formulation and Evaluation

Traditionally, urban transport planning has concerned itself with details of goal, policy and plan formulation *after* it has collected data relating to the current situation. From the information collected, emerging trends are then identified, and trends projected to a given horizon date on both a city-wide and city-zone basis. Transport needs are subsequently identified, and evaluated in response to which transport improvements are recommended within a strategy so as to meet anticipated changes in transport demand.

Although in this sequence of tasks the adopted planning process employs in its early phases some overall goals of transport and development, the major effort of their detailing usually takes place after alternative transport recommendations have been made, i.e., when it becomes necessary to assess specific alternative recommendations (see Chapter 12). In this way, the normative character of the Process is limited. Further detailing occurs during the testing of the final short-listed alternatives, a process during which more specific ends are formulated and more detailed evaluation criteria are set. Given the numerous stages in the UTP Process at which goal and policy formulation exercises arise, it may prove useful to offer the following typology of urban land use and transport planning goals:

1. city-wide general urban development goals - e.g., to stimulate the economic growth of the city.
2. city-wide general urban transport goals - e.g., to provide an integrated multi-modal public transport systems coverage of the city;
3. city-zone specific urban development goals - e.g., to stimulate the economy of the central area; and
4. city-zone specific urban transport goals - e.g., to reduce dramatically traffic congestion levels in the central area.

Transport goals may, in turn, be sub-divided into those concerned with:

1. transport systems operations - e.g., to reduce the travel costs and travel time of transport users; and
2. transport systems impact - e.g., to minimise the use of land in the provision of transport.

These may be applied either on a city-wide or zone-specific basis. In both instances, they need to be associated with supportive strategies and policies; something often lacking as a result of confusion over the meaning of key terms such as, goals, policies and strategies (1).

The goal and policy formulation stages of the UTP Process (which include strategy and plan formulation) are in fact the least formalised of the Process. In part, this is because they incorporate the interaction of decision-making undertaken by both the professional and the politician, each of whom has different perceptions, priorities and time scales, and consequently tend to favour different actions (see Chapter 2). This has the effect of clouding over goal and policy formulation procedures, and limiting the degree to which they can be simulated in a formalised manner akin to other components of the Process. Such circumstances prevail notwithstanding the fact that the possession of clearly articulated goals, policies and strategies is a prerequisite to the effective evaluation of urban transport planning proposals.

EVOLUTION OF THE PROCESS

According to Wiener (1986), the true origins of the UTP Process in fact pre-date the US pioneering work in urban transport of the 1950s. For as early as 1925, the US Federal Government promoted (for the first time) the concept of a continuous national system of highways (thereby identifying the need for a systematic approach to highway planning) which later provided the conceptual basis for the development of a standardised transport (highway) planning process.

Numerous papers have been written on the evolution of the UTP Process, most of which refer to the USA experience (see Hillegass, 1973; Weiner, 1976 and 1986; Gakenheimer and Wheaton, 1976; and Jones, 1983). The most recent and extensive account is Weiner's (1986). One of the most interesting however, is the analysis of events offered by Gakenheimer and Wheaton (1976). An expansion of the developments based upon the evolutionary periods cited by them are given below in modified form, so as to place the periods in a wider international context. The identified periods include those of:

1. conceptual development (1946-55);
2. operational development (1955-64);
3. conceptual stability (1965-69);
4. stalemate, critical review and revisionism in industrialised countries but widespread Third World application (1969-76) (2); and
5. conceptual disarray (1976 to date) (3).

Period of Conceptual Development (1946-55)

This began in the USA towards the end of the Second World War. The period is characterised by widespread optimism and a strong belief in the use of science and technology to solve social and environmental problems. The faith in science principally emerged as a result of the technological break-throughs achieved at that time by the military (and later) by space researchers. The optimism was further fuelled by the post-war US economic boom and political initiatives to stimulate other economies of the industrialised world.

The technological developments were accompanied in both the USA and other industrialised countries by urban authorities and governments experiencing rapid urban growth and extensive suburbanisation. At the same time, dramatic increases in car ownership combined with declining public transport patronage led to growing urban traffic congestion. In response to these conditions, local by-pass schemes were developed and link-specific engineering improvements were undertaken in order to alleviate points of local traffic congestion. Professional thinking simultaneously moved away from previously employed simplistic travel surveys, towards the use of more analytical techniques for travel demand analysis and a greater interest in the impact of land use on transport, and vice versa.

Given the embryonic state of professional thinking at the time, and the post-war pre-occupation of the then colonial powers with reconstructing their own economies, little was done to transfer the technical and conceptual developments of urban transport planning to the Third World. Among the earliest applications and testing of Mitchell and Rapkin's hypotheses concerning the relationship of traffic to land use was in San Jose, Puerto Rico in the 1950s (Paddilla, 1978). Because the city at the time possessed urban development characteristics and problems more akin to those of the Third World than other US cities, one may in retrospect view the San Jose Transportation Study (1959) as the first application of the UTP Process to Third World conditions.

Period of Operational Development (1955-64)

This period, as Hillegass (1973) points out, brought to an end the manual procedures employed in the earliest efforts at urban transport planning and saw the advent of the use of electronic digital computers as foreseen by Carroll (1956), and as demonstrated by him in the methodologies developed for Chicago and other cities in the USA. By 1959, major advances had been made in the development of the constituent parts of the Process for land use forecasting (Hamburg and Creighton, 1959); trip generation estimates (Wynn, 1959); trip distribution estimates (Voorhees and Morris, 1959); and traffic assignment methods (Brokke, 1959 and Carroll, 1959). These advances were all achieved in the process of working on urban transport studies for US cities, notably

Chicago, Baltimore and Washington DC. By 1961, the developments were further refined and resulted in the publication of the seminal work by Martin and Whol (1961) entitled 'Traffic System Analysis for Engineers and Planners'. Operational land use models were presented at the end of this period. These included both the Lowry series (1964) and EMPIRIC series (Hill et al 1966).

Many of the above pioneers in urban transport planning subsequently set up their own consultancy firms which later spawned the export of their planning techniques and the UTP Process to countries outside the USA. Such firms at first concentrated on the demand for their services in the US, later in Western Europe, and then in the Third World, as the demand for their expertise waned in the industrialised countries. Houston Wynn, for example, became a founder Director of Wilbur Smith and Associates - a transport planning and engineering consultancy firm that has undertaken the largest number of urban transport planning studies in the Third World. Alan Voorhees (later with Brian Martin as Martin Voorhees Associates) also established a consulting firm which became increasingly engaged in the export of the UTP Process and its derivatives from USA overseas; first to the UK, and later to Third World cities.

Period of Conceptual Stability (1965-69)

This period was greatly influenced in the USA by the Federal Government's concern with the US Interstate Highway System and the continuous financial support of the US Highway Trust Fund for the construction of highways. The adoption of the standardised UTP Process was still largely an American phenomenon, and soon became the envy of many other industrialised countries. This was even more so after 1962, when federal legislation was introduced in the USA which obliged all counties before being granted federal aid to fund and construct highways in major urban areas and to have prepared (or be in the process of preparing) general transport plans with associated land use and development considerations (Weiner, 1976).

The Process that had evolved became even more firmly established and formalised with the legislation's requirement that all urban transport planning studies had to demonstrate continuity in planning and co-operation between the agencies involved in planning transport and land use, as well as comprehensivness in

161

geographical coverage. The period saw the institutionalisation of the UTP Process in the USA, incorporating requirements of what became known as the 'Three "C" Planning Process' of:

1. continuity;
2. co-operativeness; and
3. comprehensiveness.

This led to a widespread demand for specialist urban transport planning skills throughout the USA during the late 1960s. To help overcome the shortage of skilled expertise, the American Association of State Highway Officials and the National Association of County Officials embarked on a programme to train its members to carry out urban transport planning studies, employing the standardised approach. The US Bureau of Public Roads also published guidelines defining the elements of the 'Three "C" Planning Process', together with manuals for forecasting urban travel.

Such instititional support later became a feature of national governments elsewhere such as Brazil (see Chapter 7) and Britain. In the latter case, this later manifested itself in the form of statutory Transport Plans and Programmes (TPPs) - required by central government in the mid 1970s, as a pre-requisite to their funding of local authority urban transport proposals. With the institutionalisation of the Process, came its increased standardisation and more extensive dissemination of its concepts and techniques through official and professional channels alike. By 1965 all the then 224 urban areas of the USA either had an urban transport plan conducted or had one underway.

The increased demand for urban transport planning expertise meanwhile contributed to the further expansion of US transport consultancy firms, many of which, given the pioneering nature of the work, attracted professionals from overseas. After their apprenticeship in the US, many of the overseas professionals returned home to apply their newly acquired skills and techniques to their own environments. Some were even astute enough to set up in their own country consulting services in association with already established firms in the USA, and elsewhere in the industrialised world. On the basis of the US experience, therefore, not only was the UTP Process and its derivatives exported to other industrialised countries, but also to selected Third World cities. The stabilisation period of the Process saw for example, its application to both London (1964-6), and Calcutta (1967). The same consulting practice (Wilbur Smith and Associates) was employed in each case.

Period of Stalemate, Critical Review, Revisionism and Widest Third World Application (1969-76)

The years between 1969 and 1976 saw the most paradoxical developments in the application of the UTP Process. In the US and other industrialised countries, significant modifications to the Process were made, particularly in associated environmental fields first higlighted by British professionals such as Buchanan (1963). The organisation, methodology and procedures of the UTP Process were increasingly critically viewed in the West, and public confidence in the capabilities of urban transport planners substantially declined as the transport planning environment began to alter significantly. The period was associated with: a shortage of funds, an emphasis on local management approaches, the use of shorter term horizon dates for planning, some aware- ness of the need to plan for stagnation or decline, and a greater in- terest in issues of equity and public participation (Jones, 1983).

In Third World countries meanwhile, this same period saw the widest application of the Process. Studies in which it featured significantly were conducted for (see Table 5.1) Teheran (OTCA, 1970); Kuala Lumpur (Wilbur Smith and Associates, 1974); Lagos (Wilbur Smith and Associates, 1974); Madras (MMDA, 1974); Jakarta (ARGE 1975); Istanbul (Jamieson Mackay and Partners, 1975); and Bangkok (Kocks Gk/Rhein-Ruhr Eng. Gmbtt, 1975) - to mention but a few.

The growing disillusionment with the UTP Process in the industrialised countries was principally a product of the emergence of the 'highway revolt', the subsequent re-orientation to alternative public transport solutions and the growth of the environmental and conservationist lobby, especially after the 1973 energy crisis. In the US, most metropolitan urban transport planning studies had been completed by the mid 1970s, thereby limiting the 'hands-on' modifications to what had by then become well-established (if not entrenched) procedures. In the face of new issues, such procedures appeared increasingly inflexible and inappropriate.

Table 5.1 Some Major Transport Planning Studies in Third World Cities: 1955 — 1984

Place	Date	Title	Consultants	Nationality
Bombay	1955	Bombay Traffic & Transportation Study	Wilbur Smith & Associates	American
San Jose City Puerto Rico	1959	San Jose Urban Transportation Study	Wilbur Smith & Associates	American
Kuala Lumpur	1964	Kuala Lumpur Transportation Study	Crooks, Mitchell & Peacock	Australian
Calcutta	1967	Culcutta Traffic & Transportation Plan	Wilbur Smith & Associates	American
Bogota	1970	Phase 1: Bogota Transport & Urban Development Study	Freeman Fox & Wilbur Smith & Associates	British/ American
Teheran	1970	Urban Transportation System for Teheran	Japan Overseas Technical Co-operation Agency	Japanese
Delhi & Madras	1972	Rapid Transit Studies for Delhi and Madras	Town & Country Planning Organisation	Indian
Manila	1973	Manila Urban Transport Study	Japan Overseas Technical Co-operation Agency	Japanese
Cairo	1973	Greater Cairo Transportation Planning Study	RATP Sofretu	French
Hong Kong	1973	Comprehensive Transport Study for Hong Kong I	Wilbur Smith & Associates	American
Singapore	1974	Singapore Mass Transit Study	Wilbur Smith & Associates in assoc. with Parsons Brinckerhoff Tutor, Bechtel	American
San Jose Costa Rica	1974	San Jose Urban Transport Study	Wilbur Smith & Associates	American
Bogota	1974	Phase II: Bogota Transport & Urban Development Study	Freeman Fox & Wilbur Smith & Associates	British/ American
Madras	1974	Madras Area Transportation Study	In-house: Madras Metropolitan Dev. Authority	Indian

Table 5.1 Some Major Transport Planning Studies in Third World Cities: 1955 — 1984 (Cont.)

Place	Date	Title	Consultants	Nationality
Kuala Lumpur	1974	Urban Transport Policy & Planning Study for Metropolitan Kuala Lumpur	Wilbur Smith & Associates	American
Lagos	1974	Lagos Metropolitan Area Transportation Planning Study	Wilbur Smith & Associates	American
Bangkok	1975	Bangkok Transportation Study	Kocks. F.H/Rhein Ruhr	German
Istanbul	1975	Instanbul Urban Transport & Land Use Study	Jamieson Mackay & Ptnrs	British
Jakarta	1975	Jakarta Metropolitan Area Transportation Study	Arge Intertraffic Lenz Consult.	German
Tehran	1976	Tehran Urban Transport Project	Freeman Fox and Associates	British
Manila	1977	Metroplan Metro Manila Transport Land Use & Development Plan	Freeman Fox and Associates	British
Surabaya	1977	Surabaya Area Transportation Study	Freeman Fox & Associates (later Halcrow Fox & Assoc.)	British
Penang	1979	Urban Transport Survey in Greater Metropolitan Area	Japan International Co-operation Agency	Japanese
Jakarta Metrop. Area	1979	Jabotabek Metropolitan Development Planning: Report on Transportation	Staff of Jabotabek Metropolitan Development Planning Project	International
Metro Cebu	1980	Metro Cebu Land Use & Transport Study	REDECON	Australian
Sao Paulo	1980	Transport Study of Sao Paulo Metropolitan Area	NATO Research Institute Brussels	International
Davao City	1981	Davao City Urban Transport & Land Use Study	Japan International Co-operation Agency	Japanese

Table 5.1 Some Major Transport Planning Studies in Third World Cities: 1955 — 1984 (Cont.)

Place	Date	Title	Consultants	Nationality
Johor Bahru	1982	Transplan: Urban Master Plan for the Johor Conurbation	Japanese International Co-operation Agency	Japanese
Metro Manila	1983	Metro Manila Urban Transportation Strategy Planning Project	Pak-Poy & Kneebone Pty L in Association with R.J. Nairn & Ptnrs	Australian
Jakarta Metrop. Area	1983	Jabotabek Traffic Management & Road Network Development Study	Colin Buchanan & Ptnrs in Assoc. with T.P.O. Sullivan & Ptnrs.	British
Metro Manila	1984	The Metro Manila Transportation Planning Study	Japanese International Co-operation Agency	Japanese

Source: Adapted from Table 1, Rimmer, 1986 with additional information furnished by Wilbur Smith & Associates, Hong Kong.

Meanwhile the introduction of environmental legislation and commmunity participation measures in the USA, and the evolution of similar developments in the UK, helped to create a 'shadow planning process', operating in tandem with the conventional UTP Process (a development that did not exist in Third World Countries). In the US this took the form of associated legislation, whilst in the UK, decisions could more easily be turned-over through the public enquiry procedure. The net result of both developments was that environmental and political constraints were increasingly imposed upon the standardised procedures of the Process, which in turn eroded its 'scientific' image. The combined effect was the emergence of a more 'open study' approach to urban transport planning. This reduced the pressures of the 1960s that had sought fully to institutionalise urban transport planning procedures and looked toward a greater role for public transport, supported in the USA by funds diverted from the highway sector.

The years between 1969 and 1976 saw the consolidation of transport planning expertise in other industrialised countries, notably in France, Germany, Denmark and Japan. The significance of this, apart from the impact on the urban transport sector of each of these countries, was that it contributed to the creation of additional foci in the industrialised world (both educational and professional) for the later export of urban transport planning expertise to the Third World.

Capitalising on the specialist developments in urban transport planning practice in their own countries, numerous North American, European and Japanese consulting firms more readily offered their professional expertise to Third World countries - often in association with technical assistance programmes. By the mid-1970s, certain of these countries had developed specialist fields; North American, German and British consultants became renowned for their highway expertise (particularly in transport systems management in USA [see Chapter 10], and traffic management in UK and Germany). Whilst the French and Japanese developed a greater specialisation in rapid transit planning, benefiting from technological advances made in their own countries. The Japanese also marketed their expertise in transport planning for intermediate sized settlements based upon minibus technology (Rimmer, 1986).

The focus on urban public transport during this period took on growing significance following the increased disenchantment in the industrialised countries with urban highway developments, and as the role of public transport became more appreciated by governments of Third World countries. Urban public transport became so widely appreciated that numerous rapid transit, metro and bus transport feasibility studies were conducted.

The planning of many of these public transport systems employed steps similar to those of the conventional UTP Process or its derivatives, but were usually confined to a particular line-haul section of a city. Other types of public transport studies were a product of earlier city-wide analyses of movement patterns and needs, in which a rapid transit/metro or other public transport component was proposed. These had the effect of accentuating the division of opinions between those favouring further urban highway investment and others preferring greater investment in higher capacity public transport systems - be they bus, light-rail or conventional rail based systems. Such studies also opened up the debate of the relative merits of high versus lower public transport cost options, as witnessed at the time of the Singapore Mass Transit Study (Wilbur Smith et al 1974-7). Together, these events led to the current emphasis on improved public transport systems management (see Chapter 3).

Period of Conceptual Disarray (1976 to date)

It is difficult to be precise about the commencement of this period, for there was no abrupt replacement of the highway planning tradition by another professional ethic to mark the clear start of a transition. Rather, it became increasingly noticeable over time that urban transport studies failed to employ the whole UTP 'package' of standardised assumptions, concepts and techniques. Instead, a very much wider spectrum of approaches emerged. If anything, the period of 'conceptual disarray' may be said to have started when many of the established professions in the urban transport field (i.e., civil, highway and traffic engineering) began to confess openly their own reduced confidence in the long-range forecasting capability of the UTP Process, and subsequently advocated a return to traffic engineering and traffic management as the most 'practical' alternative to earlier city-wide studies.

Apart from the wholesale de-emphasis of long term planning and the movement away from the use of aggregate to disaggregate data (see Chapter 8), this period saw the technology-transfer of conventional wisdom, both as a single package (with only partial refinements), as well as in the form of particular techniques and sub-models usually associated with the study of modal choice. The period furthermore has been associated with a growing divide between developments in transport planning research and practice, against a backcloth of numerous changes in urban transport policy directions. The major change in this regard, has been the replacement (in many industrialised countries) of the planned approach to transport provision with the market approach.

Technical developments of the period (also see Chapters 8 and 9) include the greater use of micro-statistical disaggregate analyses to reformulate and extend traditional urban travel demand models, underpinned by a theory of discrete choice and based on random utility theory. Modelling of this kind is seen as a means of better understanding different traffic flow and movement patterns, and represents a departure from the classical approach to travel demand analysis in that it adopts as its starting point the travel characteristics of the individual traveller (see Ben-Akiva and Lerman, 1985).

Among modelling developments during this period in land use/transport interaction (see Mackett, 1985), have been the work of Putman (1983) and Brotchie et al (1980). Of note for the Third World is the LUTO model, applied in Hong Kong (Choi, 1986), and the research of Zahavi (1979 and 1981). Zahavi's earlier work analysed urban travel patterns with a view to establishing underlying behavioural phenomena that could be used to describe travel without recourse to complex computer based models. This work was later related to Third World cities and was further developed to incorporate transport policy decisions influencing urban structural change. Concepts of travel time budgets figured significantly in this second phase of Zahavi's research, as it did in activity-based approaches to urban transport analysis (Jones, 1983).

Research advances in activity-based approaches developed at the Transport Studies Unit of Oxford University constitute another significant development in the field. These are believed to offer a possible overall re-orientation to transport planning, based upon travel behaviour analysis conducted within a household activity framework (see Carpenter and Jones, 1983). The approach emphasises constraints rather than choice on locational and travel behaviour factors of transport. However, unlike advances in discrete choice models which have been used and further developed in practice, activity-based approaches have not been operationalised, nor applied to Third World situations.

Other developments in the field include: efforts at improved valuation of project benefits, the re-examination of concepts such as shadow pricing, parking policy enforcement, and the provision of relevant comprehensible travel information (Jones, 1987). In addition to this, there has been a call for a return to basic principles through the better understanding of human needs (Dimitriou, 1982 and Bannister et al 1984); a greater focus on particular target groups (Linn, 1983); more attention to strategic and integrative planning (Dimitriou, 1977; Banjo, 1984 and Thomson 1984); a greater emphasis on institutional building (Barrett, 1983), and the derivation of origin and destination matrices from traffic counts (see Chapter 11). Most approaches to urban transport planning likely to emerge from these developments - as in the case of activity-based approaches - are however less formal in character and more 'open' than their predecessors. They are also less conducive to packaging and standardised use.

It is difficult to ascertain which combination of these evolutionary paths, urban transport planning practice in the Third World is likely to follow. Certainly, so long as international development agencies and consultancy firms are dominated by those from or educated in the industrialised world, the likelihood is that professional practice in the Third World will continue to reflect the 'state of the art' in the industrialised countries. Such an outcome can be avoided however, if the new cadre of indigenous professionals in the Third World are more willing to systematically learn from the errors of urban transport planning in the industialised countries rather than repeat them. In this way, benefits of past conventional wisdom can be combined with local knowledge of conditions and planning objectives so as to arrive at more appropriate approaches. Evidence of such a group of professionals emerging is now evident. It however, remains to be seen to what extent this cadre will ultimately be able to influence key policy-makers, and thus investment decisions, in both their own governments and international development agencies.

APPLICATION OF UTP PROCESS AND ITS DERIVATIVES TO THE THIRD WORLD

The UTP Process

The fact that practitioners still employ marginally revised versions of the UTP Process, as well as component models long ago discredited by researchers, emphases the continuing need for concern with the limitations of the Process. Earlier discussions in this chapter indicate that many such deficiencies can be traced back to underlying assumptions employed, of which several have particularly significant implications for the Third World.

Assumptions of this kind include (after Banjo and Dimitriou, 1983):

1. the belief that the urban transport problem is essentially one of how to overcome motorised traffic congestion - whereas the overwhelming majority of households in Third World cities are not vehicle owning;
2. the premise that increasing vehicle-ownership levels are inevitable - because saturation levels of these projections are likened to those of the industrialised countries, they become self-fulfilling;
3. the idea that informal public transport does not warrant detailed study - transport studies thus exclude important means of mobility and employment for the urban poor;
4. the belief that benefits are best derived by improving the operational efficiency of transport systems - for Third World cities, where transport systems are often planned and managed in favour of selective sections of the community, this aggravates equity issues in transport;
5. the premise that variables affecting travel demand do not experience unexpected changes - questionable even in medium term planning where unexpected changes and robust circumstances in the Third World can jeopardise forecasts for ten years hence; and
6. the idea that urban transport problems are essentially the same world-wide - examples of the very different evolutionary developments of transport problems in Third World cities however contradict this.

Other deficiencies of the UTP Process have been ascribed to its pseudo scientific features which portray a false sense of accuracy and comprehensive coverage (Dimitriou, 1977). These features have been said to have 'wall-papered' over many aspects the Process cannot cope with, as well as provide the urban transport planner with a false sense of technical competence. The pre-occupation of the Process furthermore, with detailed modelling of traffic movement and selected transport user aspects, has led to an excessive in-depth analysis of transport user matters ('comprehensive-vertical analysis'), rather than an examination of wider contextual policy issues and non-user considerations ('comprehensive-horizontal analysis'). A graphical presentation of this imbalance in the development of the UTP Process is given in Figure 5.5.

Additional limitations of conventional urban transport planning as applied to Third World contexts have to do with (after Khan and Willumsen, 1986):

1.   the high cost of its modelling efforts - traditional techniques are very demanding in terms of data, technical skills, computer resources and time;
2.   limitations of data - good and reliable data in Third World countries are a scarce resource;
3.   perceptions of the problems addressed - these are often so different from those of the industrialised countries that new models are required;
4.   scarcity of technical resources - appropriately qualified and skilled personnel are a rare commodity in the Third World; and
5.   problems of communication - the complex and heavy modelling emphasis often alienate decision-makers.

One of the conclusions that can be drawn from the above is that an approach which would de-emphasise large-scale modelling would be more appropriate for Third World needs (see Chapter 9 and 12).

UTP Derivatives

Whilst revisions to components of the UTP Process have been on-going, these have mainly taken place outside an overall planning

Figure 5.5: Vertical Versus Horizontal Analysis in Urban Transport Planning

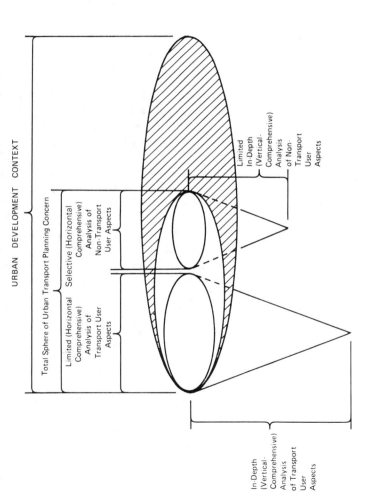

URBAN DEVELOPMENT CONTEXT

Total Sphere of Urban Transport Planning Concern

Limited (Horizontal Comprehensive) Analysis of Transport User Aspects

Selective (Horizontal Comprehensive) Analysis of Non-Transport User Aspects

Limited In-Depth (Vertical-Comprehensive) Analysis of Non-Transport User Aspects

In-Depth (Vertical-Comprehensive) Analysis of Transport User Aspects framework, and as indicated above, principally in the testing of individual traveller responses to policy changes in circumstances unrelated to the Third World. If one carefully examines these derivatives - i.e., the so called 'second-generation' (disaggregate) and 'third-generation' (behavioural models) - some can be seen to reinforce the conventional wisdom of urban transport planning on three counts: first, by their omission of reference to other problem areas of the UTP Process with which they associate; second, through their use and service of many of the same misconceived assumptions referred to earlier; third, by relating only to the travel demand analysis and forecasting parts of the Process.

Quite apart from criticisms of urban transport modelling with regard to their insatiable appetite for data, additional limitations of UTP derivatives when examined from a Third World perspective, arise from the limited understanding of household causality when modelling travel behaviour in societies with very different cultural attitudes towards the value of time, and very different priorities in travel needs (see Modak and Patkar, 1984). Similarly, the emphasis of such models on 'choice' in environments where in reality, options are either extremely limited or just do not exist, is inappropriate for Third World conditions. The treatment of uncertainty in transport service supply and demand in Third World urban transport modelling is also in need of further refinement. Activity-based approaches to urban transport planning on the other hand, appear to be more capable of accommodating many of these limitations, and seem to hold more opportunities for future application in the Third World. However in view of their limited application to practical situations, much applied research is still needed to develop further the field.

Presented in this way, derivatives of the UTP Process are in fact of less far-reaching significance than one might have wished.

Implications of Developments for the Third World

An understanding of the contribution of transport to city development is fundamental to urban transport planning - yet the conceptual review and application of the UTP Process and its derivatives suggests that much more is understood about traffic engineering, transport operations and travel behaviour aspects than the impact of transport improvements on urban communities, land use and wider urban development policies. This has major implications for

Third World cities, where progress towards development, however this may be defined (see Chapter 1), is more highly prized than in the industrialised world.

Urban transport planning for such settlements thus requires an enhanced understanding (and simulation capability) of the dynamics of Third World city development, greater than is traditionally represented in the UTP Process and most of its derivatives. It also requires a clearer appreciation of the development goals and policies of these cities, in order to direct more positively the role of transport in their achievement. This demands a greater knowledge base about among other things, the patronage, operations and functions of informal public transport systems (including non-motorised movement), and a more objective appreciation of the impact (and opportunity costs) of past urban transport planning practices, both in the Third World and industrialised countries. Finally, greater attention needs to be paid to the institutional capacity, manpower, energy and financial resources as well as constraints of planning, managing, operating and maintaining transport systems.

To incorporate adequately the above into Third World urban transport planning practice, the transport specialist needs to familarise himself thoroughly with local efforts to assist government and public sector agencies in providing the city with: the essentials of urban living (i.e., basic needs), a means of enhancing its economic productivity, a means of improving its distribution of opportunities, and within this context, plan transport as an instrument in their achievement. From this perspective, each urban transport investment should be capable of evaluation from not only the point of view of the operational efficiency of transport systems, but from the perspective of the investment's contribution to:

1.   the maintenance of economic growth;
2.   more efficient use of 'real' resources per capita; and
3.   decreasing poverty.

The evaluation is to be done in a manner which promotes the improved accessibility to, and responsiveness of public sector administration, as well as the management and encouragement of the adaptability of spatial arrangements of the city to needs in a way that enhance its cultural and social identity (Dimitriou and Safier, 1982).

CONCLUSION

In summary, it may be said that the application of the UTP Process and its derivatives to the Third World exhibit at least three mis-matches (see Figure 5.6). First, is a mis-match between the socio-economic and political environments in which the conventional wisdom of urban transport planning evolved, and that of the Third World in which it was subsequently applied. The second mis-match is between the dominant (motorised) modes of transport traditionally encouraged and serviced by the Process, and the means of transport employed by the majority of Third World urban inhabitants. And third, is the mis-match between characteristics of metropolitan areas of industrialised countries (for which the Process was initially designed), and settlements (large and small) of the Third World (see Chapter 12).

Figure 5.6:   Shortcomings of Conventional Urban Transport Planning: Mismatches with Third World Context

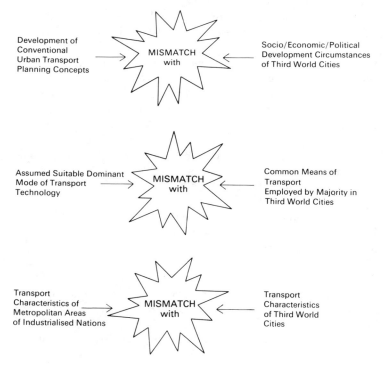

Of all the factors discussed in this chapter which will help ensure the development of a more sensitive approach to transport planning for Third World cities, is the formal inclusion in the transport planning exercise of measures of 'development effectiveness', intended to acknowledge better the contextual importance of transport planning. This is an aspect that has hitherto been underemphasised in new developments, which has contributed to many of the limitations of these achievements. Such an approach (see Chapter 12) needs to make reference to import ant issues of resource constraints, institutional and political contexts, and development policies, at a level of strategic planning to which transport-user considerations and matters of operations efficiency are subservient.

NOTES:

(1)   Goals are desired ends towards which efforts and resources are focused. Policies are guidelines in the form of combinations of 'operational objectives', designed to determine how to achieve pre-set goals. Strategies concern the arrangement of policies and goals in a sequence of time and place and in terms of pre-agreed priorities to achieve targetted ends.

(2)   The widespread international transfer of the Process during this period is a phenomenon not referred to in the article by Gakenheimer and Wheaton.

(3)   The belief that conceptual disarray continues to date (particularly in Third World transport planning practice) is an extension by the author of Gakenheimer and Wheaton's evolutionary stages.

REFERENCES

ARGE Intertraffic-Lenz Consult (1975) **Jakarta Metropolitan Area Transportation Study,** Arge Intertraffic-Lenz Consult, Jakarta.

Atkins, S.T. (1986) 'Transportation Planning Models - What the Papers Say', **Traffic Engineering and Control**, September, Printerhall Ltd., London.

Banjo, G.A. (1982) 'Towards an Appropriate Time Valuation Practice in the Third World', **Proceedings of PTRC Annual**

Meeting, University of Warwick, PTRC Education and Research Services Ltd., London.

_____ (1984) 'Towards a New Framework for Transport Planning in the Third World', **ARRB Proceedings**, vol. 12, Part I, August, Canberra.

Banjo, G.A. and Dimitriou, H.T. (1983) 'Urban Transport Problems of Third World Cities: the Third Generation', **Habitat International**, vol. 7, no. 3/4, Pergamon Press, Oxford.

Bannister, D., Bould, M. and Warren, G. (1984) 'Towards Needs Based Transport Planning', **Traffic Engineering and Control**, Printerhall, London.

Barrett, R. (1983) 'Institution Building for Traffic Management', **World Bank Technical Paper**, no. 8, IBRD, Washington DC.

Ben-Akiva, M. and Lerman, S.R. (1985) **Discrete Choice Analysis: Theory and Applications to Travel Demand**, MIT Press, Cambridge, Massachusetts.

Black, J. (1981) **Urban Transport Planning: Theory and Practice**, Johns Hopkins University Press, Baltimore.

Blunden, W.R. and Black, J.A. (1984) **The Land-Use/Transport System**, Second Edition, Pergamon Press, Oxford.

Brokke, G.E. (1959) 'Program for Assigning Traffic to a Highway Network', **Highway Research Board Bulletin**, no. 224, HRB, Washington DC.

Brotchie, J.F., Dickey, J.W. and Sharp, R. (1980) **TOPAZ - General Planning Techniques and its Applications at Regional, Urban and Facility Planning Levels**, Springer-Verlag, Berlin.

Bruton, M.J. (1970) **Introduction to Transportation Planning**, Hutchinson Technical Education, London.

Buchanan, C.D. (1963) **Traffic in Towns**, HMSO, London.

Carpenter, S. and Jones, P.M. (1983) **Recent Advances in Travel Demand Analysis**, Gower Publishing Company, Aldershot.

Carrol, J.D. (1956) General Discussion, **Highway Research Board Bulletin** no. 130, HRB, Washington DC.

Chicago City (1955-61) **Chicago Area Transportation Study**, Final Reports: vols. I, II and III, Chicago.

Choi, Y. (1986) 'Land Use Transport Optimization (LUTO) Model on Stategic Planning in Hong Kong', **Asian Geographer**, vol. 5, no. 2, Hong Kong Geographical Association, Hong Kong.

Creighton, R.L. (1970) **Urban Transportation Planning**, University of Illinois Press, Urbana.

Darbera, R. (1978) 'Methodological and Institutional Issues in Urban Transportation Planning for Less Developed Countries', **Proceedings of PTRC Annual Meeting**, University of Warwick, PTRC, Education and Research Services Ltd., London.

Detroit City (1953-5) **Detroit Area Metropolitan Traffic Study**, Final Reports: vols.I and II, Detroit.

Dickey, J.W. (1975) **Metropolitan Transportation Planning**, McGraw-Hill, New York.

Dimitriou, H.T. (1977) 'A Call for the Effective Integration of Urban and Transport Planning in Developing Countries', **Proceedings of PTRC Annual Meeting**, University of Warwick, PTRC Education and Research Services Ltd., London.

_____ (1982) 'Transport and the Urban Poor in the Third World', Paper presented to Habitat International Council (NGO Committee on Human Settlements) at Town and Country Planning Association, London.

Dimitriou, H.T. and Safier, M. (1982) 'A Developmental Approach to Urban Transport Planning', **Proceedings of Universities Transport Study Group Seminar**, University College, London.

Echenique, M. (1975) 'Urban Development Models: Fifteen Years of Experience' in **Urban Development Models** edited by R.Baxter, The Construction Press, Cambridge.

Foot, D. (1981) **Operational Urban Models: An Introduction**, Methuen, London.

Freeman Fox, Wilbur Smith and Associates (1964 and 1966) **London Traffic Survey**, vol. I and II, London.

_____ (1970 and 1974) **Bogota Transport and Urban Development Study**: Phase I and II, London and New Haven, Connecticut.

Gakenheimer, R.A. and Wheaton, W.C. (1976) 'Priorities in Urban Transportation Research', **Transportation**, vol.5., Elsevier Scientific Publishing Company, Amsterdam.

Hamburg, J.R. and Creighton, R.L. (1959) 'Predicting Chicago's Land Use Pattern', **Journal of the American Institute of Planners**, May, AIP, Chicago.

Hill, D.M., Brand, D., and Hansen, W.B. (1966) 'Prototype Development of Statistical Land-Use Prediction Model for

Greater Boston Region, **Highway Research Record**, no. 114, Washington DC.

Hillegass, T.J. (1973) 'A Brief History of the Evolution of Urban Transportation Planning Techniques: 1940-1970', Federal Highway Administration, Washington DC.

Hutchinson, B. and Batty, M. (1986) **Advances in Urban Systems Modelling**, North Holland Elsvier, Amsterdam.

Jamieson Mackay and Partners, (1975) **Istanbul Urban Transport and Land Use Study**, Greater Istanbul Master Plan Bureau, Istanbul.

Jansen, G.R.M., Nijkamp, P. and Ruijgrok, C.J. (ed.) (1985) **Transportation and Mobility in an Era of Transition**, North- Holland Press, Amsterdam.

Jones, P.M. (1977) 'Assessing Policy Impacts Using the Household Activity-Travel Simulator', **Transport Studies Unit, Working Paper**, No. 18, Oxford University.

_____ (1983) 'The Practical Application of Activity-Based Approaches in Transport Planning: An Assessment', in **Recent Advances in Travel Demand Analysis**, Gower Publishing Company, Aldershot.

_____ (1987) Response to Questionnaire on Behavioural Analysis, Network on Transport, Communications and Mobility Project, European Science Foundation, Strasbourg.

Khan, M.A. and Willumsen, L.G. (1986) Modelling Car Ownership and Use in Developing Countries, **Traffic Engineering and Control**, November, Printerhall, London.

Kocks, KG/RHEIN-RUHR Eng. GMBH, (1975) **Bangkok Transportation Study**, Final Report, Dusseldorf and Bangkok.

Lane, R., Powell, T.J. and Prestwood Smith, P. (1971) **Analytical Transport Planning**, Duckworth, London.

Linn, J.F. (1983) **Cities in the Developing World**, World Bank Research Publication, Oxford University Press, Oxford.

Lowry, I.S. (1964) 'A Model of Metropolis', **RAND Corporation Report**, no. RM-4035 - RC, Stanford.

Mackett, R.L. (1985) Integrated Land Use - Transport Models, **Transport Review**, vol. 5, no. 4, Taylor and Francis, Philadelphia.

Madras Metropolitan Development Authority, (1974) **Madras Area Transportation Study**, vols. I, II, and III, Transportation Unit, Directorate of Town and Country Planning, MMDA, Government of Tamil Nadu, Madras.

Martin, B. and Whol M. (1961) **Traffic Systems Analysis for Engineers and Planners,** McGraw-Hill, New York.

McNeill, D. (1977) 'Urban Transport in Developing Countries', **Development Planning Unit Working Paper,** no.1, University College, London.

Meyer, M.D. and Miller, E.J. (1984) **Urban Transportation Planning: A Decision-Orientated Approach,** McGraw-Hill Book Company, New York.

Mitchell, R. and Rapkin, C. (1954) **Urban Traffic: A Function of Land Use,** Colombia University Press, New York.

Modak, S.K. and Patkar, V.N. (1984) 'Man and His Transport Behaviour', **Transport Review,** vol. 4, no. 3, Taylor and Francis, Philadelphia.

Mohan, R. (1975) 'Urban Economic and Planning Models: Assessing the Potential for Cities in Developing Countries', **World Bank Staff Occasional Paper,** no. 25, Johns Hopkins University Press, Baltimore.

Morlock, E.K. (1978) **Introduction to Transportation Engineering and Planning,** McGraw-Hill Book Company, New York.

Nijkamp, P. and Reichman, S. (ed.) (1987) **Transportation Planning in a Changing World,** Gower Publishing Company, Aldershot.

Overseas Technical Co-operation Agency, (1970) **Urban Transportation System for Teheran,** OTCA, Government of Japan, April, Tokyo.

Paddilla, R. (1978) Text of Recorded Interview Held in Puerto Rico with H.T. Dimitriou.

Putman, S.H. (1983) **Integrated Urban Models,** Pion, London.

Rimmer, P.J. (1986) 'Look East: The Relevance of Japanese Urban Transport Planning and Technology to Southeast Asian Cities', **Transportation Planning and Technology,** vol. 11, Gordan and Breach Science Publishers, London.

Supernak, J. and Stevens, W.R. (1987) 'Urban Transportation Modelling: The Discussion Continues', **Transportation Journal,** vol. 14, Martinus Nijhoff Publishers, Dordecht.

Thomson, J.M. (1984) 'Toward Better Transport Planning in Developing Countries', **World Bank Staff Working Papers,** no. 600, IBRD, Washington DC.

US Department of Transport (DOT), (1977) **The Urban Transport Planning Process,** UMTA and Federal Highway Administration, Washington DC.

Viola, P. (1976) 'Large Scale Land-Use Transport Studies: How Relevant to Asian Cities', **Proceedings of PTRC Annual Meeting**, University of Warwick, PTRC Education and Research Services Ltd., London.

Voorhees, A.N. and Morris, R. (1959) 'Estimating and Forecasting Travel for Baltimore by Use of a Mathematical Model', **Highway Research Board Bulletin** no. 224, HRB, Washington DC.

Weiner, E. (1976). 'Evolution of Urban Transportation Planning', Urban Analysis Programme, US Department of Transportation, April, Washington DC.

_____ (1986) 'Urban Transportation Planning in the United States: A Historical Overview', **US Department of Transportation Report,** no. DOT-1-86-09, DOT, Washington DC.

Wilbur Smith and Associates (1963) **Athens Basin Transportation Survey and Study**, New Haven, Connecticut.

_____ (1967) **Traffic and Transportation Plan: 1966-86,** for Calcutta Metropolitan Planning Organisation, Sree Saraswaty Press Ltd., Calcutta.

_____ (1974) **Lagos Metropolitan Area Transportation Planning Study**: Final Report, for Federal Ministry of Public Works, Military Government of Nigeria, Lagos.

_____ (1974) **Urban Transport Policy and Planning Study for Metropolitan Kuala Lumpur,** Wilbur Smith and Associates, New Haven.

Wilbur Smith and Associates in Association with Parsons, Brinckerhoff-Tudor-Bechtel, (1974-7) **Singapore Mass Transit Study**, Government Printers, Singapore.

Wilson, A.G., Bayliss, D., Blackburn, A.J. and Hutchinson, B.G. (1969) 'New Directions in Strategic Transportation Planning', **Centre for Environmental Studies Working Paper,** no.36, CES, May, London.

Wynn, F.H. (1959) 'Studies of Trip Generation in the Nation's Capital: 1956-58', **Highway Research Board Bulletin** no. 230, HRB, Washington DC.

Zahavi, Y. (1979) 'The UMOT Project', Prepared for US Department of Transportation, Washington DC. and Ministry of Transport of the Federal Republic of Germany, Bonn, **US Department of Transport Report**, no. RSPA-DPB-20-79-3, Bonn and Washington DC.

Zahavi, Y., Beckman, M.J. and Golob, T.F. (1981) 'The UMOT/ Urban Interactions, **US Department of Transportation Report**, no. DOT/RSPA/DPB-10/7, DOT, Washington DC.

Chapter 6

Issues in Third World Urban Transport Project Appraisal

John W. Dickey

INTRODUCTION

Urban transport project appraisal is undertaken for different purposes, according to the situation under investigation and the persons involved. The scope of such assessments has also tended to change over time. Less than twenty years ago, for instance, the appraisal of transport projects in a Third World country would have been concerned almost entirely with the economics of the benefits and costs to potential transport users and providers. Now, although the economic emphasis is still of overriding importance, the breadth of factors taken into account is considerably greater.

Currently, an appraisal of a transport project is often concerned with more than one mode of transport and a wide variety of impacts, including institutional capacity considerations of the urban transport sector. Project appraisal as presently practised can be so broad in scope that it takes into account many factors difficult to assess in quantitative terms. Although this inevitably leads to a greater degree of subjective judgement, certain appraisal aspects can, however, still be viewed in quantitative terms, and therefore be assigned a price, indicative of their economic value to society.

Urban transport project appraisal in Third World contexts especially needs to take into account the uncertainties and risks associated with their environments. For there is a tendency for such projects to be affected by man-made and natural upheavals. Those responsible for the appraisal process thus need to try and anticipate likely problems, otherwise, uncertainties are passed on to decision-makers unable to gauge their impacts.

Given that the nature of project appraisal for urban transport varies according to geographical and temporal situations, this chapter commences with a description of a simplified approach to project appraisal. This is followed by a detailed treatment of each of the steps involved. Issues occurring in the course of making an appraisal study are then highlighted, and matters important to the formulation of more appropriate approaches to transport planning for Third World cities are raised.

OVERVIEW OF APPRAISAL PROCESS

A general approach to the urban transport project appraisal has seven principal steps as shown in Figure 6.1.

Figure 6.1: A General Version of the Urban Transport Project Appraisal Process

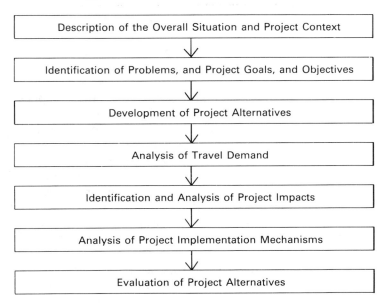

The first step sets the stage for the proposed project as it is intended to fit into the overall development process and plans are

made for the country, the transport sector as a whole, and the urban area under study. Attention, at this point, turns to macro-level issues such as energy saving policies that could influence the choice of projects.

It should then be possible in Step Two to identify the kinds of problems inherent in the urban transport system studied, as well as in other affected sectors. Urban transport project goals, and more specific objectives, can subsequently be derived to address problems, offering guidance towards the achievement of desired ends.

In Step Three, a limited set of alternatives is formulated. These are intended to highlight different ways in which the transport project, in conjunction with other services, can bring about desired project goals.

Since traffic congestion and excessive travel times are the impetus for undertaking many urban transport projects (see Chapter 2), it is necessary in Step Four to analyse urban travel demand. This analysis focuses on numbers of trips, trip destinations, travel modes, selected routes, and peaking characteristics of travel under the various alternatives represented in the traditional 'Four Stage Model' (see Chapter 5).

The impacts of projected travel upon factors such as land use development, economic growth, social equity, environmental conditions, can then be ascertained in Step Five. However, because these impacts are rarely the main focus of the appraisal process, they are usually not addressed in depth, unless otherwise specified. This is, in part, because many Third World countries do not have the resources for such an extensive task, but also because of the strong sectoral approach often pursued.

Step Six involves an analysis of the implementation of specific project measures and components. These might focus, for example, on agency organisation improvements, personnel training needs, new financial mechanisms, and better means of co-ordination with other sectoral plans, programmes, and projects.

In the last step of the project appraisal process (Step Seven), results from previous analytical stages are compiled and compared for each set of project alternatives, incorporating political, economic, social, and technical considerations (often in that order of priority). A decision can then be made as to which project alternative(s) is to be pursued.

OVERALL URBAN TRANSPORT PROJECT APPRAISAL ISSUES

Discussed below are a number of issues (see Table 6.1) that arise in attempts to implement a generalised appraisal process such as that outlined above.

Table 6.1   Some Issues in the Overall Project Appraisal Process

---

1. What degree of co-ordination with the overall planning process is required?
2. Who should do the appraisal?
3. What role should citizens play?
4. How much of the process should be based on Western experiences?
5. How much time and effort should go into the project appraisal?
6. What alternate sequencing of analytic steps are possible?
7. How should the appraisal process relate to other contemporary project appraisals?

Co-ordination

The first issue concerns the association between projects and plans. In theory, a co-ordinated and time-staged plan should exist for the overall growth of every city and subsequently for its transport sector within that scheme. On this basis, urban transport projects can then be proposed and implemented as part of that plan. This approach has worked well in Qatar and Kuwait, where there were sufficient resources to carry their plans to fruition, and also in South Korea which is known for its precision and directness in planning and project implementation. However, in less affluent Third World countries, up-to-date urban plans tend to be inadequate to provide an effective framework for project appraisal.

There are however several reasons why the appraisal process described above may not be appropriate to many Third World cities, among which are the political factors that must be taken into account. There are, for example, so many agencies, vested-interest groups, firms, and individuals involved in the project appraisal process (see the Sao Paulo case discussed in Chapter 7), that decision-making is often beyond the control of a single planning or project implementation agency. Another consideration is financial. As most project funding for urban transport is on a project basis, it is often seen as advisable to accept the funding offered rather than wait for a better match of the project with the urban plan. This then can (and often does) lead to transport projects pre-determining the strategies of urban plans, as currently illustrated in Hong Kong where a new airport project proposal under review is in danger of re-orientating the whole strategy plan for the territory. The dangers of sector and sub-sector projects having a wider impact on urban plans than their scale warrants has in fact in part given rise in Indonesia to integrated urban infrastructure development programming (IUIDP) (see Chapter 12) as a response to too much emphasis being placed on single project, and single sector approaches to urban development.

Selection of Project Appraisers

The question of who selects the experts to conduct project appraisal is an important issue. Ideally, where the project is to be financed from public sector funds, this exercise is often better undertaken by representatives of a national, provincial or municipal government agency. In many parts of the Third World, however, such agencies do not have sufficient in-house expertise to conduct appraisal studies. They are therefore usually undertaken by consultants commissioned for the task, especially where international development institutions or foreign governments are involved in the financing. In other instances, particular transport hardware vendors, such as those supplying rapid transit equipment, buses or railway rolling stock, conduct appraisal studies free of charge for government agencies. Where this is done, it is generally expected that the appraisal findings will be biased in favour of the vendor's commercial interests (see Chapter 2) and thus possibly deprive the city of a truly cost-effective choice in transport developments.

Where international agencies are involved, there are often conflicts of priority between aid donors and aid recipient governments over which sector or type of project to focus on. Similar differences occur in the case of international development banks and country government borrowers. In addition, there are issues related to the terms and conditions of loans (see later discussion) and to the preference that development banks show for projects yielding higher rates of return, over projects which are less financially rewarding but of higher social, cultural and political significance. In both cases, the allegiance of the appraiser and the guidelines for project appraisal are critical.

Citizen Participation

The role of various citizen groups in the urban transport project appraisal process is more commonly discussed in the industrialised countries than in the Third World. In the latter case,the issue of where participation is to take place and the stages at which the citizen groups should have greatest participation has become very important.

In many Latin American countries, a strong tradition of informally constituted urban communities exist (formed mostly in response to commonly confronted urban development and housing problems) which often provide a basis for citizen participation. In southeast Asia, in Indonesia in particular, more formal urban community groups have been created with government encouragement. Members are assigned particular roles and duties over time by the governing body of their community, and on this basis are seen to contribute to (read, participate in) the development of their community.

Whilst these kinds of Third World citizen participation offer very different indigenous brands, few examples of citizen participation in the Third World appear compatible with Western concepts. As a result, this aspect is rarely incorporated in the project appraisal process, despite its potentially important contribution.

Appropriateness

Many of the concepts and techniques employed in transport project appraisal in Third World cities are derived directly from industrialised countries which have quite different development and resource contexts. As in the case of other urban transport planning methods, the environment in which such techniques have evolved is so different that their application to Third World situations can be inappropriate (see Chapters 2 and 5). This in turn raises the question of whether - and how - the techniques can be modified to render them appropriate.

Although the appraisal process has now been applied to transport projects in almost all major cities of the industrialised world, these projects have focused primarily on automobile, metro and bus trips. Very few studies have included pedestrian, bicycle or motorcycle travel, let alone animal-drawn movement. In most Third World settlements, however, the use of these latter modes predominates. Clearly, this is one area where an extension of the scope of appraisal could make it more relevant to Third World city circumstances. It would require as has already been argued in this book, a greater understanding of trip purposes and trip-makers associated with these means of movement. This is particularly so because costs and benefits of city transport project improvements which serve trip-makers not traditionally incorporated into the appraisal process require realistic estimates of travel time savings.

Time Budget for Appraisal

The time required for the appraisal of Third World projects can be extensive and can range from months to years, depending on the scale and complexity of the project. Appraisal can thus seriously delay project implementation. For example, the World Bank Regional Cities' Urban Transport Project in Indonesia took four years from the project identification stage to the commencement of its implementation in April 1987.

To avoid delays, an alternative approach is to start the construction of a project almost immediately, as in Pusan in South Korea. Here a metro system has been constructed along a major corridor where the high volume of traffic made the need for a subway obvious. Analyses were for more peripheral routes where the marginal benefits of the system required investigation. Such an approach can better take advantage of the 'window(s) of opportunity' that exist, and may be justified on the grounds that ultimately the most important project output is its implementation, rather than the appraisal process per se.

In instances where funding is available only for a particular period, it is especially important to conduct the apppraisal process quickly, so as to identify the main alternatives and benefits, rather than to spend time in detailed analysis and thereby risk losing the money. In support of this approach, the aim of numerous recent World Bank training programmes is to help build-up a local professional capacity among both central and provincial senior management government staff so that they can undertake their own project appraisal efforts in urban transport. In so doing, it is hoped to help shorten the time-consuming procedures currently involved in hiring consultants or using World Bank staff.

Relationship with other Projects

Another consideration in project appraisal is that professionals (especially of international development agencies) as well as government officials, responsible for conducting or directing public sector project appraisal, rarely become involved from the begining of an appraisal process, or indeed remain involved throughout the process. Instead, previous efforts at appraisal have usually already been made, and professionals are thus often asked to enter at an intermediate stage in the appraisal process.

The longer the appraisal process, the more likelihood there is of a high turnover of persons. This was shown in the case of Delhi's rapid rail system which was appraised over many years and involved a varying cast of characters. This kind of turnover can often lead to changes in the interpretation of project objectives, if not a change in the objectives themselves. In other instances, the passing of time brings to the forefront different priorities as changes occur in economic circumstances, and in policies of those agencies' funding projects. In either event, the net effect is to lengthen and further complicate appraisal studies.

Sequences of Analytical Steps

In the sequencing of the steps in urban transport project appraisal (see Figure 6.1) conventional wisdom places goal development first. Yet, many involved in the development of the urban transport sector, particularly elected and appointed officials, do not know in advance what their goals are (see Chapter 1). An important part of the project appraisal process, therefore, is to present the decision-makers with alternatives beforehand, so they can better appreciate the available choice and the likely impacts. In many cases, the development of project appraisal goals and alternatives, proceed in parallel, with much interaction between the appraisers and the decision-makers.

STEPS IN URBAN TRANSPORT PROJECT APPRAISAL

Step One: Description of the Overall Situation

The first step is intended primarily to convey a picture of the important features of the project area of concern, as well as the economic and social setting in which the urban transport project is to operate. A socio-economic portrait is required, both of the present situation, and of the likely situation after the project's implementation.

The description of the overall situation (i.e., the project context) generally concerns eight major types of information (see Table 6.2). If the project is part of a larger effort (e.g., a comprehensive urban transport plan), then background information is also needed regarding other urban sectors, organisations, and activities associated with the project focus.

Table 6.2   Types of Project Context Descriptions

1. The national and urban sector (i.e., non-transport context)
2. The transport sector
3. The organisational and institutional framework for transport and urban development
4. The transport network and associated travel
5. The industry which provides transport
6. Studies and procedures undertaken and proposed
7. Construction practices
8. Maintenance practices

Issues in Project Context Description. There are three major issues requiring investigation when looking at the description of the overall situation (see Table 6.3).

Table 6.3   Issues in Project Context Descriptions

1. What data is available?
2. How good is the data?
3. What "unofficial" data might be relevant and obtainable?
4. What breadth and depth of impact-analysis data collection is required?
5. Should the focus be on crises or on general problems?

The first regards the kind of data that is available and its validity. Some Third World countries do not conduct a census; others do so only at 15 or 20 year intervals. In some countries or regions, especially in the Middle East, the census data may be classified on defence grounds and therefore not readily available for appraisal purposes. It may thus be necessary to make an informed guess at urban population levels.

Usually urban transport project data is obtained from a variety of different agencies. The appraisal team may not find the information they require until they examine in depth the participation of the different agencies in the project. In the process, further insight may be gained about unofficial views concerning the level of political support for various project alternatives. This is especially important in the case of urban road maintenance projects, for if the political support is lacking for what some may perceive as an uninspiring (but still important) effort, it may be more practical to assign the limited personnel resources elsewhere.

Another major issue which concerns the overall scope of an urban transport appraisal study, is the breadth of impact analysis, and therefore the amount and type of data collected. The degree of government concern for environmental factors needs to be established from the outset, so as to guide the level and type of information gathered. Concern for the urban environment has been rather limited in the Third World, even though the World Bank has recently embarked upon efforts to promote environmental considerations in the appraisal of projects.

Also important is the issue of whether to focus on recent or anticipated crises that might significantly affect a project. Political decisions are often greatly influenced by such events, as was revealed during the energy crisis of the 1970s. It might thus be important to collect data on these events and focus on them as part of the overall project-context description.

Step Two: Identification of Problems, Goals, and Objectives

Many transport project appraisal exercises in urban areas commence by concentrating on problems that are considered to warrant urgent attention, such as traffic congestion along strategic routes or in important parts of the city, elongated travel times for freight and journey-to-work trips, and retarded development in

193

productive sectors of the economy requiring improved transport infrastructure. These problems are then re-structured as goals so that the problem of urban traffic congestion, for example, is re-expressed in terms of the goal of reducing congestion. For each goal, objective verifiable indicators are then identified. The goal of increasing safety, for example, might have several such indicators, including:

1. the annual number of fatalities on a given street section;
2. the average loss of property value per accident; and
3. the proportion of accident victims receiving aid within one hour of the accident.

A technique used by many agencies, especially international development institutions (see Dickey, 1983), is to set out goals in what is called a 'logical framework' (LOGFRAME). In this technique the various goals are shown in the first column (see Table 6.4). In the second, objectively defined verifiable indicators are stated, of which there may be several for each goal. The next column contains the methods and measures of collecting data for the indicators. The last column contains the major assumptions associated with the goals.

Table 6.4   Outline of a Logical Framework (LOGFRAME)

Goal(s)	Objective Verifiable Indicator (s)	Means of Verification	Assumption(s)
Input 1	(1) ———————	(1) ———	(1) ———
.	(2) ———————	(2) ———	(2) ———
.		(3) ———	(3) ———
.			(4) ———
Output 1			

Goals of the kind employed in LOGFRAME may be divided into three categories, which relate to:

1. inputs needed for the project, (i.e., resources required for implementation);
2. desired outputs; and
3. project impacts, including those of an economic, social and environmental kind.

In addition to the above, there may be project constraints which need to be identified at the goal-setting stage. One example is the construction of the Hong Kong metro system, where it was decided at the outset that the system was not to be a financial drain on the treasury, and must thus pay its way. Project parameters and constraints of this kind need to be identified beforehand so that the planning and design of project alternatives can proceed within pre-set limits from the outset.

Issues in Identifying Problems, Goals and Objectives. There are at least six major issues that can arise in the process of identifying problems, goals, and objectives for urban transport project appraisal. They are posed as questions in Table 6.5.

Table 6.5   Issues in Problem and Goal Identification

---

1. How can the often large number of goals be identified?
2. Who decides which goals are to be included?
3. How comprehensive should the set of goals be?
4. What time horizon(s) should be considered?
5. Should all goals be stated formally and publicly?
6. What consideration should be given to additional goals as they become known over time?

The first of these concerns the difficult and exhaustive exercise of identifying project goals and objectives. There can be hundreds of different types of goals associated with the impacts of urban transport projects, since transport serves almost all activities of an urban area. Urban transport projects for example can affect the availability of city water supply, the method of sewage disposal, and the provision of city drainage facilities. The influence of transport can also be more subtle, as is the case where it affects communication among particular groups and inhabitants in the city. It is also the case when peripheral low-income areas are provided with better bus services, giving rise to enhanced access to educational facilities and jobs which in turn, helps to increase local incomes and subsequently the ability to pay for improved services.

The second issue concerns who decides what the project goals and objectives should be? In many Third World countries, central governments have considerable influence over their major cities and regions, whereas in the industrialised nations, local government has greater decision-making powers. In some countries, such as in China, central government in conjunction with citizen groups, determine the factors that are important as urban transport project goals and objectives.

The comprehensiveness and depth of the set of goals and objectives of project appraisal is yet another issue. The scope of problem restriction is important because of the widespread impact of urban transport on almost every sector of the urban economy and city social life. Despite (or perhaps because of) this, some delineation of project scope is required. This will depend on the general aims of the study and the size of the project. Although many subject areas can be studied in considerable depth, the investigation of *all* key aspects may take much longer than is politically acceptable (see Chapter 5), as in the case of environmental problems resulting from urban transport improvements.

Selecting an appropriate time horizon for project analysis, in view of the long lifetime of transport facilities, is the fourth important issue of project problem and goal identification. Many transport appraisal studies need to try to anticipate possible impacts of the following 15 years.

A politically sensitive issue is whether it is useful to state a project's goals and objectives publicly? There are countries, for example, where certain urban transport projects are implicitly intended to benefit particular political interests and, as such, it is not expedient for project planners and appraisers to state this publicly. The setting of project goals is usually an iterative process, with some goals set at the beginning only being tentative. As alternatives are periodically suggested, those in a position to make decisions may become more aware of the kinds of impacts that are important and therefore later alter or modify their goals. This is an inevitable phenomenon particularly brought about by the rapid and erratic change of circumstances experienced by many Third World countries which need to be accommodated in the project appraisal process.

Step Three: Development of Project Alternatives

The development of project alternatives covers a wide variety of possibilities (see Table 6.6). The first requiring investigation is the 'do nothing alternative'. Some problems will disappear and goals be achieved simply as time passes. Rapid transit systems are often forwarded as solutions to the mobility problems of many Third World cities. However, while such systems have advantages, it is only when compared with the 'do nothing alternative' that their high capital and foreign exchange costs become very apparent.

Table 6.6   Types of Project Alternatives

1. Do nothing
2. Construct new facilities
3. Reconstruct existing facilities
4. Better maintain existing facilities
5. Alter emphasis on use of vehicle types
6. Integrate with urban development schemes
7. Integrate with order non-transport projects that influence transport
8. Change taxes, fees, and other financial mechanisms related to urban transport

Looking at other project alternatives, one may find that construction might involve various geometric design and structural changes, as well as alternatives in equipment and personnel needs. Alternatively, it may be necessary to employ labour-intensive construction techniques which have to be accomplished through a redesign of construction methods or through special programmes like 'food-for-work schemes'. This latter approach has been recently employed in Trivandrum, South India, where a road was constructed with gravel pounded from large rocks by hundreds of workers living along the roadside.

Road maintenance has, up until recently, been a commonly overlooked project alternative. It has now become important, since the economics of road maintenance are (increasingly) favourable when compared to new road construction alternatives.

Changes in the emphasis and use of vehicle types is another important project alternative that has been inadequately explored in project urban transport appraisal. The wide variety of transport modes in many Third World cities used for both freight and passenger travel (see Chapters 3 and 4) offers scope for numerous permutations of modal choice emphasis which need to be incorporated within the project appraisal process.

In the light of the important role transport fulfills in urban development (see Chapter 1), it is also essential to examine options which integrate urban transport projects with other urban development schemes, in fields such as education and health and urban infrastructure projects (see Chapter 12). In so doing, special emphasis may be given to serving these sectors by re-routing public transport services to improve, for example, access to new schools and employment opportunities; and by constructing strategic corridors of urban infrastructure to encourage future urban growth and investment along carefully planned and pre-selected routes (see Chapter 10).

Non-transport alternatives for resolving urban movement problems can also offer scope for action. This could include preparation of various schemes designed to reduce urban travel by introducing changes in work schedules, as well as policies for industrial location and residential development.

Still other possibilities involve the introduction of urban transport cost revenue options. This might include the levying (or increasing) of transport related fuel taxes, the raising of public transport fares, the introduction of highway tolls, the increasing of vehicle licensing costs, the reduction of transport sector subsidies, and so on. There is, furthermore, no reason why an urban transport project should not focus on the taxing of petrol as a means of reducing private car travel in urban areas.

Issues in Project Alternative Development. The first of the issues (see Table 6.7) focuses on the type of alternative to be considered. Many countries do not have the resources in manpower, equipment, or investment funds to pursue certain project alternatives. The imposition of a petrol tax scheme, for example, requires a relatively sophisticated tax collection mechanism which may not exist or be practicable in certain countries. Similarly, in the case of a metro system proposal, the reliance on outside technical and financial assistance may be too great for the scheme to gain political acceptance in some less affluent countries.

An additional issue (also referred to in Chapter 2) is whether or not the professional should acquiesce to government officials when choosing among project alternatives? This is especially difficult where influential political leaders prefer a particular project alternative (such as a metro system) because of its association with 'modernity'. Under such circumstances, the selection of alternatives in the appraisal process becomes limited by virtue of the project being selected by those in power, rather than on objective and technical performance grounds. In these instances, urban transport project appraisal sometimes turns into an attempt at legitimising the choice of a single alternative.

Table 6.7   Issues in Project Alternative Development

---

1. What type of alternatives should be considered?
2. Who should decide on the alternatives to be investigated?
3. What response should be made to "windows of opportunity?"
4. What choice should be made between capital intensive and "appropriate" technologies?

This consideration again brings to the forefront the 'window of opportunity' concept, where the alternative to be considered is often dominated by the opportunity of obtaining funding tied to a particular kind of technology or idea. Some international development institutions, for instance, are more anxious to fund project alternatives which have positive impacts on low-income groups (through for example, the provision of improved bus systems or pedestrian schemes), rather than concentrate on major capital expenditures, such as light rail rapid transit systems, metro schemes or major circumferential road projects. On the other hand, vendors of transport hardware interested in selling their technology, and eager to set up export loans at reduced interest rates to help buy that technology, sometimes make the issue of choosing among alternatives a fiction (see Chapter 2).

Where government decision-makers do not succumb to commercial pressures, they must decide whether to opt for the alternative offering the newest technology or for an 'appropriate technology' option. Although, the latter may accomplish important development goals, its often limited political appeal raises the problem of attracting funds, unless championed by a particular influential political figure or international development agency.

Step Four: Analysis of Urban Travel Demand

The analysis of travel demand is an important component of any urban transport project appraisal effort. The 'Four-Step Process' of travel forecasting, as part of an overall urban transport planning process, is outlined in Chapter 5. There is, therefore, little need for a discussion here concerning this aspect. However, there are certain modifications and additions to the 'Four-Step Process' which are appropriate at the project level (as opposed to its application on a city-wide basis). These include the conducting of corridor analysis, and specific route analysis, with particular emphasis on passenger and freight vehicle load variations and peaking characteristics.

Corridor analysis (see Chapter 7) focuses on a broad strip of land, perhaps from three to six kilometres wide, usually emanating from the city centre. Within this corridor, there may be three or four possible routes for major street improvements or rail line developments. Origin-destination pairs for trips are obtained from the city-wide estimates (where they exist), and applied in more detail to the routes along the corridor under study. Route analysis is even more specific, and might involve, for example, an estimation (in the case of a public transport study) of the number of passengers embarking and disembarking at each bus stop.

An aspect of urban travel that needs to be investigated at both the corridor and route level is peaking. Unlike cities in the industrialised nations where the focus of urban transport studies is on weekday traffic movement during the two peak periods in the morning and evening, comparable routes in some Third World cities have much longer peak periods. However, in other Third World cities, there is only a slight hint of a peak, with traffic volumes almost flat throughout the day. In Shanghai, China, for example, major traffic peaks occur on Sunday, the only day most people have free for shopping and family activities. By contrast, in Rio de Janeiro, Brazil, peaks occur throughout the weekday, with traffic volumes often at a continuously congested level on major routes. The same holds true (but with lower congestion levels) for several cities in Korea, including Seoul and Pusan.

There are also variations in urban traffic volumes on account of religion and culture. In many Islamic nations, for example, Friday is the day of prayer and rest, as Sunday is in Christian countries. As a result, in Saudi Arabia and Iran for instance, traffic is very light on Friday with much of the traffic being associated with religious or recreational purposes. In other Islamic countries with significant non-Muslim populations, such as Malaysia and Indonesia, the colonial tradition survives, so that although Friday is the day of prayer, Sunday is the day of rest. In these Islamic countries, as in most other Asian and Third World nations, working and retailing hours tend to be more extended than in industrialised countries, with the result that peak traffic periods are less accentuated. In Latin-based cultures, in countries such as Mexico and Brazil, four peak periods during the weekday can be observed. These result from the custom of the afternoon *siesta* or rest, after which work resumes, and shops re-open, often until seven or eight in the evening. In these countries, particularly in the coastal areas, the affluent leave home for long weekends, causing high volumes of out-bound traffic on Friday afternoon, and returning peak traffic on Sunday evening.

Data for the analyses of urban transport project alternatives may be derived from a variety of sources. An appraisal of a project which has as one of its alternatives the implementation of a petrol tax increase, could, for example, require city-wide vehicle-mile travel data, as well as some indication of the trip-maker's response to increased travel costs. By contrast, a project aimed at creating reversible bus lanes would need relatively micro-level route-demand figures.

Travel Demand Analysis Issues. The issues that urban travel demand analysis presents (see Table 6.8) will be discussed here only briefly, since it is for the most part (particuarly the city-wide aspects) covered in Chapter 5.

Table 6.8   Issues in Project of Travel Demand Analysis

1. What is a "trip?"
2. How should the multiplicity of modes be addressed?
3. What variations are there in travel times?
4. How can travel forecasting be accurate given rapid changes in technology as well as economic and social conditions?

A central difference in the transport field between industrialised and Third World countries, is the nature of a 'trip'. In most urban transport studies in industrialised nations, a 'trip' primarily refers to motorised movement which usually excludes short distance trips. As already indicated in a number of the preceding chapters, such a limited concept of trip-making is rarely valid in Third World countries. The treatment of the multiplicity of modes in project appraisal also poses problems in travel demand analysis in many Third World cities. Some analyses in India for example (see Chapter 4), account for as many as eight different modes of urban travel compared to say, three in the industrialised world. This makes the project appraisal process much more difficult and complex because of the variations in mode speeds and other advantages that need be examined.

Travel time distributions also vary considerably from industrialised to Third World city contexts. Studies in Bombay for the development of a second major city, for example, found that average trip times often exceeded an hour; indeed sometimes ranged up to as much as two hours, thus suggesting that many trips were made on foot and/or by slower modes of transport. Similar findings were found in Lagos. Many of the parameters used in urban transport project appraisal analysing trip distribution in the industrialised countries are therefore obviously not directly transferable to Third World situations.

New technologies for forecasting are rapidly being introduced to the Third World urban scene (see Chapters 8 and 9). These have been warranted by dramatic changes in traffic composition and volumes that have taken place. Such changes have been no more marked than in Saudi Arabia over the last two decades, with its growth of motor vehicle ownership, and in less affluent countries such as India and Indonesia, where most cities have experienced major increases in motorcycle travel (see Chapters 1 and 2). In retrospect, many transport planners would not have forecast the latter development, even though today it represents the fastest growth of motorised travel in Asia.

Other forecasting considerations warranting consideration in urban transport project appraisal relate to the dynamics of economic and social changes that constantly occur in many Third World countries and which are impossible to predict accurately. These changes (many of which are discussed in Chapters 1 and 2) are influenced by exogenous factors, such as fluctuations in international trade relations, changes in import tarrifs, and commodity price hikes and slumps. Together, such factors influence the price of imported goods, vehicles, and (crucial for the transport sector of oil-importing countries), fuel and petroleum-based products. They in turn can ultimately affect the viability of an urban transport project and thus must be taken into account in the risk factor of the appraisal process.

Step Five: Identification and Analysis of Urban Transport Project Impacts

As indicated earlier, urban transport has an impact on almost all aspects of urban development. Various kinds of analyses have been developed for the investigation of the impacts of transport on different activities and sectors of an urban area. From the broadest perspective, impacts can be identified under the categories of human (and groups), the natural environment, the man-made environment, and human activities (or behaviour). The first might relate to people of different ages, races, religions, political leanings, incomes, educational backgrounds, etc. In addition, there may be various types of firms, government agencies, military organisations, and the like, involved.

The focus on the natural environment might be on air, water and noise pollution, as well as on vegetation and wildlife. Concerns for the man-made environment may be for food production and distribution, and access to industrial sites, as well as health care facilities. These concerns are intertwined with those for human activities, such as child-rearing, spiritual development and, on a longer-term basis, migration.

Often the analysis required varies with the problem. If, for instance, migration is viewed as a problem, special studies might be undertaken with regard to the role that transport plays in encouraging migration, particularly *within* the city.

Issues in Project Impact Identification and Analysis. An overriding issue in project impact analysis is which consequences to consider and in how much depth? The most immediate impacts of urban transport project execution are on:

1. urban travel behaviour and trip patterns;
2. the construction and transport industries (involving public and private sector organisations participating in the building, operation and maintenance of transport facilities); and
3. the surrounding environment and strategic development activities to the project.

Environmental impacts of urban transport projects are increasingly being investigated in 'middle-income' Third World countries. These are found to be greatly influenced by, among other things, local topographical considerations. However, transport is only one contributor to urban environmental problems. A coal-fired electricity generating plant located in close proximity to an urban area may, for example, be a much greater cause of air pollution than transport facilities.

An extremely complex issue in the analysis of urban transport project impacts concerns the 'multiplier effect', where it is sometimes debatable who gains from the use of a newly introduced or improved transport facility, and who will make use of the time or money saved. Project beneficiaries may, for example, rent better housing or move from an undeveloped land plot to one with some kind of shelter. The owner of the new property may in turn increase land rental prices, knowing that the newly improved transport facility will increase the value of his property. Local retailers may then increase the prices of their goods to cover increased rental charges, and so on.

The above explained spiral effects (see Figure 6.2) demonstrate that questions of how benefits are generated and distributed, how they flow through the urban economy, and who really benefits in the end, are very complex. Such considerations in Third World city studies, although sometimes critical to the success of a project, are made even more difficult to analyse by the absence of adequate data, particularly with regard to those impacts affecting the informal sector.

Figure 6.2: Simplified Example of Money Flow and Multiplier Effect

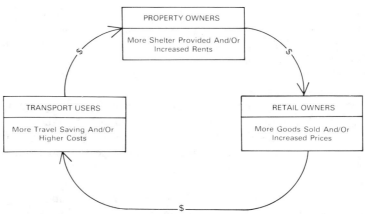

From the preceding discussion, it is obvious that the treatment of risk and uncertainty are crucial aspects of project appraisal. Many cities located in earthquake zones, such as Mexico City, Managua in Nicaragua, and several cities in China, necessarily warrant even more careful treatment of the risk factor.

Finally, particularly difficult to estimate and forecast, are impacts of fluctuations in the cost of major urban transport system components, including labour, fuel, construction materials. An illustration of such uncertainty is the price hike of oil in the early 1970s, and the subsequent price level drop after 1982. These fluctuations are particularly problematic in countries which depend heavily on petroleum imports.

Step Six: Analysis of Project Implementation Mechanisms

Project appraisal is generally required to investigate four aspects of project implementation, namely:

1. the organisational capabilities of the agencies and/or firms involved in project implementation;
2. the financial status of the project in terms of expenditures and revenues for the relevant transport agencies involved;
3. the related policies, plans, programmes, projects, and regulations of both transport and non-transport agencies affected; and
4. the level of personnel development for those expected to be involved in project implementation.

An analysis of organisational capabilities is required in order to examine the types of functions agencies involved in the project must undertake. Of particular importance are their procurement capabilities. Sound capabilities in this field are essential for the provision of goods and services required to carry out the project. There is, furthermore, the need to establish whether the structure of the organisation has the capacity to accomodate the kinds of activities and options being considered.

In the financial field, it is important to ascertain an organisation's financial capacity, in order to establish whether current expenditures are being made at the right time with proper guidance, and at sufficient levels. Where revenue is concerned, it is valuable to determine the type of funding available (both internal and external). Information about this may be derived from a variety of different sources, such as details of fuel taxes, driving licence revenues, customs and excise taxes, gross receipt taxes, public transport fare revenues, and loans or grants from external agencies. Revenues and expenditures taken together contribute to an agency's cash flow, which help it maintain a sustainable effort to implement both proposed and current projects.

A third important consideration regarding project implementation mechanisms is that of related endeavours. These include policies, plans, programmes, projects, legal decisions, executive orders, and regulations which originate from a wide variety of agencies, and may relate to an equally wide spectrum of sectors. The Indonesian government, for example, despite the export of petroleum products, provides a subsidy to the state-owned petroleum company to help finance below market price petrol sales in Indonesia. There was at one time a proposal to raise the price gradually and end this subsidy. However, as it was feared that this would affect overall inflation, and particularly millions of low-income kerosene users, the policy was not pursued.

The fourth category of concern in project implementation is personnel development. Some general questions requiring examination in this field are presented in Table 6.9 (also see Chapters 2, 5 and 8). As might be expected, many Third World countries lack adequately trained personnel to manage and maintain their urban transport systems. There is subsequently, a need for much on-site, in-country, and (in some cases) out-country training. Training takes many years. There is, furthermore, the risk of trained personnel subsequently leaving their agencies in the public sector to join the private sector for better pay.

Table 6.9   General Questions Related to Training

---

1. What is the overall support in government and in the private sector for training?
2. Who requires training?
3. What types of training are required?
4. What individuals or groups should do the training?
5. What training facilities and equipment are needed?
6. What personnel and financial resources are needed?
7. In what way should the training be evaluated?

Issues in Analysis of Implementation Mechanisms. A major dilemma in the analysis of implementation mechanisms for urban transport projects is to decide which of the many organisational, financial, programming, and training considerations should be given priority attention. Since transport affects and is affected by both innumerable urban development factors and groups of people, those responsible for implementation can easily be trapped into focusing their attention in the wrong direction thereby endangering the likely success of project implementation.

Until recently, for example, it has been common practice for governments and international development agencies alike, to focus more on the physical (engineering) aspects of project development, than on the institutional and financial capabilities of those agencies assigned the task of implementation. This was despite the fact that the financial, management and personnel resources were typically inadequate to support the scale and schedule of proposed public works. In Indonesia, for example, a study of manpower development and training needs of a proposed multi-million US dollar urban transport infrastructure project (Dimitriou, 1988), identified:

1.   the educational and seniority profile of agency personnel requiring training;
2.   the type of training needed;
3.   the manpower, space and equipment needs of the proposed training; and
4.   the costs and institutional framework for such training.

The study concluded that the failure to positively respond to the above training needs could jeopardise the viability of the project, and that therefore, certain training efforts required in their own right, substantial plans and programmes spanning a number of years, during which agency personnel management and technical skills should not only be systematically upgraded, but also evaluated.

Efforts of this kind, however, raise a number of issues (see Table 6.10) which are further discussed by the author in another publication (Dickey and Miller, 1984). Observations from the field suggest that some of the most significant issues include: government and private sector support for training (without which valuable resources are wasted); the need for the training to be

207

appropriate; and the need to introduce financial and promotional incentives for those who complete the training.

Table 6.10   Some Issues in Project Alternative Evaluation

1. Who should do the evaluation?
2. What role should international development institutions play?
3. Who should benefit from and who should pay for the project?
4. What factors (social, economic, political, etc.) should be considered?
5. What prices should be employed?
6. How should the effect of the project under study on other projects be assessed?
7. How should travel time savings be valued?
8. What discount factor, if any, should be employed?

A further problem of project implementation is the weak budgeting practices of many Third World municipal agencies. In many Latin American countries, for example, central government has such power over the cities that many municipalities have very limited ways of raising local revenue, except through central government channels (see Chapter 7). The result is that adequate financing of projects in these settlements is hard to achieve. Even where funding sources are available, these may be unstable. Given the considerable fluctuations in the past of revenues received, precedents do not provide adequate stability or, therefore, the confidence needed to execute substantial on-going urban transport projects.

Related to the issue of revenues and cost-recovery are questions associated with accepting financial backing from international development institutions, such as the World Bank and the Asian Development Bank. These agencies provide not only project finance, but also valuable technical assistance for carrying out projects and ensuring their appropriate execution, within acceptable financial and economic bounds. In addition they provide an important access to considerable foreign exchange funds for many Third World countries. A difficulty, however, is that the money must be repaid in the same currency. Many loan-receiving countries such as Brazil, have as a result, encountered problems in repayment, since their currency has experienced much greater inflation than the currency being repaid. In southeast

Asia, where many development projects are financed from Japanese sources, the appreciation of the Japanese yen since the mid 1980s has been so great it has offset any low interest rates that might have been offered in conjunction with such loans, and thus also presents problems of repayment.

Step Seven: Evaluation of Project Alternatives

Project alternative evaluation is the final step in the urban transport project appraisal process. It should lead to an assessment of the relative costs and benefits of different options, and their economic (including financial), social, environmental, and other physical impacts. Where employment and growth in the domestic product are significant, economic impacts generally will be the most important.

Project appraisal evaluation can be divided into two parts: the overall economic evaluation; and a broader evaluation, involving all impacts of a transport project. Before discussing either of these, it is appropriate to highlight the economic evaluation techniques which may be employed in the evaluation of project alternatives. These include:

1. the Net Present Value (NPV) method;
2. Benefit Cost Ratio (BCR) method;
3. the Internal Rate of Return (IRR) method; and
4. the Payback Period (PP) method.

Each of the above will be described here only briefly, since they are discussed in other texts (see, for example, Heggie, 1972; Fabrycky and Thueson, 1974; and Dickey and Miller, 1984).

The NPV method takes changes in project alternative costs over different periods, and weighs them by the time value of money for the same durations. These weighted estimates are then added over the periods and subtracted from a similar estimate for benefits. A 'discount factor' must be employed in the calculation which generally represents (in percentage terms) the value of the dollar one year from the base year. The BCR method is similar to the NPV method but instead of taking the difference between benefits and costs, it takes the *ratio*. Again, the discount rate is featured in this technique. In the IRR method, varying values for the discount rate are tried until one is found which equates the costs and net present benefits. Unlike the other methods, the PP method is used sparingly. In this technique, the cumulative benefits and costs of each project alternative are looked at over time (not discounted). The time at which cumulative benefits catch up to cumulative costs is referred to as the 'payback period'.

In each of these four techniques, it is necessary to make a comparison between benefits (measured in terms of the monetary value of user savings) and the costs of implementing and operating the project. Transport project user savings relate to such items as: fuel and oil consumption levels, travel time budgets, and sometimes safety rates (measured in terms of loss of life and/or damaged property). The 'cost' side of the project alternative ledger focuses on land, labour and capital requirements.

To undertake a broader evaluation involving all impacts, an urban transport project must go through three 'hoops' in the appraisal process, leading to its eventual success (see Figure 6.3). It must first obtain the necessary project inputs. In the case of an urban road construction project for example, requisite labour, land, and materials are generally included. The next 'hoop' is the attainment of the desired types and levels of project outputs. These are exemplified by actual road kilometres constructed, the amount of maintenance carried out, or in the case of a public transport project, the number of new buses acquired and put into service.

The last 'hoop' is the 'impact' hoop. If adequate project inputs are received, and defined outputs provided, the project is then deemed successful. Measures of impacts could include Internal Rate Return estimates, as well as estimates of other factors such as:

1. increased employment generated by the project;
2. accessibility provided to people living at the periphery of a city; and
3. air pollution reduction.

Putting together an appraisal of all these factors is a difficult and complex exercise. For not only does it usually involve a spectrum of professionals, including engineers, planners, and economists, but also elected and appointed officials, and representatives from international development institutions, all making judgements on presented findings. There is, therefore, no single way in which an appraisal criterion of an urban transport project alternative can be developed which encompasses this wide diversity of interests. However, some techniques which are helpful, are the Goals Achievement Method of evaluation, and the Cost Effectiveness Technique.

Figure 6.3   Example of Hoops to be Overcome for an Urban Road Project

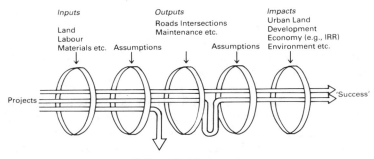

'Failure' Readjustment

Adapted from Be-Akiva, M.E. et al 1976

In the former, project inputs, outputs, and impacts are listed for each alternative, together with whatever quantitative measurements are available. These are scaled, so that the best value equals 100, and each value on the other alternatives is a proportion of the best. The factors are then weighted in importance, and a total score derived for each project alternative. The Cost Effectiveness Technique avoids any weighing, and thus inappropriate quantification. It simply lists the kinds of objective verifiable indicators available for each cost and measure of effectiveness, whether it be a project output or impact. Decision-makers then have a clear picture of the different types of factors involved, and make judgements accordingly. It should be noted that the CBR, IRR, or other economic measures can be used within the the context of either of the above two approaches.

Part of the appraisal stage involving project alternative evaluation also needs to be devoted to the setting up of a continuing monitoring and evaluation process, to ensure that anticipated results occur. Some kind of scheme is thus required to assess project inputs, outputs, and impacts over a given period of time, during which the project is to be completed. Though various types of designs for this kind of monitoring and evaluation exist, they are not discussed here in detail. However, some of the important factors which need to be taken into account, include (after Dickey and Miller, 1984):

1.   the costs of their implementation;
2.   the accuracy of the timing of various project inputs, outputs, and impacts; and
3.   project results compared with those expected.

Particular attention also needs to be paid to 'unexpected' project outcomes, with a view to establising whether they can be anticipated more fully in the future.

Issues in Evaluation of Project Alternatives.   There is a long list of issues associated with the evaluation of project alternatives in the appraisal process. Some of these are given in Table 6.10.

One of the main issues however, is who should do the evaluation? Ought it, for example, to be the lead agency or should it involve the co-ordination of a variety of agencies, in conjunction perhaps with various citizen groups? Since the evaluation occurs within a broad political process, appointed and elected officials are in any case usually involved in the various steps.

International development institutions also play an important role in Third World countries in determining the kind of evaluation that best satisfies the project and its circumstances. Whether this role is excessive or not often depends on the nature of the project and terms agreed. Apart from the influence exerted on particular projects, some international development agencies such as the United Nations and the World Bank, conduct training programmes on project appraisal. Through these programmes, combined with their international publications programme, they disseminate ideas and guidelines on project appraisal which considerably influence the state of the art.

More specific issues concerning the evaluation of project alternatives deal with such matters as:

1.   who benefits from, and who pays for, proposed urban transport improvements?
2.   whether perceived or actual costs ought to be used in the evaluation;
3.   how should inflation be taken into account?

4.   to what extent should actual prices be used, instead of those which would occur in a truly competitive situation (represented by shadow prices)? and

5.   how ought various factors in the evaluation be made commensurate (i.e., converted into equivalent units such as US dollars)?

The last of the above is especially difficult for those involved in the calculation of project costs and benefits, as illustrated by efforts at travel time valuation in the evaluation of transport project alternatives (see Table 6.11). Research findings about travel habits in Nigeria revealed that the common approach to such an assessment (which assumes that the value of time is the same as the average wage rate in the study area), has several drawbacks which need to be taken into account in the making of travel time estimates. These include (after Banjo, 1980):

1.   the wage rate may not reflect work done in the informal sector;

2.   in some cities wages are low but wage increments (including social security, reduced house rents, and use of company cars) are high and not included in the wages;

3.   saved time may not be used for further work (at the given wage rate), but for leisure; and

4.   wage rates may not reflect the 'willingness to pay' of tripmakers, who may have sources of income other than their wages.

Table 6.11   Issues in Travel Time Valuation

1. Is time actually saved?
2. Is time saved used productively?
3. Does the wage rate adequately represent the value of labour?
4. What considerations should be made for wage increments and hidden wage subsidies?
5. From whose viewpoint should time savings be considered?

Another issue concerns the 'system-effect' of urban transport projects. Not only do benefits accrue for example, to the users of a particular road project involving transport improvements, but also to users of other roads which may benefit from the reduced congestion. In the case of a traffic management scheme, where the operation of buses is enhanced by taking street vendors off the streets, this incurs costs for the displaced street vendors and perhaps for pedestrians who normally shop in the area (see Chapter 11).

The question of which unit prices to employ in the evaluation of project alternatives is usually an integral part of the appraisal process, especially when international development institutions are involved. To take the Indonesian illustration mentioned earlier, where the government charges its own nationals less for petrol than would be paid on the open international market, the question here is whether the former or the international price should be employed as the basis for calculating project costs and benefits? If it is the former, this will then encourage a tendency to use more petroleum-related products (e.g., petrol and asphalt) in projects. On the other hand, if the international price operates, fewer of those products are likely to be used thus enabling more of Indonesia's oil to be sold on the international market at a higher price than domestic levels. This would bring in revenue to the country which in turn could finance a variety of other projects. There is, therefore, a real cost associated with using the lower (domestic) price in the benefit/cost calculations, from which it can be seen that prices utilised in analysing alternatives can significantly influence the output of the appraisal process.

CONCLUSION

Overall, many of the issues discussed in this chapter revolve around the attempt to place the urban transport project into some broader framework of goals achievement, cost-effectiveness, or LOGFRAME. It is reasonable that an evaluation of an urban transport project alternative should be conducted relative to the goals set at the outset of the project. As this approach, however, has not been common, it becomes an appraisal issue in itself.

Finally, we return to the concept of the 'window of opportunity'; although it is of paramount necessity to conduct a highly professional appraisal on a project using the latest appropriate theories and techniques, the ultimate objective is to introduce an urban transport project that benefits the public. If the appraisal process itself tends to prevent this, then the method of appraisal should be reconsidered. This comment is made to emphasise the importance of project product (i.e., outcome) over the appraisal process itself.

REFERENCES

Banjo, G.A. (1980) 'The Theoretical Basis for Travel Time Savings Valuation in Developing Countries', **Department of Civic Design Working Paper,** no. 15, University of Liverpool, Liverpool.

Dickey, J.W. (Senior Author) (1983) **Metropolitan Transportation Planning,** Second Edition, McGraw-Hill, New York.

Dickey, J.W. and Miller L.H. (1984) **Road Project Appraisal for Developing Countries,** John Wiley, Chichester.

Dimitriou, H.T. (1988) 'Urban Transport and Manpower Development and Training Needs for Four Asian Cities: A Case Study of Bandung, Medan, Semarang, and Surabaya, Indonesia', **Habitat International,** vol. 12, no. 3, Pergamon Press, Oxford.

Fabrycky, W.J. and Thuesen G.J. (1974) **Economic Decision Analysis,** Prentical Hall, Englewood Cliffs, New Jersey.

Heggie, I.G. (1972) **Transport Engineering Economics,** McGraw-Hill, London.

United Nations, Economic Commission for Latin America (1976) **Information Classificaton Manual for the Transport Sector,** Report E/CEPAL/1008, New York.

World Bank, (1979) **Highway Design and Maintenance Standards Model: Model Description and User's Manual,** World Bank, Washington, DC.

____ (1986) **Urban Transport: A World Bank Policy Study,** IBRD, Washington, DC.

Chapter 7

Institutional Frameworks for Planning Transport in Third World Cities

Josef Barat

INTRODUCTION

Of the many different characteristics typifying Third World cities, the most common is their limited and often inadequate institutional framework for planning. In countries as diverse as Brazil and Tanzania, India and Mexico, it is common for urban transport plans (where they exist) to be formulated in a way whereby their implementation is frustrated by an inability to direct efforts towards the achievement of pre-specified objectives. Furthermore, even in countries which have a strong planning tradition, such as India and Mexico, urban transport planning is hampered by the fact that urban movement problems are generally treated by central government as a purely local matter. As a result, the local and state urban transport planning agencies tend to draw up plans and proposals which reflect very little of the national development priorities.

Given the central bureaucracy's attitude towards urban transport (except in the notable case of capital cities and major industrial centres), most urban transport planning agencies in the Third World receive very little funding or staffing support from central government, expecially in non-metropolitan areas. Even in those cities which have had the assistance of central government in the preparation of transport plans, the local institutional capacity to implement the plans, is invariably inadequate, (see Chapters 2 and 5). This inadequacy is generally of two kinds: institutions concerned with the urban transport sector are not very capable of preparing plans and programmes for *different types* of areas, and are often unable to *implement and enforce* any proposals emerging from prepared plans and programmes. In both instances, these limitations are of critical importance for the planning institutions themselves, and for the approach to urban transport planning that they employ.

The position taken in this chapter is that a major contributor to the failures of planning urban transport in Third World countries arises out of a structural incompatability between institutional planning frameworks, which Friedmann calls 'societal guidance systems' (Friedmann, 1973), and the environment they are to serve. As a result, what is planned often has little relevance to community needs and aspirations, and simultaneously takes scant account of the resources available to pursue the stated goals. Such circumstances suggest ignorance of the necessary conditions for the formulation and implementation of transport projects which should take place within the context of an institutional planning framework for transport. Without this framework, institutions are likely to pursue conflicting objectives and suffer from a mis-allocation of resources.

To illustrate these points further, this chapter examines the evolution of the institutional planning framework for transport in the Sao Paulo Metropolitan Area, and its capacity to implement transport plans and programmes that have been put forward. As a prelude however, it is first important to define clearly the term 'institutional planning framework', both in general and as it relates to the transport sector of Third World countries.

DEFINITION OF INSTITUTIONAL PLANNING FRAMEWORKS

Nature of Institutional Planning Frameworks

An institutional planning framework may be defined as a set of organisations and agencies (usually government institutions or government-sponsored) *with* their linkages. Together, they provide the means for undertaking planning action by dependent institutions, as well as the mechanisms for deciding and designing such action. Such planning frameworks can be highly formalised and characterised by their statutory requirement for one or other organisation to involve specified institutions in particular aspects of their work. Alternatively, institutional planning frameworks may be informal in nature and be based upon ad-hoc linkages between particular organisations, arising from a recognition of mutual benefit. In many cases, planning frameworks incorporate both a formal and informal set of characteristics - the mix of which changes over time or as a result of different political and development circumstances.

Institutional planning frameworks are intended to promote actions that both contribute to goal/objective achievement (e.g., for urban development or for the development of a particular sector), and discourage those actions likely to have adverse effects on such efforts. In this respect, such frameworks may be seen as agents of development, introducing change in a structured and consensual manner. Equally important, however, they may be used as tools for monitoring the impact of change - whether these changes are deliberately introduced or the result of unforeseen events.

It can be argued that the effectiveness of any institutional planning framework is directly related to its ability to cope with unplanned change, since it is under these conditions that institutions have to demonstrate their ability to act complementarily towards the resolution of the problems confronting them. In fact, it is under crisis situations of unexpected changes that deficiencies in the existing frameworks are most likely to be revealed.

Because planning is by nature continuous, the institutional framework set up to undertake planning tasks must similarly be able to accommodate continuous activities. Linkages between organisations forming the institutional framework for instance, normally maintain contacts in the form of meetings, letter correspondence, telephone conversations etc. In so far as the efficient operation of an institutional network relies upon the maintenance of a system which facilitates speedy interaction at low cost, an institutional planning framework with all its networks is analagous to a transport system.

This analogy likens the hierarchy of transport systems to the hierarchical structure of links within an institutional planning framework. Links of the institutional planning framework are seen as akin to networks which commonly converge on major decision-making points, similar to the convergence of transport routes to a town. Institutional links also have capacity limitations (as do transport links). The former are constrained in their ability to accommodate information about traffic from one organisation to another, or between different units of the same organisation at different levels of administration. In this way, the performance of an institutional planning framework and its constituent links are subject to constraints as well as opportunities found within the system, as in the case of the transport systems. Self-contained or autonomous organisations can therefore be expected to have minimum inter-institutional connections - analogous to the private car user who is relatively free in the use of the overall road transport network. On the other hand, less autonomous organisations are expected to be more interdependent; as in the case of the bus passengers whose reliance upon public transport is also determined by the needs of other bus users, the operational constraints of the bus operator and the characteristics of the bus route.

Just as it is possible to regulate the use of transport infrastructure by the private car and bus, so it should be possible, if this analogy has any real meaning, to regulate the use of links within an institutional planning framework. This can be done, indeed is done, through the manipulation of the institutional relationships and resources made available to each organisation.

Functions of Institutional Planning Frameworks

From the description of institutional planning frameworks given so far, one can appreciate that accommodating the exchange of information and resources in the pursuance of specified ends is one of the principal functions of such frameworks.

An alternative way of viewing frameworks of this kind is as a management context for institutional actions taken by specific agencies and organisations pursuing certain interests and acting upon given responsibilities. The institutional planning framework in these circumstances becomes a medium through which the different organisations involved operate and interact.

More specifically, the framework accommodates activities related to:

1. the planning toward the achievement of specified goals and objectives;
2. the identification of resources needed for the attainment of these ends;

3. the marshalling of these resources in a manner which reflects the priorities attached to the various elements of policy actions;
4. the clarification of the roles and actions to be performed by each of the agencies involved;
5. the regulation and coordination of the interaction of those policies and actions associated with one sector, with those of other sectors; and
6. the monitoring and evaluating of activities of the sectors.

An institutional planning framework may be seen to consist of three elements: organisations, procedures and resources (see Figure 7.1). The employment of these in a directed, rational and coherent manner (i.e., the management and control of these elements toward the attainment of sector and non-sector objectives) is what identifies the existence of an institutional planning framework and what determines its output.

Another principal function of an institutional planning framework is to select the planning philosophies, procedures and techniques most appropriate for addressing the issues that have to be resolved. In so doing, it is necessary to be clear about what is being planned for whom, and how and when the plans will be carried out. These decisions must then be translated into action for particular agencies in specified sectors and geographical areas. Such decisions involve a careful distribution of planning responsibilities and resources among the relevant organisations. They also require a clear statement of the procedures to be employed in these tasks, and an indication of the expected output. To guide these actions, priorities over time need to be set and related to different geographical and institutional areas of responsibility for the implementation of planned action.

In establishing procedures for the development and operation of the above tasks, it is important to appreciate that 'planning' is essentially a multi-disciplinary activity requiring a wide variety of expertise. More importantly, it has to be recognised that there are several styles of planning, arising from (among other considerations):

1. the *level* of planning - e.g., district, city, metropolitan etc.;
2. the *method* of planning - e.g., incremental, comprehensive, strategic etc.;

Figure 7.1: Elements of an Institutional Planning Framework

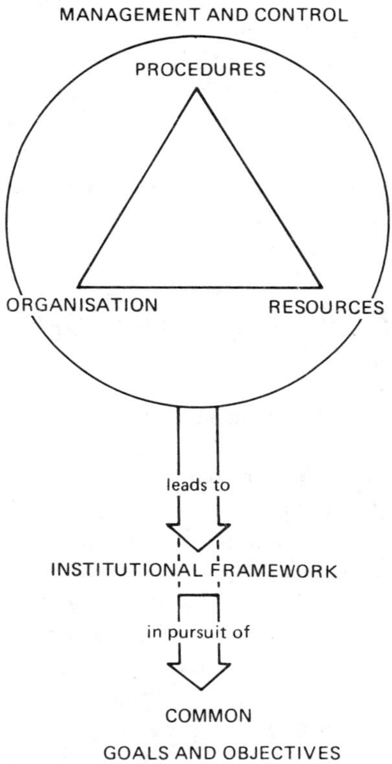

MANAGEMENT AND CONTROL

PROCEDURES

ORGANISATION   RESOURCES

leads to

INSTITUTIONAL FRAMEWORK

in pursuit of

COMMON

GOALS AND OBJECTIVES

Source: Banjo G.A. and Dimitriou H.T., 1983

3.   the *type* of planning - e.g., sector, economic, physical etc., and
4.   the *environment* of planning -e.g., political, cultural, development etc.

Although planning procedures are more commonly articulated in relation to the level and type of planning, their effectiveness is more often dependent upon the planning methods and techniques employed, and their associated philosophical assumptions. Institutional planning procedures are thus only as good as the means available to them to operate, and are subject to the constraints of their environment. They may be enhanced by addi-

221

tional technological and legislative support, but ultimately the criteria determining the effectiveness of the actions of institutional planning frameworks go well beyond this. This is not to undervalue the importance of legislative support for planning, for it is often a prerequisite for the successful implementation of many institutional procedures. However, legislative support alone cannot ensure the success of institutional planning actions, even though it gives a legitimacy to their enforcement and (in an enlightened context) should be concerned with the obligations and accountability of institutional action.

DEFICIENCIES OF INSTITUTIONAL PLANNING FRAMEWORKS (1)

Characteristics of Institutional Planning Framework

Despite the acceptance of planning in most Third World nations, one of the principal problems in such countries (indeed in some of the industrialised nations also), is the lack of understanding of what is meant by 'planning'. This is confirmed by the fact that in many Third World countries, planning is characterised by the drawing up of shopping lists of projects for implementation, rather than by any process of articulating objectives, and designing efficient and effective means of attaining them.

Another common feature of such countries is the concentration on the organisational structure for projects on the one hand, and national economic plans on the other, with little (if any) interface between the two. The ultimate outcome of this situation is an inconsistency in policy making and project implementation, largely brought about by a difference in priorities at the two levels of decision-making and poor communication between different tiers of government.

As indicated, one of the major purposes of establishing institutional planning frameworks is to resolve conflicts which invariably arise in the course of planning. This requires that resolutions emerge from *within* the planning process, through a process of justification rather than imposition. Whilst every planning framework usually has some mix of both, if the emphasis is on imposition the institutional planning framework is less likely to be effective in the long run. Unfortunately, however, many planning institutions in the Third World resort to imposition measures quite soon after their establishment. As they usually have inadequate resources to enforce such decisions, the result is that their overall effectiveness is very limited as will be seen in the Sao Paulo case study discussed later in this chapter. In part, this problem is associated with the fact that goverments of many Third World countries imitate institution models of planning frameworks of the industrialised world in their institution-building efforts. Such models possess inherent assumptions about the availability of professional and administrative resources which Third World countries do not have. Hence, unrealistic demands are made on the planning framworks of such nations.

The degree of centralised control over institutional planning frameworks is an extremely important and sensitive issue in many Third World countries. This is especially apparent in much of Africa, where large proportions of diverse populations have only a partial alliegance to the nation, state or administrative region in which they reside. Instead, such populations show a greater loyalty to their local, ethnic or tribal group which may or may not be represented in the established planning framework.

In instances where institutional planning frameworks fail to adopt structures which reflect the social, cultural and spatial differences of a country, and where they are more representative of administrative interests, there is a general lack of commitment by the local populations to national development priorities. This in turn, weakens any institutional planning efforts undertaken within such frameworks, and subsequently reduces the capacity to plan change.

Institutional Planning Frameworks for Transport

Translating the preceding institutional planning deficiencies and limitations usually associated with Third World countries into the transport sector of such nations, the over-concern for projects (as against planning) is very apparent. One need only refer to cities such as Mexico City, Lagos, Cairo and Calcutta, where many large-scale transport projects have been constructed outside of (and sometimes contrary to) wider strategic planning considerations of development. In smaller Third World settlements, characteristics of transport 'projectitis' are even more visible. For there, roads are mostly constructed before any urban planning study has been undertaken.

The overemphasis on projects in the transport sector is in part due to the fact that government implementation agencies, such as State Highway Departments and Municipal Engineering Departments, are predominantly staffed by professional engineers, who as an elite are far more influential than professionals in the newly emerging planning fraternity. Furthermore, such agencies often have good direct links with international development agencies such as the World Bank: institutions which themselves usually view 'development' from a project by project perspective.

What is equally important in determining the influence of transport projects over plans, is the fact that construction work such as urban highway and metro projects, are visible to the electorate as symbols of 'progress' epitomising development. The attention such projects attract is very often so great that they distract the public eye from more important development issues. In this way, 'projectitis' generates far more political capital for the government than any planning exercise can.

The relative infancy of institutional planning frameworks for transport in the Third World, coupled with a shortage of expertise, has furthermore created circumstances whereby planning agencies are unable to meet expectations made of them. Their general performance (in comparison with the individual performance of the older, more established government agencies), is seen to be relatively ineffective. As a result, two types of action are often resorted to (sometimes in sequence): either additional institutions are created to expand the capacity to plan for transport, or planning functions are merely re-assigned to existing agencies. The former, however, has the effect of creating more complex and diffused institutional planning frameworks, thus creating conflict rather than integration. Complex over-elaborate planning frameworks for transport are commonly found in (and proposed for) metropolitan areas.

Dissatisfaction with the performance of transport planning institutions can alternatively lead to their disbandment, and to the re-assignment of their planning functions to existing and better established agencies which have longstanding responsibilities in the construction, financial or operational spheres of transport.

In fact, both types of action were ultimately taken in Sao Paulo, as the latter part of the chapter illustrates. It should be said however that 'institutional adding' and 'responsibility re-assigning' are common to metropolitan governments of both the

Third World and industrialised nations. In the transport field, this comes about particularly when a transport co-ordinating agency attempts to impose its planning decisions, or when its decisions are challenged, and it does not have sufficient resources and political support to take *effective* action.

Centralisation of Institutional Planning Frameworks

The degree of government centralisation in general does, of course, greatly determine the powers of planning institutions. In the Third World transport sector for example, since in many countries highways play a major role in forging a national identity out of automonous cultural and ethnic entities, national and state highway agencies have traditionally received widespread backing from central government. This explains the centralised decision-making structure of institutional planning frameworks concerned with the provision of national and regional transport infrastructure.

At the local level, especially in non-metropolitan settlements, central government involvement tends to be much more limited. Not everyone considers this desirable. Some, for example, argue that limited involvement constitutes governmental negligence and aggravates local transport problems in urban and rural areas alike. Others, on the other hand, such as Friedmann (1973), argue that centralised institutional planning responses to local problems are likely to alienate local populations and local government. Furthermore, those who belong to this way of thinking point out that centralised responses are commonly associated with endless delays in adminstration and usually favour capital projects over small ones.

A more decentralised approach to transport planning would however, require greater political and financial autonomy at the local level - particularly for urban areas, where infrastructure costs are much higher. Decentralisation also requires an institutional apparatus for the devolution of decision-making which may be more extensive than is politically acceptable or too much for the administration to cope with. Hence, most Third World countries do not favour a decentralised approach. The reluctance to decentralise the institutional planning framework for transport in part explains another common institutional feature of many Third World governments: namely the widespread leading role given in the transport sector to highway planning agencies of national or state governments. These agencies are typically located in Ministries of Public Works, as in Indonesia and Nigeria, and coexist with much less influential (and often newly established) Ministries of Transport. The institutional responsibilities of the two ministries often become confused where they concern road transport, contributing to unclear spheres of accountability. Furthermore, there is a tendency for such agencies to fail to recognise that transport problems are more than just highway problems. This is particularly apparent in urban areas.

In the urban context, problems of accountability are highlighted in efforts to implement transport plans, since many such plans and their associated programmes are often formulated with little regard to the institutional characteristics of the agencies which ultimately execute the projects. Often, urban transport plans are drawn up with the assistance of central or state government agencies which involve international development agency personnel and foreign consultants. Such personnel have, however, tended to accentuate the mismatch between plans and the capacity to implement plans by employing approaches to transport planning which assume a greater institutional and professional manpower capacity than actually exists at the implementation phase (see Chapter 5).

On the basis of the preceding discussion (also see Banjo and Dimitriou, 1983), the following general conclusions may be arrived at concerning the institutional planning frameworks for urban transport in Third World countries:

1. a tendency for the highway planning profession to have a dominating influence over the urban transport sector, resulting in the transference of its perceptions, planning procedures and techniques, into a sphere concerned with *more than* road transport issues, and more complex considerations of development and urban growth than is usually associated with inter-urban highway planning expertise (see Chapter 2);

2. a situation in which there is centralised control over major urban transport projects, paradoxically creating circumstances in which there is a specific preoccupation with organisational structures for projects on the one hand, and a general concern with national, state and metropolitan institution-building on the other;

3.   the employment of institutional structures which are inap-
      propriate imitations of institutional models in the in-
      dustrialised world;
4.   a situation in which there is a widespread shortage of
      professional and administrative staff, particularly at the
      municipal level, constraining the necessary preparation and
      implementation of urban transport improvements;
5.   an overall lack of clarity in the responsibilities of the dif-
      ferent institutions and agencies concerned with the urban
      transport sector and a subsequent lack of coordination
      among the different levels of government within the institu-
      tional planning framework for transport;
6.   a tendency, in response to performance deficiencies among
      transport planning institutions (particularly of metropolitan
      areas), either to set up new agencies (often with insufficient
      resources and political clout) or to re-assign the planning
      functions of the institutions out of favour to the better-estab-
      lished organisations in the transport sector; and
7.   an ultimate focus on transport projects, rather than trans-
      port plans; a focus which is reinforced by politicians and in-
      ternational lending agencies with vested interests in such
      projects.

INSTITUTIONAL PLANNING FRAMEWORK FOR URBAN TRANSPORT IN BRAZIL

Background

To appreciate determinants of the institutional planning framework in Brazil for the urban transport sector, it is useful first to
trace briefly the evolution of transport policy making and planning
as a whole in the country. In so doing, it will become evident that
whilst a relatively developed and coherent legal and institutional
planning framework has evolved in the inter-urban highway sector, this is not the case in the urban transport sub-sector.

     There are several reasons for this, mostly related to histori-
cal developments in Brazil during the international economic
crisis of the 1930s and immediately after the Second World War,
when opportunities emerged for newly established Brazilian industries to serve both domestic and international markets. These
developments were a reflection of the era, for this post-war period

was marked by a growing tendency of the Brazilian ruling classes to focus upon economic development through industrialisation.

In an effort to achieve greater industrialisation, it was necessary, among other things, to integrate the previous export-orientated economy with its related supporting transport infrastructure, with one directed more toward a wider domestic market. This was particularly necessary as railways had been built to transport primary production goods from the interior to the regional ports. The wide variety of gauges employed and the general deterioration of the system however, began to pose real obstacles to economic development and integration by the mid-1930s (Baer, 1979).

This situation had come about despite early attempts at the end of the nineteenth century to plan the country's transport sector, especially railways and shipping, with the clear objective of enhancing political national integration. This was principally because the strength of the export industrial interests induced railway investments into isolated areas rather than regions which required linking into the national transport network.

Expansion of the Road Sector

Given the unwillingness of the railway companies during the 1930s to invest in additional track and rolling stock in support of the country's first phase of industrialisation, the road sector was turned to in order to meet the new transport needs of the Brazilian economy. The change in reliance on the road sector was supported by the Federal Constitution of 1934, which recorded the necessity of transport plans and federal institutional instruments to bring about the change.

In 1937, the National Roads Department (Departamento Nacional de Estradas de Rodagem - DNER) was created. In 1945, it was reorganised as an autonomous federal government agency and its major functions were to co-ordinate, supervise and control road construction and maintenance, integrating federal, state and local plans within the scope of a national road development plan. DNER was also responsible for the execution of federal programmes and projects in the road sector.

The re-organisation of DNER coincided with the establishment of the National Road Development Fund (Fundo Rodoviario Nacional - FRN) on similar lines to the Highway Trust

Fund of the USA. The FRN was based on 80 per cent of the tax revenues from the sale of petroleum derivates. It was committed to the expansion of interurban highway construction and maintenance throughout Brazil, as well as to the improvement of municipal, feeder and farm-to-market roads. The state level agencies assigned these tasks were the State Roads Departments (Departamentos Estaduais de Estradas de Rodagem - DERs) and for the local roads, the municipalities. The funds made available to these organisations were from the FRN. These were based on a share of 60 per cent transferred to the states and municipalities, while 40 per cent was retained by DNER.

An interesting observation, if one looks back on the federal governments of Brazil since 1946, is that all these administrations, despite their different ideologies, political priorities and social backing, supported and even improved the legal and institutional capacity to plan for road transport initially set up in the 1930s. In fact, the institutional capacity to plan for inter-urban highways in the post-war period was unmatched by other spheres of transport in the country.

By imposing its technical guidelines and procedures upon the State and Municipal agencies, the DNER preserved central government control over the country's road system, particularly in non-urban areas. It did this by defining the scope of projects and plans for these agencies, and making necessary the granting of its approval prior to the execution of road schemes. The later introduction into the private sector of bidding for road construction and maintenance projects by both the DNER and DERs brought a certain amount of decentralised institutional involvement into the highway sector, although federal government control was still dominant. The same agencies also extended their involvement into other areas of road transport, including freight and passenger movement, traffic control and traffic policing.

In 1969, the federal government introduced a Motor Vehicle Ownership Annual Duty (Taxa Rodoviaria Unica - TRU) destined to form a Special Fund Committed to road maintenance and traffic safety facilities (Fundo Especial de Conservacao e Seguranca de Trafego). DNER retained 40 per cent of the revenues and 60 per cent was destined to the states, whereas the allocation to the municipalities was regulated by state laws. Also in 1969, an Inter-urban Road Passenger Transport Tax (Imposto sobre o Transporte de Passageiros - ITP), based upon 5 per cent of the inter-urban tickets, was created with the same objectives. In 1974 this tax was extended to freight transport and the name changed to Road Transport Tax (Imposto sobre o Transporte Rodoviario - ISTR) (see Figure 7.2).

These measures transferred additional earmarked resources to the states and municipalities for road improvement and maintenance. Together with regular and abundant institutional funds from the FRN, and within the institutional planning that had evolved, the federal and state paved highway network in Brazil was increased from 3,000 km in 1950 to 65,000 km in 1975. Freight tonnage transported by road increased from 108 billion tons km in 1950 to 2048 billion tons km in 1975 (Barat, 1978). These figures in freight movement represented 38 per cent of the total freight carried in 1950 and 69 per cent in 1975 - an impressive increase of 31 per cent in the road transport share.

In the long run, the highway funding mechanism and institutional planning framework described above, had three principal redistributive effects on the transport sector of the country. First, it led to funds being raised from petroleum derivates consumption and motor vehicle ownership (which were heavily concentrated in large urban areas) to support long-distance road construction, maintenance and traffic safety facilities throughout the country. Second, the rapidly increasing share of private car ownership in the total vehicle fleet and the lower prices of diesel vis-a-vis gasoline prices, encouraged heavy financial transfers from car users to trucks' and buses' long-distance movements. Third, it enabled funds to be made available for road development in the less developed parts of the country (mainly the northeast) from tax and duty generated in the more affluent parts of Brazil with higher rates of motor car ownership (Darbera and Prud' Homme, 1980).

Despite the taxation of gasoline and the introduction of an annual duty on motor cars, motor vehicle ownership between 1950 and 1980 increased from 360,000 to 11 million (see Table 7.1). This growth was a direct result of the expanding national highway programme and the increased wealth created in certain sections of the post-war Brazilian community. As the country's industrialisation policies and highway investment programmes became increasingly interwoven over the years, a strong block of converging Brazilian interests in motor car manufacturing, petroleum production and road construction industries emerged. These were supported by multinational assembling industries and other commercial interests outside the country. Together, this lobby of interests (supported by a guaranteed income derived from

Figure 7.2: Institutional Resources to Road Development in Brazil, 1976

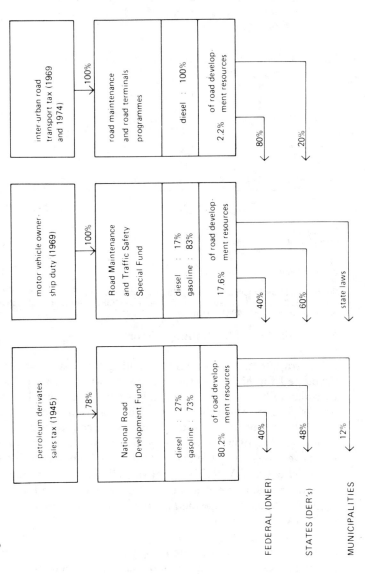

taxation on rising petrol consumption), helped to cement the dominant influence of highway planning agencies in the overall transport sector at all levels of government. This influence was later enhanced by the growth of the Brazilian motorcar industry until the late 1970s.

Table 7.1   Motor vehicle Ownership in Brazil (in Thousands): 1950-1980

	1950	1960	1970	1975	1980
Private cars[1]	195	570	2,324	4,672	8,214
Buses[2]	11	28	51	74	125
Light commercial	14	70	(5)	446	909
Trucks	140	320	454	635	968
Others[3]	(4)	(4)	193	157	883
TOTAL	360	988	3,022	5,984	11,099

(1) Including taxes
(2) including micro-buses
(3) including motorcycles
(4) non-available data
(5) included in private cars

Source: Institute Brasileiro de Geogratia e Estatistica, Anuarios Estatisticos do Brasil 1952 1962, and Ministerio dos Transportes GEIPOT, Anuarios Estatisticos dos Transportes 1976 1981, Rio de Janeiro.

Nationalisation of the Railway Sector

In contrast to the institutional planning framework which was developed for highways, the framework which evolved for the Brazilian railway sector was much less complex. With the exception of four private railway companies operating in Sao Paulo State, all the private railway companies in the country were already nationalised in 1956 and operating their networks independently. In that year was set up the Federal Railways Company (Rede Ferroviaria Federal SA -RFFSA) unifying all the railway systems. In 1972, the remaining private companies were combined to form a single Sao Paulo State owned company (Ferrovias Paulistat SA - FEPASA).

By the time the private railway companies were nationalised, many of them had accumulated heavy financial losses. In order to deal with these losses and simultaneously ensure a tighter control over railway finances, RFFSA was managed from the beginning as a highly centralised agency. The extent of this became apparent when conflicts arose with the National Department of Railways (Departamento Nacional de Estradas de Ferro - DNEF).

The DNEF, established in 1941, had the function of coordinating the railways' policies and of supervising and controlling, in accordance with agreed guidelines, the expansion and operation of the wide range of private (and the few government owned) railway companies that existed before the boom of nationalisations after the Second World War. After the creation of the RFFSA, the existence of the DNEF induced emerging major differences between the two federal organisations, mainly in relation to the elaboration of plans, studies, projects and construction programmes for the railway sector. Since RFFSA was originally conceived as an operational agency (whereas it also later became an important contractor of civil works both for new railway lines and renovated lines) conflicts between the two organisations became particularly intense in the rapidly growing metropolitan areas, and passageways or final destinations of the bulk of freight traffic of the Brazilian railways.

As a highly centralised company, RFFSA did not delegate its decision-making to suburban lines in metropolitan areas, thus increasing the gap between social needs in Sao Paulo (where RFFSA operated two suburban lines), Rio de Janeiro, Belo Horizonte, Porto Alegre and Recife, on the one hand, and the central headquarters priorities (mainly concerned with the rehabilitation of freight traffic), on the other. So, from 1956 till the mid-1970s, an insignificant part of RFFSA resources was destined to improvements in the existing suburban lines. In the Sao Paulo Metropolitan Area, the fact that suburban operations were shared between RFFSA (169 km of lines) and Sorocabana Railway (later FEPASA - 62 km of lines), created additional conflicts so long as there was not a clear definition of roles and lines of accountability in the planning, programming and budgeting aspects of suburban railway improvements between federal and state governments. The overall concern with the operational aspects of the railway sector, rather than with plans for expansion, over time led to the creation of an institutional framework for the railway sector dominated by operational issues - in stark contrast to the institutional support given to the highway sector.

Many, furthermore, argued that the very inflexible nature of railways, together with their high operating costs, made them unsuited to the economic needs of the country when domestic industrial markets had to be unified and consolidated.

233

National Interest in Urban Transport Planning

Up until 1975, urban transport planning was primarily the area of concern of the various municipalities, with federal and state government involvement limited to the funding of specific projects through the DNER and the DERSs. In 1975, however, the federal government of Brazil created an agency with the overall responsibility for the country's urban transport planning and finance decisions. This organisation, the Brazilian Agency for Urban Transportation (Empresa Brasileira de Transportes Urbanos - EBTU) was assigned the task of directing all financial and planning aspects of urban passenger transport for *all* modes of travel.

A national fund was simultaneously set up with the specific purpose of providing financial support for important urban transport projects that had already been started with state or municipal resources. Such projects included the metro schemes for Sao Paulo and Rio de Janeiro. The National Development Fund for Urban Transport (Fundo Nacional de Desenvolvimento dos Transportes Urbanos - FDTU) was mainly financed through an additional levy on petrol consumption, generating funds for use for all forms of urban public transport.

This development took place after a very long period of non-involvement by the federal and state governments in the urban transport sector. For more than 30 years prior to the establishment of EBTU and FDTU, city municipalities of the largest urban areas in particular, faced dramatic increases in the demand for public transport services for Sao Paulo (see Table 7.2). Given their financial situation, however, these municipalities were unable to raise funds to meet these demands. As a result, tramways were discarded, bus operations were taken over by private companies, and informal and illegal public transport services became widespread.

Since there was no mechanism for financing urban public transport with government support at the time, or for co-ordinating the various kinds of public transport that existed, the private bus companies looked to high fares for profits. Moreover, many such operators had the political influence to acquire the rights of operation on the profitable routes. Meanwhile, the few government owned bus companies were obliged to operate the largest share of the non-profit-making routes, thus accentuating their accumulated financial losses.

Table 7.2   Urban Public Transport Patronage in Sao Paulo
Metropolitan Area: 1960, 1970, 1980 and 1990

	1960		1970		1980		1990	
	000's Trips/Day	%	000's Trips/Day	%	000's Trips/Day	%	000's Trips/Day	%
Buses	2,640	52.0	4,808	54.0	7,830	51.4	11,580	47.5
Tramways	438	8.6	0	0	0	0	0	0
Trolley buses	182	3.5	128	1.4	138	0.9	366	1.5
Suburban trains	183	3.6	218	2.4	595	3.9	1,220	5.0
Ferries	—	—	—	—	—	—	—	—
Metro	0	0	0	0	580	3.8	580	3.8
Cars	1,330	26.2	2,984	33.5	5,261	34.5	7,800	32.0
Taxis	255	5.0	670	7.5	610	4.0	1,097	4.5
Others[1]	50	1.0	100	1.1	229	1.5	490	2.0
Public Transport Share of Total Trips	3,443	67.7	5,154	57.9	9,143	60.0	14,996	61.5
Total Trips	5,078	100.0	8,907	100.0	15,243	100.0	24,386	100.0

(1) Bicycle and motorcyles.

Note: Cars and Taxis in 1960 include informal passenger transport of light
commercial vehicles.

Source: Expresa Metropolitana de Transportes, EMTU, 1980 and Barat, J. 1987.

The above conditions prevailed in the nine metropolitan
areas of Brazil in which a total of 435 private bus companies and
seven government owned bus companies operated in 1976 (Darbera and Prud'homme, 1980).   The introduction of EBTU
however, did much to alter this state of affairs. With its access to
FDTU, and its organisational capacity to influence local decision-
making and planning in most major cities of the country, EBTU
forwarded numerous institutional schemes and proposals to improve (among other things) the urban bus services. The organisation was especially active in the implementation of bus lane
schemes and in bus route rationalisation planning. As an important agency within the overall institutional planning framework for
urban transport in Brazil's metropolitan areas and large cities (see
Figure 7.2) EBTU had also become involved in urban development strategy formulation, metro planning and suburban railway
planning.

The railways in major metropolitan areas such as Sao Paulo
and Rio de Janeiro particularly warranted attention, since between 1956 and the mid-1970s, only limited funds were made available by the RFFSA for the improvement of existing suburban lines,
even though these services performed an important role in pas-

235

senger movement for the two cities. Instead, more attention was given to the rejuvenation of rail freight movement, which in the case of Sao Paulo, generated conflicts between freight and suburban traffic and, frequently, between RFFSA and FEPASA's policies.

The resultant gradual transfer of passengers from the railways to suburban bus services in Sao Paulo and Rio de Janeiro added to the financial losses and operational decline of the suburban railway services in both cities. This in turn led to numerous civil disturbances in the 1960s and 1970s which clearly emphasised the critical need for an overall urban transport planning and coordinating agency such as EBTU.

In seeking to erect an overall institutional planning framework for transport and development in Brazilian cities - with EBTU playing a key part - a number of complex legal and institutional problems emerged. Many of these were particularly related to problems of institutional accountability in the urban transport sector between the municipalities and other transport agencies. Other difficulties were associated with the general inadequacy of local institutional and legal support for EBTU's activities. Additional problems arose from insufficient directives being provided from central government to EBTU and other centrally controlled transport agencies to indicate how federal resources should be used in the urban transport sector. There was, in other words, no real set of national policy guidelines to direct action in this field of development.

The most serious problem, however, was the irregular funding support for EBTU, since the organisation received financial contributions from central government sources on a project-to-project basis through specific convenants. This in effect meant that its funding was erratic and its actions were subsequently not as influential as those taken, for example, by the DNER, which had consistent guidance from central government and continuous funding. The implications of this and other institutional shortcomings as they affected the Sao Paulo Metropolitan Area, are discussed in the following section.

SAO PAULO METROPOLITAN AREA CASE STUDY

Urban Development and Transport Provision

In 1872, the city of Sao Paulo had a population of less than 32,000. By the turn of the century, this had increased to 240,000 - primarily due to intensive immigration from Europe. Subsequent waves of immigration prior to the First World War increased the city's inhabitants to 1.3 million by 1940. Further population movements to the city after this date were greatly increased by the country's industrialisation programme which had a considerable impact on Sao Paulo in both a physical and economic sense. For it was in Sao Paulo that a great deal of the nation's industrial plant was (and is still) concentrated.

The industrialisation programme of Brazil was in full swing during the 1950s and 1960s, although it had begun to taper off by the end of the 1970s. The development of the industrial base of the city during this period also attracted many migrants from rural areas, in addition to immigrants who had already settled in the vicinity. The combined effect of these developments, together with the rise in the natural birth rate (see Table 7.3) was to increase the inhabitants of Sao Paulo City from 2.2 million in 1950 to 8.6 million in 1980 (IBGE, 1980).

Table 7.3 Population of City of Sao Paulo:1872-1980

Date	Inhabitants	Annual Growth Rate %
1872	31,385	—
1890	64,934	4.12
1900	239,820	13.96
1920	569,033	4.51
1940	1,318,539	4.20
1950	2,198,500	5.25
1960	3,709,200	5.37
1970	5,978,977	4.89
1980	8,584,898	3.68

Source: Instituto Brasileiro de Geografia e Estatistica, Anuarios Estatisticos do Brasil, 1872–1980.

The urban development and population growth characteristics of the Sao Paulo Metropolitan Area (on occasions referred to here as the SPMA) includes not only the City of Sao Paulo but also 36 other municipalities (see Figure 7.3). Its area coverage is approximately 8,000 sq km (which compares with the City area of approximately 1,500 sq km) and incorporates 51 per cent of the population of the State of Sao Paulo. Estimates of the metropolitan population suggest that it is in the region of 12.7 million (1972-1980), and constitutes one of the fastest growing metropolitan areas in the world. It has been estimated (Echenique, 1980) that its inhabitants in 1985 was 14.5 milliion.

A close examination of the provision of transport infrastructure and public utilities in both the City of Sao Paulo and its environs during the above period of urbanisation, reveals that transport played a major and critical role in the growth of the metropolitan area. This was largely due to limited government intervention in the urban development of Sao Paulo between 1870 and 1930. For during these years, the essential urban services were provided by private companies through concessions given by the municipalities (or the state, as in the case of the railways). The private sector initiatives of providing these services were based upon operational guarantees on the services offered and on the return of invested capital from running the services. The consumers were charged the rates that the market would bear. The role of the municipalities on the other hand, was confined to regulative and development control functions on building and urban development.

In Brazil, as in many Third World countries, private companies providing urban services were constituted and organised by foreign companies from England, France, USA, and Canada. They brought to Brazil financial resources, various new technologies and administrative methods which permitted the absorption of capital goods produced in their countries. Frequently, the interests of these companies were closely connected with those of land development companies. They therefore not only attended to the demands of that time but also induced the development of new districts and suburbs.

In Sao Paulo in particular, much urban development was a direct consequence of the co-ordinated action of such private companies. This was also true in part of Boston, and numerous other North and South American cities of that era. New districts were created along the routes of public utilities and transport ser-

Figure 7.3: Sao Paulo Metropolitan Area and its Municipal Composition and Main Access Routes

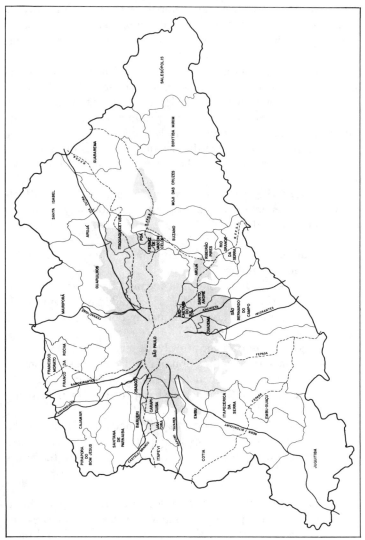

vices, especially suburban railways and urban tranways. An example of this in Sao Paulo, was the integrated provision of public utility and transport services developed by the City Company (in land development, sanitation and water supply) and the Sao Paulo Tramways, Light and Power Company (providing transport, lighting and electrical power services).

Such private sector schemes were feasible because foreign trade up until 1930 permitted the large scale import of goods and services; most of which was equipment associated with urban development projects and industrial products (Barat, 1979). Furthermore, poverty was predominantly a feature of rural Brazilian society, so that by and large the urban inhabitants of Sao Paulo were able to afford the tariffs charged by the public service companies.

Between 1930 and 1940 however, numerous factors affecting the development of Sao Paulo altered considerably. Principal among these were that:

1. urbanisation trends had become not only more rapid but also more complex;
2. the market mechanism as a means of determining tariff levels for the use of public services, failed to provide sufficient revenues to cover adequately both operational and capital costs;
3. the simultaneous monopoly of urban public service provision and the imposition of government restrictions on traffic inreases induced the concessionary companies to neglect new investments and improvements in existing facilities; and
4. the foreign trade crisis of the time made it difficult for the public service companies to import the equipment, spare parts and components they required to operate their services.

The period after 1945 witnessed an increasing trend in government ownership of urban public services through the cancellation of concession contracts to private companies and their transference to public sector agencies which in most cases were public companies specially created by the municipalities, and later in the 1970s (as a result of metropolitanisation) by the state (Suzigan, 1976).

The disruption of the earlier well-established institutional framework for public services in Sao Paulo, dependent upon market mechanisms and the involvement of large foreign companies, was not compensated for however by another institutional system capable of inducing an integrated approach to the growth of the city. As a result, the provision of urban services by government agencies became subordinate to private sector initiatives in land speculation. These initiatives were organised in a coordinated manner in such a way that they exerted considerable pressure on government to provide additional public services.

Whereas in the past, foreign companies providing urban public services attracted financial resources from the stockmarkets of their own countries (where at the time they were considered good investments), public sector agencies set up after the mid-1940s in Sao Paulo could only rely upon government budget allocations and revenues from charges levied. Public sector agencies, as a consequence, soon found themselves financially unable to respond to the increased demands generated by land developers, and to cater for the basic needs of the growing number of underprivileged inhabitants.

Transport Growth Characteristics

In the context of the general disintegration of public services in Sao Paulo after 1940, the suburban railways and urban tramways also became increasingly incapable of keeping pace with the growth of the metropolitan area. They lost passengers (and hence revenue) to bus public transport and to the private motorcar, as their services deteriorated in the face of increased competition from other transport modes. Furthermore, the government had taken the line of least resistance to these developments, thereby encouraging competition between public transport services.

The low cost of petroleum-based products until the mid-1970s placed bus services (of both the formal and informal sectors) at a distinct advantage over the railway and tramway services. The greater flexibility of the buses and the private motorcar in their response to further urban expansion forces, made feasible for private land developers the suburbanisation of enormous new areas. This process of suburbanisation was further fuelled by the growth in the domestic production of motor vehicles from 1956 onwards, and the emergence of an influential middle class during the

1960s and 1970s (the members of which were the main purchasers of these vehicles).

Motorcar ownership in all nine metropolitan areas of Brazil increased substantially during the post-war period, particularly after 1956. The ownership rates of Sao Paulo increased from 25 per cent of all households owning a car in 1968, to 44 per cent in 1975. By 1980, it was forecast that 58 per cent of all households could afford a motorcar (Echenique, 1980). These trends were greatly encouraged by the general rise in households income, estimated to have risen by a rate of 7 per cent in the 1970s, and the general vitality of the economy of Sao Paulo which by then had developed an industrial sector representing 40 per cent of the nation's industrial product and employing 35 per cent of its workforce (Echenique, 1980).

The combined effect of increased population growth, rising incomes, associated urban expansion and increased motorcar ownership in the Sao Paulo Metropolitan Area has produced, over the decades, a formidable travel demand profile. The number of daily trips in the area, for example, rose dramatically from 8.9 million per day in 1970 to an estimated 18.3 million in 1985. On the basis of these estimates, the Sao Paulo Metropolitan Area is faced with the problem of accommodating the largest number of daily trips of all the nine Brazilian metropolitan areas, since these statistics represent 44.3 per cent of the nation's daily metropolitan trips (GEIPOT, 1980).

At the same time as trip-making by all modes of transport in the Sao Paulo Metropolitan Area increased, the proportion of private motorcar trip also increased from 26.2 per cent of the total in 1960 to 34.5 per cent in 1980 (see Table 7.2). This compares with an avarage share of 27 per cent for the other eight metropolitan areas in 1975. What is interesting is that the growing reliance upon the motorcar developed despite the general deterioration of road-user access throughout the area and irrespective of the rise in the average cost of motorcar trips estimated to have increased by 22 per cent (Echenique, 1980). In part, this dependence is a direct consequence of huge investments made in elevated freeways, expressways and parking facilities (see Figure 7.4) financed both by FRN and local resources. These investments principally benefited the car-owning community and also helped to encourage a widespread transfer of reliance upon railways and tramways on the bus and motorcar transport.

Figure 7.4:   Elevated Freeway in Sao Paulo

In spite of the enormous pressures in favour of road construction in the 1960s and early 1970s, and even though government funds were not diverted in support of public transport until 1973 (when EBTU and FDTU were set up), there was widespread traffic congestion in the metropolitan area during this period. Indeed, traffic congestion was so acute that it induced certain important institutional changes in the municipal administration after 1967. These, and many other institutional developments associated with the transport sector of Sao Paulo Metropolitan Area, are discussed in the following section.

Institutional Planning Framework for Metropolitan Transport

The Sao Paulo Metro Company was created in 1968 with a brief to manage the construction of the new metro system and subsequently be responsible for its operation. By 1974, the company, which was funded basically by municipal and state budgetary resources and was ultimately responsible to the Sao Paulo city government, completed the construction of its first designated line (see Figure 7.5). This was 17 km in length with 20 stations and part of a then proposed total network of 42 km.

Figure 7.5: Sao Paulo Metro System: Proposed and Existing Lines

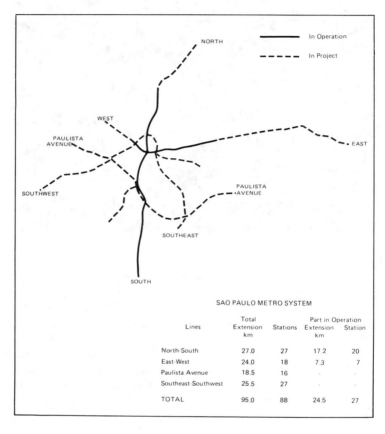

Lines	Total Extension km	Stations	Part in Operation Extension km	Station
North-South	27.0	27	17.2	20
East-West	24.0	18	7.3	7
Paulista Avenue	18.5	16	·	·
Southeast-Southwest	25.5	27	·	·
TOTAL	95.0	88	24.5	27

Among other institutional changes made in the 1970s, measures were introduced to strengthen the Sao Paulo Municipal Public Transport Company (Companhia Municipal de Transportes Coletivos - CMTC) a municipal owned company created in 1946 to operate expropriated tramways, trolley-buses and a minor part to the bus services in Sao Paulo City. The municipal area was divided in 1978 into 23 bus operation areas in order to improve the control on private operators, CMTC being the overall bus operation co-ordinator. In 1974, the Sao Paulo Municipality also set up a Traffic Engineering Authority (Departmento de Sistema Viario - DSV). Its function and responsibilities were to establish the planning guidelines necessary to improve the urban road transport infrastructures, traffic signalling and traffic operation.

Given the predominant use of road-based public transport in Metropolitan Sao Paulo (in 1977, 54 per cent of all daily trips were undertaken by bus and only 8 per cent by rail and metro [GEIPOT, 1980]), and as a result of the increased traffic congestion experienced on the roads (particularly in Sao Paulo City), the City's government through the Municipal Transport Secretariat and its planning and executive agencies (CMTC, DSV and the newly created Traffic Engineering Company [Companhia de Engenharia de Trafego - CET] as an executive body), introduced in 1975 some important measures designed to improve its bus public transport services.

The measures were intended to initiate low-cost operational solutions for the road public transport sector, simultaneously reducing petrol consumption. They were based upon guidelines drawn up by the municipal authorities and were partially supported by funds from federal sources. Among the most significant of these measures were:

1. The integration of bus and metro services - in 1980, 160 bus lines with almost 2,000 buses operating per day were integrated with the first and second metro lines - by means of the overall re-definition of bus routes designed to feed selected metro stations and create integrated fares;

2. the implementation of a pedestrianisation scheme in the central area, accompanied by measures to make better use of existing urban road space and favour the movement of buses (by restricting the use of the private car);

3. the introduction of bus lanes along selected urban corridors;

4. the introduction of bus priority traffic signals and the implementation of bus stop rationalisation schemes along the more congested corridors; and

5. the introduction of trolley-bus priority lanes along selected corridors, intended to provide the city with priority routes for high capacity, road-based public transport utilising Brazilian transport technology.

In addition to the above schemes, the Federal and State Authorities decided in 1975 also to provide financial support to two federally owned (RFFSA) suburban railway lines (Santos-Jundiai e Central do Brasil), and one state owned (FEPASA) line (Sorocabana) operating in Sao Paulo. This was done with a view to conserving fuel in the transport sector. For similar fuel saving reasons, public funds from EBTU and state and municipal budgets were also made available in 1979 for undertaking improvements to the Sao Paulo trolley-bus network and to expand the city's metro system.

The above transport improvements were predominantly restricted to Sao Paulo City, rather than extended to the wider metropolitan area. They were furthermore, primarily a set of separate projects rather than a package of proposals conceived as part of a wider institutional planning response to the transport problems of SPMA. This largely reflected the absence of an adequate institutional framework and the lack of institutional support for a more co-ordinated and comprehensive urban transport planning response for the metropolitan area.

In order to extend to the metropolitan area the transport improvements implemented in Sao Paulo City, important institutional changes were introduced in 1978. In October of that year, the State Government created a Metropolitan Public Transport Agency (Empresa Metropolitana de Transporte Urbanos de Sao Paulo - EMTU/SP). The expertise of the planning units of the Metro Company, the State Traffic Engineering Authorities, the Greater Sao Paulo Planning Agency (EMPLASA) and the 36 municipalities were all integrated into the new agency.

EMTU/SP was funded in part by the State from its Metropolitan Investments Financing Fund (Fundo Metropolitano de Financiamento de Investimentos - FUMEFI) based on budgetary resources of the state and resources transferred from federal sources of the National Development Fund for Urban Transport (Fundo Nacional de Desenvolvimento dos Transportes Urbanos - FDTU). EMTU/SP was assigned the responsibility of harmonising and co-ordinating actions which were otherwise likely to generate conflict among the various federal, state and municipal executive actions on the one hand, and between government and non-government agencies in the transport sector, on the other. Details of the decision making mechanism and conflicts in Sao Paulo Metropolitan Area and of the main federal, state and municipal agencies operating within the transport sector are given in Figure 7.6 and in Table 7.4

The principal projects actively supported by EMTU/SP were:

1. the undertaking of physical and operational improvements to the metropolitan bus and trolley-bus networks along selected major transport corridors - this was conducted with a view to improving the overall frequency of public transport services in specific corridors and to achieving a better integration of the transport modes involved (eliminating conflicts between inter-municipal and municipal bus services which converge on Sao Paulo City);
2. the introduction of strategically located metropolitan transport terminals on the periphery of the metropolitan area - this was introduced to promote further integration of various transport modes;
3. the extension of legal and administrative arrangements, such as fares clearing among operators and integrated tickets - to promote the integration of diesel/trolley-bus, suburban trains/metro and inter-municipal/municipal buses and to provide special assistance to low income public transport users; and
4. the construction of Sao Paulo's second metro line - to respond to the long-run petroleum shortages expected in the country and to influence future directions of urban development.

One of the most important characteristics of the actions of EMTU/SP from the outset, was its institutional capacity to translate certain preferences of the metropolitan community into programmes and projects. This was achieved through a process of permanent consultation and discussion with specific interest groups. For even though the nature of EMTU/SP's involvement and intervention at the implementation level was largely administrative and technical, the metropolitan setting of Sao Paulo provided local communities with a relatively strong political basis for participation in projects through both institutional and informal channels.

However, in July 1980, after two years of difficult negotiations with federal, state and municipal agencies, EMTU/SP was dismantled by the new state government on the basis that the agen-

Figure 7.6: Institutional Planning Framework for Sao Paulo Metropolitan Area Transport Sector: Decision-Making Mechanism and Conflicts in Sao Paulo Metropolitan Area

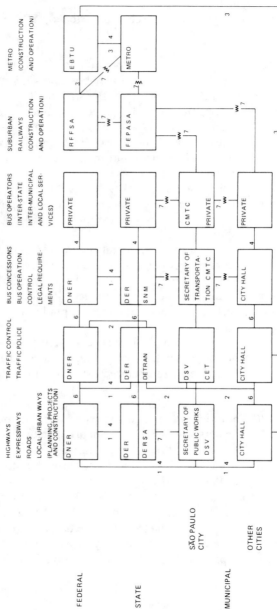

1 - Institutional resources: regular and automatic transfers (National Road Fund, Motor Vehicle Duty and/or Road Transport Tax)
2 - Institutional resources: regular and automatic transfers of a small share of the Motor Vehicle Duty
3 - Institutional resources: irregular and non-automatic transfers (National Urban Transport Fund) defined for specific projects
4 - Institutional co-ordination: technical guidelines and budgeting control
5 - Legal requirements, concessions and operation control
6 - Government level or internal co-ordination of planning and executive actions
7 - Planning and decision-making conflicts

Table 7.4 Main Federal, State and Municipal Transport Organisations Acting in Sao Paulo Metropolitan Area

Acronym	Agency	Agency Functions
DNER	National Highways Department	Inter-state highways and access
DER	State Highways Department	Inter-municipal highways and access
DERSA	State Expressways Company	Expressways construction and toll collection
DETRAN	State Traffic Authority	Urban traffic control and police
DSV	Sao Paulo City Urban Ways Systems Department	Urban traffic control and police
CET	Sao Paulo City Traffic Engineering Company	Traffic engineering
SNM	Secretary of Metropolitan Affairs	Inter-municipal bus control in the metropolitan area
CMTC	Sao Paulo City Bus Company	Bus and trolley-bus operation and municipal bus concessions and control
RFFSA	Federal Railways Company	Two suburban lines operation
FEPASA	State Railways Company	One suburban line operation
EBTU	Federal Urban Transportation Agency	Financial support to specific projects
METRO	State Metro Company	Two metro lines operation

cy was a source of conflict and tension among the different levels of decision makers and sectoral executive bodies involved. It was felt that planning was not the best mechanism to solve these conflicts and tensions. This was clearly a political decision of an administration not concerned with planning and socially oriented solutions. It was a decision taken despite the important and useful role EMTU/SP played in the co-ordination and implementation of transport programmes and projects for the metropolitan area of Sao Paulo. The breakup of EMTU/SP left the most significant metropolitan area of Brazil without an effective institutional planning framework within which to resolve conflicts among the many transport agencies. These circumstances arose, in spite of the complex institutional framework for transport that had by then evolved for the Sao Paulo Metropolitan Area, because of insufficient political support for the institutional structure that had been erected.

These circumstances in part may be accounted for by the withdrawal of federal government support for a planned response to the metropolitan transport problems of Sao Paulo. Instead the federal government funded isolated projects outside any co-ordinated effort. The fact that there was no federal legislation obliging states to create EMTU transport planning agencies for all major urban areas, or to oblige states to define the long run financial mechanisms for transferring resources to the urban transport sector (as there was for the highway sector) together weakened the very existence of EMTU/SP.

The main challenge to EMTU/SP that ultimately led to its being dismantled was the organisation's involvement in the task of formulating a detailed overall investment budget for transport project implementation in the Sao Paulo Metropolitan Area. In this exercise, resources were allocated to different institutions involved in the metropolitan transport sector, with the intention of achieving a greater degree of integration in both long-term and medium-term planning. Unfortunately, however, the assignment of resources to the various institutions met with strong opposition from municipal agencies (such as CMTC and the Transport Sectretariat) and state sectoral agencies (such as FEPASA and METRO) which wanted to maintain their independence and separate influence in the provision of transport infrastructure and facilities. Many of these agencies wanted to keep their direct channels of communication with the federal government so as to have a greater say in the resources they should ultimately receive. They could not exert such influence or maintain their power with a powerful EMTU/SP.

In addition, there are other reasons for the early demise of EMTU/SP. Important among these were the considerable delays associated with the organisation in its decision-making when compared to other agencies in the roads, communications and energy sectors, where strong alliances between the state and private sector bureaucracies were already consolidated before the establishment of EMTU/SP. Furthermore, particular concern about the status and activities of EMTU/SP was expressed when central government began to object to the organisation's efforts at introducing more democratic and representative channels of communication with local communities. Instead, the federal government attempted to impose upon the organisation (and its links with these communities) a greater degree of institutional control, thought by many to be insensitive to local grass-roots issues in the transport field.

Municipal authorities, particularly those within the City, were also pressured by the state to accept transport projects which very often did not address the real local tansport needs of the urban poor. These needs became an important concern of the 37 municipalities of SPMA. However, its mayors did not possess the technical and financial resources with which to translate any proposal they had into effective action. With the dismantling of EMTU/SP, an opportunity for the municipalities to utilise an umbrella organisation as a means of taking co-ordinated action to tackle local transport problems on a metropolitan-wide basis was taken away from the mayors almost overnight.

These developments took place despite the growth of organised community groups throughout the metropolitan area (mainly sponsored by Catholic and neighbourhood organisations) which challenged traditional government decision-making, particularly with regard to resource allocation, of public funds in the transport sector. A good example of such a group was the so-called 'Bus Movements', a pressure group organised by suburban communities in 1973 to fight for improved bus services (Telles and Bava, 1981).

The demise of EMTU/SP also took place against a backcloth of problems in the relationship between EMTU/SP and the public transport bureaucracies. The hierarchies of these public transport agencies felt threatened by the new cadre of professional engineers and planners within EMTU/SP and reacted to their efforts by presenting obstacles to the implementation of projects and programmes sponsored by the organisation. The new cadre of professionals within EMTU/SP, in turn were not able to establish a strong alliance with private sector interests in industry, such as those associated with civil engineering works, rolling stock etc. This was in direct contrast with public transport agencies which had a long-standing relationship with such interests. Furthermore, EMTU/SP's involvement in the metro, suburban railway and trolley-bus programmes were hampered by frequent hesitations of federal and state government to provide EMTU/SP with the necessary support.

The combined effect of all these limitations reduced the credibility of the organisation to a point where it was politically too vulnerable and liable to the dismantling it was ultimately subject to. On this basis, it must be concluded that the viability of a metropolitan-wide transport agency for Sao Paulo ultimately relies upon its ability to arrive at compromises among all levels of government (federal, state and municipal), and with all types of agencies involved in the transport sector. It, furthermore, requires an institutional ability to adapt its administrative and financial resources to changing circumstances; particularly as they relate to revisions in government decision-making and resource alloction for transport improvements for the public at large and the urban poor in particular.

LESSONS FROM THE SAO PAULO EXPERIENCE

Institutional Resources and Metropolitan Transport Goals

The general lessons of institution-building for the transport sector of Sao Paulo Metropolitan Area, and of the short-lived EMTU/SP in particular, show how the mere existence of a relatively sophisticated institutional planning framework for urban transport does not in itself guarantee the adoption of policies to be shared by all the agencies within this institutional framework. The lessons instead suggest that the goals and policies of transport planning in such contexts are more likely to reflect the distribution of political and financial powers among the agencies (especially those of the federal and state highway authorities), rather than any wider set of interests or perceptions.

The effort in Sao Paulo to launch an agency responsible for all aspects of metropolitan transport has, most importantly, emphasised that any conversion from a project-by-project approach to a more comprehensive and integrated one, requires more than a sophisticated institutional planning framework. It requires political commitment from all levels of government (particularly from federal government) and sufficient funding to translate this commitment into transport programmes and projects. The absence of such support, as witnessed in the case of EMTU/SP, creates merely a semblance of a wider and more influential institutional approach to metropolitan transport planning than in reality exists.

For a metropolitan transport agency to survive, therefore, the ultimate conclusion must be that its institutional framework must reflect the likely compromises it has to make with different levels of government on the one hand, and with various kinds of public and private sector agencies involved in metropolitan transport on the other. Furthermore, it may be concluded that an influential factor determining the consistency of direction of institutions with metropolitan-wide responsibilities such as EMTU/SP, has most of all to do with the political and funding support it can muster from *both* federal government and local community sources.

The lack of any effective and long-standing co-ordination among the many agencies and organisations concerned with metropolitan transport in Sao Paulo, considerably weakened any real possibility of the emergence of grass-roots responses to urban transport problems. This in turn also prevented the development of more innovative approaches. This was particularly so, since the lack of co-ordination permitted the more influential federal and state government agencies to impose their measures on local metropolitan communities in a manner which did not meet the inhabitants' travel needs. This centralised approach to urban transport planning injected a strong central government bias into the implementation of projects (Friedmann, 1973). The bias however, is not immediately recognisable, for much of the evaluation and presentation of such transport projects is wrapped in seemingly objective and standardised technical procedures which in fact are void of any real local representation or involvement. Moreover, the efforts made to introduce social welfare policies into the transport sector of metropolitan Sao Paulo were diluted by inter-group bargaining of the parties involved. Disagreements over which social welfare policies to adopt and the means of achieving them, ultimately reduced the potency of the measures.

Finally, the lack of any truly co-ordinated action also prevented the systematic use of transport infrastructure development as a powerful instrument of employment promotion and as an effective stimulus to industry. This, in turn, limited the effectiveness of projecting Brazil's national and regional transport policies into Sao Paulo's metropolitan and municipal levels of decision making.

Whatever the nature of the compromises arrived at within a particular institutional planning framework for urban transport, there is a crucial need to co-ordinate those actions agreed. The co-ordination of institutional efforts and resources in a mutually reinforcing manner thus remains an important task that *must* be undertaken by some kind of agency with overall responsibility, if a metropolitan-wide approach to transport planning is to be effective. The absence of such an umbrella organisation both creates and perpetuates conflicts in the actions being taken by the various agencies within the transport sector itself and with other sectors.

Despite the demise of EMTU/SP, therefore, a general lesson of the Sao Paulo experience is that the functions of such an organisation are important if a real desire exists to plan and co-ordinate transport provision. Alternatively, the functions should be distributed among various existing organisations, in which case a new institutional planning framework for transport emerges, which may or may not take into account the failing of the previous arrangement.

The experiences of the Sao Paulo Metropolitan Area also point to a number of more specific lessons that may be of value to other Third World cities. The most important of these can be noted as follows:

1. Project-orientated criteria alone should not be permitted to dominate decision-making at the planning phase of transport provision - the use of such criteria in excess leads to the unco-ordinated commitment of resources.

2. Urban transport plans and programmes should not contain a commitment to proposals beyond the implementation capacity and resource availability of the institutions involved - such a mismatch leads to insufficiently funded programmes and unimplemented plans.

3. Central government efforts which tend to alienate local government agencies and local community participation

should be checked if there is a genuine desire to arrive at a more sensitive approach to tackling local transport issues - failure to do this prevent the emergence of approaches from the grass-roots.

4. Planning and implementation agencies within the urban transport sector should not operate separately but have their functions integrated within the institutional planning framework - the failure to achieve this merely perpetuates the current detrimental dichotomy between planning and implementation.

5. Fields of agency responsibility and accountability within the urban transport sector should be clearly defined as ambiquities in assigned responsibilities merely contribute to inter-agency conflict and delayed decision making.

6. The prevailing conventional concern for physical and operational considerations of transport infrastructure provision to the exclusion of almost all other aspects should be modified - welfare and local community considerations of urban transport must also be incorporated if the development benefits of transport investments are to be maximsed.

NOTE

(1) For this part of the chapter, the author has, among other sources, extensively drawn upon a paper written by Banjo and Dimitriou entitled 'Institutional Planning Frameworks for Transport in Third World Cities' (1983).

REFERENCES

Baer, W. (1970) **The Brazilian Economy: Its Growth and Development**, Grid Publishing Inc., Columbus, Ohio.

Banjo, G.A. and Dimitriou, H.T. (1983) 'Institutional Planning Frameworks for Transport in Third World Cities', Unpublished Proceedings of 1982 Special Programme on Urban Traffic and Transport Planning in Developing Countries, Development Planning Unit, University College, London.

Barat, J. (1978) **A Evolucao dos Transportes do Brazil**, IBGE/IPEA, Rio de Janeiro.

____(1979) **Introducao aos Problemas Urbanos Brasileiros,** Campus, Rio de Janeiro.

____ (1987) Energia e Transportes, Estud do Caso da Regiao Metropolitana de Sao Paulo, Sao Paulo.

Darbera, R. and Prud'Homme, R. (1980) **Le Role des Transports Urbains dans le Development Economique du Brasil: Moteur ou Frein?** Institute d' Urbanisme de Paris, Paris.

Echenique, M. (1980) Sistran: **Transport Study of Sao Paulo Metropolitan Area,** NATO Advanced Research Institute on Systems Analysis in Urban Policy-Making and Planning, Brussels.

Friedmann, J. (1973) **Retracking America: A Theory of Transactive Planning,** Anchor Press, New York.

GEIPOT, (1980) **Instituto Brasileiro de Georgafia e Estatistica** Empresa Brasileira de Planejamento de Transportes, Anurio Estatistico Dos Transportes, Brazil.

(IBGE), (1980) Instituto Brasileiro de Geografia e Estatistica, Auvario Estatistico do Brasil, Rio de Janeiro.

Suzigan, W. (1976) 'As Empresas de Governo e o Papel do Estado na Economia Brasileira', **Aspectos da Participabao do Governo no Economia,** F. Rezende and W. Suzigan (eds), IPEA/INPES, Rio de Janeiro.

Telles, V.S. and Bavas, S.C. (1981) O Movimento dos Omnibus: Aspectos de um Movimento Reinvidicatorio de Periferia, **Espaco e Debates,** vol. 1, no. 1, Sao Paulo.

Chapter 8

Developments in Urban Transport Planning: Their Relevance to Third World Practice

Marvin L. Manheim

INTRODUCTION

Transport planning activities have been undertaken in many countries at urban, regional and national levels in relation to both passenger and freight movement. Since formal planning methods using large-scale models were developed in the mid-1950s in the USA and Western Europe these methods and procedures have also been applied to many Third World cities. As already discussed elsewhere in this book (in particular, see Chapter 5), much criticism has been levelled at such practice in the different environments of the Third World.

The main purpose of this chapter (1) is to discuss relatively recent developments in urban transport planning methodology and computer technology which offer substantial promise of overcoming some of the criticisms. In particular, these developments are seen as providing opportunities for undertaking transport analysis more responsive to the needs of specific situations and problems than hitherto possible.

The remainder of this chapter contains brief comments on the aim of transport analysis and of the impact of recent developments in computer technology on the range of transport analysis choices. This is then followed by an outline of disaggregate demand theory, with an illustration of its use to predict travel demand along a bus route. The chapter concludes with a discussion of how these developments allow a more innovative approach to urban transport analysis and of the challenge this poses to the transport planning profession.

ROLE OF TRANSPORT ANALYSIS

Transport planners work on different types of problems in many different circumstances, from the classical situation of producing a long-range 'comprehensive' transport plan for an urban area, to improving the design of a specific road junction. In these contrasting situations, the approach adopted by the transport planner needs to fulfil certain basic criteria. They need to be:

1. **Problem-centred.** The analysis should be tailored to the specific issues which are of concern to a particular situation;
2. **Resource-effective.** Resources (time, finance, manpower, skills, etc) have to be used in appropriate balance between the requirements of the particular problem and resources available for all the transport analysis.
3. **Result-oriented.** An analysis should be designed to produce results useful to decision makers within the time frames required for it to influence decision making; it should also provide insights into the questions at hand.
4. **Amplification of Analyst's Judgements.** Past transport planning styles have implicitly assumed that the computer-based analysis produced an objective appraisal, that the analyst operated as a neutral professional, and that there was little or no professional judgement involved in the analysis. By contrast, today's analytical style should clearly accept the need for substantial individual professional judgement on many points and should support the making of informed judgements on these elements.

In seeking to fulfil these conditions, the transport planner will have to draw upon a wide variety of skills. Some of these skills might be called those of 'the public entrepreneur' meaning the ability to interact effectively with *various* organisations and individuals in order to bring about the necessary coalition of forces to initiate or carry through some transport system change (Bradley and Casebeer, 1980; and Manheim, 1980). Other useful skills are those of the 'analyst', such as the ability to develop alternative courses of action, anticipate their consequences and present the major choices to those responsible for making a decision in terms relevant to their frames of reference. In general, the skills of both the 'entrepreneur' and the 'analyst' will be required to tackle effectively the wide variety of problems and resource constraints that transport professionals confront.

Transport planners, especially those with a background in engineering or influenced by its traditions, are usually of the opinion that there is one 'best' methodology for addressing urban transport problems. The importance of uniformity, both in methodology and its application, is probably a consequence of the role that engineers perceive as theirs in society (see Chapter 2): the role of conducting a relatively rational, objective and value-neutral technical analysis of a problem in order to provide information useful to its resolution.

With the widespread availability of computers, this problem-solving philosophy was the impetus for the development and common application of a standardised computer software package designed to analyse transport systems' problems. The use of these packages, as indicated in Chapter 5, has become so widely institutionalised that many a transport planner is thought of as an individual with expertise in running this standard battery of computer programs. This is an inadequate perception which results in a 'pre-packaged' type of analysis in which, often, more time is devoted to methodological problems than to substantive transport issues. The justification of this kind of analysis is now much weakened by recent theoretical and methodological developments in transport system analysis and advances in computer technology. Together, these developments are believed to have greatly increased the analytical approaches available to the transport planner and thus improve the profession's ability to satisfy the criteria outlined earlier.

These developments are of particular importance for Third World countries, in that, by making possible a style of analysis requiring less data and fewer resource inputs (see Chapter 9), two of the major constraints on undertaking meaningful transport analysis are removed. Moreover, such an analysis can more readily be tailored to a specific problem and appropriate effort devoted to the examination of transport issues and the assessment of alternative policy proposals.

RANGE OF URBAN TRANSPORT ANALYSIS CHOICES

Impact of Developments in Computer Technology

Until relatively recently, the range of analysis environments available to the transport professional was limited to those shown on the upper part of Figure 8.1. In that situation, once the data handling needs of an analysis moved beyond that of the slide rule or simple pocket calculator, the only recourse was to use a large mainframe computer, the cost of which renders it relatively inaccessible, especially in most Third World countries.

However, recent advances in computer technology have led first to the advent of the programmable calculator and more recently to the development of a range of micro and mini computers with analytical capabilities falling between those of the simple pocket calculator and the large mainframe computer. This 'filling out' of the middle ground of the analysis environment spectrum (see Figure 8.1) has now made it technically possible to choose an environment and analytical approach appropriate to the needs of a particular problem; moreover, these new environments are much more accessible than their forerunners through their portability and relative cheapness.

The technological innovations primarily responsible for these new middle-range analytical tools are the *miniaturisation* of components, the elimination of the need for controlled environments for housing, the large machines and the reduced costs due to mass production. In particular, the development of the microprocessor chip, of the magnetic read/write head which can read (input) or write (output) programs or data onto or from magnetic cards, and of the optical wand (which can read bar coded information by passing the wand over the information) have made possible the handling of quantities of data and the execution of complex programs by highly portable programmable calculators. Important in impact for the user of microcomputers have been the development of the ability to read (write) large data sets and program from (onto) either magnetic cassette tapes or 'floppy' or 'hard' disks, of sophisticated software including operating systems and user-oriented programs, and of especially compact and versatile desk-top and portable micro computers.

For example, a methodology employing the optical wand technique, OPSCAN (Optical Scanning) has been employed in Libya to undertake a home interview survey (Shembesh and

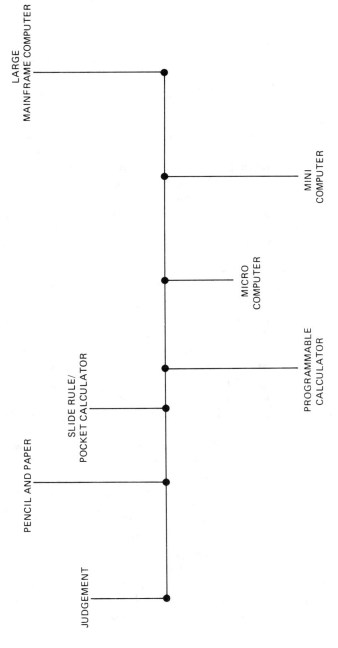

Figure 8.1: Spectrum of Analysis Environments

JUDGEMENT

PENCIL AND PAPER

SLIDE RULE/
POCKET CALCULATOR

PROGRAMMABLE
CALCULATOR

MICRO
COMPUTER

MINI
COMPUTER

LARGE
MAINFRAME COMPUTER

Brown, 1979). Magnetic cassette tapes on the other hand, can now be used as the medium for both the collection and analysis of traffic count data; the information is recorded on-site directly into the cassette and decoded and analysed in the office simply by inserting the cassette into a microcomputer with a decoding machine attached. These two are typical examples of the way in which recent advances in computer technology can be used to simplify and significantly reduce the cost of the collection and analysis in urban transport planning.

Standard pocket calculators have since their inception relied only on manual input of data and programs (in the sense of step- by-step calculations). This is a time-consuming and error-prone process. The advent of the magnetic read/write head described earlier has led to advanced professionally-oriented calculators with special pre-programmed functions, some of which allow the user to write his own programs. Particularly powerful are the user-oriented features of some of these calculators. For example, a program consisting of a sequence of operations can be executed by pressing just one key. The same program can be run a number of times, for different data inputs, simply by changing the data and pressing the one key again. Thus the user does not have to be a programmer.

Beyond the obvious advantage of working with a program entered only once, at least two more advantages are noteworthy. First, it is simple to operate, a program can be executed repeatedly by non-technical staff with virtually no training. Second, the probability of errors is reduced when fewer manual inputs are required. These are highly desirable attributes in a Third World context.

Programming pocket calculators is quite straightforward. No familiarity with computer language is required. Typically the manual provided with a calculator includes a self-tutorial section on programming which can be learned in a matter of hours and mastered within a few days. Further, as indicated above, programs can be used by transport analysts who are not familiar with programming through the provision of a library of programs which include detailed user instructions, such as in the form of structured worksheets (Manheim et al, 1978). Programming desk- top calculators varies by type and brand. Some use simple, direct programming as in the pocket calculators. Others use a simple language (BASIC) or higher-level computer languages.

Most manufacturers support their products with libraries of programs in printed form which can be input manually by the user. Some programs are permanently packaged in the pre-programmed memory modules which are inserted into the calculator and accessed directly or as sub-programs of the user's program. A large number of other programs are available. Other forms of disseminating programs are on pre-recorded magnetic cards or in printed bar codes to be read with an optical wand.

Using a microcomputer does not necessarily require learning a programming language. For example, spread sheet programs such as the pioneering Visicale or its many imitators enable a planner to develop useful models quickly. When more sophisticated programs are required, other systems can provide them, such as UMTR'S DODOTRANS II or its successor AE-I (Manheim, 1983). If programming is required, almost all microcomputers have BASIC, an easy-to-learn language; many have other high-level languages such as PASCAL, FORTRAN, COBOL, etc.

The emerging development of portable and 'briefcase' microcomputers offers especially great potential. By 1983, it was already possible to obtain for a few thousand dollars a complete portable microcomputer the size and weight of a full briefcase.

Taken together, the above developments in computer technology have greatly improved the transport planner's ability to collect and analyse data. Most importantly for the Third World, it has brought within their technical and economic resources computational tools capable of handling large data sets and serious calculation requirements. The scope this provides them with for transport analysis is further increased when consideration is given to the converging impact of parallel developments in the theory and methods of travel demand analysis.

Impact of Theoretical and Methodological Developments

The modern theory of transport systems analysis (Manheim, 1966b; Wohl and Martin, 1967; and Manheim, 1979) provides a useful starting point for discussing recent developments in travel theory related to disaggregate demand modelling. The central ideas of this theory are summarised in Figure 8.2.

In this theory, the core of the analysis of transport problems is hypothesised as the prediction of traffic flows, which requires

263

Figure 8.2: Theory of Transport Systems Analysis

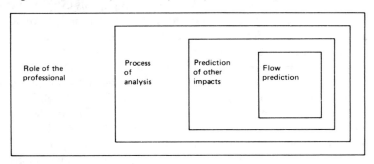

Source: Manhiem, M.L. 1979

finding the balance between the supply of, and demand for, transport services. Additional elements of prediction include activity changes (e.g., land use changes), and resources consumed. The prediction of the effects of travel demand is only one component of the overall process of technical analysis, which involves search (developing alternative actions), evaluation and choice, as well as goal formulation and revision, data collection and analysis, and the development of predictive models (also see Chapters 5 and 6). The role of the professional, as discussed earlier, includes the balancing of entrepreneurial and community involvement activities with the elements of technical analysis in an overall strategy (Manheim, 1979).

One of the major constraints on the application of the theoretical structure has hitherto been the absence from the transport planner's armoury of expertise of operational approaches with causal and behavioural validity and flexibility. The development and successful testing of such a disaggregate demand modelling approach, constitutes one of the hallmarks of recent achievements of the transport planning profession.

A key issue in assessing the effects of any transport system or policy change is to predict how consumers will respond to the proposed change. Such prediction is undertaken with demand models which represent consumer behaviour. One particularly powerful class of such models is called 'disaggregate' demand models, because the models predict the behaviour of individual travellers, households, or transporters of freight. Such models are expressed in probabilistic form, for example:

> probability of traveller in choosing the private car over public transport = function of travel times and costs for both

A particular form of these models is 'multinominal logit,' (the specific mathematical forms are discussed elsewhere; see for example, Manheim 1979 or Ben-Akiva et al, 1976). Such disaggregate demand models have been developed for predicting many aspects of traveller behaviour: mode choice, access mode choice, car ownership by type, residential location, destination choice, etc. Many behaviourally-relevant variables have been used in these models (see for example Table 8.1).

Conventional modelling uses aggregate approaches to produce generation, distribution and modal split relationships as part of the demand function. These require large quantities of data and result in some losses of behavioural validity. The advantages of disaggregate models include: explicit inclusion of relevant policy and behavioural variables, consistency with theory of consumer behaviour, efficient use of small samples of data, and flexible approaches to aggregation. The disadvantages include: the additional statistical knowledge required, the need for quality data in the small sample used, the shift in thought processes required of planners, and the need to address explicitly the issue of aggregation (which is treated only implicitly in conventional aggregate aproaches). The aggregation issue is not so much a problem as it is an opportunity, as we will see below. Once the parameters of a disaggregate model have been obtained (by statistical estimations), the model can be used for forecasting by predicting these to get an overall forecast (e.g., expected mode shares of public transport and private car usage). There are a number of techniques for providing aggregate forecasts with a disaggregate model, as shown in Figure 8.3. (Koppelman, 1976). These are discussed below.

In many respects, disaggregate models seem especially appropriate for use in Third World countries. Data collection resources can be focused on getting a relatively small number of quality observations of present travel behaviour. The significant differences in travel behaviour among different social, economic, and cultural groups can also be modelled explicitly and examined

Developments in Urban Transport Planning

Table 8.1 Illustrative List of Explanatory Variables Included in Disaggregate Travel Demand Models

Socio-economic Variables

1. vehicle ownership (can also be internally predicted)
2. household income
3. license driver status
4. number of licensed drivers in the household
5. primary vs. secondary worker
6. number of full time workers in the household
7. number of adults (and children) in the household
8. type of residence
9   occupation (used to define market segments in the vehicle ownership model)
10. sex
11. education level

Land Use and Locational Variables

12. distance
13. CBD work place
14. employer type
15. total employment
16. retail employment
17. manufacturing employment
18. gross employment density
19. net employment density
20. retail employment density
21. % vacant land
22. population
23. net population density

Level-of-Service Variables

24. in-vehicle travel time
25. out-of-vehicle travel time
26. total door-to-door travel time
27. out of pocket travel cost (fare for public transport, operating costs, tolls and parking costs for car)
28. comfort
29. convenience
30. safety

Adapted from Ben-Akiva, M.E. et al 1976

266

Figure 8.3: Aggregation Techniques

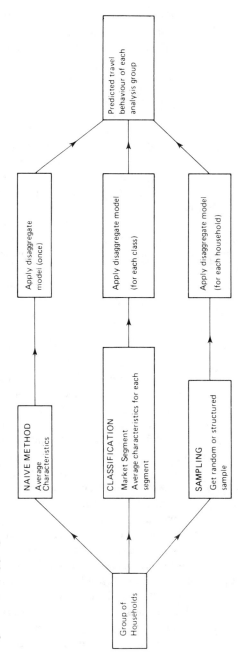

in forecasting as conducted. Particularly important, combined with the new computational environments, disaggregate models provide an especially powerful range of choices of analysis methods.

Techniques for Producing Aggregate Predictions

In the *naive* approach, average characteristics of all the individuals in the population are utilised. For example, average incomes, car ownerships, differences between private and public transport travel times and costs, etc., and other characteristics can be used with a disaggregate mode choice model to obtain average modal split shares in an area. In this respect, it should be noted that the use of simple elasticities is equivalent to aggregation with the naive method; in reality, the elasticity is different for each household in the population, and using a single elasticity for an area is equivalent to averaging in some implicit way the whole population.

A second approach is *classifications*, in which the population of a region is divided into groups, or 'market segments' and the average characteristics of each market segment are used together with the disaggregate models to predict the behaviours of each segment. This is exemplified by the typical practice of classifying travellers by the number of cars owned (and perhaps income) and then using the averages of household size and other socioeconomic characteristics and transport service attributes (such as average access time) for each geographic area or traffic zone. These average characteristics are used as inputs to the disaggregate demand model for a prediction of modal split (or trip destinations, frequencies, etc.) for each market segment and zone.

A third major approach to aggregation is *sampling*, in which a sample of, say, households is taken. The disaggregate model is then used to predict the choices (e.g., travel mode choice) for each household in the sample. The modal share for the population as a whole is the percentage of the sample choosing each travel mode, while the modal volumes are the shares expanded by the ratio of the sample size to the relevant population size. The sample can be derived from a survey (such as a household survey used for model estimation) or it can be synthesised. For example, from knowing the probability distributions over socio-economic characteristics of the population of a study area, Monte Carlo sampling from this distribution can be performed to obtain a sample of any desired size and statistical relationship to the underlying distributions. With this approach, however, the accuracy and validity of subsequent results depend on the extent to which the probability distributions utilised reflect the true multi-dimensional distribution of the population characteristics.

These three are the most important alternative approaches to aggregation. Each is in fact a family of approaches, hence various combinations of approaches can be used.

As indicated above, the conventional urban transport modelling approach of dividing a study area into geographic zones and grouping households into classes by various socio-economic and locational characteristics is (implicitly) a particular form of aggregation by classification. Disaggregate models can be applied in the same way, when it is desirable to relate the analysis specifically to the transport network in the form of, say, the traffic carried by each travel mode (Ruiter and Ben-Akiva, 1977). Alternatively, classification can be used in other ways, and other aggregation methods can be used, alone or in combination with classification.

Estimating the Model

Model estimation is primarily concerned with defining the parameters that should enter into a model and determining the values of its constants and coefficients. For example, it may be hypothesised that the probability of a traveller choosing to make a particular journey by public transport depends on the relative difference in cost, time, comfort and convenience between public transport and private transport. The model (equation) explaining this relationship could take the form as shown below:

$$(8.1)$$

probability of choosing
public transport $(\text{Prob.}_{P.T.}) = a + bC + cT + dV$

where: C, T, and V are the differences between public and private transport in travel cost, in-vehicle travel time, and out-of-vehicle travel time (including walking, waiting, etc.); b, c, and d are their respective coefficients and a is a constant. Much more general expressions, including many variables such as those in Table 8.1, are used in practice. An exponential model is also often used in practice as is the multinomial logit, rather than the single linear model (see Manheim, 1979; and Ruiter and Ben-Akiva, 1976).

The task in model estimation is to determine the values of a, b, c, and d, so that, for given values of c, T, and V, representing existing or future proposed conditions, the appropriate probability of choosing public transport can be found.

An additional aspect of model estimation is that of defining the number of parameters that should be specified to achieve good predictive accuracy. For instance, in the above example, the statistical test of significance may indicate that the transport convenience parameter could be omitted from the model without significantly decreasing its predictive accuracy.

Typically, complete estimation of a model involves formulating a number of alternative sets of variables and statistically estimating the values of the parameters for each model formulation. Specification of model variables is an important part of model formulation and estimation because it can lead to significant savings in the data collection and analysis tasks. For example, by conducting a pilot survey with quite a detailed questionnaire, it is possible to determine which responses are actually pertinent to the issue at hand by specifying and testing for significance a different combination of parameters in an appropriate model form. Those questions related to parameters that are found not to contribute noticeably to the accuracy of a tested model form can then be excluded from the main survey. In this way, unnecessary data collection and analysis is avoided.

The disaggregate modelling approach to travel demand analysis is quite suited to the above type of model specification approach, since it can yield useful results with small data sets. There are a number of ways in which a model can be estimated (i.e., determine the values of a, b, c, and d in an equation such as 8.1 above). A number of options are given as an illustration below:

1. **Econometric Estimation.** Using reasoning from prior theory and empirical evidence to suggest model specifications, employing a good data set, and utilising the best standards of statistical practice to estimate most likely parameter values consistent with available data.

2. **Transfer with Updating.** Taking models and model parameters that were developed by 'best practice' at another location and/or another point in time and applying them to a new situtation, using data on the new situation to test the

quality of the transfer and to adjust the models in some systematic way to the new context (Atherton and Ben-Akiva, 1976). For example, in one city, equation 8.1 above may have been found to display good predictive accuracy when it had the following parameter values:

$$(8.2)$$
$$prob._{P.T.} = 0.95 - 2.3C - 0.5T - 3.30V$$

The basic form of this equation may initially be assumed to be still valid in a second city and the appropriate values of C, T, and V used to obtain the probability of public transport being chosen. In doing this, however, it may be found that the model underpredicts the number of people choosing public transport. This reflects the differences in social and economic characteristics of the two cities. A correction is made by adjusting the constant a (0.95 in the example), so that the model duplicates existing observed public transport usage. The relative values of the level-of-service coefficient b, c, and d, are kept at the values originally estimated (see Atherton, 1978 and Ben-Akiva 1976; Salomon, 1978).

3. **Comparison with Partial Observation.** Developing a model by making judgements about model parameters and comparing model outputs with observed data. For example, coding of the transport network is often accomplished by making judgements about transport link characteristics, coding these parameters into a network and then computing travel times over minimum paths, and comparing these with a small sample of actual travel times along some selected links. Continuing the above examples, estimates of parameters a, b, c, and/or d might be made based on judgement and then the resulting forecasted volumes compared with whatever limited data is available on existing transit usage.

4. **Judgement and Transfer of Experience.** Development of a model by making judgements about variables, model form and key relationships, based upon theory and experience from other situations or other points in time. For example, using values of elasticities derived from other locations, or using volume-travel time functions estimated elsewhere without any checks on the ground in the present situation.

In each of the above examples, existing theory, prior experience, and judgements play some part. The major differences are in the extent to which data from the situation being modelled are used and how systematic and powerful the techniques employed have proven to be.

No single model estimation approach is the most appropriate in every situation. While econometric estimation may be the ideal in many situations, the transport analyst will often face situations in which time, data, and other resource limitations require that other forms be used. Moreover, there are instances where an econometric model can be built only at the cost of having little time or other resources left for working on the substantive transport problem. Therefore, choices of model estimation styles are always present.

Traditionally, greatest attention has been given to the systematic estimation or calibration of demand models (whether traditional aggregate trip generation models, modal split models, etc. or the newer disaggregate models), with progressively less attention being given to models of changes in traffic generating activities (e.g., land use), transport service factors (e.g., volume-travel time functions), available resources, and balance between travel demand and supply (e.g., network assignment procedures). Serious questions could be raised (as they indeed are in Chapter 5) about the relative balance of effort among these various components, and whether the resulting systems of models are sufficiently 'balanced' with respect to their degree of validity in representing the real world.

APPLYING SOME RECENT DEVELOPMENTS

The preceding discussions have provided an indication of the character of relatively recent developments in theory and methods of transport analysis, and the way in which advances in computer technology have made their exploitation easier. The result is that there is now a wide range of choice as to how to approach a transport analysis. Each approach has advantages and disadvantages; each differs in time, data, personnel and other resource requirements: and each has different degrees of precision and validity in particular situations.

The aim of this part of the chapter is to illustrate briefly how some of the developments outlined above can and have been put into practice. One survey of simplified methods oriented to short-range transport policies (Cambridge Systematics, Inc, 1979) identified twenty or more such methods for examining travel demand, facility performance and related environmental impacts. Case studies examined included investigation of the impact of:

1. reserving expressway lanes for buses and multi-occupancy cars;
2. car restraint measures;
3. bus priority strategies;
4. busway networks;
5. expressway ramp measures; and
6. area-wide analysis of traffic engineering and transport measures.

For the purpose of this chapter, examples of applications to be presented include: the prediction of passenger volume changes over a bus route, calculator methods of travel demand analysis, and the use of mixed continuous-discrete transport models. These are all applications which, in their own specific ways, are particularly relevant to transport analysis in the Third World. Additional applications, especially using micro computers and focusing on performance models, are discussed elsewhere (Manheim, 1983).

Example 1: Predicting Changes in Passenger Volumes Along a Bus Route

Consider the example of predicting changes in the number of passengers over a bus route. Some of the choices now open to the transport planner are as follows (note that the first two are at the two extremes of detail and complexity):

1. **Traditional Urban Transport Network and Zone-oriented Analysis**. An approach representing, as indicated above, classification (implicit or explicit) by geographic location, traffic zones, and one or more socio-economic categories (such as car ownership).
2. **Aggregate Elasticity**. Use of a single elasticity of travel demand, for example that of travel cost or time for the population as a whole. Knowing the present number of

travellers choosing say, each mode, the difference in mode volumes for a given change is estimated using the elasticities and the proposed service change (for example, price or time increase). This is called a 'pivot-point' approach (Manheim, 1979) because the elasticity is used to 'pivot' around the existing volume.

3. **Classification with Elasticities.** Estimating the population in each of several market segments (e.g., income groups) and using the average socio-economic characteristics for each in the transport demand model, calculating the different elasticities for each segment and then using these elasticities to estimate changes in passenger volumes by the pivot-point approach as above.

4. **Incremental Demand Model.** Certain forms of transport demand models lend themselves to ready use for calculation of change in passenger volumes corresponding to proposed changes in transport service attributes. For example, with the incremental form of the logit model, new passenger volumes can be calculated knowing only the base volumes, the magnitude of the change (for example, travel time decrease), and the corresponding coefficient of the demand model (the coefficient of time is the utility function). The incremental model can be used in a naive approach to estimate the change in passenger volume over the bus route as a whole (Manheim, 1979).

5. **Incremental Model with Socio-economic Classification.** For a more precise estimate, the population can be divided into market segments and the incremental model applied separately to each market segment, the total change being the sum of the segment changes. This produces a better estimate than the naive approach, only if socio-economic variables enter into the incremental form being used (for example when the coefficient of price is a function of household income).

6. **Incremental Model with Geographic Classification.** Another obvious approach is to divide the bus route by origin-destination zones or by groups of stops, and apply the incremental model for each origin-destination pair (i.e., combine 5 and 6 above).

7. **Sample Enumeration with Incremental or Synthetic Models.** Using an appropriate sample of households drawn from a previous survey, the appropriate disaggregate model

is used to predict behaviours of each household in response to changes proposed. The prediction is expanded to the population as a whole on the basis of the sample and population sizes. The model can be used directly to predict (for example) transport mode choice probablities (i.e., *synthetic prediction*) or in incremental form (*incremental prediction*). The sample size can range from a few households in a corridor to several hundreds city-wide.

8.   **Sampling with Classification.** The corridor population can be classified into market segments by socio-economic or geographic characteristics or both. Households are then sampled within each cell of classification; alternatively cells of the classification can be sampled, or both. (Manheim, et al, 1978, vol. II).

9.   Sampling with a Synthetic Sample. Similar to (8) above except that the sample is synthesised. For example, given a probability distribution over the population income for the area as a whole, and the mean income for each census area or zone, a distribution for each area can be determined which gives the mean for that area. A sample of N households can then be drawn from the income distributions for each area, for a sample of M areas. This disaggregate model is subsequently applied to the sample of (MN) households, and the resulting predictions expanded to the corridor as a whole (Salomon, 1978).

10.   **Structured Sampling.** A stratified sample can be constructed, using a classification as a sampling frame. 'Structured' includes cases where there is no random sample within each cell. For example, one method that has been used (Kocur et al, 1977) was to classify origin-destination zones by their characteristics and then to take a sample of origin-destination zone pairs from each group. Within each zone, households were classified by socio-economic category (car ownership) and by access to public transport within walking distance only of feeder services, or beyond walking distance of any public transport service. Then mode choice changes were predicted for each cell in the sample - about six origin-destination pairs, three access conditions and three socio-economic groups; in total, 54 trip types.

The above methods of predicting changes in passenger volumes along a bus route are a few of the many possible combinations of ways in which disaggregate models can be used to assess changes in travel demand.

Example 2: Pocket Calculator Methods or Travel Demand Analysis

A number of travel prediction procedures have been developed for use with programmable pocket calculators (Manheim, et al, 1978). In developing such procedures, the capabilities and limitations of the programmable pocket calculators have been important stimuli to the development of analytical methods which exploit both the computational environments and the developments in analysis methods described in the preceding sections.

A key feature of the approaches adopted in designing the various procedures has been the emphasis on user-oriented design. For example, user-oriented worksheets have been designed to be employed in conjunction with many of the programs. These worksheets assume the user does not know how to program the calculator, and so lead the user step by step through the stages involved in entering the necessary data and executing the computational routines (see Figure 8.4).

Some programs deal with the performance of the transport system. These include the computation of travel time on a link (considering acceleration, deceleration and congestion), computation of intersection delays using Webster's model and a combination of these programs which can simulate movements of a bus along a line. The programmable calculator's ability to deal with procedures for balancing transport supply and demand is limited. A single link equilibrium model has been implemented. However a more practical use is to examine issues related to the environment (e.g., air pollution emissions) and energy consumption.

A number of programs for pocket calculators are designed to enhance the analyst's capabilities for operating in environments with very limited data. Research findings suggest that, for difficult situations such as the analysis of a single bus route, a major problem is to obtain data on the characteristics of the riders of the line or of the population in the area being served (Lerman and Manski, 1978).

Several programs have been developed which, given boarding and alighting counts along a public transport route, can draw inferences about the stop-to-stop origin and destination matrix. A

Figure 8.4: Calculator Method – Intersection Delay Calculation Example

Step	Procedure	Enter	Press
1.	Read Cards		push cards through read slot
2. a.			XEQ ALPHA INTN ALPHA
b.	Enter intersection characteristics:		
	(1) Vehicle capacity per lane at saturation flow (vpm/lane) (30)	q_{CL} = _30_	STO 04
	(2) Signal cycle length (min.)	c = _1.17_	STO 05
	(3) Fraction of cycle length which is effective green time	λ = _0.60_	STO 06
	(4) Total vehicular volume (vpm)	q_T = _25.2_	STO 07
	(5) Number of lanes in direction of flow	n = _2_	STO 08
3. a.	Compute delay:		USER B
b.	Read average delay per vehicle from display: Delay = _0.1744 min_		
4.	To vary any elements, repeat only necessary parts of Step 2, followed by Step 3.		

Source: Manheim, M.L. et al 1978

* To enter the default value it is sufficient to press only E in USER mode.

USER WORKSHEET – Intersection Delay Calculations – (HPHIC Programmable Calculator)

Notes: All units are in minutes, or vehicles per minute (vpm)

second group of programs is designed to generate two, three or four dimensional cross-classifications of households from the limited published socio-economic data, using the technique of iterative proportional fit. Given marginal distributions of such characteristics as income, household size, car ownership, etc, the procedure can be used to derive a joint distribution over the several relevant dimensions. Once derived, the resulting classification of households can be used as a whole, or sampled to produce an aggregate forecast.

A third type of program generates a synthetic sample of households from published census (or district) data of interest and, using assumptions about the marginal and joint distributions of the sampled population, generates a sample of households by Monte Carlo methods. Such approaches are particularly useful for capturing (in a probabilistic sense) the variations in characteristics from area to area within the corridor served by a bus route (only a sample of households from a sample of streets would be used for prediction). Again, the sample would be used for producing an aggregate prediction as described previously.

These programs are immediately useful in a Third World context of resource and data deficiencies, since all were designed to be used by transport professionals without the ability to program pocket calculators themselves. However, given the simplicity of programming, it is indicative of a style of analysis which can be adjusted by individual analysts to their own needs. In many cases, the user of a specific program would want to adapt the procedure to the specifics of his problem situation and perhaps develop new programs.

Example 3: Mixed Continuous-Discrete Models

Most transport planning methods are based on a discrete representation of urban space and its transport system by the division of the former into zones and the representation of the transport facilities as links (the conventional urban transport modelling approach). The performance of the transport system can be expressed through link-specific performance functions (e.g., speed-flow relationships). One of the advantages of this approach is that it permits detailed representation of a number of transport policies dealing with the network by means of changes in transport link characteristics and performance functions. However, for many planning contexts, the use of these discrete network models is inefficient or unresponsive because of their high level of detail and high costs in time and resources for preparation and analysis. Moreover, they require access to a large standard mainframe computer and this makes them highly inappropriate for many Third World countries (see Chapters 5 and 9).

An alternative class of approaches needing only a programmable calculator or microcomputer is based on continuous models employing continuous functions for the representation of origins, destinations and transport facilities over the urban space. One of the advantages of using continuous functions is that the data requirements and the required storage space of the computational equipment are reduced. Also, in continuous models the power of integral calculus can be used to derive closed-form solutions and thus to reduce the computational effort. However, it should be noted that continuous models, by their very nature, may lack the necessary details required for some important types of analysis.

In practice in Third World cities, the policies to be analysed are often focused primarily on a particular sub-area of urban space and on a portion of the urban transport network (see Chapters 10 and 11). In these cases, a suitable methodological analysis can use a mixture of continuous and discrete approaches. A detailed, discrete representation of the transport system and the urban space elements is used for those areas where the policies are to be applied, while the rest of the urban area and transport system is modelled by a continuous representation (Litinas and Ben-Akiva, 1980). Important features of this methodology are: the use of joint destination and mode choice disaggregate models, consideration of choice-set constraints, and the use of both analytical and sampling techniques for aggregate demand prediction.

Simple versions of the methodology and features mentioned above have been incorporated into programs for pocket calculators and used to examine public transport policies. A more complete methodology has also been developed, including, in addition to the above mentioned features:

1. representation of the transport system by a mixture of speed and link-specific performance functions; and
2. a combined balancing of travel demand and transport system performance in the network and the continuous travel spaces.

Full implementation of all the features of the above methodology is likely to require a desk-top micro computer. Once implemented however, it should prove to be a powerful tool for transport analysis.

The use of continuous models is another way in which disaggregated travel demand models can be used. This methodology is flexible and policy-sensitive, and is potentially very useful in the Third World where severe limitations on data and computational capabilities often exist.

CHALLENGE AND TRAINING REQUIREMENTS OF RESPONSIVE ANALYSIS

Responsive analysis methods, though relatively new, have now been applied in a number of countries; they are no longer research ideas but practical tools. Applying these approaches however, presents a challenge to the transport planning professional - especially with regard to how to develop a repertoire of methods and models appropriate to different problem situations. In particular, it requires the development of a new perspective on the appropriate roles of models and a willingness to accept the subjective nature of analyses.

For the above challenge to be successfully met, there is clearly a need to train transport planning professionals for their new role. The remainder of this chapter is given over to outlining some points on how this challenge may be met.

The Challenge

The preceding sections illustrated a variety of ways in which a specific analytical approach can be designed for a particular situation involving: choice of computational environment, choice of travel forecasting procedure including (if disaggregate models are used) the choice of estimation styles and aggregation techniques, as well as many other elements of an analysis. In deciding on the appropriate technique however, it is important to resolve the question of how best to go about doing a responsive analysis.

Analysis is not an end in itself, it is a means by which the transport planning professional can potentially increase his/her ability to contribute effectively to the decision-making process. Therefore, analysis must be context-specific. To enable transport analysts to operate effectively and to be truly responsive, a rich variety of theories, methodologies and specific analytical approaches is essential.

Clearly today there is already a substantial variety of choices available. Some transport planning professionals may feel uncomfortable with this; once the notion of a single standard of professional practice is intimately abandoned one must confront the difficult problem of how to design and implement an analysis strategy which facilitates the effective operation of the transport planner in the dual roles of analyst and entrepreneur (see Figure 8.5).

Many subsidiary questions must be answered in resolving this problem:

1.   What models and methodologies are potentially applicable in particular circumstances?

2.   Which models are sufficiently promising that they should be given careful consideration?

3.   What can the role of technical analysis be in the overall process of reaching a decision on selecting a course of transport planning action (if any) - what should be the role of technical analysis, and what should be the role of the analyst?

4.   What are the roles of predictive transport models - do they relate closely to an objective assessment of reality or are they basically intended to reflect the analyst's judgements?

5.   Are models essentially devices to force consistency on judgements, and provide some degree of rationality for decisions?

6.   How can (or should) outputs of transport models be used - as if they were accurate, or as if they were reasonable approximations of reality proving useful in gaining subjective insights into problems?

7.   How should the consequences of alternative judgements, assumptions, and/or data be examined - what emphasis should be placed on developing and examining internally-consistent scenarios of exogenous events as opposed to the systematic use of formal models?

8.   What criteria should the transport planning professional consider in designing an analytical method and in choosing among alternative analysis strategies?

These are some of the questions that must be thought through in order to undertake a responsive analysis. Clearly, technical analysis - and analysts - can and should have some role. The challenge is in determining this role in a particular context. Recent developments in travel theory and computation technology can increase the flexibility with which the transport planning profession can respond to this challenge. It also however makes the responsibility more difficult to fulfil.

Figure 8.5: Responsive Transport Analysis

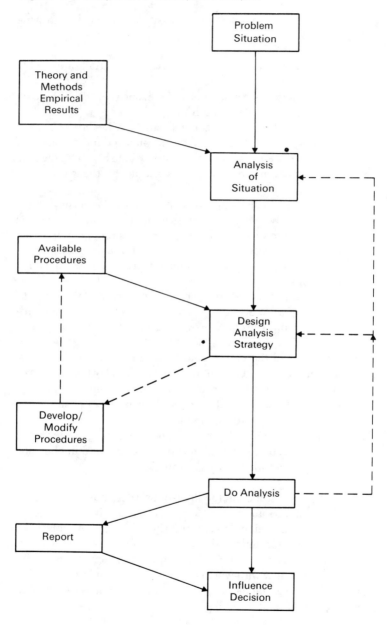

The challenge in undertaking responsive transport analysis can be seen as two-fold: that of conducting a responsive analysis in a particular context (as suggested by Figure 8.5) and that of developing the information needed to undertake such responsive analysis. It requires consideration of the range of analytical techniques that should be developed and of the research and/or transport system development tasks that need to be undertaken.

Perhaps the most important factor to emerge from the preceding discussions is the need for flexibility. The availablity of a very wide spectrum of computational approaches provides an opportunity for substantial experimentation in designing different approaches to transport analyses for different contexts. To exploit this opportunity, it is necessary to provide alternative analytical styles within each particular type of computational approaches, and to provide the same style in several alternative environments. Care should be taken not to develop analytical tools which constrain the analyst to a single mode of thought like the pre-packaged approaches. Innovation should be through more than just computation capabilities, it needs also to be through a much more flexible, responsive style of analysis that has been used in the past.

Clearly, there is a need for much more research and experimentation in the development and use of alternative technical methods. Just as necessary however, is open criticism of the uses of different strategies, since there are many different ways of developing a potentially useful analysis. Different professionals may legitimately reach different conclusions as to what is the most relevant and reasonable analysis strategy in a particular context (Manheim et al, 1980).

The Training Task

The training requirements for responsive transport analysis at first glance may appear to be quite formidable in the Third World, especially given the limited cadre of its trained transport professionals. However, training needs (see Chapters 2 and 6) should be analysed quite carefully before reaching such a conclusion.

The first training need is for specialised skills. There are clearly specialised skill areas of transport planning which require a significant degree of formal training. For example, for statistical skills for knowledgeable formulation and estimation of models, computer programming skills for making significant changes to computer programs (although microcomputer programming is very accessible to most professionals), urban planning, and perhaps some other areas.

The second training need lies in the more specific aspects of transport planning practice. This concerns the ability to use a variety of analytical tools for a variety of policy situations, which obviously requires training. However, in some ways the simpler transport models and simpler computational approaches may be significantly easier to master than the traditional urban transport modelling approach. In the latter, what was learned was how to run specific batteries of computer programs, and the substantive issues were so far removed from the analytical tasks that the educational content and motivation were weak. Responsive transport analysis methods on the other hand, can be effectively taught in a much more learn-by-doing style, with practical applications to immediate on-going issues and problems. Responsive transport analysis methods are easier to learn because the concepts underlying them are more readily understood and therefore easier to accept. The behavioural foundation of disaggregate travel demand models makes them appealing, whilst practical experience in their application can be provided to a large number of staff at relatively low computational cost. Their portability and access to computing tools (such as programmable pocket calculators and microcomputers) allow professionals to explore and experiment with analytical approaches at their own pace; and in private, without loss of status or embarrassment. Particularly promising are possible tutorial programmed or computer-assisted instruction modes for self-paced and guided instruction.

The biggest challenge, however, is likely to be the re-education of transport planners who were educated to believe that the conventional urban transport modelling and planning tools are the desirable approaches. In the limited application of responsive transport analysis to date, the unfortunate finding is that experienced planners are often reluctant to deal explicitly with simplified analyses, limited data, and to rely heavily on professional judgement.

Clearly, the whole transport planning and analytical style that is being argued for is one requiring flexibility and thoughtfulness. It would therefore, be highly inconsistent to take the position that none of the previously developed transport planning tools or techniques should be used in future. On the contrary, it is possible to conceive of large computer urban transport models (with improved behavioural structures) still playing a role, being representative of one end-point of the spectrum of approaches. There still will be analyses and situations calling for long-range, comprehensive area-wide studies with detailed networks and large-scale data collection exercises. What is important to recognise is that the large-computer urban transport models will be only one among many possible styles of transport analysis, and will probably not be the dominant one, especially in the Third World.

NOTE

(1) Special acknowledgements are due to Sergio Gonzales, Nicholas Litnas and Ian Solomon whose publication written with the author entitled 'New Conceptual Environments: Opportunities for More Relevant Transportation Analysis' (1980), provided the basis for this chapter.

REFERENCES

Atherton, T.J. and Ben-Akiva, M. (1976) 'Transferability and Updating of Disaggregate Demand Models', **Transportation Research Record**, no. 610, Transportation Research Board, Washington DC.

Ben-Akiva, M.E. (1977) 'Aggregate Forecasting with Disaggregate Travel Demand Models Using Normally Available Data', **Proceedings of World Conference on Transport Research**, April, Rotterdam.

Ben-Akiva, M.E., Lerman, S.R. and Manheim, M.L. (1976) 'Disaggregate Models: An Overview of Some Recent Research Results and Practical Applications', **PTRC Summer Annual Meeting**, University of Warwick, PTRC Education and Research Services Ltd., London.

Binder, R.H. (1973) 'Major Issues in Travel Demand Forecasting'. in Brand and Manheim (eds) (1973).

Bouchard, R.J. (1973) 'Relevance of Planning Techniques to Decision-Making', in Brand and Manheim (eds) (1973).

Bradley, R.H. and Casebeer, E.M. (1980) 'A New Role for Transportation System Managers', **Proceedings of World Conference on Transport Research**, April, London.

Brand, D. and Manheim, M. L., (ed) (1973) Urban Travel Demand Forecasting, **Transportation Research Board**, Special Report, no. 143, TRB Washington DC.

Cambridge Systematics (1979) 'Sketch Planning Methods for Short-Range Transportation and Air Quality Planning', vol. 1, Analysis Methods; vol. II, Case Studies, Office of Transportation and Land Use Policy, US, Environmental Protection Agency, Washington DC.

Kocur, G.A., Rushfeldt, T. and Millican, R. (1977) 'A Sketch Planning Model for Transit System Analysis and Design', Paper presented to Transportation Research Board, Washington, DC.

Koppelman, F.S. (1976) 'Guidelines for Aggregate Travel Prediction Using Disaggregate Choice Models, **Transportation Research Record**, no. 610, Transportation Research Board, Washington DC.

Lerman, S.R. and Manski, C.F. (1978) 'Sample Design for Discrete Choice Analysis and Travel Behaviour: The State-of-the-Art', **Transportation Research,** vol. I, no. 13A, Pergamon Press, Elmsford, New York.

Litinas, N. and Ben-Akiva, M. (1980) 'Simplified Transport Policy Analysis with Disaggregate Choice Models', **Proceedings of the International Conference on Research and Applications of Disaggregate Travel Demand Models,** July, University of Leeds.

Manheim, M.L. (1966a) **Hierarchical Structure: A Model of Planning and Design Processes**, MIT Press, Cambridge, Massachusetts.

_____ (1966b). 'Principles of Transportation System Analysis', **Highway Research Record**, no. 293, Transportation Research Board, Washington, DC.

_____ (1979) **Fundamentals of Transportation Systems Analysis**, (vol. I), MIT Press, Cambridge, Massachusetts.

_____ (1980). 'What do we Want from Travel Demand Analyses?' in **Transport and Public Policy Planning**, edited by Bannister, D. and Hall, P., Mansell, London.

_____ (1983) 'Microcomputer Applications in Transportation: A Strategy for Improving Organisational Effectiveness', **Proceedings of Third World Conference in Transportation Research**, Hamburg, Germany, April 1983.

Manheim, M.L. et al (1972) 'Community and Environmental Values in Transportation Planning: Summary of Findings and Recommendations to the State of California', Research Report, nos. 72-2, TCV Project, Urban Systems Laboratory, Massachusetts Institute of Technology, Cambridge, Massachusetts.

Manheim, M.L., Furth, P. and Salomon, I. (1978) 'Responsive Transportation Analysis: Pocket Calculator Methods', vol. I "Introduction to calculator methods"; vol. II, "Examples of transportation analyses using pocket calculators"; vol. III, "Program Library", Part 1 - Using calculator programs, Part II - Technical documentation; Working papers prepared by the Responsive Analysis Methods Project (RAMP), Center for Transportation Studies, Massachusetts Institute of Technology, Cambridge, Massaschusetts.

Manheim, M.L., Gonzalez, S., Litinas, N. and Salomon I. (1980) 'New Computational Environments: Opportunities for More Relevant Transportation Analyses', **Proceedings of PTRC Summer Annual Meeting,** University of Warwick, PTRC Education and Research Service Ltd., London.

Moore, G.T., (ed) (1970) **Emerging Methods of Environmental Design,** MIT Press, Cambridge, Massachusetts.

Ruiter, E.R. and Ben-Akiva, M.E. (1977) 'A System of Disaggregate Travel Demand Models: Structure, Component Models and Application Procedures', Paper presented to Transportation Research Board, Washington, DC.

Salomon, I. (1978) 'Application of Simplified Analysis Methods: A Case Study of Boston's Southeast Expressway Carpool and Bus Lane', Responsive Analysis Methods Project (RAMP), vol. IV, **Working paper CTS** RAMP 79-1, Massachusetts Institute of Technology, Cambridge, Massachusetts.

Shembesh, A. and Brown P.J.B. (1979) 'Data Collection in Developing Countries: Problems and Pitfalls of Survey and Management', **Proceedings of PTRC Summer Annual Meeting,** University of Warwick, PTRC Education and Research Services Ltd., London.

Simon, H.A. (1969) **The Sciences of the Artificial,** MIT Press, Cambridge, Massachusetts.

Wohl, M. and Martin, B.V. (1967) 'Traffic Systems Analysis for Engineers and Planners.' McGraw-Hill, New York.

Chapter 9

Urban Traffic Modelling with Limited Data

Luis G. Willumsen

INTRODUCTION

A model is a simplified representation of selected aspects of reality which are of interest to decision makers. In this sense, model development and use are fairly common activities. We use conceptual or mental models (perceptions) to understand, interpret and modify reality in our daily life. Mental models are the most frequently used type and a prerequisite for the existence and use of mathematical models run on a computer. For example, we use maps (iconic models) to plan journeys in an unfamiliar city. As we get to know the city and its transport system better we develop an improved mental map (model) which facilitates more precise and efficient journey planning.

An essential feature of modelling activities is the frame of reference or viewpoint employed. A model is a simplified representation of an aspect of reality from a *particular point of view*. A model highlights certain aspects of reality and leaves aside others. What is included is partly determined by the problem in hand and partly by the subjective preferences of the modeller.

One of the most important advances in modelling has been in the development and use of models in which the main features of an area of interest are represented by mathematical equations. These models have proved to be quite powerful in many subject areas and appear particularly attractive when dealing with problems of high complexity over which only limited control is possible. Transport problems usually have these characteristics and for the last three decades there has been a continuous effort in the industrialised world to produce better mathematical models to assist rational and effective transport planning.

The main stream of this effort has resulted in modelling techniques of increased complexity, data requirements and cost. Considerable resources have been spent by central and local government in industrialised countries in carrying out studies based on large scale models. In recent years, several of these exercises have been undertaken (often by foreign consultants) in Third World countries. In many instances the results, in both settings, have been disappointing - see for example Atkins, (1977) and chapters 2, 5, and 8 of this book.

The most relevant criticisms of conventional transport modelling exercises are the following:

1. A large amount of expensive to collect data is required. Although some relatively recent (disaggregate) models use data more efficiently than older ones, they are still 'data intensive' and more often than not, these data have little alternative use.

2. Despite the great advances in computer power, conventional transport models seem to be insatiable. The computational and processing effort involved in running them are such that only few alternative plans or policies can be tested.

3. Large scale models tend to be problem specific. Some suites of programs have become popular in the industrialised world because most of their cities share common problems. But there is also a reason of convenience for this common usage as argued in Chapter 5. In many cases, models have been chosen before identifying the major issues to be tackled or the policy options to be assessed.

4. There are serious doubts about the theoretical basis of most transport models. Disaggregate models have been developed in order to represent travel behaviour better (and use data more efficiently) but even these have been criticised as lacking a sound theoretical basis, see for example Heggie (1978) and Supernak (1983).

5. The dominant modelling and planning style requires a considerable administrative overhead and assumes that society has a wide margin for absorbing resource losses or improving solutions to unanticipated problems falling outside the (technical) 'system'.

Anticipating some of the arguments presented below, two additional problems are particularly relevant to the use of conventional models in Third World countries:

6. Conventional transport modelling requires considerable resources, some of which are scarce in most Third World countries. In particular, these models require highly qualified professionals and often expensive computing facilities, the opportunity cost of which is very high. If these services are provided by foreign consultants it is often the case that few of the indigenous staff will be able to use the models once the consultants have left. Furthermore, if the best local professionals are allocated to the modelling effort, other planning functions will be weakened and internal inefficiencies in planning agencies will be created, in particular in the implementation of plans.

7. Conventional transport models do not lend themselves for regular use in revising, updating and monitoring plans. They are based upon the assumption that the future will not be *too* different from the past. This assumption is particularly inappropriate in Third World countries where high rates of growth and change are to be expected (see Chapters 1 and 2), but cannot be forecast with confidence.

The remaining part of this chapter will provide some guidelines for more appropriate modelling techniques in Third World countries, beginning with a section discussing the trade-off between model sophistication and data availability; this suggests that simpler models may be better suited to conditions where data is scarce and unreliable. This section is followed by one in which possibilities for model simplification are discussed and a few model types offering promise in the transport field are characterised. The fourth section describes in greater detail the case of network models based on available data and in particular traffic counts. Finally, the chapter closes with a consideration of the use of simplified models in the context of continuous transport planning.

ERRORS AND COMPLEXITY IN MODELLING

In considering the major transport problems faced by Third World countries, it is very tempting to try to use 'the most advanced and sophisticated tools and models' available. This has been an underlying theme in some of the large scale modelling exercises undertaken by foreign consultants. However, use of these refined techniques may not always be appropriate. Indeed some of the problems faced in transferring advanced 'hard' technology to the Third World also point in this direction: technology, manpower and organisation must be tuned to the needs of the client country.

The aim in this section is to review the problem of choosing the most *accurate* model for certain problems under two sets of considerations, namely: model complexity and data errors. The discussion loosely follows the lines put forward by Alonso (1968).

The accuracy of any model may be seen as depending on two broad types of error: specification and data errors. *Specification errors* are generated because the model is not a completely faithful representation of reality. This is usually reflected in a wide use of simplified and not too realistic assumptions or in the use of short-cut methods or approximations. Because the reality to be modelled is complex, one would expect a better model representation also to be more complex.

In general terms, models are improved by including new variables, sub-dividing existing ones, including new relationships or linking models together. It is also possible, in principle at least, to produce a better model by starting from better assumptions, but this will usually require some of the actions above, resulting in a more complex model. For example, a trip generation model may be improved by allowing different trip rates for different household types. This is certainly better than assuming that all households are very similar in respect of the generation of trips. The finer the household classification scheme the more realistic the model is likely to be. However, a large number of household types increases the data collection and processing effort, and complicates the forecasting process. An estimation of trips in the future requires an estimation of the number of households of each type in each zone for the planning year. This is more difficult and less reliable than simply estimating total households per zone.

A reduction in specification errors then normally requires an increase in the complexity of the model in order for it to gain in realism. This complexity can loosely be 'measured' in terms of the number of variables and relationships included in the model and the sequence of calculations for solving it. Increasing complexity can be expected to lead to greater data, technical and other resource requirements, i.e., greater modelling cost.

On the other hand, *data errors* occur as part of the process of assigning values to key variables in the model. For example, sampling, coding and data transcription errors will occur during any data collection exercise to obtain values for population, employment, income distribution, trip generation rates and so forth. Even larger errors will become associated with the values given to these variables for some future planning horizon (say ten years ahead) because of the greater uncertainty attached to them. Moreover, certain parameters in a model are assigned values through a calibration (estimation) process. Not all calibration techniques are equally robust and in some cases only approximate methods are available. The calibration process also introduces data errors into the models. There are however, some ways of reducing data errors; namely by:

1. **Using larger sampling fractions and making more observations.** This approach increases the cost of data collection in general and may not be possible within many budget and time constraints. The adoption of strict quality controls on the data collection exercise will also reduce data errors but again at an increased cost.

2. **Selecting models that use data more efficiently.** This is certainly an attractive proposition. Some models, in particular of the disaggregate type, make a better use of data than others. However, these are not available for all types of problems and there are still unresolved questions in many areas of application (see Ortuzar, 1982).

3. **Selecting more robust calibration techniques.** This usually requires a good deal of expertise and resources. Moreover, robust and well tried calibration techniques are only available for a limited number of models.

4. **Using models requiring data which is easier to collect and verify.** For example, it may be decided to base transport models on data such as population and employment statistics collected by other institutions on a regular basis. These data are also likely to be better understood and their values in the future can probably be forecast with greater confidence.

It is interesting to reflect on the impact of model complexity on data errors. When arithmetic operations like subtraction, multiplication etc. are performed on variables with associated errors, the results are figures which in general display a larger relative error than each of the individual variables (exceptions are additions and raising a variable to an exponent between -1 and +1).

For example, consider the following hypothetical model of the number of non-car trips, G, generated in a zone as a function of car-ownership c, the number of households in the zone H and a parameter for calibration g:

$$G = (1 - c)g\,H \qquad\qquad (9.1)$$

Assume now that the exact values for c, g and H are unknown but that they have only a specific single value and a range, for example:

$$c = 0.2 \pm 0.02$$

$$g = 8 \pm 1$$

$$H = 500 \pm 20$$

The error of G can be estimated (Wilson, 1952) as:

$$e_G \times \sqrt{8^2 \times 500^2 \times 0.02^2 + (1 - 0.2)^2 \times 500^2 \times 1^2 + (1 - 0.2)^2 \times 8^2 \times 20^2} \qquad (9.2)$$

$$e_G \approx \pm 427$$

where $\approx$ means approximately.

Then:

$$G = 3200 \pm 427$$

Errors tend to be amplified by a sequence of arithmetic operations and these are likely to increase as model complexity increases. At least in these broad terms, increased complexity seems to have a favourable effect on specification errors (reduction) and an unfavourable effect on data errors. A more realistic (complex) model is not necessarily a more accurate one.

This rather qualitative explanation of the way in which model complexity and model accuracy are related can be further illustrated with the help of Figure 9.1. In this figure the vertical axis is used to represent total model error in suitable units (for example per cent root mean squared error of the trip rate by a certain household type). The horizontal axis represents model complexity as some function of the total number of variables and relationships in the model. The curves are hypothetical and only meant to represent the problem in qualitative terms.

Figure 9.1: Model Error and Complexity

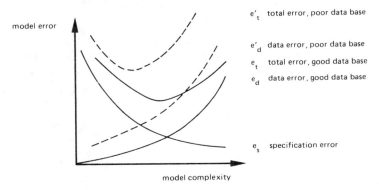

As model complexity increases, the expectation is for a decrease in specification errors (e_s) albeit at an increased cost for the model. However, an increase in complexity is likely to imply an increase in *data errors* (e_d). From the point of view of model accuracy, the aim is to select the model that produces the minimum total error (e_t), that is specification error (e_s) plus data error (e_d). From Figure 9.1 this point of minimum error lies somewhere in between very complex and very simple models.

Consider now the transfer of a model which produces minimum total error in a country with a relatively good data base (reliable data, little change expected in the future) to a country with less reliable data. Because of greater errors in the data a new curve e'_d, represented in Figure 9.1 by a dotted line should be used. Even if it is assumed that the specificatiom error remains the same, it is now necessary to choose a less complex model in order to minimise the total error (e_t) in the predictions. Less reliable and limited data should be used in combination with simpler rather than more complex models.

SIMPLER TRANSPORT MODELS

It is generally recognised that conditions in Third World countries are such that data are scarce and often unreliable. This is at least partially explained by the rapid change and growth prevailing in these countries, as well as their limited experience in mounting and maintaining consistent efforts in extensive data collection and their quality control. Following the argument advanced in the previous section, this situation calls for the use of models of less complexity than those in use in countries where data is more abundant and reliable. If that is the case, what types of models are available to assist in the formation of a technical model-building toolkit for these conditions? Does the request for simpler models imply using older ones?

While it is fair to say that the mainstream of research and development in transport modelling has concentrated on improving model realism and hence its complexity, there are other minor streams pursuing alternative approaches. These have received less attention in the learned journals, although there has been a recent trend to give them a better coverage. The intention here is to explain some of these alternative modelling approaches, moving from the more general and abstract to the most specific. As space prevents a discussion of *all* existing simplified models, this exploration is intended only as a general pointer to the variety of alternative approaches.

One of the aspects affecting the complexity of a model is its treatment of space. Transport problems take place in specific locations, that is why most conventional models give a detailed treatment to zoning systems and transport networks. However, it is possible for certain purposes to simplify the treatment of space or even omit it altogether.

The seemingly simplest option is to use no formal model at all to assist decision making. This is certainly a widely used approach. To advocate the use of *no explicit* models in transport planning however, is equivalent to accepting that only the implicit mental models of the planning actors will be employed. These mental models play a critical role in defining the character and range of transport problems to be considered, the framework for their analysis and the type of solutions which are politically feasible and attractive as argued in Chapter 2. The mental or conceptual models of the planning actors are reflected (and perhaps refined) in meetings, discussions, written reports and political negotiations. Despite their importance and because of their nature, it is difficult to discuss mental models and this often gives rise to quite intractable communication problems. Techniques like scenario writing and Delphi methods have been developed to improve the use of mental models and expertise in forecasting, and some applications have been reported in the transport field (Hupkes, 1974).

Structural Modelling

Grouped under this description are simple techniques for making explicit and visible the implicit mental models held by politicians and planners. The idea behind them is to develop an explicit and often graphic representation of the relationships thought to be important in a particular problem. One example of this is depicted in Figure 9.2, often used to represent (model) the way in which growing car ownership, congestion and public transport are interrelated.

If only arrows link one block to another, indicating what causes what, the diagram is said to be a 'directed graph' or a 'digraph'. If weights are attached to the arrows indicating, for example, that a 1 per cent increase in the number of cars implies a 0.8 per cent reduction in public transport passengers, the diagram is said to be a weighted di-graph. The weights can be obtained from observations but more generally from the opinions of 'experts' in the field (see for example Roberts, 1975).

Despite its simplicity, even the model depicted in Figure 9.2 (without weights) is useful to facilitate discussion. The model is in a sense a description of the problem, highlighting a few of its real life elements. It even suggests possible strategies for dealing with the problem, for instance subsidies to operators, bus priority schemes along corridors and car restraint policies in congested areas. But even at this level of simplicity there are dangers in transferring models. Readers familiar with problems in Third World countries will have noted that the model in Figure 9.2 applies only to areas where the total number of travellers remain more or less constant over time. This model is nevertheless implicit in most textbooks on the subject.

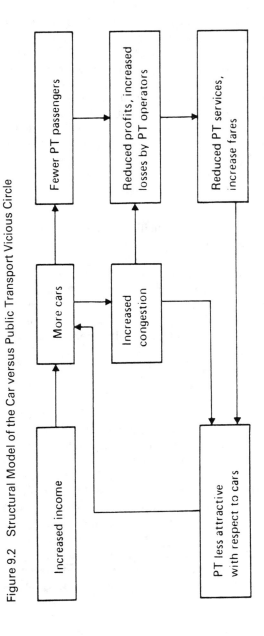

Figure 9.2   Structural Model of the Car versus Public Transport Vicious Circle

Manual or simple computer-assisted techniques can be used to integrate and combine the expertise and conceptualisation of several planning agents. For a good general description of this approach see Warfield (1976). Despite their simplicity and non-spatial character, structural models can also play a cost-efficient role in broad policy analysis. As only structural relationships are explored, this approach can consider qualitative implications of policy options. Indeed, there is a very good case for making more extensive use of this type of approach, in particular to clarify discussions and to improve the interface between politician and technical advisors.

Idealised Models

The simplest transport models explicitly considering *space* are probably of the 'idealised' or 'continuous' type. In these models, space is treated as a continuum over which population and employment (trip ends) and sometimes network densities are distributed. Often, some symmetry condition is also assumed. Possibly the best known model of this type has been put forward by Smeed (1967). Smeed considered the road capacities of city centres as a function of the length of the peak period, bus and car occupancy rates, the area of the city centre and the proportion of it used for carriageway. Under these circumstances and with some mathematics, it is possible to show that the total number of commuters who can travel into the city centre is limited and will be maximised if all go by public transport. There is no space to reproduce these calculations here but the interested reader may consult Smeed (1968) where these theoretical results are compared with data from major urban centres.

The main advantage of idealised models is the opportunity they provide for studying optimum design problems directly, rather than by trial and error as in conventional models. Typical problems are: optimum parking policies, optimum location for a ring road or a supplementary licence scheme. Because of their highly idealised character, the solutions thus obtained can only be considered as general guidelines. They certainly provide however, a focus for discussion and consideration of policies with spatial implications in a way impossible in simpler structural models. The presentation of these idealised models in technical publications is often obscured by mathematical formulae. However, these formulae can be handled by a small computer program requiring the user to insert and interpret simple commands and messages.

Gaming-simulation

This is a technique developed for training purposes which has gained wider acceptance in the last decade or so. It has been suggested that extensions of the technique might be used to assist actual decision-making, as well as teaching and training. In the area of urban transport and traffic management, Ortuzar and Willumsen (1978) have developed GUTS, a computer-based gaming-simulation exercise used in more than ten countries. This will be used as an example to illustrate the approach.

The city simulated in GUTS has perfect symmetry around its centre, and is divided into a number of concentric bands or zones. Its configuration and strategic network are depicted in Figure 9.3. The strategic network is made up of a number of radial routes and of up to two ring roads. Each of these radial roads has several nodes which can be deemed to represent intersections, and the links between them may have different characteristics. Each link is defined by its length, its uncongested speed and its capacity. The secondary network is not described in detail, but under certain conditions some trips are assumed to take place in it. The distributions of employment, residences and car ownership, which also follow a symmetric pattern, are depicted in Figure 9.3 as well. They grow every year (or run of the game) and the shape of these distributions may also change with time.

Only car and bus movements are considered in the model and there are only two person types: car owners and non car owners, with different characteristics in terms of location, trip generation rates, and value of time. In general, the model follows the lines of conventional aggregate transport models (Wilson, 1970). The basic parameters may be specified by the controller of the exercise. It is possible to simulate in this way a wide range of different cities to make the exercise more realistic in different environments.

The user of GUTS takes the role of decision maker and is invested with most of the powers usually associated with a local authority in relation to transport: traffic management measures, control of bus operations, and investments in road and public

Figure 9.3: Simplified Urban Transport System in GUTS

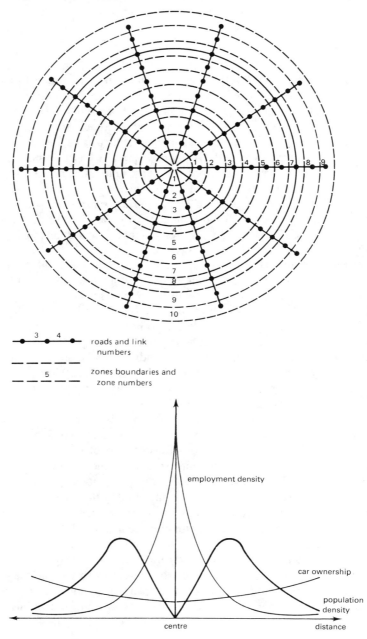

transport improvements. In particular, the user can specify the following measures:

1. **Public Transport Management:**
    a. Fares -The fare structure can be specified in terms of a fixed part and a variable part dependent on the distance travelled. Flat fares, and even free fares, can also be specified in this way. The combination of fares, travel demand and costs will determine the level of subsidies to the bus undertaking, if any.
    b. Services. - Bus services are affected by the total number of buses available. Traffic management schemes may also affect the amount and quality of service that can be offered with a given number of buses.
2. **Traffic Management:**
    a. Bus lanes - These can be established in *all* links and can be peak only or all-day bus lanes.
    b. Parking control - It is possible to control all parking in the six innermost areas. There are two types of parking: long stay and short stay parking. The parking charges at each zone and for each type of space can be specified.
    c. Supplementary licence scheme - As in Singapore and proposed elsewhere are car restraint measures which can also be simulated.
3. **Investment Decisions:**
    a. Acquisition of new buses - These are to replace old equipment and increase the supply of public transport services.
    b. Engineering projects - Projects of this kind include widening roads, building car parks, or installing area traffic control systems.

The model also simulates fairly realistic financial constraints which the *user* has to meet. The output from GUTS includes:

1. traffic information on link capacities, average speeds and flow levels;
2. traffic characteristics, including the number of vehicles parked in each zone, parking revenue and a qualitative indicator of the excess of demand for parking spaces. Modal

split, cost, time and distance travelled by type of user are also printed out. It is also possible to obtain accessibility indices for different journey purposes and zones in the city;

3.   a financial report for the appropriate year of operation and made up of the following three parts:

    a.   A Bus Operations Report - This contains costs and revenues and calculates the number of buses required to maintain a given level of service and the subsidy levels;

    b.   A Revenue and Expenditure Report - This contains all the sources and destinations of funds for that year - these include loan payments and bank balances; and

    c.   An Investment Report - This gives up-to-date information on the amount of money spent in each of the possible investment projects.

Simulations, like GUTS, are essentially training tools, but they may also help to improve decision making in real cases. Firstly, they can be used in their normal 'training tool' capabilities, to train the staff of planning agencies and to achieve a common 'language' throughout the office, as they offer a reference point helpful in defining a common vocabulary. For example, GUTS seems ideal to explain what is meant by 'managing transport in a city as a total system'. Second, a model of the kind incorporated in GUTS, because of its simplicity and speed in operation, can be used advantageously to test and discuss broad strategies and particular conceptions of decision makers. This again leads to a better understanding among those involved in the simulation and about the transport *system* itself. GUTS is no substitute for more sophisticated models in dealing with specific projects and detailed analyses, but it can help to bridge the gap between broad policy proposals and specific modelling exercises.

A third use of simulation models such as GUTS is in demonstrating the advantages and weaknesses of mathematical models. The obviously simplified character of GUTS coupled to its capacity to depict interactions between modes and decisions provides a good example, albeit exaggerated, of what the modelling approach can offer. The use and subsequent critique of the game by politicians and planners would help them to understand each other's activities and interests better. For more details about GUTS the reader is referred to Willumsen and Ortuzar (1985).

Sketch Planning

These models have been put forward as tools for long range decision making by many institutions as reported in OECD (1974), and Sosslau et al (1978). They are models with a greater level of detail than idealised ones, but much simpler than conventional packages. This facilitates the analysis of broad transport and land use strategies at a coarse level of definition but without requiring some of the stricter assumptions of ideal space models. Their practical implementations range from scaled-down conventional computer packages to ad-hoc programs developed for microcomputers or programmable calculators (see Chapter 8). Most sketch planning models rely considerably on transferring parameters and relationships from one area (country) to another. Only certain aspects of the model are made location-dependent and these are usually network characteristics, population, income levels and so on.

One of the simplest sketch planning transport models is the Unified Mechanism of Travel (UMOT), put forward by Zahavi (1979). The UMOT model requires three types of *input*:

1. the number of households in the study area and their sizes;
2. the income distribution of households; and
3. the unit cost of travel by mode (at present up to 3 modes can be handled).

The UMOT model assumes that the following relationships are transferrable over space (countries/cities) and over time (past/future):

1. the average daily travel time per traveller;
2. the average daily travel money expenditure as a function of income and car ownership;
3. the average number of travellers per household as a function of household size and car ownership;
4. the unit cost of owning and operating a car;
5. the speed-flow relationships by road type;
6. the threshold of car daily travel distance which justifies owning a car.

These relationships are not calibrated from observations but are already built into the model. The UMOT model produces the following outputs:

1. car ownership per household by income group/type of car/number of cars;
2. number of travellers and their average daily travel distance;
3. modal split;
4. travel speeds;
5. relationship between network size and travel (time and money) budget utilisation; and
6. distribution of car daily travel distance by purpose and time of day.

All these calculations are carried out at a high level of aggregation and the results are deemed to be representative of the whole study area. The model may be run on a small microcomputer with 48K bytes of memory. There is evidence that daily travel time and travel cost expenditure may also be a function of transport systems quality (Banjo and Brown, 1982) and this has significant implications for the use of the UMOT model in a Third World context.

Other sketch planning models, for example the Community Aggregate Planning Model, require much larger mainframe computer resources (Schleifer et al, 1976). In a review of sketch planning techniques in transport, Sosslau et al (1978) identified 40 models or procedures and the number has no doubt increased since that time. Sketch planning techniques seem to offer several advantages for Third World countries in terms of simplicity, fast response and low data requirements. However, several considerations should be borne in mind when attempting to transfer such a model to a different context:

1. Like any model, sketch planning techniques are only reasonable representations of reality from a particular viewpoint and frame of reference.
2. Most sketch planning techniques rely considerably on assumptions of model and parameter transferability. Although in some cases evidence is offered to support this assumption, these findings are not universally accepted.
3. Sketch planning techniques usually operate at a level of aggregation too high for the analysis of many local problems.

NETWORK MODELS BASED ON TRAFFIC COUNTS

As shown above, it is possible to analyse several important transport problems using simplified techniques, albeit at a rather high level of aggregation. For certain groups of problems more localised performance indicators would be required. A typical example is the design of traffic management schemes for the relief of congestion.

This type of project is likely to include measures such as the introduction of one-way schemes, the banning of certain turning movements at some junctions, the banning of specific classes of vehicles from some streets, etc. These modifications to the network may result in important changes in the routes followed through the area and will in turn produce new flows, travel times (delays), fuel consumption and expenditure levels for different groups of users. Because of its potential contrasting impacts, the simple observation that average speeds have increased is not enough to justify a traffic management scheme (Thomson, 1968). For example, higher speeds might be achieved at the cost of longer routes thus increasing performance indicators such as travel time and cost through the system.

A good assessment of a traffic management scheme requires the identification of the origins and destinations of the journeys likely to be affected by it. The most practical way of achieving this is by estimating an origin-destination (O-D) matrix. This is a matrix which depicts the total number of trips in the study area made between each trip origin and each destination. A traffic management scheme is likely to affect some of these trips, perhaps lengthening some and shortening others. The value of the scheme from the point of view of congestion will depend on whether there has been an overall reduction in travel time. An O-D matrix is required for both the design and evaluation of traffic management schemes. At the other end of the spectrum, it is quite important from a planning point of view to be able to predict the changes in flow levels resulting from a major modification to a transport network, as in the case of the construction of a new high capacity link.

The possibility of developing transport models based on traffic counts is particularly attractive. This is first of all because traffic counts are relatively inexpensive to obtain (compared with interview and other survey methods) and their collection costs can be shared over several projects, for example intersection design, accident analysis and traffic flow monitoring. Secondly, the technology for automatic collection of vehicle counts is well advanced and there are several computer packages providing an efficient pre-processing of them. Moreover, it is much simpler to count vehicles, passengers or pedestrians than to carry out surveys requiring interviews and form-filling. Most counting operations can be performed without interrupting traffic and without causing delays.

Simplified transport models based on traffic counts are being developed for two related objectives:

1.   The estimation of O-D matrices in local, probably central areas, to assist in the design of traffic and transport management measures. Traffic counts are less expensive than number-plate surveys, roadside interviews or aerial photography.
2.   The development of full transport demand models which require much less data and processing power than conventional ones and make possible regular re-running to update and modify decisions and plans.

For a concise review of the most important models put forward for these two applications, see Willumsen (1981). In this chapter the discussion will focus on the general characteristics of these approaches and describe in detail only a couple of examples.

Consider a study area where M zones have been defined and each one has been connected to a centroid. These centroids could represent towns or parts of cities in an inter-urban study. Alternatively, in an urban study, some centroids may represent roads entering the areas, internal residential zones, or large parking areas. The road network will be coded into N nodes and L links connecting pairs of nodes. Some of these links may simply represent particular turning movements while other links stand for major stretches of road. In this system there will be M^2 unknowns to form an O-D matrix.

A key issue in the estimation of a trip matrix from traffic counts is the identification of the origin and destination pairs whose trips use a particular link; the variable p_{ij}^{lm} will be used to this end. This is defined as the proportion of trips from origin i to destination j which use link lm. If no trips between i and j use the link lm, the $p_{ij}^{lm} = 0$. On the other hand if all these trips use link lm, then $p_{ij}^{lm} = 1$. The variable p_{ij}^{lm} is obviously related to the type of route choice model thought to be realistic for the system of interest. In congested urban areas, more than one route between i and j will be attractive and accordingly at least some of the route choice proportions p_{ij}^{lm} will take intermediate values between O and 1. In general

$$0 \leq p_{ij}^{lm} \leq 1 \qquad (9.3)$$

If T_{ij} is the (unknown) number of trips from i to j and the (observed) flow on link lm, the fundamental equation of a trip matrix from traffic counts is

$$\hat{V}_{lm} = \sum_i \sum_j \quad T_{ij} p_{ij}^{lm} \qquad (9.4)$$

Given a route choice model and the corresponding proportions p_{ij}^{lm}, there will be as many linear equations of the type above (9.4) as traffic counts $\hat{V}_{lm}$. This number will, in general, be far less than the number of unknowns M^2 and the problem will be under-specified in the sense that there will be more than one trip matrix which, when loaded onto the network, reproduce the observed counts. The method of selection of one of these matrices leads to two different groups of models.

EXPLICIT TRAVEL DEMAND MODEL APPROACHES

One way of selecting an appropriate trip matrix consistent with the observed flows is to assume that travel behaviour in the study area can be explained by some accepted model. The most common assumption is that there are three important types of factors which are determining travel demand:

1. trip generation or origin factors;
2. trip attraction or destination factors; and
3. separation or travel cost factors.

Most of the travel demand models in this group rely on a limited amount of information (in addition to the traffic counts) to provide some estimation of the above three types of factors. The approaches differ mainly in the particular variables selected for this purpose, but the most frequent functional form chosen for the model is of the gravity type. In its simplest form, the gravity model may be written as:

$$T_{ij} = b_1 O_i D_j c_{ij}^{-d} \qquad (9.5)$$

where O_i and D_j represent information regarding trip ends at origin and destination (say population and employment), is the cost of travel between i and j, and b_1 and d are parameters for calibration. In this case the parameter b_1 takes the role of a trip generation factor. The flow levels estimated by this model will be:

$$\hat{V}_{lm} = \sum_i \sum_j b_1 O_i D_j c_{ij}^{-d} p_{ij}^{lm} \qquad (9.6)$$

In practice, there will be trips that do not leave a zone (intra-zonal journeys) and these will not be well represented by a gravity model. However, they may appear in the network and in the corresponding traffic counts. One way of tackling this problem is to assume the presence of local traffic b_0 absent from the gravity model but present in the count. In this case:

$$\hat{V}_{lm} = b_0 + b_1 \left[\sum_i \sum_j p_{ij}^{lm} O_i D_j c_{ij}^{-d} \right] \qquad (9.7)$$

The problem then becomes one of estimating d, b_0 and b_1 from as many equations (of the kind given in 9.7) as observed link flows so that some measure of the differences between modelled flows V_{lm} and observed flows V_{lm} is minimised. If this measure is the square of these differences, a least-squares method can be used to solve it. It is possible to assume different values for the exponent d (say between 1.5 and 4.0) and solve (9.5) by ordinary linear regression, once for each value of d. The values of d, b_0 and b_1 which provide the best fit can then be chosen.

It is possible to extend this model to more than one journey purpose, each one with a different trip generation parameter b_k, and still use a multiple linear regression technique to calibrate the parameters d, and b_0, b_1, b_2 ..... It is also desirable to include in the model a normalising factor for each origin (and journey purpose). This normalising factor may take the form of:

$$B_i^k = \frac{1}{\sum_j D_j^k c_{ij}^{-d}} \qquad (9.8)$$

In this way the following, more general, model may be written and calibrated from traffic counts:

$$T_{ij} = \sum_k b_k O_i^k B_i^k D_j^k c_{ij}^{-d} \qquad (9.9)$$

and

$$\hat{V}_{lm} = b_0 + \sum_k \left[b_k \sum_{ij} p_{ij}^{lm} O_i^k B_i^k D_j^k c_{ij}^{-d} \right] \qquad (9.10)$$

If software for non-linear regression is available even more general normalising (or balancing) factors and deterrence (or separation) functions may be used. Several of these models have been applied to practical problems in different countries, see for example Holm et al, (1976), Smith and McFarlane (1978) and Tamin and Willumsen (1988).

This approach assumes that the explicit demand model realistically estimates trip-making behaviour in the study area. This assumption is probably reasonable in self-contained areas, and has been accepted in the past in much larger studies. The assumption is less attractive when the study area is small and many of the trips have their origin or destination (or both) outside it, making trip end factors much more difficult to identify.

MODELS BASED ON NETWORK DATA ONLY

An alternative approach is to search for the trip matrix which is closest to an 'a priori' matrix but is consistent with the information contained in the traffic counts. The author (Willumsen, 1978) has developed such a model from entropy maximising considerations (see Wilson, 1970). In outline, the model results from solving the following optimisation problem:

maximise

$$S(T_{ij}/t_{ij}) = -\sum_{ij} (T_{ij} \log T_{ij}/t_{ij} - T_{ij}) \qquad (9.11)$$

subject to the constraints:

$$\sum_i T_{ij} p_{ij}^{lm} - \hat{V}_{lm} = 0 \qquad \text{from (9.4)}$$

and $\quad T_{ij} \geq 0$

where t_{ij} is the prior, or 'a priori, number of trips between i and j.

The solution to this optimisation problem can shown to be the following mode:

309

$$T_{ij} = t_{ij} \prod_{lm} x_{lm}^{p_{ij}^{lm}} \tag{9.12}$$

where $\prod_{lm} x_{lm}^{p_{ij}^{lm}} = x_1^{p_{ij}^1} \cdot x_2^{p_{ij}^2} \cdot x_3^{p_{ij}^3} \cdot \ldots$

The derivation of the model above is analogous to the derivation of the gravity model from entropy maximising principles (Wilson, 1970) but the customary total cost and trip end constraints have been replaced by *link flow constraints*. The variables X_{lm} can be interpreted as balancing factors forcing the estimated matrix to reproduce the observed flows. The model can be solved using a multi-proportional adjustment algorithm which is quite simple to program and efficient in execution.

The prior trip matrix may be obtained from:

1. an old trip matrix;
2. a matrix 'cordoned out' from a larger study; or
3. a trip matrix synthesised with a travel demand model.

Of course, if no information is available to produce a prior matrix, a reasonable assumption is to make all 'prior' trips equally likely, that is all $t_{ij} = 1$. This and other related approaches are discussed in some detail in Van Zuylen and Willumsen (1980).

The model has been tested using real data in the central area of Reading, England (Van Vliet and Willumsen, 1981). The trip matrices estimated by the model *without* using any prior information were found to be within the range of *daily variations* of the observed trip matrices. In other words, the estimated matrices were as close to the observed one for a particular day as this was close to the observed matrix of another day of the same week. The model has also been applied to other cities in Britain and the results have been very encouraging (Hall, Van Vliet and Willumsen, 1980).

Some of the properties of the model are worth stating at this stage:

1. The model does not require counts on all links in the network. Guidelines have been worked out to select links for counting in order to improve the accuracy of the matrix t_{ij} .

2.   The solution always reproduces the observed link flows. The convergence criterion of the algorithm is precisely a comparison of observed and modelled flows.

3.   The model can make use of a wide range of additional information through the use of the prior matrix t_{ij}.

4.   The model does not require large computer resources and the algorithm for its solution is quite robust and efficient.

5.   The model is ideal for updating trip matrices.

The author has been involved in at least two applications of this model in the Third World (in Jakarta and Santiago), in both cases using low cost microcomputers. In Jakarta, for example, the trip matrices for the metropolitan area were calculated using a network with 158 zones, 1,200 links and 250 counts. The initial or prior, trip matrix was synthesised using a gravity model. Information in the form of trip length distributions was incorporated in the model through additional equations. In the second case, a number of small trip matrices was estimated for areas of Santiago, Chile. These were used to design and evaluate traffic management schemes. The initial trip matrices were produced by local engineers from their personal knowledge of the areas. In both cities, trip matrices were produced at a fraction of the time and cost of conventional techniques.

AN EXAMPLE OF MODELS BASED ON TRAFFIC COUNTS

A very simplified example will be used to illustrate the way in which models based on traffic counts operate. Consider a network with two origins A, and B, and two destinations, E and F, as depicted in Figure 9.4. There are 5 links in this network but traffic counts are only available for 3 of them:

Link	Count
A - C	5
C - D	15
D - F	6

There are only 6 matrices (whole trips) compatible with these counts as depicted in Table 9.1. This table shows the value of the objective function (9.11) under the assumption of no prior information, that is all $t_{ij} = 1$.

Figure 9.4: Simple Network

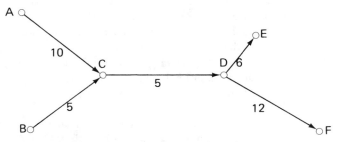

Note: The figures represent the cost in minutes on each link.

Table 9.1   Feasible Trip Matrices and their Entropy

Matrix Number	Trip matrix				Entropy $S(T_{ij}/t_{ij})$
	A to C	A to D	B to C	B to D	
1	5	0	4	6	- 9.34
2	4	1	5	5	- 6.64
3	3	2	6	4	- 5.98
4	2	3	7	3	- 6.60
5	1	4	8	2	- 8.57
6	0	5	9	1	-12.82

The entropy maximising model described in the preceding section selects the trip matrix that maximises this entropy measure. Thus, the model selects matrix 3 as the most likely trip matrix consistent with the information contained in the traffic counts.

The use of the gravity model based approach described previously follows a slightly different path. Firstly, one would need information regarding the trip generation and trip attraction factors O_i and D_j. Secondly, the costs of travelling between each origin and destination pair have to be calculated. These two sets of data are given below.

Trip end factors by zone

	A	B	.	E	F
O_i	10	18	-	-	
D_j	-	-	7	9	

Travel costs (time)

from/to:	E	F
A	21	27
B	16	22

With this data, it is possible to calibrate the model:

$$T_{ij} = b_1 \frac{O_i D_j d_{ij}^{-d}}{\sum_j D_j c_{ij}^{-d}} \tag{9.13}$$

using regression techniques and to obtain the values $b_1 \approx 0.53$ and $d \approx 2$, resulting in the following trip matrix:

to:		E	F
from	A	3.0	2.2
	B	5.6	3.9

This second matrix has been obtained using information on travel costs and trip ends in addition to traffic counts; accordingly, it cannot be expected to yield exactly the same result.

SIMPLIFIED MODELS AND PLANNING STYLES

In this chapter we have examined the types of models that may be used in conditions of rapid change and limited data. It has been argued that in these situations it is more appropriate to use simpler models offering a fast response than to try to adapt complex models with an unreliable data base.

A whole range of simplified models with modest data requirements has been identified. These modelling techniques will not solve all transport planning problems of Third World countries, but compared to the conventional alternatives of using no models at all or hastily adapting a large-scale package of programs, they are particularly attractive. The adaptation to local conditions of most of these simplified models does not require highly sophisticated expertise and is probably best performed by local institutions. Each of these models has particular strengths and limitations. What is advocated in this chapter is their use at the appropriate level and stage in the decision making process.

It is not possible to identify a unique set of models for each type of application. The choice will depend on the local availability of skills, computer equipment and programs and, above all, experience in planning. However, some pointers may help in this search for more appropriate models.

Firstly, certain transport problems such as public transport finance or the implications of continuous growth on vehicle ownership can be treated in a non-spatial manner. In this case, structural models or a simplified sketch planning model like UMOT may play a helpful role. If the problems are more localised geographically, some kind of network representation (idealised or not) is required. In this case, a more ambitious sketch planning model may be chosen. The models based on traffic counts may be considered to be of this type and they offer interesting potential. If the problem is long-term planning, the approach based on the gravity model seems to be more suitable. This is because it can explicitly handle growth in origin and destination factors such as population and employment. This type of model may also be used for freight studies. Modal split problems are probably better treated by a disaggregate model of the type discussed in Chapter 8. An interesting combination of these two approaches in Santiago is described in de Cea, Ortuzar and Willumsen (1986).

Monitoring urban traffic and design of traffic management schemes can be assisted by the use of the entropy maximising model described above in the section dealing with models based on network data. Training of understanding between decision makers and analysts can be assisted by the use of gaming simulation.

CONCLUSION

The era of (one-off) large scale transport modelling exercises *should* now be over. The development of a single definitive, comprehensive and behaviourally sound transport model is no longer feasible or desirable, either in an industrialised or a Third World context. A new planning style is being sought that is better adapted to the uncertainty and errors inherent in modelling and forecasting. The issues likely to be stressed are:

1. the identification and examination of key issues and problems in detail using modelling techniques developed to their specific requirements;

2.   the need to incorporate all actors in the planning process and hence provide means of participating effectively in modelling activities;

3.   the need for continuous updating of plans and forecasts;

4.   the monitoring of the performance of transport systems and the use of controlled experimental changes; and

5.   ways of learning better from experience and incorporating the accumulation of knowledge into the modelling and forecasting process.

The simplified models discussed in this chapter can contribute to all these areas in conditions of limited data.

Structural and idealised models are quite useful in the identification of problems and broad strategies for their resolution. Structural models and gaming-simulation techniques provide an attractive framework for incorporating the experience and perceptions of different actors in the planning process and improving the dialogue between decision makers and professional planners.

Sketch planning techniques may again contribute to a quick analysis of transport problems provided the issues of model transferability are dealt with in the recipient country.

Models based on traffic counts offer a very attractive low-cost technique, in particular within the context of a continuous updating of forecasts and plans. Models using prior information when available and updating it with current and easily obtained data such as traffic counts seem very suited to this new planning style.

All these simplified models offer two additional advantages in a Third World context. First, their reduced resource requirements make it easier to de-emphasise the modelling effort so that a better deployment of the limited resources of qualified professionals is facilitated. Second, the simplicity of the models enables a more balanced appreciation of the advantages and limitations of transport models and a better interpretation of their output.

In some cases there may be good reasons to combine simpler and more sophisticated aproaches to transport modelling. One would use a simplified method to discuss broad policies and to provide a background for problem identification and assessment. If a particular problem requires a detailed analysis of modal choice then a disaggregated model should be applied just where it is critically needed. If a problem requires long-term planning of a road network with regular monitoring of traffic levels a simpler model based on traffic counts and basic planning data may be all that required.

The availability of low-cost microcomputers makes these simpler models even more attractive to Third World countries. A microcomputer costing less than half the price of a small car provides enough data processing power to run the majority of the models discussed in this chapter. Computer programs to run some of these models on microcomputers is already available. For example, one suite of programs for 256k bytes machines can handle the models based on traffic counts for study areas of up to 300 zones and 6000 links. The availability and quality of suitable computer programs is bound to improve and it would be to their advantage for Third World countries to pool resources to ensure that the programs satisfy their specific requirements.

REFERENCES

Alonso, W. (1968) 'Predicting Best with Imperfect Data', **Journal of the American Institute of Planners**, July, Chicago.

Atkins, S.T. (1977) 'Transport Planning: Is There a Road Ahead?' **Traffic Engineering and Control**, vol. 18, no. 2, February, Printerhall Ltd., London.

Banjo, G.A., and Brown, P.J.B. (1982) 'Patterns of Time Budget Expenditure in Nigeria', paper presented at Annual Meeting, Transportation Research Board, Washington DC.

de Cea, J., de Ortuzar, J.D., and Willumsen, L.G. (1986) 'Evaluating Marginal Improvements to a Transport Network: An Application to the Santiago Underground', **Transportation**, vol. 13, no. 3, Elsvier Science Publisher, Amsterdam.

Hall, M.D., Van Vliet, D., and Willumsen, L.G. (1980) SATURN - A Simulation-Assignment Model for the Evaluation of Traffic Management Schemes, **Traffic Engineering and Control**, vol. 21, no. 4, Printerhall Ltd., London.

Heggie, I. (1978) 'Putting Behaviour into Behavioural Models of Travel Choice', **Journal of the Operational Research Society**, no. 29, Pergamon Press, Oxford.

Holm, J., Jensen, T., Nielsen, S., Christensen, A., Johnson, B., and Ronby, G. (1976) Calibrating Traffic Models on Traffic Census Results Only', **Traffic Engineering and Control**, vol. 17, April, Printerhall Ltd., London.

Hupkes, G. (1974). DELPHI Opinion Poll FUCHAN-I. 'An Evaluation of Changes Affecting the Passenger Car', **Transportation**, vol 3, no. 1, Elsvier Science Publisher, Amsterdam.

OECD (1974) **Urban Traffic Models: Possibilities for Simplification**, OECD Road Research Group, Paris.

Ortuzar, J.D., (1982) 'Fundamentals of Discrete Multi Model Choice Modelling, **Transport Reviews**, vol. 2, no.1, Taylor and Francis, Philadelphia.

Ortuzar, J.D., and Willumsen, L.G. (1978). 'Learning to Manage Transport Systems', **Traffic Engineering and Control**, vol. 19, no. 5, May, Printerhall Ltd., London.

Roberts, F.A., (1975) 'Weighted Di-graph Models for the Assessment of Energy Use and Air Pollution in Transportation Systems', **Environment and Planning A**, vol. 7, Pion Press, London.

Schleifer, H., Zimmerman, S., and Gendell, D. (1976) 'The Community Aggregate Planning Model', in **Transportation Research Record**, no. 582, Transportation Research Board, Washington DC.

Smeed, R.J., (1967) The Road Capacity of City Centres', **Highway Research Record**, no. 169, Transportation Research Board, Washinton DC.

_____ (1968) Traffic Studies and Urban Congestion', **Journal of Transport Economics and Policy,** vol. 2, no. 1, London School of Economics, London.

Smith, R, and McFarlane, W. (1978) 'Examination of a Simplified Travel Demand Model', **Transportation Engineering Journal of ASCE**, 104 (TEI), Institute of Transport Engineers, Washington DC.

Sosslau, A.B., Hassam, A., Carter, M., and Wickstrom, G. (1978) 'Quick Response Urban Travel Estimation Techniques and Transferable Parameters', **NCHRP Report** no. 817. Transportation Research Board, Washington DC.

Supernak, J. (1983) 'Transportation Modelling: Lessons from the Past and Tasks for the Future', **Transportation** vol. 12, no. 1, Elsvier Science Publisher, Amsterdam.

Tamin, O. and Willumsen, L. (1988) 'Freight Demand Model Estimation from Traffic Counts', **Proceeding PTRC Summer Annual Meeting**. PTRC Education and Research Services Limited, London.

Thomson, J.M. (1968) 'The Value of Traffic Management', **Journal of Transport Economics and Policy**, vol. 2, no. 1, London School of Economic, London.

Van Vliet, D., and Willumsen, L.G. (1981) 'Validation of the ME2 Model for Estimating Trip Matrices from Traffic Counts', **Proceedings of the 8th International Symposium of Traffic and Transportation Theory**, Toronto.

Van Zuylen, H.H., and Willumsen, L.G. (1980) 'The Most Likely Trip Matrix Estimated from Traffic Counts', **Transportation Research,** vol. 14B, Pergamon Press, Oxford.

Warfield, J.N. (1976) **Societal Systems, Planning, Policy and Complexity**, John Wiley, New York.

Willumsen, L.G. (1978) 'O-D Matrices from Network Data: A Comparison of Alternative Methods for their Estimation', **PTRC Summer Annual Meeting**, Universtiy of Warwick, PTRC Education and Research Services Ltd, London.

_____ (1981) 'Simplified Transport Models Based on Traffic Counts', **Transportation**, vol. 10, no. 3, Elsvier Science Publisher, Amsterdam.

Willumsen, L. G. and Ortuzar J.D. (1985) 'Institution and Models in Transport Management', **Transportation Research**, vol. 19A, no. 1, Elsvier Publisher, Amsterdam.

Wilson, A.G. (1970) **Entropy in Urban and Regional Modelling**, Pion Press, London.

Wilson, B.E. (1952) **An Introduction to Scientific Research**, McGraw Hill, New York.

Zahavi, Y. (1979) 'The UMOT project', **US Department Transport Report**, no. DoT-RSPA-DPB-20-79-3, Washington DC.

Chapter 10

Urban Transport Corridor Planning

Ralph Gakenheimer and Michael D. Meyer

INTRODUCTION

Transport corridor planning concentrates techniques of traffic management along a particular access way to reduce congestion and make the best use of the roadway. It takes advantage of a multiplying effect among the different traffic management measures. The urban corridor usually centres on a single radial or circumferential highway and public transport route, but may also include related minor facilities and impacts on nearby land development.

Corridor planning arises from the general emphasis on traffic management techniques that have been topical in the field since the mid-1970s. It has evolved in the industrialised countries, but with certain adaptations it is particularly suited to tackling the urban traffic problems of the Third World countries. Corridor planning incorporates a number of diverse actions, all achievable in the short term, and requiring limited public investment. Actions such as the synchronisation of traffic signals, preferential lanes for high occupancy vehicles, redesign of intersections, parking enforcement, reduction of crossings, motorway ramp metering, and improved public transport service, have all been used either alone, or in combination with other traffic management actions, to improve the transport service in urban corridors.

The authors of this chapter argue that the major adaptations of corridor planning that will ensure that the concept works in the Third World must respond to special problem characteristics, the urban environment of the problem, and the administrative en-

319

vironment of the problem. The form discussed here that these modifications should take is based upon applications of transport corridor planning in Cairo, Egypt and Guadalajara, Mexico.

EVOLUTION OF URBAN TRANSPORT CORRIDOR PLANNING IN THE USA

The characteristics of transport corridor planning in the industrialised countries need to be understood as a prelude to its adaptation to the Third World. It should then be possible to identify which of its aspects can be directly transferred to a different culture and to highlight those less transferable aspects, linked to conditions unique to the countries in which the approach was first developed.

Initial Efforts

As early as 1959, traffic engineers in Washington DC, were examining the application of traffic management actions and their joint effect as a programme for traffic improvement along major urban corridors (Carter, 1962). They were doing so in the belief that traffic management actions, such as signalisation, signing, channelisation and better separation of vehicles and pedestrians, could dramatically increase the vehicle-carrying capacity of major urban streets. This approach remained of interest to some US transport professionals throughout the 1960s. Indeed, it gradually matured as a potential alternative to comprehensive transport planning and large scale highway construction programmes which dominated transport planning (and associated thinking) during this period.

By the late 1960s, several US cities began to experience the public opposition to highway construction that, by the mid-1970s, brought to a halt most of the major urban highway projects in the country (see Gakenheimer, 1976 and Pill, 1976; also Chapter 5). Still facing a problem of growing vehicle congestion on urban highways, and yet prevented from expanding the vehicle-carrying capacity of these routes, transport planners were forced to examine other means of enabling urban highways to handle their vehicle demand. The focus of many transport studies thus changed to one of making the *existing* transport system more efficient through the use of service, regulatory, and operational improvements. Because the performance of an urban highway must be measured in terms of its ability to handle the traffic along all its length, and not just for short sections, a planning methodology had to be developed in which were considered both traffic demand and system performance characteristics within the entire area served by the highway; hence the birth of transport corridor studies.

National Programme

The focus on urban travel corridors, and the related traffic management actions to improve traffic flows, were further encouraged in 1970 when the US Department of Transportation (US DOT) sponsored the Urban Corridor Demonstration Program in selected parts of the US. This was a measure aimed specifically at encouraging local transport planners to consider corridor planning approaches in their transport planning programmes (US DOT, 1974). Eleven US cities participated in the programme, the actions under consideration including reserved highway lanes for high occupancy vehicles, improved public transport services, car-sharing schemes, traffic surveillance/control systems and road improvements.

The concept of transport corridor planning was soon extended to streets serving the central areas of US cities (Rose and Hinds, 1976; Cox, 1975; Elias, 1976; and Ourston, 1976). Transport planning and management actions that were considered included intersection and signalisation improvements, parking restrictions, street conversions to one-way systems and preferential bus treatment. With the announcement by the US DOT of the Transportation System Management (TSM) Program in 1975, these types of actions have since become known as TSM planning and have been widely applied in the US (US DOT, 1975 and Meyer, 1976).

Transport planning is also leading in this direction elsewhere in the industrialised world. In the UK for example, a concern for improved public transport services led to several experiments with preferential treatment for buses on urban streets, as in London's major retail area in Oxford Street (Britton, 1978) and to an extensive range of measures throughout the London area (Bradlam and Hurdle, 1981). In France, 'Plan Circulation', a programme similar to the US DOT's TSM program, has generated a significant experience with traffic management actions since it began in 1970 (Ministere des Transports de France,

1974). A corridor orientation of urban traffic and transport has been an important aspect of the 'Plan Circulation' approach since the first plans were put into practice in Rouen in 1970.

Corridor planning, as a transport planning methodology, has thus gained acceptance in several Western countries. Its emergence can be partly explained as a response to the pressing needs of the mid-1970s, and partly attributed to the latent interest of many transport professionals in the use of traffic management measures to increase the efficiency of existing transport facilities (Gakenheimer and Meyer, 1979).

Before discussing the application of transport corridor planning in a Third World context, it is useful to specify the elements of an urban transport corridor plan in more detail.

ELEMENTS OF URBAN TRANSPORT CORRIDOR PLANNING

A transport corridor study methodology involves five major steps (after Meyer, 1982):

1. identifying corridors;
2. establishing overall policy objectives for the selected study corridors;
3. using socio-economic, travel, and transport system data to identify existing or potential problem areas;
4. analysing potential strategies; and
5. detailing the design of the favoured strategy and its related proposals, chosen in the light of the transport and development goals and policies for the study area in question.

Each of these steps will be discussed below.

Corridor Identification

The first step in this planning approach is to define the transport corridor(s) that will be the subject of study. In an urban area, this usually means a radial set of parallel roads or a cone-shaped service area focusing on the central area (see Figure 10.1).

Other factors which need to be considered when defining a corridor's boundaries include:

Figure 10.1: Example of Transport Corridors in an Urban Area

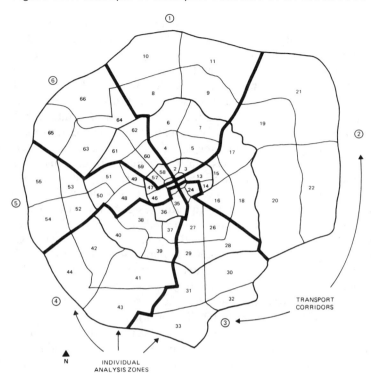

1. the area of domain's perceived problems;
2. physical barriers to trip crossing e.g., rivers, rail lines, canals, etc.;
3. existing transport facilities;
4. concentrations of economic activities;
5. concentrations of population;
6. local government boundaries; and
7. spatial units of data availability.

This last consideration is often one of the deciding factors in the definition of a corridor, since prior data is important in the identification of problems and in assessing the impact of alternatives.

323

Establishing Overall Policy Objectives

Transport corridor studies are carried out for different purposes. One is to identify a set of short-range transport improvements that can be implemented to provide temporary relief, while long-term, high-cost facilities are examined and/or implemented. A second purpose as a final objective, is the improvement at low cost of vehicle flows along major arterial streets. A third purpose is to increase the *person flows* along the corridor - an orientation that favours the road-space saving characteristics of public transport.

Transport corridor planning can be dominated by a concern for a specific issue. Actions can be assembled to minimise fuel consumption, to minimise accident costs, to reduce localised contamination of air quality, to enhance the economic viability of a business district, or to ensure quieter residential environments. Plans can also be directed toward providing better transport service to low-income populations. They can further be applied to increasing the financial viability of public transport operators. Each objective suggests different measures of effectiveness by which proposed actions need to be judged.

It is important to establish at the outset what the exact goals of the corridor study are to be. This is not an easy task, because the various public agencies and private companies that participate in urban transport necessarily have different mandates and interests. Nevertheless, every effort should be made to ensure that the set of policies employed by any transport corridor planning approach is internally consistent, i.e., that the likely actions resulting from one component policy are compatible with the actions resulting from another.

Data Collection and Problem Identification

The data needed to conduct a transport corridor study range from specific details of the transport system (e.g., road widths, lane designations, medians, public transport stops, etc.) and the conditions or performance of elements of a particular facility's network (e.g., pavement and drainage conditions, parking characteristics, accident records, traffic volumes, etc.) to more general information on the legislative, regulative and planning control aspects of the transport system (e.g., extent of policy enforcement, pedestrian use of road space, adherence to speed restrictions, etc.).

Table 10.1 illustrates the kind of information needed to conduct a transport corridor study, based largely upon US experience.

Table 10.1   Type of Data Required for Transport Corridor Planning

Socio-Economic Data	Travel Data	
	Private Transport	Public Transport
* population by sub-areas	* volumes	* passengers' trends in patronage
* employment locations	* accidents	
* income levels	* vehicle/capacity ratio	* passengers per seat miles
* car ownership/availability	* speed and travel time	* passengers per hour
* minority, urban poor and elderly concentrations	* energy consumption	* percentage of passengers who transfer
	* air pollutant emissions	* average fare
* major activity centres	* noise levels	* revenue per seat mile
* residential densities	* road condition	* revenue per seat hour
* land use types	* parking provision	* manpower utilisation
	* traffic control measures	* speed and travel time
		* energy consumption
		* air pollutant emissions
		* route location
		* revenue collected

There are several ways of identifying problem areas within a corridor, the specific approach being dependent upon the overall goals of the transport corridor study. In the case of street performance, for instance, volume to capacity ratios, number of accidents and average vehicle speed could all be used to pinpoint problem locations. In the case of public transport service performance, average bus speeds along sections of the route, passenger loads, bus fares collected and bus frequencies, can all be used to indicate which bus routes are experiencing problems.

Analysing Potential Strategies

There are several basic studies which provide yardsticks by which to evaluate the consequences of corridor strategies:.

1.   speed and delay studies show the level of achievement in reducing bottle-necks;

325

2. critical movement studies show the level of expected accomplishments in reducing accident risks and delays at intersections; and

3. portrayals of public transport service patterns reflect improvements of service coverage through more efficient use of existing equipment.

The use of descriptive accident records in evaluation is basic. For purposes other than safety, however, objectives can only be anticipated from hopeful experimental actions or inferred from similar cases of prior experience. This is especially true of the more complex objectives, such as raising the financial viability of a business district. For most actions, the general studies, together with a background of experience in the performance of particular actions elsewhere, can be used to identify their contribution to corridor objectives.

Designing the Actions to be Recommended

Having chosen the actions of measures to be used, it is necessary to tailor them to site requirements. This includes specifying, for example, the particulars of bus service provision, including route, frequency, stops, and fares. It includes the design of movement control and channelisation at intersections. It involves identifying affected institutions, organisations and individuals and their participation in complicated collaborative projects such as the preparation of pedestrian zones.

APPLICATION TO THE SPECIAL NEEDS OF THIRD WORLD CITIES

There are several reasons why transport corridor studies can be of special importance to urban transport planning in the Third World:

1. Transport corridor planning is generally aimed at low-cost improvements. It is therefore appropriate to the circumstance of scarce resources for public capital investment often found in Third World cities.

2. It adjusts to various levels of technical inputs. If there are origin-destination trip matrices and functioning travel

demand models, they can be profitably used to examine the demand for travel along the corridor. If there are refined traffic engineering studies, and public transport route and schedule planning, they can be used to good advantage. In most cases, however, these are not available in Third World cities. In those cases, significant indications of transport system performance can be found from simple field observations.

3.   Using a single general methodology (created by a national agency), it is possible to propose transport corridor planning actions which are easily replicable, and applicable to cities of all sizes, once officials learn how to implement them. This is important where there is limited professional expertise available.

4.   Most of the actions recommended are incremental and cancellable. They can be introduced cautiously and later expanded. Unlike roadbuilding, where the initial step commits government to a large, expensive and permanent facility, they can be discontinued at little loss of resources. This is an important attribute in the environment of considerable uncertainty that characterises Third World cities and lack of prior experience with the solutions. Growth in travel demand can be met as it appears, without undue dependence upon the use of unreliable forecasting. Errors can be corrected. For example, if the prevention of traffic from crossing a corridor leads to congestion elsewhere, the measures can be cancelled at limited cost. Or actions can be cancelled where driver discipline has been overestimated. It is difficult to know in advance, for example, whether drivers will respect a bus-only counterflow lane.

5.   In most Third World cities there has been little attention to actions of this kind. This means that limited effort can yield substantial results. Simply installing traffic signals that work, or renewing nearly impassable paving spots, would be very important actions in many cases.

6.   Corridor level analysis, when used on industrial corridors, enables planners to focus on urban industrial development. Components include facilitating goods movements through the city, a major problem in many cities in the developing world. Industrial corridor planning can also be part of a strategy to stimulate employment, since industrial areas are often far from parts of the city where residents need work.

In addition to those aspects of transport corridor planning that apply to travel in the specific corridors, it is important to consider objectives at the strategic level of metropolitan planning that are especially appropriate for the Third World. Such objectives include raising the overall travel efficiency within an area that comprises several transport corridors. This might be done with a view to saving fuel, if that is important. There is reason to believe that considerable savings could be attained in some countries by taking actions that yield high returns such as restrictions on non-essential use of private cars. It is important to emphasise this, since professional opinion in the industrialised world generally does not anticipate significant fuel savings through traffic management. The increments of efficiency possible in fuel savings in these countries are too small compared to the objective, and in any case, they have only a limited scope for introducing aggressive new traffic management measures. Consider, for example, the failure of high occupancy lanes in US highways when opposed by pressure groups of inconvenienced motorists.

Transport corridor planning can significantly increase the number of public transport trips in Third World cities by improving the operational performance and capacity of public transport systems. In these countries, public transport vehicles are typically used to capacity, and there is a good deal of latent demand (see Chapter 3). Therefore increased efficiency inevitably means greater use. Thus important benefits may be gained by increasing total trip-making opportunities. These opportunities can be provided to urban groups who are especially suffering from a lack of public transport. Increased use can also aid the viability of the (often marginal) public transport industry.

It should be mentioned that in the Third World, such increases in public transport capability are not likely to cause private car users to switch to public transport in significant numbers. The small percentage of the population owning cars see such ownership as a status symbol to be used both conspicuously and to the full. The difference in quality of service offered by the two modes is typically very dramatic. Furthermore, car ownership involves such very high expenditures when compared to current costs of public transport use that modest fare reductions would not have measurable effect on choice.

Transport corridor planning also provides a rational framework for minor capital improvement allocations in Third World cities, which are otherwise often ineffectively distributed. For example, weak public authorities are likely to spread their work programme more broadly among constituent communities to satisfy political pressures, or simply concentrate on the most serious local spot problems such that each improvement has only a small effect on its respective corridor. Either way, the value of such actions is dissipated and cannot add up to significant system impact.

Transport corridor planning is potentially a good tool, as already indicated above, for the distribution of the benefits of access to the poor. It can be particularly useful, for example, as part of a squatter upgrading programme. In these and other low income areas, access to jobs and social services is generally a serious problem; distances are often great and travel speeds very low. Conditions in general do not encourage public transport operators (especially of the formal sector) to provide needed services.

The limited car ownership in such low income areas, and their predominant residential character, means that on current design criteria, multi-lane roads are difficult to justify. Thus, roads of inadequate standard for bus operation and requiring constant repair owing to the density of use, come to typify low income areas. Low-cost actions that alleviate these problems for modest volumes of traffic (especially public transport vehicles), can be a very important contribution to the improvement of conditions.

Transport corridor planning can have an impact on land development patterns and thus alleviate important problems unique to Third World cities. Consider the following situation in a city where employment and businesses are highly concentrated in the central area (see Figure 10.2). The immediate surrounding area is very densely built up, with narrow streets and paving from building-line to building-line. The city centre is penetrated only by a few high traffic volume arterials, which already form the spines of urban development at the outer periphery of the urban area. These radial arterials are typically found in the high-income parts of metropolitan areas.

Local officials, in this case, want to encourage urbanisation at new locations on the urban periphery but there is little opportunity to do so without providing more adequate road access to the centre. Furthermore, demolition in the dense inner residential areas is not feasible. The most effective means of peripheral access is by organising a travel corridor made up of several of the parallel, narrow, radial streets and facilitating movement along them as a unit. In this way, access between the central city and the

Figure 10.2: Transport Corridor Planning as an Agent of Urban Development in Guadalajara, Mexico

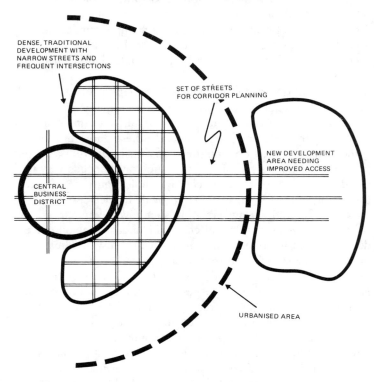

DENSE, TRADITIONAL DEVELOPMENT WITH NARROW STREETS AND FREQUENT INTERSECTIONS

SET OF STREETS FOR CORRIDOR PLANNING

NEW DEVELOPMENT AREA NEEDING IMPROVED ACCESS

CENTRAL BUSINESS DISTRICT

URBANISED AREA

peripheral hinterland is facilitated through the densely built inner urban area. An example of the application of this approach can be seen in Guadalajara, Mexico, discussed later.

PROBLEMS OF IMPLEMENTATION

The technical aspects of transport corridor planning in Third World cities need not be difficult. The major problems of implementing the approach are more likely to be institutional in nature. Several of these problems are worth mentioning.

In many Third World countries, responsibility for traffic planning and management actions is divided among numerous different agencies. Traffic management initiatives, for example, tend to be in the hands of local government (with too few professional staff to undertake them), or the traffic police (who often enforce traffic regulations without the help of appropriate transport planning guidelines). On the other hand, construction responsibility lies mostly with national or state public works agencies; whilst a large proportion of the urban public transport systems is operated by the private sector (generally in multiple small ownerships). Also, since public transport is often subject to political controversy and labour disputes, government agencies tend to be unwilling to become involved in its operation and co-ordination. Thus, they resist entering into the collaborative action necessary to maximise the effectiveness of transport corridor planning.

Under these circumstances, it would be very difficult to conceive of a 'budget' for traffic and transport corridor management. It is much more feasible to budget for actions of a particular kind which are the responsibility of a single agency. However, this contradicts the very principle of corridor planning, which rests upon the need to take various actions to tackle the transport and development problems within a single corridor.

Transport planning professionals, both in industrialised and Third World countries, do not generally take the approach, nor have the skills needed for transport corridor planning. In the US there were problems in the early stages of the Transportation Systems Management Program on this account. Professional staff skills are mostly directed to the design and execution of high-capital road transport projects and the tradition of the field emphasises these skills. This is reinforced by the fact that the system of vested interests normally surrounding the transport sector is one that profits from heavy construction programmes and not from low-cost service-oriented actions, despite the latter being the most appropriate for many Third World cities.

There are two potential answers to these implementation problems. One is to find a reasonably comprehensive organisation in the existing governmental structure that can undertake a significant number of different corridor actions. The other is to create a new organisation that can undertake such actions with full responsibility (except, perhaps, for operations) as in the case discussed in Chapter 7 of this book. The creation of a new organisation should not present great difficulty if there is a commitment to the objectives of traffic management through transport corridor planning. Most ministries of public works or transport could house such a group and make it effective, provided it is given enough independent strength and is internally cohesive. It would also be confronted with the question of priorities among the cities in which it is to work, but that could be handled without disturbance to the basic objectives.

EXAMPLES OF APPLICATION

The two cases that follow are very different from one another in the adaptations they make of the general method proposed above. In Cairo, transport corridor planning was based on a reasonably complete set of travel data and made use of some advanced analytic techniques. It was in good measure focused on increasing the capacity of public transport operations. It was viewed as a pilot study to be replicated later throughout the network in order to increase the entire system's effectiveness.

Guadalajara on the other hand, was based on very limited trip-making information (excluding origin-destination data). The analyses accomplished and the actions chosen were simple and pragmatic. The focus was on a special urban development problem facilitating access to a peripheral reserve of developable land rather than evolving a replicable technique. The method chosen for achieving the desired objective was primarily that of increased street vehicle capacity.

Transport Corridor Planning in Cairo

With a population of over eight million people and an average annual growth rate of over 5 per cent, Cairo has great difficulty in maintaining city services at acceptable levels. One of the government services especially pressured by this population growth is metropolitan transport - both the public transport service and the urban street system. In the case of public transport, approximately four million passengers are carried daily, accounting for approximately 75 per cent of all vehicular trips. The average of 165 passenger-trips per vehicle per bus- hour indicates how heavily the public transport bus system is used. The annual growth rate in patronage of 6 per cent indicates that even more significant problems of overcrowding and congestion are likely to occur in future years. The fact that almost all of Cairo's metropolitan public transport is operated by a single government agency provided an unusual opportunity for urban public-transport based traffic management.

In the case of the street system, limited urban land area and very high population densities in Cairo have resulted in a street network that is extremely congested and has few opportunities for expansion without destroying large numbers of buildings. In the last decade, car ownership in Egypt increased by over 150 per cent to 245,300 cars, of which half are in Cairo. During the same period, the population increased by 30 per cent. Problems are rapidly becoming more serious (Wyatt, 1980).

A preliminary master plan for the metropolitan area was prepared in 1970. It focused on large-scale facilities and proposed a number of bridges and a few urban highway segments. Secondary population centres of the metropolitan periphery served by an outer ring road were later to be the basic foci of regional physical growth. Another study, centred on the proposal for a metro system, was undertaken in 1973 and has served since then 'officially' as the master plan for urban transport in the region (RATP Sofretu, 1973).

With the status of the urban transport system continually changing from one year to the next because of rapid population shifts, and with a constrained budget for all the projects in the master plan, it became apparent to Cairo transport planners and public officials that a new approach to planning was needed. This was to focus on operational improvements to the public transport system and traffic management schemes for the street network. The approach adopted was transport corridor planning.

Corridor Identification

The first step in the transport corridor planning approach was the identification of a well-defined set of travel corridors in the urban area. In Cairo, this was a fairly easy task because topographical conditions and a strong radial orientation of the street system has resulted in easily defined, densely populated corridors.

Cairo was divided into four corridors (see Figure 10.3) with the Shoubra corridor, north of the central city, chosen for a pilot application of the planning methodology . The boundary definition of Shoubra corridor illustrated quite well the concept of an urban corridor. The western boundary bordered the Nile, the national rail line with no crossing permitted was to the east, and the

Ismailia Canal to the north. There were five major north-south streets that transversed the corridor, with only two major points of extrance/exit from the south and one from the north. The Shoubra corridor, as the focus of a planning study, thus provided a well-controlled set of boundary conditions within which a detailed examination of the transport flows internal to the corridor, and those with origins or destinations outside the corridor, could be undertaken. Further, its level of congestion was among the most serious, yet the corridor was served by through-ways providing opportunity for improvement. Thus, it was in all respects a good place to start.

Figure 10.3: Cairo: The Four Transport Corridors

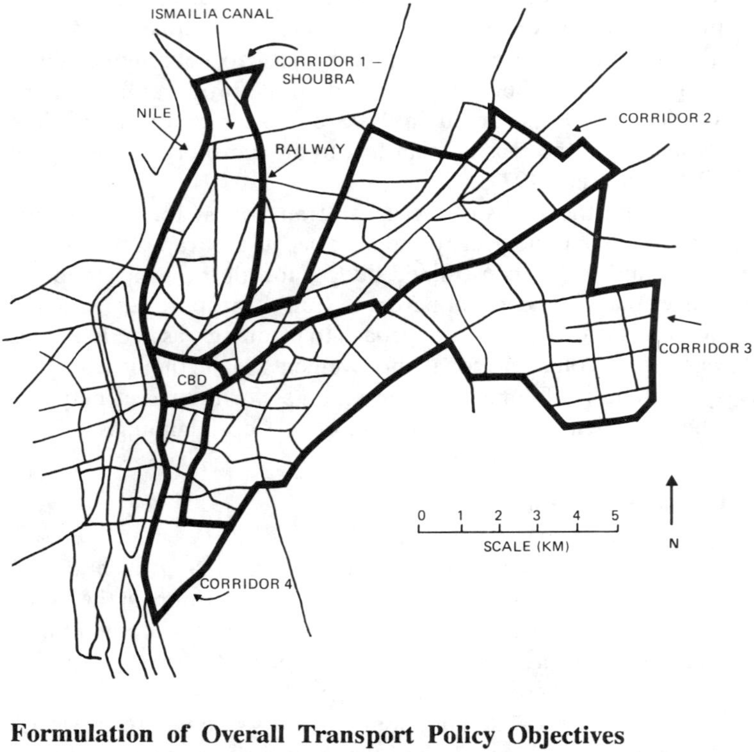

Formulation of Overall Transport Policy Objectives

Since public transport plays an important role in the Cairo metropolitan area, the Shoubra corridor study focused on the identification of actions that could be taken to improve the overall effectiveness of the public transport service in the corridor. There were two major elements of the study: an investigation of alternative operational improvements that could be made in the public transport system itself (e.g., scheduling of buses, rationalising the bus route structure, etc.) and the identification of traffic management improvements for the street system to facilitate the movement of buses.

Data Collection, Problem Identification, and Analysis

The two major components of the corridor study utilised different analytical techniques which will be discussed separately under the sub-headings Traffic Management and Public Transport Service Planning.

Traffic Management Study. The most important constraint in this study was the limited availability of useful data. Although the Cairo Transit Authority (CTA) maintained a fairly extensive data bank of operational statistics (e.g. of patronage, revenue, headways, etc.), there was no up-to-date information on overall road traffic growth and volumes at specific locations. Aggregate measures of accidents by district were available, but the site-specific accident information used to obtain these statistics was not kept on computer file, thus the identification of dangerous intersections would have to be the result of traffic police judgement.

The planning methodology consisted of three major procedures (after Wyatt, 1980):

1. identification of problem sites;
2. identification and screening of feasible strategies; and
3. impact analysis of strategy/site matchings.

As can be seen from this methodological structuring, the purpose of the study was to identify specific problem areas and arrive at possible 'solutions' rather than to provide a master plan for the entire transport corridor.

Procedure 1: Identification of Problem Sites. This procedure was based on the formulation of specific tests that could be used to identify problem locations in the corridor's public transport system. These tests had to be clearly related to the operating objectives of the government agency or agencies responsible for the public transport service in question. For example, like most public transport agencies, the CTA was very concerned about vehicle productivity, operating costs and quality of service to passengers. Because these can all be related to the amount of time a vehicle spends in travel and its average operating speed, a good diagnostic measure was the average vehicle operating speed by route segment. A colour-coded map of a network of such route sections in the Shoubra corridor was used to indicate average bus speeds on major streets, and thus to pinpoint those sections along which serious delays occured.

Procedure 2: Identification of Feasible Alternatives. Once a problem area had been indentified, the next task was to define the possible actions that could be taken to improve the situation. In Cairo, institutional considerations played as important a role in this definition as did technical constraints. Technical constraints included design criteria such as road widths, turning-radii and pedestrian movements. Institutional constraints were imposed by the roles, objectives and capabilities of the agencies involved with traffic management schemes (also see Chapter 7). An institutional factor affecting the selection of traffic management actions for example, was the conflicting objectives of the Cairo Transit Authority (which wanted priority in road use to be given to its buses), and those of the Traffic Police (which viewed the buses as a nuisance to the smooth flow of private car traffic). Any traffic management action taken to improve public transport service would have to be agreeable to both of these agencies; a requirement which in the past, had impeded the implementation of several projects.

One traffic management action in Cairo that satisfied both the technical and institutional requirements was the implementation of bus lanes - the reservation of at least one lane of traffic for buses, in this case travelling in the same direction as the general traffic flow. The technical criteria that had to be satisfied to justify such a project included:

1. exceeding a minimum volume of buses per hour travelling in the lane;
2. no significant reduction of the car carrying capaity of the road section ;
3. its capability of being enforced; and
4. no serious safety problems being created.

Institutional conflict did not arise because, on the one hand, a with-flow bus lane would obviously help the operation of buses, thus gaining CTA support. On the other hand, the Traffic Police would be supportive (assuming the safety criteria were met) because as the lane segregated bus flows from the general traffic, the overall flow was no longer being hindered by buses stopping in the roadway to discharge passengers.

Procedure 3: Impact Analysis of Strategy/Site Matchings. The basis for the analysis was a set of evaluation criteria (or measures of effectiveness) that were related to the overall objectives defined previously for the sponsoring agency. For example, evaluation criteria that could be used in the project of the with-flow bus lane include:

1. the impact on average bus and car operating speeds;
2. pedestrian/bus accident levels;
3. revenue miles per bus; and
4. service reliability.

Straightforward manual computational methods could be used to estimate these impacts for a series of projects, with the results then being compared with alternatives, in order to determine the most cost-effective set of project investments under the prevailing budget constraints.

Public Transport Service Planning. The second component of the corridor study focused exclusively on public transport changes which if adopted, would improve the capacity of these services along the corridor. The specific areas examined included:

1. the present allocation of buses among the existing bus routes;
2. the identification of possible new bus routes which could provide a more direct service between points of high origin and destination travel; and
3. the scope for new express bus service operations along existing routes.

An extensive, system-wide origin-destination survey conducted in 1978 served as the data base for the procedures used in this analysis (El-Hawary et al, 1979); riders on all bus services in the city were surveyed.

Bus Allocation Procedure. The purpose of the bus allocation procedure was to examine the allocation of buses to bus routes in a way intended to satisfy the demand that occurs along specific routes. The procedure consisted of four major steps:

1. establish network of nodes and links within the corridor;
2. develop a nodal origin-destination matrix based on the network;
3. assign trips between each origin-destination pair to the minimum transfer/minimum time path; and
4. calculate the number of buses needed to carry peak loads on each route.

The network that was established in Shoubra corresponded to the major transfer points and network links of the corridor's public transport service (see Figure 10.4). Given the origin-destination data from the travel survey, it was possible to assign trip origins and destinations to each of the nodes in the network. The trip volumes between each origin-destination pair were then assigned to the bus route with the shortest travel time (with or without transfers). The total volume for each network link could then be determined by adding all of the trips. From this estimate, bus frequencies needed to satisfy the peak-period loads and the total number of buses required for corridor service were determined.

The application of this methodology to the Shoubra corridor indicated that more buses were being used than was necessary to satisfy demand, thus reducing the system's efficiency.

Express Bus Service. New express bus services were desirable where high passenger volumes existed with origins near one end of a route and destinations near the other. In this situation, it is practical to have direct buses that skip the intermediate stops. The procedure for analysing the potential express bus services is principally determined from the origin-destination data of the demand for the service between outlying and inner zones. This is done to discover whether the demand is sufficiently high to benefit both the public transport operator and the passengers. Benefit to the passengers was defined as the saving in travel time. Using these

Figure 10.4: Major Transport Transfer Points and Links Along the Shoubra Corridor, Cairo

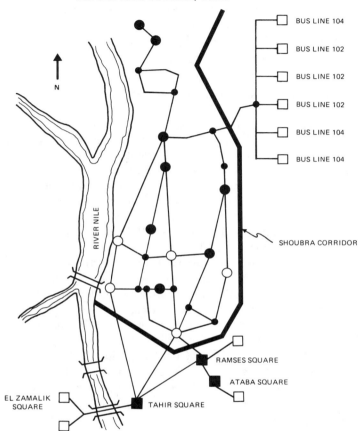

estimates, the public transport planners were able to identify several routes in the Shoubra corridor where potential express bus services could be implemented.

Direct Bus Service. The indentification of bus routes which would, if implemented, provide more direct service to some passengers, was based upon identified origin- destination traffic pairs with high volumes of transfer passengers (which were then ranked). In this case, a direct bus service was considered between spatial zones within the Shoubra corridor and zones in the rest of the metro-

339

politan area. As in the express bus procedure, the determination of the feasibility of a direct bus service was based on benefits to the operator (i.e., ability to reduce the existing service by at least one bus) and benefits to the passengers (i.e., travel timesavings). Using this procedure, six possible direct service lines were identified and later implemented by CTA.

Transport Corridor Planning in Guadalajara

Guadalajara is a setting for transport corridor planning quite unlike Cairo and the planning objectives were completely different. A metropolitan area of two and a half million in a more affluent Third World country, Guadalajara is the centre of a rich agricultural region in northwest Mexico. It attracts heavy in-migration, and the current population growth rate around 1980 was 5.7 per cent. It has a very active urban planning and development programme, including an enormous central city urban design and historic restoration project. The central business area is large and thriving, including over half the city's economic activity. The urban structure includes a traditional Latin American high-density urbanised area, surrounded by lower density modern urban areas with very large regional shopping centres.

Public transport carries 80 per cent of trips in Guadalajara. The growth rate of public transport use is 6.5 per cent per year - but the rate of increase of the system's capacity is only 2 per cent. In the metropolitan area 160,000 cars are registered, about one for every 16 people. The organisation of public transport in Guadalajara is typical of Latin America; private sector bus companies operate on renewable concessions to the state. The State of Jalisco itself, in which Guadalajara is located, owns two trackless trolley lines - a very small part of the total service and the only non-bus component.

As in many Third World cities, the public transport companies have a long record of conflict and confrontation with the government. The public transport system, as a result, does not provide the logical organising basis for transport corridor planning in Guadalajara that it does in Cairo. Instead, urban transport planning is unified by a remarkably close collaboration between the public works department of the city, the planning department of the State of Jalisco, and the regional delegation of the national Ministry of Human Settlements and Public Works. Transport planning was developed in the work team made up of members of these agencies, and within it transport corridor planning has been given a significant role. The problem most underlying the interest in transport corridor planning in Guadalajara, is the need to penetrate the inner city residential shell to reach land for new development at the periphery. Reasons for the need to do this have already been implied by the description above, but require further explanation.

Land planning is very important in Guadalajara. Rapid population growth and other considerations have raised the value of land to the extent that a minimum size house plot is beyond the means of 75 per cent of the population. Some 60 per cent of the population are regarded as having incomes too low to participate in the open housing market. As a result, illegal settlements account for 10 per cent of the metropolitan land area, and house approximately 500,000 people. The quest for land that can be urbanised with assistance from the government is complicated by difficulties of the constraining topography - such as the need to save the rich surounding agricultural land, high land costs on the affluent periphery, and the surrounding *ejidos* (1).

These problems have been addressed by a focused urban development plan prepared by the collaboration of the State of Jalisco Planning Office and the Regional Delegation of the national Ministry of Human Settlements and Public Works. One aspect of this plan is to locate carefully a 'reserve' for future urban development within given planning criteria and the constraints of the setting. This urban reserve lies beyond a large portion of the high density inner shell of the city at the periphery (see Figure 10.2).

The form of the intervening urbanisation is the traditional Latin American chess-board street plan. Ground coverage is very high and for the most part there are no pavements. The construction is mostly old but in good condition. The streets are narrow with many crossings, some of them are used very heavily by buses. The problem is how to make the urban reserve usable by facilitating travel between the urban growth 'reserve' and the centre of the city. There are no broad arterials, not to mention highways, near the corridor. Given the use of narrow streets, simple straightforward techniques of corridor management were required. Under these circumstances, the variety of actions considered included the following:

1. **Traffic Control:**
   a. the reduction in number of kerb entries and crossing streets (both very numerous in this corridor);
   b. the improvement and repair of signs and electrical signals;
   c. the provision of synchronised signals;
   d. the removal of parking, enforcement of parking regulations (since illegal parking impeding traffic was very common);
   e. the removal of encroaching obstructions (such as ambulant vendors); and
   f. the separation of fast vehicles from slow vehicles (speed differences between different types of vehicles in use were notable).
2. **Public Transport Planning:**
   a. the creation of bus lanes (or bus streets) in the corridors;
   b. the relocation of bus stops (to be less numerous) and provision of adequate terminal points;
   c. the provision of signalisation that favours public transport vehicles;
   d. the redesign of public transport routing and scheduling (in the case of collaboration with the concessionaires) to remove duplicated services on major routes near the centre of the city, and provide special non-stop service for clusters of passengers with the same destinations, etc.; and
   e. the introduction of public transport (perhaps introduction of small vehicles, including the implementation of regulations permitting fixed-route taxis).
3. **Minor Construction:**
   a. intersection redesign;
   b. street surfacing and resurfacing (since pavement of poor condition sometimes constituted a significant obstacle to smooth traffic flow);
   c. the provision of street drainage (so undrained run-off of rainstorms does not impede traffic; and
   d. street widening (in the few spots where conditions permit).

The planning team formulated and refined a study methodology designed to prepare and present technical information for choice of actions. The information was quite basic. Although some traffic and critical movements studies had been conducted, there were no reliable origin-destination surveys available, either of public transport or vehicular traffic, and more were to be undertaken within the scope of the study.

The general approach which emerged contained four components:

1. the determination of a radial set of parallel streets on which to focus attention;
2. the preparation of a Corridor Condition Diagram for information purposes - describing the corridor to be provided on a facility map. It includes such items as street widths, lane designation, pavement widths, medians, kerb entries, public transport stops, etc. (i.e., the corridor geometry). It also describes physical conditions, such as areas of poor pavement, poor drainage, illegal parking, institutions with sensitive entry problems (e.g., schools and hospitals), accident records and traffic volumes;
3. the preparation of a Corridor Dossier for noting spatial or general corridor information. It includes notes on police enforcement of parking regulations, overall conditions of paving and drainage, detailed descriptions of accident records, observations about public transport vehicle manoeuvres, the mix of fast and slow vehicles, etc.; and
4. the preparation of Special Studies including an analysis of critical traffic movements, speed and delay studies, and public transport routing and scheduling.

CONCLUSION

Transport corridor planning has a great deal to offer Third World cities, provided the general methodology is adjusted to the special dynamics of urban transport in the city of application, and it fits in with local urban development strategies, as well as the constraints and potentialities of the institutional setting. The prior history of this tool and its use in on-going development and gradual improvement of transport corridor planning in the industrialised world are advantageous to the Third World. For the experience provides a basis for relevant methods increasingly being included in professional education and training programmes.

The particular relevance of transport corridor planning and management approaches to Third World cities arises from its low cost, its flexibility in the force of different development realities, the possibility for a national agency to guide it with a single set of model methods,and the fact that the approach's techniques can be applied incrementally and cancelled at any time.

Given the poor performance of traffic management schemes in many Third World cities, transport corridor planning and management has much to achieve in its early stages of application. It should however be emphasised that transport corridor schemes are not to be confined to isolated projects for this dissipates the potency of the methodology. They should instead be applied in accordance with a plan that begins with definite transport and development objectives that reinforce one another. Such objectives are numerous and range from reducing energy consumption to increasing access to populations suffering travel disadvantages.

The basic requirements for the effective adoption of transport corridor planning and management efforts are trained professionals, and an institutional coherence across the affected institutional planning framework as advocated in Chapter 7.

The examples of transport corridor planning outlined in this chapter suggest a variety of alternative uses of the approach. In Cairo, advantage was taken of a unified public transport system and a largely public transport-orientated scheme was planned. In Guadalajara, on the other hand, the emphasis of application was on traffic enforcement and control, generating anticipated benefits which facilitate the development of planned urban form.

NOTE

(1) Ejidos in Mexico are lands held in common by groups of peasants, which cannot, within practical limitations of time and effort, be bought or expropriated.

REFERENCES

Armstrong-Wright, A. (1986) 'Urban Transit Systems: Guidelines for Examining Options', **World Bank Technical Paper**, no. 52, IBRD, Washington DC.
Bradlam and Hurdle (1981) 'Programming for Houses in Greater London', GLC, London.

Britton, E.K.B. (1978) 'Transportation Systems Management in Europe: The Research Results', EcoPlan International Centre for Economic Research and Industrial Planning, Department of Transportation, Washington DC.

Carter, Jr., A.A. (1962) 'Increasing the Traffic-Carrying Capacity of Urban Arterial Streets', Bureau of Public Roads, Government Printing Office, Washington DC.

Cervero, R. (1986) 'Unlocking Suburban Gridlock', **Journal of the American Planning Association**, vol. 52. no. 4, Chigaco.

Cox, M. (1975) 'Reserved Bus Lanes in Dallas', **Texas Transportation Engineering Journal**, vol. 101, no. TE4, Institute of Transportation Engineers, Houston.

El-Hawary, M. and others (1979) 'Cairo Urban Transportation Project Public Transportation Survey', Technology Adaptation Program, MIT Technology Adaptation Program, Massachusetts Institute of Technology, Cambridge, Massachusetts.

Elias, W.J. (1976) 'The Greenback Experiment, Signal Pre-emption for Express Buses: A Demonstration Project', California Department of Transportation, Sacramento, California.

Englen, R.E. (1982) 'Coordination of Transportation System Management and Land Use Management', **Highway Research Board, NCHRP Report**, no. 93, HRB, Washington DC.

Gakenheimer, R. (1976) **Transportation Planning as Response to Controversy**, MIT Press, Cambridge, Massachusetts.

Gakenheimer, R. and Meyer M. (1979) 'Urban Transport Planning in Transition: The Sources and Prospects of TSM', **Journal of the American Planning Association**, vol. 45, no. 1, Chicago.

Gakenheimer, R., Thomas F. Humphrey, McNeill S. and others (1987) 'National Survey of Transportation Actions in Suburban Corridors', MIT Center for Transportation Studies, Massachusetts Institute of Technology, Cambridge, Massachusetts.

____(1987) 'Measures to Deal with Transportation Congestion in Suburban Corridors in Massachusetts', MIT Center for Transportation Studies, Massachusetts Institute of Technology, Cambridge, Massachusetts.

Jalisco, Gabierno del Estado de, and Secretaria de Asentamientos Humanos y Obras Publicas (1978) **Guadalajara: Region y**

Zona Conurbada: Ordenamiento, Instrumentacion Guadalajara: Delegacion 13.

Massachusetts, Commonwealth (1986) **Proceedings of National Conference on Suburban Expressways and Beltways**, Executive Office of Transportation and Construction, Boston, Massachusetts.

Meyer, M.D. (1976) 'A Review of Transportation Systems Management Plans Submitted in Response to New Federal Policy', **MIT Center for Transportation Studies Working Paper**, no. 76-3, Massachusetts Institute of Technology, Cambridge, Massachusetts.

_____ (1982) 'Urban Transportation Planning', **Journal of Urban Planning and Development**, American Society of Civil Engineers vol. 108, no. UPI, New York.

Meyer, M.D. and E.J. Miller (1984) **Urban Transportation Planning: A Decision-Oriented Approach**, McGraw Hill, New York.

Ministere de l'Equipement (1974 and subsequent publications) **Les Plans de Circulation: Paris**, The Ministry, Paris.

Ourston, L. (1976) **Timing Traffic Signals to Reduce Fuel Consumption: The Outer State Experiment**, City of Santa Barbara, California.

Pill, J. (1976) **Planning and Politics: The Metro Toronto Transportation Plan Review**, MIT Press, Cambridge, Massachusetts.

RATP Sofretu (1973) **Greater Cairo Transportation Planning Study**, Ministry of Transport, Arab Republic of Egypt, Cairo.

Roark, J.J. (1981) 'Experiences in Transportation System Management', **National Cooperative Highway Research Program Report**, no. 81, Transportation Research Board, Washington, DC.

Rose, H.S. and Hinds, D.H. (1976) 'South Dixie Highway Contraflow Bus and Carpool Lane Demonstration Project', **Transportation Research Record**, no. 606, Transportation Research Board, Washington, DC.

Urban Mass Transportation Administration of the USA (1976) **Transit Corridor Analysis: A Manual Sketch Planning Technique**, US Department of Transportation, Washington, DC.

US Department of Transportation (1974) **Urban Corridor Demonstration Program,** US Government Printing Office, Washington, DC.

World Bank (1985) **Transportation in Urban Management and Planning,** IBRD, Washington, DC.

_____ (1986) **Urban Transport: A World Bank Policy Study,** IBRD, Washington, DC.

Wyatt, E.M. (1980) 'A Framework for Identification and Evaluation of Low Cost Public Transport Improvements in Cairo', Unpublished Master's thesis, Department of Civil Engineering,Massachusetts Institute of Technology, Cambridge, Massachusetts.

Chapter 11

Street Management

Alan Proudlove and
Alan Turner

INTRODUCTION

The management of urban traffic to achieve particular circulation objectives is widely accepted as an alternative to major capital works. Its primary objective is to improve traffic flow and safety, the premise being that streets (1) are for movement and that motorised traffic flows should be as unimpeded as possible.

However, while it is true that undue congestion has economic disadvantages, the city streets of the poorer Third World nations have additional functions which are absent from either wealthier Third World countries or the industrialised countries where the techniques of traffic management were originally devised. Living, sleeping, working and trading all take place in the streets of many major Third World cities, and while these activities may be a nuisance to the traffic engineer they represent part of the economic and social life of the city and as such they should be planned for. Unfortunately increasing motor vehicle traffic is causing more and more congestion, and engineers and planners charged with providing for the motor vehicle are coming to regard non-transport activities (together with non-motorised traffic) as anachronistic.

In order to focus attention on the existence of non-traffic activities and the needs of slow-moving and non-motorised traffic in determining a policy for street use, the term 'Street Management' was coined during the preparation of a development plan for Madras with which the authors of this chapter were involved

(Turner et al, 1980). The term includes not only traffic management, but also street maintenance and socio-economic management; the aim is to involve not only the highway authority, the public transport agencies and the police, but also agencies responsible for social services, housing, education and perhaps commerce.

A conventional response to the chaos and confusion in many Third World streets is to say that since it is too difficult to change people's habits or to adjust the physical layout of streets within their current (sometimes narrow) widths, major changes are needed. The contention is that unless streets are widened, and new roads and intersections built, the city will grind to a halt. Although new construction will always have a place in a balanced programme, there are few countries with the resources to 'solve' all their problems in this way (assuming that construction could ever 'solve' Third World urban transport problems).

> To relieve congestion, many countries have opted to expand road networks....... But these solutions are costly and strain already hard pressed budgets....... Some traffic specialists claim that with a package of far less expensive measures, designed to re-organise road space more efficiently, congestion....... can be dramatically reduced ...... (Koepell, 1982).

In most Third World countries the emphasis must be laid very clearly on making the best use of existing street networks through the adoption of innovative approaches to urban traffic management. Comprehensive management of streets to achieve their more effective use by making provision for a range of wide activities is the subject under discussion in this chapter.

TYPICAL STREET CONDITIONS OF THIRD WORLD CITIES

It is difficult if not impossible to describe the street and traffic conditions which apply to all Third World cities, as emphasised in Chapters 1 and 2, for customs and urban characteristics obviously vary considerably. Nevertheless, these are often variations on a common theme, so that it is possible to derive some generalisations which can lead to a policy approach. The following paragraphs describe experiences from several countries; examples from a poor country (India) and a wealthier Third World country (Iran) are used as illustrations.

Streets in urban settlements are laid out principally to give access to land which is to be developed or else is developed but inaccessible. All kinds of traffic may be generated in the street by urban development, but the dominant means of access, especially in the Third World, is on foot. Most streets will also attract some through-traffic, the amount and type depending on the streets' location in the road network. Through-traffic is in conflict with most other street activities; its character, speed and volume coexist unhappily with slow-moving and non-motorised traffic and with other activities such as street-trading. Both types of traffic, (i.e., through-traffic and that seeking access within the street,) include pedestrian, animal and motorised movement; the traffic itself may be fast or slow-moving - depending on its propulsive method. There is a further distinction between traffic which is slow-moving because it is at the beginning or end of its journey, and that which is in mid- journey, wishing to encounter a minimum of impediments.

Vehicular traffic in Third World cities characteristically contains far higher proportions of trucks and buses than in more industrialised countries, and also larger numbers of animal drawn vehicles. In some cities, taxis and minibuses form a high proportion of the motor vehicles; in India the various forms of rickshaw take the taxi's dominant place (see Chapter 4). In virtually all cities there is a high volume of pedestrian traffic. In many countries where the urban topography is reasonably flat, bicycles are the next most important means of transport.

Other important street activities are those associated with the urban informal sector which covers a wide spectrum of social and economic activities. These include trades and crafts (such as leather work or shoe-making), selling and marketing, entertainment and, in some cases, living. In many instances these activities are viewed by local governments as a blight on the city, an administrative nuisance and an unnecessary impediment to a 'smooth traffic flow'. Whereas in fact, they simply reflect the state of the urban economy; they would not exist if they were not necessary.

> There is a tendency among some economists, as well as officials, to treat the informal sector with contempt regarding its work as unnecessary, inefficient, un-

profitable, undignified and even counterproductive...
yet it manages to serve the urban poor by providing
employment and training opportunities, using appropriate technologies and local resources, recycling
materials, producing affordable goods and services
and distributing profits to those with the greatest need
(Werlin, 1982).

It is precisely for these reasons that it is so important for
planners and engineers to understand and make provision for this
type of activity. The economic life of the city may not be best
served simply by providing traffic flow at the expense of a large (if
un-vocal) section of the community.

A particular characteristic of the streets in many Third
World countries is the poor (in many cases unusable) state of the
sidewalks. They are generally narrow and badly maintained, with
irregular surfaces, holes and obstructions. Often heaps of garbage
or building materials make progress along them impossible; in
other instances, street traders and their customers take up so much
space that pedestrians are forced into the road where they may
have to walk alongside deep and unprotected storm water drains.

Bicycles are frequently parked on the footway, and it is not
uncommon to find some or all of the width taken up by constructions such as electrical sub-stations or traffic police control-cabins,
among other official and unofficial structures. The result is that
the pedestrian is often forced to walk in the roadway along an intermediate zone between the sidewalk and the motor vehicles
which he must share with bicycles, hand-carts and animal-drawn
vehicles. This is often a zone of chaotic profusion, where the
greatest mix of traffic occurs; cyclists weave in and out among
pedestrians and carts, while the occasional parked vehicle causes
people to squeeze by or spill still further out into the roadway. It
is on the edge of this tide of movement that the crowds waiting for
public transport must also stand, to flag down passing taxis or get
near the front of the bus queue. This intermediate zone is often
muddy or dusty as it is seldom swept by motor traffic (see Figure
11.1).

Pride of place goes to the motor vehicle whose right of way
is usually the smoothest and best maintained part of the street.
Though the width between sidewalks may be sufficient to carry
four to six lanes of traffic, motor vehicles tend to travel in the
central lanes unless they are slow moving or stopping, leaving the

Figure 11.1: Typical Street Use in Madras

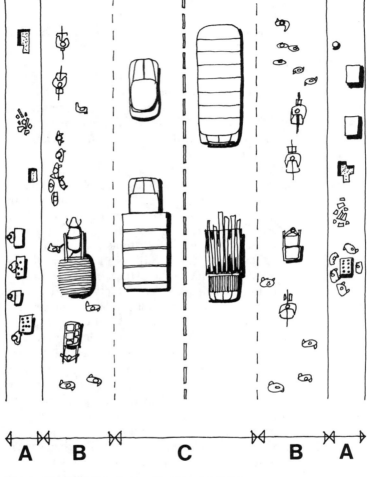

The street is divided into three main zones of activity:
a. Narrow sidewalks obstructed by piles of rubbish, street vendors, missing manhole covers, excavation or municipal equipment.
b. Inner lanes used mainly by cars, bicycles, pedestrians, parked vehicles and groups of people waiting for buses. Muddy or dusty surface is evidence of lack of use by motor traffic.
c. Outer lanes used by motor traffic; cars, buses, lorries, taxis, auto-rickshaws.

remainder of the roadway to the miscellaneous uses described above. If these lanes become congested the authority's approach is either to call for road widening or to subjugate other road users to the needs of the motor vehicle by confining pedestrians behind barrier fences and seeking to ban slow moving vehicles.

Neither of these 'solutions' is commendable to Third World cities - there are usually more urgent needs for scarce financial resources than the widening of roads and the relocation of those displaced by such widening. Pedestrian and other slow moving traffic have as much right to consideration by the authorities as have motor vehicles, particularly in cities with low vehicle owner-ship rates. The solutions must lie in more socially sensitive and in-novative approaches aimed at securing reasonable conditions for all street users. The following paragraphs illustrate the situation in two very different cities; Madras (India) is a large city with very low vehicle ownership rates, whereas Tehran (Iran), being weal-thier, has many more vehicles per capita.

Madras

Madras is a city of some 4.5 million people and is expanding rapid-ly. One third of its inhabitants are extremely poor and live in huts with mud walls and thatched roofs. The rates of unemployment and under-employment are very high and are unlikely to decrease significantly in the medium term. The enormous importance of the informal sector is reflected in the large numbers of bullock carts, hand-carts, bicycles, cycle rickshaws and other slow moving traffic, not to mention the street traders and those whose only home is the street. Except in the narrow streets of the central busi-ness district, traffic moves along relatively well, although to Western eyes the disordered nature of the streets prevents vehicles making proper use of the roadway (see Figures 11.2 and 11.3).

Public transport of all kinds is vital in Madras since private vehicle ownership is extremely low. The road network is extensive and, on the whole, well maintained. Both the bus and rail systems are efficiently managed and carry vast numbers of passengers. Nevertheless some 40 per cent of all trips are on foot or bicycle. In the past, traffic studies carried out in the city have been based on American or European models and too much emphasis has been given to improving the flow of vehicular traffic and reducing 'slow moving' traffic.

Figure 11.2:   Typical Streets in Madras: Pedestrian Movement
              and On-Street Parking

In 1979-80 the authors were involved in the preparation of a
development plan for the Madras Metropolitan Area which
covered all sectors including transport (Turner et al, 1980). The
main findings in the transport sector related to improvements to
existing rail lines and bus services, but in the context of this chapter the following observations are particularly relevant:

1.   The majority of journeys in the urban area are made by
     pedestrians and cyclists, hence facilities for these two
     categories need to be radically improved.
2.   The improvement of sidewalks is essential in order to dis-
     courage people from walking in the roadway. This is the
     single most important measure to which transport policies
     should be addressed.
3.   The efficient use of the existing road network should be im-
     proved before further capital costs are incurred in new high-
     ways. The key lies in improved traffic management and
     enforcement. The government should formulate integrated
     policies of Street *Management,* including traffic manage-
     ment and highway maintenance, and should coordinate the
     activities of the local bodies.

354

Figure 11.3:   Typical Streets in Madras: Public Transport
                Operations and Street Vendors

Most people in Madras prefer to walk in the roadway, owing to the narrowness and
poor conditions of the sidewalks. This, together with bad lane discipline, reduces the
effective width of the roads and causes a great deal of traffic congestion. A solution
to this problem is one of the most important of the improvements to which transport
policy should be addressed; the efficiency of existing infrastructure could be
increased significantly by good management.

These three findings illustrate very clearly some of the major
problems.

Tehran

Tehran is another city where the inefficient use of streets prevails.
A study of pedestrian movement revealed that most of the

355

problems identified were related to impediments to pedestrian traffic and the consequent loss of road space (Turner et al 1976). Crossing the road in Tehran appears to be relatively more dangerous than in some other cities of comparable size, although accident data are collected in such a way that it is difficult to be precise. Even where pedestrian crossings are installed there is often no integration with footpaths so that the pedestrian may have to climb over a physical barrier (see Figure 11.4).

Figure 11.4:   A Pedestrian Crossing in Tehran

Anyone using the crossing has to clamber over a low wall and **djube** (open drain). Needless to say few people use the crossing.

In Tehran, obstacles varying from building materials to large unlit holes or trenches litter the sidewalks. The *djubes* or open storm drains which line most streets make matters worse. These conditions force people onto the roadway where large groups of people wait for buses and the popular orange taxis. As in Madras a significant width of the road is unavailable for vehicular movement (see Figures 11.5 and 11.6).

In neither Tehran nor Madras is there an easy solution to a problem of this kind, since it has many contributary causes. Once

Figure 11.5:   A Major Street in Tehran

The people in the road are waiting for shared taxis. They have no choice owing to the uncovered djubes; as a result the inner lane is hardly used by moving traffic.

again co-ordination is the goal; co-ordination among the agencies responsible for traffic management, highway maintenance, education, social, economic and institutional aspects. Clearly the enforcement of traffic regulations (sadly lacking in Tehran) will alone do little good unless a comprehensive view is adopted and other measures concerning management, street maintenance, education in road safety and social attitudes to the use of street space are taken at the same time. It is not enough to rely on the traffic police, the highway authority and the public transport agencies; organisations dealing with many other aspects of urban life must also be brought into the picture.

Figure 11.6: A Typical Minor Street in Tehran

Where there are no **djubes**, cars park on the sidewalk, forcing pedestrians to walk along the road.

AN APPROACH TO STREET MANAGEMENT

Policies for Street Management

The foregoing sections of this chapter illustrate the range of street activities in many Third World countries. We have also suggested that a conventional 'solution' to reducing traffic congestion is often inappropriate. Nevertheless, the higher levels of activity in all sectors of urban development which arise from the increase in population densities and the use of motor vehicles, contribute to the over-use of streets. Friction between different types of street activity is dangerous and leads to aggressive behaviour. Some order must therefore be introduced into the streets.

The more important street functions can be classified into three groups:

1.   those connected with access to adjoining lands and properties;

2.   movement through the street; and
3.   those which take place within the street such as trading or social exchange.

Any policy for street management which aims to reduce over-use of street space in a fair and rational way must recognise the legitimacy of all these activities. Policy must also underlie the laws relating to the use of streets and their physical design, layout and construction. A policy for street management must also recognise that different streets have different functional priorities. Therefore, certain rules of relativity, connectivity and continuity need to be introduced and maintained to secure effective functioning. This functional hierarchy of use is similar to, although much more complex than, the hierarchy of traffic routes which has become a commonly accepted feature of highway planning.

The need to provide for all recognised street activities must be taken into account as must the space available in the existing street system. The safety of street users, harmony of activities and efficient use of limited resources are the aims. Legal measures alone to confine particular activities to specific parts of the street are not sufficient. Appropriate priorities of use must be determined and the street surface suitably designed.

Determining Street Functions

In the highly motorised cities of the industrialised countries, a philosophy of functional use has resolved itself into the adoption of hierarchies of urban roads for vehicular movement and access. There, the road classification ranges from the urban motorway - permitting only vehicular movement and no direct access to adjoining lands - to the access way which primarily serves to bring vehicles to adjoining land and buildings (simultaneously recognising that many other non-vehicular activities will also take place in these access ways).

However, such an approach is inappropriate to deal with the street problems of many Third World cities where in many streets there is no justification for vehicular traffic to take precedence. In circumstances where appropriate laws and regulations do not exist, it will be necessary to enact statutory instruments to define and delimit desirable activities, so as to provide the legal foundation for street management, design and use-enforcement. The

outcome of a policy appraisal should, therefore, include the definition of the scale of broad groups of street activities along the following lines:

1. traffic - sub-divided into:
    a. motor vehicular,
    b. slow-moving vehicular, and
    c. pedestrian;
2. public transport - including facilities for passengers joining
    or leaving vehicles;
3. access - which will include loading and unloading into ad-
    joining properties (but not the use of the street surface for
    storing goods in-transit); and
4. socio-economic activities of an informal and transitory na-
    ture.

The policy will then assign priorities of use in the street on
the basis of the scale of each of these various activities and the
street's dimensions and location in the network.

As a rule, vehicular through-traffic has the most urgent
need, not simply because of its scale (which it may not be possible
to accommodate together with other justified street activities) but
because a rational and continuous network for through-traffic
movement must be created. Access to properties must also be allowed for, though it may be reasonable in certain streets to adopt
policies limiting vehicular access to particular times of day or requiring rear access to be provided for vehicles.

The appropriate balance between the provision of space for
pedestrians, and slow vehicular and motor traffic in particular
streets should be a major aspect of a street management policy.
Just as a network for through-motor traffic should form one
aspect, another could arise from the presence of large volumes of
slow-moving traffic which justify either an independent street network or a network giving priority to this kind of traffic; for example, an independent cycleway, or routes for cart traffic in the
vicinity of a port or market.

In some situations, the scale of pedestrian movement could
justify the closure of a street to all through vehicular traffic. The
street would then become a pedestrian area with limited access for
vehicles which would be required to move at slow speed and to
give way to pedestrians. In some pedestrian areas, a high level of
non-traffic street activity could then be tolerated, though extreme

pressure for street-trading activities would be the priority factor determining a street's use. In most streets there is scope for all the activities to co-exist and street management should, therefore, seek to achieve the right balance between them. However, this principle cannot succeed unless activities which have no reason to take place in the street are removed.

Principal unacceptable street uses are mostly those associated with public utilities, such as transformer stations, switchgear and poles, or the dumping of building materials onto the sidewalk. These unacceptable uses are invariably permanent or semi-permanent and interfere significantly with pedestrian movement; this, in turn, has a cascade effect on other types of traffic.

The whole cycle of street-activity conflict largely originates in the inadequacy or mis-use of the sidewalks. So it is essential that policy is clear on permitted uses and on measures to secure these. Implementation of a policy should be through design and enforcement, recognising that the mark of good design is that it should be basically self-regulating. The design process is likely to identify deficiencies in supply - for instance, insufficient street space. It is in these circumstances that the common reaction to favour traffic movement (and vehicular traffic in particular) must be resisted and a fair balance maintained between the needs of *all* street users.

SOME TYPICAL PROBLEMS AND RESPONSES

It was suggested earlier in this chapter that despite considerable local variations, there are recurring street problems common to many Third World cities. These problems are so complex and interrelated that it is difficult to influence them with conventional traffic management approaches. Clearly experimentation is necessary to lead to innovative solutions. A traffic engineer whose education and experience have led him to concentrate exclusively on improving the flow of vehicular traffic may find it retrogressive to encourage street traders by making provision for them. Nevertheless, such measures are necessary if any real progress is to be made.

Pedestrians in the Roadway

Problem. People do not walk on the roadway out of sheer wilfulness; they do so because in a tropical climate walking is tiring and it is easier to walk on a well-maintained and well-paved surface. Traditionally, road surfaces are considered more 'important' than pedestrian routes; this attitude may not be entirely unrelated to the fact that decision makers usually travel by car and rarely if ever walk or cycle to their offices.

Response. The best way to remove pedestrians from the roadway (and simultaneously improve safety and traffic flow) is to offer a more attractive alternative. In other words, sidewalks should be wide and *maintained to at least as high a standard as the roadway*. A greater share of total resources would then have to be allocated to sidewalks and, with a fixed budget, it would be necessary to accept a lowering of the standard of road maintenance. There is, however, a strong argument for satisfying the needs of the majority of street users - the pedestrians. The agencies involved in this response is primarily the Municipality's Highways department.

Slow-moving Vehicles

Problem. Conventional thinking also tends to divide street users into pedestrians, slow-moving traffic and motor vehicles with the aim of segregating each group. This is usually not only impossible but may also be totally unnecessary. There is little danger to pedestrians from bicycles, animal carts or hand-drawn carts which can all continue to mix freely. The only segregation necessary is between traffic powered by human or animal energy and that powered by internal combustion engines.

Response. Where street width allows, animal or human drawn vehicles could use the same smooth wide tracks as pedestrians, so that the roadway proper is reserved for motor vehicles. The agencies involved would be the Municipal Highways department and the traffic police.

Obstruction of Movement by Street Trading

Problem. Humane solutions to the problem of street trading have been carried out in Indonesia and Malaysia (Werlin, 1982) and usually involve providing space which will not interfere significantly with pedestrians. At present in many cities, a trader selects a pitch anywhere on any sidewalk from an almost infinite number of available locations. However, once the locations are reduced by a policy of control, competition for space can cause problems. Obviously, adequate spaces must be provided.

Response. Where the width of the street allows, marked out spaces for trading should be designated on specially widened sections of the sidewalk. However, it must be stressed that over-ambitious regulation should be avoided; excessively complicated licensing systems or attempts to charge rents for trading creates over-bureaucratic administrative procedures and opportunities for corruption. It should be adequate to designate spaces where trading is allowed and where it is not. The corollary is, of course, that improved supervision and enforcement is essential. Agencies involved would include the municipality's departments concerned with employment and commerce as well as the police department.

Street Dwellers

Problem. Clearly, solutions must be sought over the long term; there is no way in which homeless families can be prevented from sleeping or cooking in the streets (as is common in India) until other opportunities are provided for them. An emphasis in housing policy on sites and services developments for low income groups (in accessible locations) and on the upgrading of slum housing will do much to improve the situation. However in the short term, other measures may be necessary such as the provision of small off-street areas with water, sanitation and some supervision, where homeless families could live temporarily (but not build shacks) until they could be offered a serviced lot.

In Indian cities, as in many Third World settlements, there are basically two types of street dweller:

1. those who (in cities such as Bombay or Calcutta) build shacks in the street and stay in one position for considerable lengths of time; and
2. those who (as is often the case in Madras) sleep on the sidewalk but move away during the day. They often return to the same place night after night, for advantages such as proximity to water, employment or the shelter provided by overhanging canopies or arcades.

The first type is clearly an impediment to movement and where possible the families should be offered alternative basic serviced lots. The second category has little effect on traffic movement and can be tolerated.

Response. Housing policy should be directed to making the best use of resources in solving the shelter problems of the lowest income groups. In many programmes, the concentration is on building conventional public housing which is not affordable by the poor and hardly affects the problem of homelessness. Where this is the case, a change in emphasis to slum upgrading and sites and services projects can enable the same resources to cater for the needs of many more low-income families. However, in the short-term it should be possible to provide temporary off-street spaces for homeless families with some basic services and supervision. A possible approach to street use where these conditions exist is shown in Figure 11.7 and Figure 11.8. Agencies involved in such a response should include municipal departments concerned with housing, social services, water and sanitation.

AN EXAMPLE OF STREET MANAGEMENT

An illustration of the type of street management problems and solutions to them is given in Figure 11.9 and Figure 11.10 which represent a hypothetical plan of an inner area in a Third World city. Three types of street are examined and their problems analysed to produce suggested street management policies and programmes to benefit each group of street user. The problems posed are not, of course, the only problems, and the suggested solutions are not necessarily appropriate in all circumstances. Planners, engineers and urban designers must above all keep an open mind about street management and be prepared to adopt un-

Figure 11.7:   A Possible Street Layout Where There is
Sufficient Width

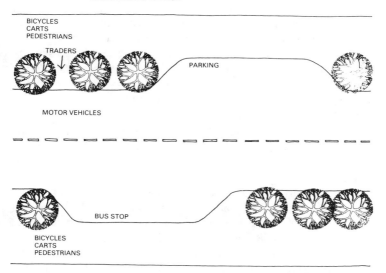

The idea behind this sketch is to recognize the zones of use shown in Figure
11.1 and to allocate space accordingly. 'Zone B' (in Figure 11.1) is divided
between vehicles (bus stops and parking) street vendors and other static uses.
It also provides space for shade trees. The wide pavement provides for carts,
bicycles and pedestrians.

Figure 11.8:   A Sketch Section of the Street Shown in
Figure 11.7

conventional solutions - at least until more experience of street management has been gained and its techniques become established.

The area illustrated in Figure 11.9 and Figure 11.10 contains one of the city's main shopping streets, together with a network of old minor central area streets, housing a variety of land uses, although shopping and services predominate. The area is bordered by a more recent arterial road which is one of the main traffic arteries serving the centre. Streets are open to all types of traffic, but only the arterial and the main shopping street carry buses. Parking is allowed in some of the narrow streets and also in the main shopping street which, like some others, is a one-way street. Sidewalks are narrow, ranging from one metre in some of the narrowest streets to three metres in the main shopping street areas.

Streets are also used for many non-traffic activities and constructions. The utility companies, in addition to buried services, have erected poles on the sidewalk to carry overhead services. They have also built transformer and switching stations on or beneath sidewalks, which in some places occupy its full width. The traffic police control every vehicle intersection by traffic lights, but operate these manually from observation cabins on sidewalks at the intersection. Street vendors occupy the best sales pitch they can find, usually areas of maximum pedestrian activity. They are not averse to taking up the greater part of the sidewalk to lay out their wares or set up their food or drink stalls.

The main problem of the area is disorderly congestion. Vehicular traffic, although it can penetrate any part of the area, is often delayed at junctions by slow-moving traffic and by numerous obstructions. Pedestrian movement is grossly congested in the main streets, especially on sidewalks and in narrower streets, because the footway is frequently completely blocked by permanent constructions or temporary stalls. During shopping hours street vendors occupy all the likely pitches, favouring the main shopping street, adjoining side streets, and the vicinity of bus stops. Food and drink stands favour bus stop locations, and also areas of office employment. Cyclists encounter fewer problems, because they are able to cycle round the parked vehicles, pedestrians, crowds waiting for buses, and other obstructions along the edge of the roadway.

The best approach to street management lies in determining priorities of street use. In the main shopping street, pedestrian movement must have first priority, but bus traffic, delivery vehicles

Figure 11.9:   A Typical Central Area Street Pattern: Pre-Street
Management Scheme

A   MAIN SHOPPING STREET
Shops at ground level, offices
apartments/hotels over
Large pedestrian flows
One-way traffic, bus route,
parking allowed

> *PROBLEMS*
> *Sidewalks overcrowded,*
> *much used by street-*
> *vendors*
> *Deliveries obstructed by*
> *parked cars Buses cannot*
> *reach kerb, passengers*
> *must wait in roadway*

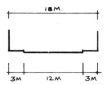

B   NARROW DOWNTOWN
STREETS
Mixed land uses, shops/
services offices at ground
One or two-way traffic flow,
some parking allowed

> *PROBLEMS*
> *Sidewalks too narrow*
> *to pass comfortably*
> *Sidewalks blocked by*
> *police or utilities*
> *equipment*
> *Roadway blocked by*
> *delivery vehicles*

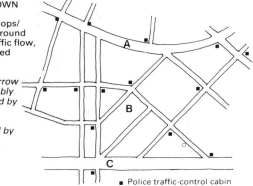

■ Police traffic-control cabin
○ Transformer sub-station

C   ARTERIAL STREET
Mixed land uses fronting
street, institutional buildings
Two-way mixed traffic, cycle
lanes, slow moving traffic
Many bus routes, much
pedestrian movement

> *PROBLEMS*
> *Sidewalks overcrowded,*
> *obstructed by street*
> *vendors parked bicycles*
> *and motors vehicles, etc*
> *Pedestrians have difficulty*
> *crossing wide roadway*
> *Bus passengers must await*
> *bus stranding in roadway*
> *Motor vehicles restricted to*
> *travel in two centre lanes*

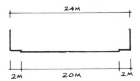

Figure 11.10: A Typical Central Area Street Pattern: Post Street Management Scheme

MAIN SHOPPING STREET

SOLUTION
widen sidewalks to about 6m,
mark out trading area
Create a 6.5m bus and servicing
way
Prohibit access of general traffic
and parking

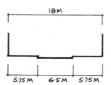

DOWNTOWN STREETS

SOLUTION
Rapave whole street as a
pedestrian area
Allow servicing vehicles to enter
parts of pedestrian area subject
to restrictions on time, etc
Designate areas where street
trading is permissible

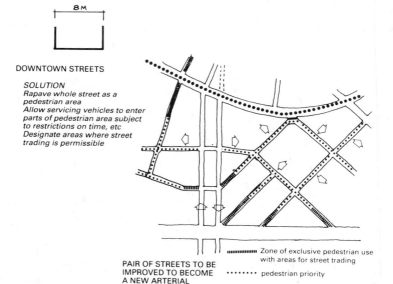

PAIR OF STREETS TO BE
IMPROVED TO BECOME
A NEW ARTERIAL

⊪⊪⊪⊪⊪⊪⊪ Zone of exclusive pedestrian use
with areas for street trading

•••••• pedestrian priority

ARTERIAL STREET

SOLUTION
Widen sidewalks and keep clear
of all obstructions
Divide roadway to create
pedestrian refuges
Designate an alternative route for
slow-moving vehicles

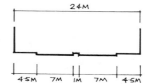

A hierarchy of use is suggested based on function, location and width.
These physical measures would need to be supported by social and
economic measures as suggested in the text.

and some street trading also have their place. Once these activities are accommodated there is unlikely to be enough space for general traffic and parking needs. The priority of use of the arterial road is also obvious; to accommodate the movement of large volumes of motor traffic. Nevertheless, this requirement must co-exist with the provision of reasonable facilities for the pedestrian, including improved facilities for crossing the wide roadway. Reducing the number of interruptions to motorised traffic caused by intersections of many minor streets, will compensate for the reduced roadway width required to improve pedestrian facilities. Slow moving vehicular traffic should be redirected to other streets where possible. The street management study shown in Figure 11.9 and Figure 11.10 reveals the need for improved facilities for arterial traffic in an orthogonal direction. Plans can be made, for example, to develop an arterial from a pair of parallel city centre streets in the long-term renewal of the area. In the short term, they could be used as a pair of one-way streets, serving a limited arterial function, with traffic speed kept low by frequent controlled intersections, which will also assist pedestrian crossing.

The remaining network of small streets provides the important basic function of access to adjoining properties, although vehicles will not necessarily be allowed access to every property. In many cases it will be sufficient to get vehicles within about 30 meters of a property, accepting that deliveries may have to be carried up to this distance. However, the function of access should not necessarily predominate in these streets. Because these streets are so narrow, it may be appropriate to remove the distinction between areas for walking and areas for vehicles - converting the whole surface into a pedestrian area, or pedestrian and bicycle domain. Motor vehicles could then be allowed into parts of this area subject to strict controls, as to permitted time of day, type and purpose of vehicles, permitted speed and the precedence of pedestrians and cyclists. No parking would be allowed in these pedestrian areas, although vehicles would be able to load or unload. In the enhanced newly vehicle-free environment street traders could set up semi-permanent stalls.

A plan of this kind would have to be reviewed to check that each type of street user has had a fair deal; that there are good facilities for movement on foot, particularly along direct routes to and from the main pedestrian traffic generators (such as public transport stops and termini, educational establishments, etc.); that there is adequate capacity for arterial vehicular movement;

that all buildings have reasonable access facilities; and that non-traffic street activities can still take place in suitable locations. It will be necessary to discuss the proposed changes generally in the planning and implementation stages so that users will have had representation and will not subsequently feel that unwarranted changes have been imposed.

STREET MANAGEMENT THROUGH DESIGN

General Design Principles

The foregoing examples indicate among other things, a need for good design. The authors advocate design as the medium for conveying to the user the appropriate use for particular streets, and for the component parts of those streets. Designs must, however, be created within the statutory and regulatory system adopted by each city and state. Design can be much more than an aid to regulation and correct functional use. In particular, it can become the principal element (apart from the street user) in the achievement of street safety and an aesthetically satisfactory environment.

In order to achieve his objectives the designer must allocate appropriate parts of the street surface to appropriate uses, so as to achieve a degree of segregation in order that each street can function satisfactorily and safely by providing surfaces in a way to define clearly the limits of each street function. Supplementary to these basic elements of design are other details which can contribute to the success of street management, such as street furniture and street lighting, parking controls, street signing, and in particular the design and policing of junctions.

Design for pedestrians

To summarise the arguments so far: pedestrians are the most numerous users of Third World city streets, yet are the worst provided for. Walking is a physical activity with a natural tendency to minimise effort, even at the expense of personal safety. This is emphasised by the risks commonly taken crossing a street, or walking on the vehicle way. It follows that smoothness of street surface and lack of interruption or discontinuity are important. This is why developed design for sidewalks has adopted large, smooth paving slabs of fine textured asphaltic surfacings. The former is preferred for tropical countries for its coolness - in slab form rather than in-situ concrete, or asphalt if services are buried beneath. The shortage of highly skilled tradesmen to lay this kind of paving may be a problem in some countries.

Ideally, sidewalks should not have sudden changes of level nor should they be broken too often by vehicle crossings. Where vehicles must cross the footway, they should be made to mount the sidewalk. In so doing they are more likely to give precedence to the pedestrian, as the law should require.

An adequate footway width is important: it should never be less than 1.5 metres (preferably 2.5 metres). Its proper width and position in relation to vehicular traffic will be affected by the speed and volume of traffic, and by more and/or faster traffic requiring a greater separation of pedestrians from vehicles. Where other sidewalk activities occur, minimum widths of three to six metres are appropriate.

In many Third World cities some shading of sidewalks is most desirable, in which case the sidewalk must be wide enough to contain fully the spread of trees. It is also important to select species of trees which will not damage buildings or pavings, and will not grow branches below head height.

Good drainage of the footway is also important - this is achieved by raising the sidewalk above the roadway where the two adjoin, arranging for the surface to have a fall towards the road. Separate footway drainage will then be unnecessary. However, drainage is no justification for holes or channels in the sidewalk. Drainage equipment, such as grids and entries to piped drains, should be placed in the roadway edge or finished with a smooth cover if in the edge of the sidewalk. Good maintenance of equipment mounted in the sidewalk is important; all too often there are missing drain covers or unfilled excavations in the sidewalks.

Good design is an aid to securing a high level of maintenance. Street lighting of sidewalks is more important than lighting the vehicle way, and requires different techniques and equipment. The use of light coloured pavings will enhance the illumination of footways.

Design for Vehicular Traffic

This aspect of design is well covered in the technical literature, so there is no need to deal with many of its details here. However, in the context of street design for Third World cities it is important to point out the dangers of over-design for vehicular traffic at the expense of other elements of the street. Apart from the possibilities already mentioned of making the vehicle-way too attractive for pedestrians and other non-vehicular activities, there is a danger that over-design will waste resources which should be devoted to other parts of the street. Where over-design exists, drivers sometimes behave aggressively towards other street users, driving too fast and menacing other road-users. This comment applies particularly to aspects of the design width of the roadway, where space ought instead to be used for greater sidewalk width, for slow-moving traffic and for vehicle parking or bus stops.

Some streets must, however, be identified as giving priority to motor-vehicle traffic - the arterial streets. These should form a rational network to serve the main vehicular traffic flows of the city, and for public transport, offering continuity of route and good connectivity. Few such arterial streets need to be designed for high speed. Maximum capacity probably occurs at speeds close to 50 kph and is more affected by stationary vehicles and interruptions to flow than by lane width or curvature. It is generally more important to provide separate facilities for loading and unloading, including buses, than to provide great width for moving traffic.

Street crossing is a problem for pedestrians that increases with greater roadway width. Where this exceeds eight or ten metres it is important to provide pedestrian refuges in the centre of the road at points where pedestrian crossing is envisaged, especially at the junctions.

Design for Other Street Activities

A case has already been made for accommodating other, non-traffic activities in the street, provided that these are transient in nature, that is to say that they must not occupy a place in the street for the full 24 hours of any day. Where special circumstances make longer occupation desirable, such as building or maintenance operations, or perhaps street sales kiosks, then these might be sited in the street under licence, provided that adequate spatial provision can first be made for other activities.

In terms of street use priorities, these transient but non-traffic activities must take third place, after pedestrian and vehicular traffic. Occasionally, it might be appropriate to give priority to non-traffic activities, where there is a centre of commercial activity or where there is a severe deficiency of other space for these activities. Where transient activities are to be accommodated together with traffic, the areas available must be clearly defined and located so as not to interfere with movement. This would be best achieved by identifying residual surface areas after defining footways and vehicle-ways, and by marking these residual areas as being available for trading by using a different surfacing material and preferably by raising their level.

In situations where streets have irregular or badly defined edges, or where unused adjoining land can be included in the street, these pieces of land would be the most suitable for non-traffic activities. Small parks can be created, adjoining one or two streets as places for congregation and trading. Unfortunately, traders usually want locations where there is plenty of passing traffic, whereas people in premises fronting the street do not want itinerant traders on their doorsteps. Thus there is some conflict within the general philosophy outlined here. However, given a sympathetic view of the problem, it should be possible to find locations for a reasonable amount of non-traffic activity.

In many cities there are good opportunities in the older areas to devote lengths of narrower streets almost wholly to non-traffic activities, provided that access can be maintained. The rededication of some streets to 'social functions', for pedestrians and trading, could have advantages in vehicular traffic control by simplifying the arterial street network. Such an approach has been employed in Europe, and is incorporated in the Dutch Woonerf and Winkelerf techniques for recovering streets from the traffic function, and restoring former residential and shopping functions (Royal Dutch Touring Club, 1977).

In other cities, some streets have been made pedestrian 'precincts' or joint pedestrian and public transport areas. In most cases limited vehicular access has been preserved. Changes of this kind have frequently been made in order to improve the commercial potential of areas and their environment; given the high pedestrian densities of Third World cities, that alone could well justify a more extensive adoption of pedestrian - priority streets.

Design of Junctions

Between junctions a rational approach to the allocation of street space can be devised in such a way as to favour whatever activity is appropriate to the particular street's place in the functional hierarchy. Junctions, however, pose many problems in that they create an inherent conflict between different activities. Pedestrians must cross vehicular-traffic streams; traffic activity is greatest at junctions; trades see them as their best locations; and bus stops are usually located close to junctions.

Techniques of vehicle control at junctions, by conventional automatic traffic lights, for example, may be too crude to deal with the multitude of conflicts which occur, especially where there is heavy pedestrian or cycle traffic. Some form of manual control and regulation will be necessary at busy times. Traffic light signals may be appropriate, provided that they include all- red pedestrian-crossing phases, are guaranteed a continuous power supply, and are reinforced by traffic police to ensure compliance. In some Third World cities, every street crossing is independently manually controlled. There are dangers in this in that there is no continuity of vehicular flow on the arterials, which in turn reduces their effective capacity and leads to calls for roadway widening. In such situations, traffic police controllers often see their responsibility as being solely towards the motor vehicle. There may therefore be some overall advantage in adopting automatic linked control (provided that adequate pedestrian facilities are incorporated into the system) supported by traffic police to assist with enforcement.

Advantage should be taken of topographical opportunities to secure pedestrian grade-separation without the use of steps. A slight elevation of the vehicle-way may be all that is necessary.

An Approach to Street Design

While these design criteria are set out, it must be recognised that few streets in the inner parts of many Third World cities have space to accommodate all three components of street activity to reasonable standards. In such circumstances the choice lies between accepting sub-standards, (with unsatisfactory environmental and safety consequences) or determining priorities. In many cases, there may be no real alternative to the first choice, but where possible a plan should be devised for assigning functional priorities to all streets in an area. This plan would take into account the socio-economic character and needs of the area, the overall vehicular traffic circulation plan, public transport requirements and the capital available to make the necessary changes to the street fittings.

Planning would start with measurement of current traffic volumes of all types, followed by forecasts of volume changes with time and following the rationalisation of the street network. A socio-economic study of non-traffic activities should be carried out, to include adjoining land uses and their access requirements. The same study would examine deficiencies in the provision of facilities for informal socio-economic activities in the area.

The resources required to implement proposals emerging from the kind of study described would be compared with the resources available in the streets of the study area. Where shortfall arises (probably the most common case) priorities must be assigned to each street. Some streets will form part of the arterial vehicular-way network, others will be too narrow to serve more than pedestrian traffic adequately. In all cases it is important to give priority to the provision of adequate space for pedestrians and public transport, making reasonable provision for non-traffic activities (where possible by the addition of land to the street) and giving lowest priority to motor vehicle traffic, except in the few streets identified as arterials. Even there, pedestrian needs should first be properly provided for. Where practicable, separate networks for slow-moving vehicular traffic should be identified.

Demonstration Programmes

Street management, being a relatively new concept, is best introduced on a street-by-street basis, although it may be necessary to produce a plan for a wider area, giving details of how the plan affects the arterial street network. In its other aspects, such as designation of areas to be used by street traders, and particularly the improvement and clearing of sidewalks, street management can be introduced on a street-by-street basis as design and funds permit. This gradual procedure is best regarded as a 'demonstration programme' with the objective of generating a public awareness of its benefits, and encouraging the demand for an extension of the programme to further streets and other areas. It should be borne in mind, however, that any demonstration programme needs to be very well planned and executed. If it fails through poor management, rather than because the idea is wrong, the result may be to convince decision-makers that the new ideas do not work; in short, a badly conceived demonstration programme can be counterproductive.

ENFORCEMENT

Streets in the inner areas of Third World cities are under intense competition for use of space, but as we have argued, most of these uses have a certain social legitimacy. It has been suggested that a comprehensive street management plan should be adopted to ensure reasonable opportunities to all legitimate users, with priorities specified for certain streets. The plan is put into operation by the appropriate design and layout of the street surface, with the objective of being self-regulating as far as possible. However, in conditions of intense use and competition, conflict between users is inevitable which the design will be unable to resolve on an hour by hour basis. It will therefore be necessary to reinforce the management plan by some degree of enforcement.

Consequently, it is important that the enforcement agency (normally the traffic police) should be party to and involved in the preparation and execution of street management plans. Both in this role and in their subsequent enforcement role, it is imperative that a sympathy should be developed within the police authority and its officers for the rights of all street users. A part of police officer training should therefore be concerned with the *sociology* of street use, the laws relating to street use, and techniques of street management. Traffic police could then extend their enforcement role into one of education and management of street users, particularly of vehicle drivers, staff of the public passenger transport authority and children.

The need for extensive enforcement against any particular category of legitimate street user can generally be taken to be an indication of the need for the introduction of street management, or for the review and perhaps modification of the management plan in operation.

EDUCATION IN THE USE OF STREETS

The measures that have been advocated in this chapter, while themselves aimed at creating a street environment that can be readily understood and properly used by the public, will be of little use unless the public becomes aware of the objectives of street management and related street design. A characteristic of Third World cities is, however, that a large proportion of the population are recent migrants to the city from rural areas. The task of educating them in the use of streets is, therefore, particularly difficult. Indeed, behaviour towards motorised traffic by many residents of many Third World cities is especially alarming. They often behave as though motor vehicles do not exist, and do not appear to comprehend the limits on motor manoeuvrability, and the dangers to which they are exposing themselves. In spite of this many drivers act aggressively towards pedestrians.

To be able to benefit from the street management approach advocated requires that attention should also be directed to changing the attitudes of the street user. The poorest people of many Third World cities are too burdened by the complacency of despair to do other than accept their lot, and it is, therefore, very difficult to command their attention on such matters. The media in Third World countries is, however, well able to mount attractive programmes on the proper use of streets, directed particularly towards the young and to vehicle operators, concentrating on the proper use of each part of the street, on the rights of users, and on safety and environmental aspects.

Equally important is the re-education of the establishment, particularly of government officials associated with the use and management of streets: the police, passenger transport staff, administrators and engineers, financial controllers, and many others. It is important that they should appreciate the need to revise the conventional view that streets are only for (motorised) traffic. The lack of concern in many countries for pedestrians, cyclists, slow moving traffic and other street activities has focused attention forcibly onto the need to demonstrate to the policy maker and planner that a great deal of progress can be made without massive investments. A change of attitudes alone could significantly improve street conditions in many Third World cities and towns.

NOTE

(1) The word 'street' has been used to convey an urban quality
and therefore means a roadway and sidewalks lined by continuous buildings.

REFERENCES

Koeppel, B. (1982). 'Breaking up LDC Gridlock', **Report** World
Bank, Washington, DC.
Royal Dutch Touring Club (1977) **Woonerf**, RDTC, The Hague.
Turner, Alan and Associates (1976) **Pedestrian Movement in
Tehran**, Tehran Urban Transport Project, Freeman Fox and
Associates, London.
_____ (1980) '**Structure Plan for Madras Metropolitan Area**',
Madras Metropolitan Development Authority and Overseas
Development Administration, London and Madras.
Werlin, (ed) 'Supporting Businesses of the Urban Poor', **The
Urban Edge,** Council for International Urban Liaison, vol.
6, no. 3, Washington, DC.

Chapter 12

Towards a Developmental Approach to Urban Transport Planning

Harry T. Dimitriou

INTRODUCTION

This chapter outlines the parameters and characteristics of a 'developmental approach' to urban transport planning. The first part of the chapter offers a theoretical presentation and the latter an illustration of such an approach consistent with principles of integrated urban infrastructure development programming (IUIDP) proposed for Indonesia.

The IUIDP framework described is one which commences with the recognised need for a policy study of a country's urban transport sub-sector and focuses on the requirements of cities of different sizes and characteristics. The developmental approach advocates the use of a sketch-planning method capable of implementation at low cost at the municipal level designed to encourage the use of the transport modes and related infrastructure that most efficiently contribute to IUIDP objectives.

This planning approach is presented in a professional environment where current expertise in urban transport planning rests more on developments in planning *for* urban transport than on *planning* transport for urban development. This is because those involved in transport are well equipped with tools and techniques to design and plan operationally more efficient networks but lack the expertise to provide transport systems that are also effective in terms of achieving pre-set development goals.

In view of this situation and the increasingly huge investments being made in the urban transport sub-sector of the Third

World (see Chapter 2), it is necessary to ask whether these investments are, in fact, 'adequate', 'effective' and 'justified'.

Goals and benefits of urban development associated with transport planning as a result need not only to be well articulated but capable of disaggregation for both targeted socio-economic groups and particular geographical areas. This contrasts with more conventional approaches to urban transport planning which have in the past paid less attention to this aspect by presuming that the efficient operation of transport systems as a rule automatically yields positive development spin-offs. Although this assumption has attracted considerable investment, it is nevertheless inadequately researched and not necessarily substantiated by project experiences.

COMPARATIVE EXPERIENCES IN URBAN TRANSPORT PLANNING

Goals of Transport Planning

It has already been argued in earlier contributions to this book that whereas industrialised countries have traditionally placed a great deal of emphasis on consumption and economic growth as the main generators of development, it has become increasingly apparent that the different circumstances of Third World countries warrant an alternative emphasis and mix of priorities. Economic and development functions of urban transport planning practice thus pose very different questions in the Third World than in the industrialised world.

Since many countries of the Third World (particularly the poorest but excluding the NICs) have not experienced the consistent benefits of economic growth to a widespread degree, they cannot presume their development aims will be automatically well served by trends of *laissez-faire* economics and associated infrastructure provision. For this reason, the governments of many of these nations see the need for their active participation in their own development process. This is especially necessary as the private sector of many Third World countries is usually not strong enough to sustain the development pace required to channel efforts towards the achievement of specific national goals and policies. The implication of this on the urban transport sub-sector is that, whereas industrialised countries have by and large relied upon a greater degree of free market forces in both urban land and transport developments, the resources needed for this approach are insufficient in most Third World countries, whatever their development aims. While much can be gained by stimulating private sector initiatives, the wholesale re-orientation towards privatisation and away from public sector planning and co-ordination, is an approach that many Third World countries can ill afford given their limited resources and the need to tackle development problems on a wide, multi-sectoral front.

Types of Resource Constraints

At least four kinds of constraints make many of the underlying assumptions and goals associated with conventional urban transport planning studies in the Third World inappropriate (see Chapter 5). They include shortages of:

1. institutional resources to plan, co-ordinate and manage the transport system;
2. financial resources to invest, construct and maintain transport infrastructure and hardware;
3. technological resources required to modernise transport systems and their services; and
4. skilled manpower resources to maintain and operate the system adequately.

The above types of resources have traditionally been more readily available in the industrialised countries, which have long had a distinct advantage over Third World nations through their ready access to financial resources, and to accumulated skilled manpower. They furthermore possess well-developed institutional resources and have continued access to indigenous new technologies. Only since the recession periods as from 1973 have some in the industrialised countries begun to appreciate many of the real resource constraints in the urban transport sub-sector that much of the Third World has been grappling with for many generations.

ELEMENTS OF A DEVELOPMENTAL APPROACH TO URBAN TRANSPORT PLANNING (1)

Principles of Urban Development Planning

Before detailing prerequisites of a 'developmental approach' to urban transport planning, it is prudent to outline the scope and principles of urban development planning and its potential contribution to transport planning in urban areas.

The tradition of urban development planning has been described (after Dimitriou and Safier, 1982), as:

> ....one founded upon the systematic application of evaluation criteria derived from the diagnosis of urban development seen as a process of social, economic, technological and physical change that has been managed (or mis-managed) by government operations and interventions.

Urban development planning is based upon the premise that selected and organised guidance in the planning of urban areas and the management of public sector action can enhance the productive potentials and distribution of opportunities in cities. It takes as its unit of operation, individual cities and towns which it regards as 'public enterprises', each with its own contribution to the overall national development of the country. In so doing, urban development planning takes into account four principal considerations; namely:

1. the role of urban areas in achieving national development strategies;
2. the role of urban areas in contributing to rural and regional development economies and policies;
3. the capacity of urban areas simultaneously to generate economic wealth and provide for the 'basic needs' of its own population; and
4. the capacity of urban areas to provide for the absorption of migrants.

The principles and practice of urban development planning are not intended to replace the already operational traditions of urban planning, town and country planning, or urban traffic and transport planning. Rather, they are intended to support a continuing dialogue with other types of planning - whether based upon scale, subject or sector. The model and format of this dialogue is, of course, open to debate. The debate, however, should be a continuous and evolving one, since this enhances the understanding of the relationships involved. What follows is a presentation of one such model for the treatment of the relationship of transport to urban development in which the former is seen to be subservient to the latter.

Guidelines for a Developmental Approach to Urban Transport Planning

As the criticism of the failures of urban planning have mounted, and as consequent attempts to improve the concept of 'development' utilised in such planning exercises have taken place (see Chapter 1) a series of interrelated development planning performance criteria have evolved. These are applicable to elements of the urban economy, society and their environment, and may be grouped into four sets of equally important development facets. These are (Dimitriou and Safier, 1982):

1. the creation and maintenance of growth of real resources per capita;
2. the decrease of poverty and deprivation;
3. the encouragement of increased accessibility to, and responsiveness of public sector decision-making in urban affairs; and
4. the promotion of more adaptable spatial and physical arrangements of urban infrastructure to accommodate community needs as well as social and cultural identities.

When applied to urban transport, the translation of these four performance criteria suggest the following development guidelines:

1. With regard to the creation and maintenance of growth of resources per capita, urban transport systems need to be planned, provided and operated in a manner whereby they:
    a)   stimulate economic growth by means of simultaneously increasing the appropriate and efficient use of ex-

isting local resources and avoiding the use of transport technologies which are not consistent with the development constraints of the study area;

b) improve the mobilisation of presently unused or idle resources, so that the best use is made of existing transport facilities through improved management and administration before additional facilities are provided; and

c) maximise energy conservation and minimise negative ecological and environmental impacts, penalising for example, motorised vehicles typically associated with excessive air pollution (which in the case of non-petrol producing countries, would also reduce the expenditure of valuable foreign exchange).

2. With regard to decreasing poverty and deprivation, urban transport systems need to be planned, provided and operated in a manner whereby they:

a) decrease the inequality of access to transport services and in the provision of transport infrastructure for different groups which, for example, may be achieved by subsidising selected public transport fares or operations for the poor;

b) improve the opportunities for the less privileged through the provision of public transport services linking, for example, the places where they live with those of work, education, recreation; and

c) improve the capacity of the city to accommodate the basic needs of the majority of inhabitants by providing not only essential means of transport but also, through such efforts, by generating additional associated employment opportunities. This entails avoiding indiscriminate restrictions on useful informal public transport operations (and their related repair and manufacturing activities), purely in the interests of increased government control over the transport sector.

3. With regard to promoting an increase in the accessibility to local decision-making and administration of urban affairs, urban transport systems need to be planned, provided and operated in a manner whereby active government support is given to local groups involved in providing and maintaining additional transport capacity outside the formal sector.

This, for example, can be done by central government selectively providing grants, loans and advice on local transport technology improvements to help raise the performance of the local urban transport sub-sector and make it more self-sufficient.

4. With regard to promoting an increase in the adaptability of urban areas spatially and physically better to accommodate community needs that are consistent with their cultural and social identity, urban transport systems need to be planned, provided and operated in a way whereby they support desirable urban form patterns, city structures and development densities, in harmony with the historical evolution of the settlement and its resource constraints. In this way, new transport technologies which dramatically and indiscriminantly alter the social life styles of a society for the worse, and impose new urban form patterns contrary to those planned for, should wherever possible be prohibited.

Of the above, it can be said that the first set of criteria is particularly pertinent to transport technology and production considerations. The second refers especially to issues of transport pricing, levels of mobility and the contribution of transport to meeting basic needs. The third set has relevance to the organisation and management of transport, especially measures concerning informal paratransit modes. The fourth set has to do with the design and arrangement of transport systems and their integration with the city as a whole, together with its constituent parts.

MATCHING URBAN POLICY, TRANSPORT TECHNOLOGY AND SETTLEMENT SIZE CONSIDERATIONS

The Need for a Theoretical Framework

The guidelines above are intended to encourage the use of developmentally more effective and operationally more efficient transport systems and technologies consistent with national and local development goals and resource constraints. The practical application of such guidelines, however, warrants a more structured planning framework that relates the performance of different transport technologies to the size of settlements, their related movement needs, and to the development policies of the contexts in which they operate.

A framework of this kind, presented by the author (see Dimitriou, 1989), incorporates 'operational efficiency' measures of a range of transport technologies presented by Bouladon (1967a and 1967b) and Sasaki (1970), as well as criteria measuring the levels of 'developmental effectivness' of urban transport systems of the kind advocated by the author in earlier writings (see Dimitriou, 1977; Dimitriou and Safier, 1982; and Banjo and Dimitriou, 1983).

Transport Technology and Operational Efficiency

Bouladon, in his seminal research at the Battelle Institute, Geneva, in which he investigated the operational engineering efficiency of various transport systems (1967a), identified two transport gaps (see Figure 12.1):

1. one occurring between pedestrians and car users on the urban scale, and
2. the other occurring between the conventional aeroplane and the space travelling rocket.

The concern of this chapter, is with the first of these 'gaps'. However, to appreciate the significance of Bouladon's work as it relates to Third World cities, one first needs to elaborate upon his use of the 'Unified Theory of Transport' in which each transport mode is seen to have its own rightful place among a spectrum of modes from the point of view of demands made upon it.

The theory is briefly outlined below in the form of a paraphrased extract from an article by Bouladon in the Science Journal (1967a):

> ....The diagram (see Figure 12.1) emphasises that, as one might expect, the greatest demand (for transport) is for very short distance transport. The graph shown is really three dimensional. It forms a tri-angle, the top line of which represents optimum use as defined by maximum satisfaction to users. The line below represents the point at which 50 per cent of the

Figure 12.1: The Transport Gaps

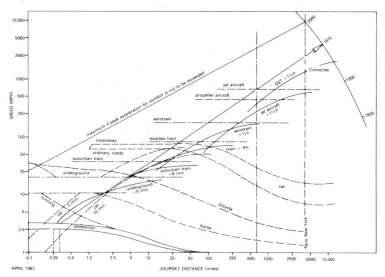

Source: Redrawn from Bouladon, 1967b.

Note: DEMAND FOR SPEED is closely related to distance to be travelled; greater distances always demand greater speed. With time, all forms of transport tend to become faster, as shown by the pivot arrow. All systems falling above this pivot can be regarded as fast enough, those falling below as too slow. Dotted horizontal lines show the theoretical performance of transport systems and continuous curves show practical performance, including waiting time. When the car was not widely used, and average waiting time on a car journey was 3 minutes, it compared favourably with many other forms of transport. Now that waiting time is at least 10 minutes, the car is far less satisfactory and falls below the pivot line. Uppermost line shows limits imposed by acceleration and suggests it will never be possible to cross the Atlantic in less than one hour (assuming maximum allowable acceleration of 0.25 *g*); this limit may be reached by 1990. Figure also highlights importance of transfer systems.

users would declare themselves satisfied and thus marks a lower limit for reasonable use.

In each of the five areas into which the figure is divided there should be an optimum means of transport. In practice, this is so only in three areas in which pedestrian, car and air transport dominate the whole hierarchy of transport. Between these three regions many other methods of transport are currrently in use, but they give less satisfaction. It can be seen

> therefore that there are two signficant transport gaps,
> one in the second area and the other in the fourth ......

When referring to Bouladon's findings it must be appreciated that they are based solely on observations from industrialised countries. Had he extended his research to
encompass Third World nations, particularly those of Southeast
Asia, Bouladon would have found the first of his 'transport gaps'
not so immediately apparent. For there is in fact a wide selection
of non-motorised transport modes in this part of the world that actually bridge this transport gap (see Ocampo, 1982 and Chapters
3 and 4). This suggests that the transport planner has, as a result,
a much broader basis upon which to plan urban movement in
Southeast Asia than his counterpart in industrialised countries.
The editors of this book have argued (Banjo and Dimitriou, 1982)
that many traditional transport planning practices in the Third
World are, in fact, in danger of creating the very 'transport gap'
Bouladon has identified at the urban scale, because of the failure
to design adequate and appropriate infrastructure for non-
motorised modes, and in some instances, indiscriminately banning
their operation.

Transport Technology and Settlement Hierarchy

Although Bouladon's main interest was in the development of new
transport systems and the more efficient use of existing modes, his
work did much to popularise the transport hierarchy concept first
developed by Sasaki and subsequently employed as a corner-stone
to the 'developmental approach' to urban transport planning for
Indonesia.

The work of Sasaki conducted at the Athens Centre of Ekistics (1970) sought to correlate transport technology efficiency to
settlement size. His thesis rested on the assumption that a given
type and size of settlement requires a consonant type of transport
mode, and that if the internal organisation of a settlement follows
a hierarchical pattern it may have several types of transport modes
serving different functions and distances operating at maximum
efficiency.

Sasaki concluded that the absence of a hierarchy of transport technologies consonant with the needs of a settlement hierarchy is one of the fundamental causes of many urban transport

problems. He subsequently argued that since settlement growth and transport development are closely interrelated, urban transport technologies must match the needs of the settlements they serve.

Sasaki substantiated his conclusions by positively relating the hierarchy of a settlement with its constituent communities and hierarchy of trip distribution frequencies for each type of community. He thereby concluded that different kinds of communities within the same settlement generate a demand for consonant means of transport.

Observations from Sasaki's research suggest that:

1.   motorcar use is most efficient in cities with populations in excess of 300,000;
2.   because there is often no appropriate transport mode for the kind of trip-making usually associated with communities and settlements with populations of 300,000 and less, the use of the motorcar in such circumstances constitutes a sub-optimal use of transport technology; and
3.   more generally, settlements and their transport systems are too often poorly integrated.

Sasaki's work, like Bouladon's research, was also confined to cities in the industrialised world, and as such his conclusions warrant re-examination in the light of different development contexts. Even so, it should be emphasised that the principle of seeking to correlate a hierarchy of transport technologies with that of a settlement and community hierarchy is pertinent whatever development context one works within, as confirmed by Zahavi (1980).

Policy Context, Transport Technology and Settlement Hierarchy

For the work of Bouladon and Sasaki to be made relevant to cities in the Third World, much more needs to be known about how development circumstances and policies of the environments in which transport technologies operate affect transport operation.

Apart from the more conventional categorisation of Third World environments of the kind discussed in Chapter 1, development contexts may also be identified by making reference to:

1.   their level of resource constraints (and riches);
2.   the nature of their institutional and political contexts; and
3.   the kind of national development policies and priorities employed.

Various combinations of these features generate different development contexts and policies within which transport technologies operate and city growth takes place. What this suggests is that whilst a specific transport system may in accordance with Bouladon's and Sasaki's criteria be considered most appropriate for a city of a particular size, the local unavailability of certain resources such as the technical expertise to manage, operate and maintain this system, could transform the systems' viability into one which is not developmentally practical, until such time as other actions are taken.

A similar conclusion may be arrived at for very different reasons, regarding the introduction of a technically superior urban transport system, which if it makes a large number of persons unemployed in an economy where unemployment is already very high, can be called into question on development grounds.

In order to illustrate further and more explicitly the value of injecting development considerations into technical aspects of transport planning for Third World cities, the remaining part of this chapter outlines a 'developmental approach' to urban transport planning proposed for settlements in Indonesia.

TOWARDS A DEVELOPMENTAL APPROACH TO URBAN TRANSPORT PLANNING IN INDONESIA (2)

Background

In the light of the government of Indonesia's decentralisation policies and its concern for the implications of fast-rising rates of urbanisation, there is a growing realisation that settlements other than the capital and the four largest provincial cities, now have an increasingly important role to play in national development and associated efforts at arresting trends of over-urbanisation and achieving a more balanced population distribution.

Since both public transport and road infrastructure facilities in Indonesian cities are limited, and given the critical role transport plays in the well-being of such settlements (see Chapter 1), central government with selected municipalities (under the management of an inter-ministerial co-ordinating committee - *Tim Ko-ordinasi*) have recently embarked upon an integrated urban infrastructure development programme (IUIDP). One very important component of the programme is the planning and development of transport services and related road infrastructure.

To assist in the implementation of this programme, the Ministry of Public Works and UNDP/UNCHS commissioned a study (TDC S.A., 1988) to recommend national guidelines for the urban transport sub-sector that are consistent with IUIDP objectives. The study recommends a planning approach and a set of techniques based on: windscreen surveys of five settlements of different sizes (3), a literature review of numerous government and consultancy reports, plus other technical literature which build on many of the ideas articulated earlier in this chapter, regarding:

1. principles of urban development planning;
2. the concept of an integrated transport hierarchy for urban areas;
3. the need to match transport hierarchies with settlement hierarchies; and
4. the moulding of transport technology proposals with characteristics of the development context and policies of the situation under study.

The recommended approach also draws upon several of the concepts and techniques advocated elsewhere in this book, namely:

1. urban traffic modelling with limited data (see Chapter 9);
2. urban transport corridor planning (see Chapter 10); and
3. street management (see Chapter 11).

In arriving at the recommended study guidelines, the consultants employed two underlying principles. First, that the kind of errors observed in many of the bigger cities of the industrialised world associated with full-scale attempts at meeting the needs of the private motorcar should be avoided. Second, that there is an urgent requirement in Indonesia to shift attention to planning and managing the movement needs of small and intermediate sized cities.

Identifying Indonesia's development context as one which is resource-rich but severely constrained by public sector funds, rapid population growth and the maldistribution of its population, the UNDP/UNCHS sponsored study advocates that those involved in urban transport investment decisions take into account the following:

1. National development policies concerning urbanisation, population distribution, energy consumption and manpower development - a recently completed national urbanisation and strategic development study (NUDS) of Indonesia (UNDP/UNCHS, 1985) provides useful background information regarding national urbanisation policies as they affect urban transport.

2. Ongoing/existing settlement policies, plans, and programmes, especially of intermediate and small sized cities - most such settlements do not possess urban development plans, let alone plans for future transport movement, even though they are widely recognised prerequisites to effective transport planning exercises.

3. Transport technologies (both of the formal and informal sectors) and their relative operational efficiency - the wide choice of transport modes available in Indonesian cities warrants study with a view to arriving at assessment of urban transport operations efficiency along the lines advocated by Bouladon.

4. Transport technology and urban patterns - following an analysis of the operational performance and potential of various urban transport modes of the kind suggested above, further study is called for along the lines advocated by Sasaki to investigate the suitability of different modes of transport for cities of particular sizes and urban form patterns.

5. Institutional support to oversee and execute urban transport schemes and proposals - these have been diagnosed as extremely weak in Indonesia at the municipality level. Efforts at strengthening central and local institutional support for transport have already been embarked upon in the five largest cities (Dimitriou, 1988). Similar efforts are now required for other cities.

6. Capital, manpower and material resources available to plan, manage, operate and maintain proposed urban transport projects - although public resources available to the In-

donesian urban transport sub-sector are severely over-stretched, those of the private sector (both formal and informal) have yet to be fully exploited and co-ordinated, and thus offer substantial scope for future increased participation.

National Urban Transport Policy Considerations

The approach to urban transport planning recommended by the UNDP/UNCHS funded study emphasises, at the national level, the function of urban transport in its 'facilitating role', whereby urban areas are seen as intersections of the nation's highways (Gakenheimer et al, 1984). It also highlights the 'service of freight function', particularly for food and semi-processed agricultural products related to consumption requirements of urban areas.

At the city level, the approach emphasises the role of urban transport in its 'link function'. For whilst the importance of transport to urban development is multi-dimensional, its prime purpose is to link together residence and employment, as well as producers and users of goods and services (see Chapter 1). Additionally important is the 'stimulant function', whereby urban transport systems are seen to influence the provision of other urban infrastructure, such as solid waste, drainage and electricity networks. The 'employment function' is also recognised to be of considerable significance, both where transport is an important employer in its own right and where it acts as a stimulant to the creation of employment opportunities.

Additional considerations taken into account by the proposed approach include:

1. on the transport demand side - the settlement's physical characteristics, socio-economic features, and local travel patterns;
2. on the transport supply side - the nature and condition of the urban transport system, and related transport cost and investment considerations; and
3. regarding institutional and financial policy matters - the complexity of the urban transport sub-sector's institutional framework and related agency responsibilities, plus associated institution-building and financial management requirements.

Urban Transport Demand

Physical Characteristics of Settlements. Physical aspects of urban development seen to influence travel demand and taken into account in the urban transport planning approach advocated, include considerations of city size, settlement structure, urban form and topography. Whilst there is insufficient space to discuss each of these fully here, it is relevant to point out that recent studies in Indonesia suggest that small cities with populations of between 20,000 and 100,000 (of which there are 369 - see Table 12.1) tend to generate short trips. Observations (Gakenheimer et al, 1984 and TDC S.A., 1988) indicate that there are few problems with non-motorised travel in such settlements, apart from the need for competent traffic management measures and improved roads. In intermediate sized cities of 100,000 to 500,000 inhabitants (of which there are 27), average trip lengths begin to reach levels at which motorised travel takes on increased importance.

Table 12.1   Size, Distribution and Growth of Indonesia's Cities and Towns, 1980

Size of City	Total Inhabitants in Cities of this Size (million)	Number of Cities (% per Year)	Average Population (% per year)(a) 1961–71	1971–80
Less than 20,000	4.3	369 ⎫		
20,000–100,000	6.8	293 ⎭	3.0	3.2
100,000–500,000	6.1	27	2.4	3.8
500,000–1 million	2.5	4 ⎫		
More than 1 million	13.1	5 ⎭	3.5	4.1
Total	21.8	698	3.2	3.9

Source: Adopted from Table 9, Hamer, A., Steer, D. and Williams, D.G. 1986, Indonesia: The Challenge of Urbanization, World Bank Staff Working Paper No. 787, IBRD, Washington DC, Adapted from Table 9.

The threshehold at which more complex urban travel patterns commence occurs in settlements with populations of between 100,000 and 150,000 (TDC S.A., 1988). In large cities of between 500,000 and 1,000,000 inhabitants (of which there are four) trip lengths increase to a point where walking to work is no longer a realistic option. This class of settlement is growing at the fastest rate in Indonesia and potentially presents the greatest problems regarding the use of motorised vehicles in central areas.

Urban areas in excess of 1,000,000 inhabitants (of which there are five) receive most attention. These are especially prone to the development of multi-nuclear urban patterns of the absorbing settlements on the surrounding periphery. This exerts additional pressure on new infrastructure investments and results in longer average trip distances, the development of heavy corridor movements, more traffic congestion, and the increased marginalisation of non-motorised travel.

Socio-economic Features of a Settlement. Two of a city's most influential socio-economic characteristics affecting travel demand are changing profiles of the household (a key domestic decision-making unit determining travel choice) and its community structure. In the former are included changes in household size, income, vehicle ownership, and age and sex structures. Of these variables, household studies indicate income to be an overriding factor in the choice of travel mode. Soegijoko (1986) has revealed cycle rickshaws (*becaks*) and motorcycles used as public transport (*ojeks*) to be the most common public transport mode for those whose monthly disposable income exceeds Rp 50,000 (US$77). Bus transport was revealed to be popular with those with spending power over Rp 25,000 (US$38) per month. The same research showed that the motorcar is most favoured by those with monthly expenditures in excess of Rp 100,000 (US$154) and that household heads with a monthly disposable income of less than Rp 25,000 per month are hard pressed to make a transport mode choice they can afford.

Considerations of community structure are also important in determining transport demand because the travel patterns it generates reflect the hierarchies of urban activities that such communities accommodate. This is particularly apparent in Indonesia, where settlements are made up of a hierarchy of formally assigned communities (see Table 12.2):

1. the *Kecamatans* (with populations between 20,000 and 100,000 inhabitants),
2. the *Kelurahans* (between 3,000 and 20,000 inhabitants),
3. the *Rukan Wargas* (between 1,000 and 3,000 inhabitants), and
4. the *Rukun Tetanggas* (between 150 and 1,000 inhabitants).

These are all units of community governance which offer promising opportunities for self-help and locally funded projects.

Table 12.2 Typical Community Size and Trip Length
Characteristics in Indonesia

Community Level or City Size	Median Population	Median Area (ha)	Typical Trip Length (km)
Rukun Tetanggas	250	2.5	0.08
Rukun Warga	1,500	15	0.19
Kelurahan	10,000	100	0.5
Kecamatan	70,000	700	1.3
Medium City	300,000	3,000	2.8
Large City	750,000	7,500	4.4

Source: TDC S.A., 1988.

Local Travel Patterns. An obvious expression of urban transport demand is travel patterns. Details of observed average speed and trip lengths for principal urban transport modes in Indonesia are given in Table 12.3. Numerous studies confirm walking to be critically important, irrespective of settlement size. Even in the Greater Jakarta (DKI) area, estimates indicate that one third of all person movements are on foot (Buchanan and Partners et al, 1983). The proportion of walk trips is anticipated to be even greater in smaller settlements where trip distances are far more conducive to this mode of travel. Second to walking as a mode of urban travel is public transport. Most public transport trips are undertaken for work and education purposes. In larger cities such as Bandung, they take between 10 to 30 minutes for distances of between 1 and 5 kms (Soegijoko, 1986). In intermediate sized cities such as Yogyakarta, travel times are significantly less, with almost half of the trips covering distances of between 0.4 to 1.5 kms (Kartodirdjo, 1981).

Urban Transport Supply

The Transport System. Between 1973 and 1984 private car registrations nearly doubled in Indonesia (much of this growth concentrated in urban areas). The number of registered trucks

Table 12.3   Average Speed and Trip Lengths by Urban
            Transport Modes

	Average Speed (km/h)	Average Trip length (km)
Pedestrian	3.5	1.1
Becak	5.3	2.3
Public transport (Bus)	7.8	4.4
Bicycle	6.0	2.8
Motorcycle	9.0	5.6
Car	8.3	4.9

Source: TDC S.A., 1988.

and buses for the same period more than tripled (UNDP/UNCHS, 1985). In contrast to these trends, the increase in the provision of urban road infrastructure has been very slow - only eight kilometers of new roads (excluding toll roads) were added each year to the national urban road network for the same period.

A survey of 64 cities in Indonesia, excluding Jakarta (Ministry of Home Affairs, 1983) revealed, furthermore, that 50 per cent of the mileage of the main urban network was physically deficient and 32 per cent would be unable to carry anticipated traffic volumes by the end of the current Five Year Plan period. Unless remedial measures are taken, it is feared that rapid growth in the demand for transport together with the excessive amount of deferred road maintenance will produce widespread poor urban road conditions on a scale that will be detrimental to both national and regional traffic movement, as well as local urban development.

An analysis of infrastructure provision in small and intermediate sized cities in Indonesia (Gakenheimer et al, 1984) indicated a widespread need for through-road widening to dual-carriageway standards, greater emphasis on traffic management, an extension of public transport services, as well as additional regulations concerning informal public transport operations. Larger cities of 500,000 and more inhabitants are reported by the same source urgently to require the completion of by-passes, updated strategic land-use/transport plans (including O&D surveys). They also need better consultation and co-ordination among government agencies, commercial interests, transport operators and representatives of the public, as well as improved financial management; and sufficient public transport services at an affordable cost to the public at large.

Provision of Public Transport Services. The rich of mix of public transport modes (legal and illegal) operating in urban areas of Indonesia has evolved in response to diverse levels of affordability and need. In the larger settlements, public transport services are made up of city buses, motorised paratransit vehicles (including minibuses) and *becaks* - although it should be stressed that these modes are rarely co-ordinated. The low capital requirements of more traditional modes, such as the *becak*, the *gerobak*, (goods-carrying cart pushed or pulled by a pedestrian), and the *delman* (a type of horse-drawn carriage), especially predominant in cities of 500,000 inhabitants and below, have different capital and operation requirements, both in terms of money and labour.

While not all cities operate regular bus services, where they do exist they are run by government-owned or subsidised companies on fixed routes with scheduled services and set routes. Such services provide the backbone of the formal public transport system for the capital and five other large cities in Indonesia. Also operated on fixed routes (but not to a fixed schedule) are minibuses which constitute the predominant mode of motorised public transport in most cities of 300,000 inhabitants and above.

Transport Costs and Investments. Funding levels and financial mechanisms for urban transport throughout Indonesia are deficient. This is borne out by the fact that although urban roads account for 15 per cent of the national mileage, they only receive 8 per cent of road financing against 16 per cent devoted to public transport (see Gakenheimer et al, 1984).

In terms of fares per passenger/kilometer, after the taxi the highest in Indonesian urban areas are for pedicabs (*bajaj*), and the cheapest (following the *becak*) for buses. Public transport studies (Soegijoko, 1986) indicate that revenues per passenger/kilometer is lowest for the bus and highest for the *bajaj*. Comparing revenue to costs, the same source suggests *becaks* have the highest ratio, followed by the bus and minibus. The lowest ratio of revenue to cost is offered by the *bajaj*. Buses clearly require the greatest investment, while *becaks* require the least. Minibuses yield the quickest financial return on capital, and buses the slowest.

Of all urban transport modes in the country, bus and freight traffic are more seriously affected by congestion than are private cars because of the importance of labour costs, the lesser degree of flexibility in timing, and losses through uncertain schedules and delayed delivery times.

Institutional and Financial Management

Complexity of Agency Responsibilities. A number of government agencies are involved in the urban transport sub-sector at the national level in Indonesia (see Figure 12.2). Their functional relationship is complex and their realms of responsibility often overlap (Buchanan and Partners et al, 1983). At the municipality level, the formal allocation of responsibilities in the sub-sector appears similar in most cities but in practice there are significant variations.

Figure 12.2:   National Level Urban Transport Project
Organisation Chart for Indonesia

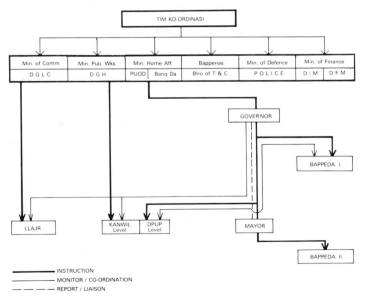

An executive body (*Tim Ko-ordinasi*) with representatives of all key national agencies involved in urban development has recently been set up to try and facilitate the interface of different agencies in the field. The agency is among other things, responsible for the preparation of national urban transport policy and guidelines, plus the co-ordination of large urban sector projects requiring inter-ministerial involvement.

Institution Building. Since an integrated approach to urban transport planning at the local level is unlikely to come about through the mere establishment of a new national co-ordinating body (however powerful it may be), it is now widely recognised in Indonesian government circles that municipal institution building aimed at enhancing local government capabilities (especially in financial management) is a prerequisite to the successful implementation of projects.

The institutional framework for Indonesia's urban sector has therefore recently experienced transition and a re-orientation toward a more inter-ministerial and inter-sectoral approach to project development and implementation, reflecting the principles of IUIDP. One of the main aims of this re-orientation is ultimately to develop an institutional municipal capacity (at least in the larger cities) enabling cities to appraise and implement their own projects with little if any assistance from central government.

Funding Sources and Revenues. Funding for urban services in Indonesia has for some time now predominantly come from central government sources (some of it from property tax) through sectoral development expenditures or the grant system. Recent government of Indonesia estimates indicate that central funding covers approximately 64 per cent of total services, while local (provincial and municipal) government sources account for the remaining 36 per cent. The relative proportion of central government financing for urban services varies considerably - from a low of 4 per cent for public transport to over 60 per cent for urban roads and traffic management.

Among the most important provincial government revenues from the transport sector are incomes from royalties on gasoline tax (accounting in 1983/4 for 3 per cent of provincial tax revenues); taxes on ownership of motor vehicles (yielding in the same period 40 per cent of provincial government revenues); and the transfer of motor vehicle tax (accounting for 56.6 per cent of such revenues over the same period). In addition to these, provincial governments impose user charges (i.e. *retribusi* and *dinas* incomes) for public utilities and services for water supply, medical treatment, parking, bus terminals, taxi stands etc. These make up the largest category of provincially administered and locally-generated income which (with better management) holds the most promise for cost recovery in the urban sector.

APPLYING IUIDP PRINCIPLES TO URBAN TRANSPORT PLANNING IN INDONESIA

Issues and Principles

In the context of the aforementioned background, the study conducted by TDC S.A. advocates the use of Indonesia's guidelines for national development planning (*GBHN*) and programming (*Repelita*) as the starting point of its proposed approach to urban transport planning within a policy framework of integrated urban infrastructure development programming (IUIDP) (see Figure 12.3).

Issues. The approach is intended to confront various issues at the national and urban level.

Regarding national development functions of urban transport, it can help discover the most effective way of enhancing the sub-sector's national administrative and management capacities, of creating sufficient new resources for the sub-sector, and of introducing measures to arrest the rapid growth in vehicle ownership. The existing fragmentation of policies concerning the sub-sector is also a problem to be tackled with this approach.

Regarding city development functions of urban transport, the approach can indicate what action to take to deal with the problem of inadequate and poorly integrated public transport services, of insufficient infrastructure (especially in local communities), and of central government imposing road improvements not in keeping with master plan priorities.

Where urban transport demand is concerned, the issues are the pace at which central area congestion should be allowed to increase, how future traffic should be dispersed, how best to tackle the transport needs of those who work and live in the same locality,

Figure 12.3: Tracing National Development Strategies Through to Urban Transport Sub-Sector

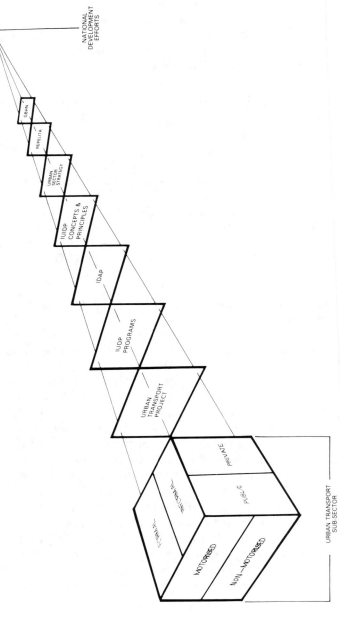

Source: Redrawn from Figure 4.1 TDC S.A., 1988.

and how to respond to the continued rapid increase in motorcycle ownership and use.

Two further issues are concerned with the supply of urban transport and its institutional and financial management. With regard to supply, the problems are how to match functional classifications of urban roads with their capacities and geometric characteristics, the range of transport modes to encourage in different types of cities and their integration. In the long run, however, the important questions are not those of investment levels but of selecting non-transport policies which promote better patterns of travel demand within available resources.

Regarding institutional and financial management in urban transport the questions are whether to establish throughout the country new multi-modal public transport authorities, and how best to overcome staff shortages in the sub-sector at the municipal level. It is also important to know what to do where city agencies have developed low-cost proposals generating strong local benefits but have insufficient resources; and what kind of government credits, loans and subsidies (if any) should be provided for urban public transport operators.

Principles. In order to bring the planning and management response to urban transport in line with IUIDP principles employed in other urban sub-sectors in Indonesia, the UNDP/UNCHS commissioned study emphasised the importance of certain measures. One of these is the optimisation of existing transport infrastructure and services before providing additional facilities. Another is the co-ordination and synchronisation of road infrastructure improvements with the programming of other related facilities. The planning and programming of transport facilities needs to be integrated with other urban development programmes. Finally, revenues must be generated locally from the road transport sub-sector to assist its further funding.

The application of IUIDP principles in the urban transport sub-sector is especially supportive of selected low-cost traffic management schemes and road maintenance efforts, as well as the rehabilitation of surfaced and unsurfaced roads and footpaths essential to the development of local communities. It also by implication, gives priority to the importance of strengthening the technical and managerial capabilities of provincial and municipal agency staff concerned with the preparation and implementation of transport projects.

IUIDP represents a cross-sectoral and multi-agency approach to urban transport and as such requires all parties concerned at each level to understand and agree on at least six fundamental principles. These are:

1. Transport infrastructure and service improvement in support of strategic self-sustaining economic growth - this implies that plans and projects which stimulate self-generating economic growth, especially at the local level, would receive the highest ranking in plan evaluation and project appraisal.

2. Urban transport in the service of basic needs of the economically weaker sections of the community - this indicates that plans and projects which assist the economically weaker members of the community and help them become more productively involved in the economy will receive high priority in plan evaluation and project appraisal.

3. Multi-sector integration of urban infrastructure development efforts - this suggests that urban transport facility plans and projects which limit the duplication of efforts in the provision of infrastructure and recommend balanced investments among various sub-sectors will also receive high ranking.

4. The adoption of low cost transport solutions - this ensures that transport plans and projects which save resources, be it by investment synchronisation or use of low-cost technologies and methods, should also receive high ranking.

5. The employment of cost recovery principles in both public transport operations and infrastructure provision - this applies in two kinds of instances, namely when cost-recovery is a prerequisite to the plan or project going ahead, and in instances when it is not, but recognised instead as important.

6. The need for decentralisation and institutional strengthening in local government agencies responsible for urban transport - this implies that where urban transport plans and projects are to be implemented in cities with an already proven technical capability and adequate institutional support, they would receive high ranking in plan evaluation and project appraisal. Where such capability and institutional support, however, does not exist or is deemed to be weak, the ranking would be proportionately lower.

Focus on Strategic Self-sustaining Economic Growth

At the same time as it serves the transport needs of the economically weaker section of the community, an equally (some would claim more) important focus of IUIDP in urban transport planning is to service the needs of economic activities known to be highly productive and strategic to self-sustaining economic development. Such an emphasis, however, requires clarification and specification as to which urban activities are 'highly productive' and instrumental in the generation of further development.

On the understanding that opportunities for local financial participation in the urban transport sub-sector will in the future be enhanced, and that local revenue generation will increasingly help finance the sub-sector, and assuming that efforts to develop the sub-sector will be synchronised and co-ordinated with other urban development programmes, certain kinds of urban transport needs are envisaged to warrant IUIDP attention in Indonesia (TDC S.A., 1988). These are:

1. National and regional highway links passing through cities - particularly major junctions with sections of the city network, and requirements of freight traffic needs (e.g. lorry parks, lay-bys, lorry routes etc).

2. National and regional public transport services and related infrastructure, transversing, terminating and/or commencing in cities - with particular attention given to public transport terminal provision, public transport routing requirements and their service needs by local public transport facilities.

3. Selected city-wide major and minor road networks, particularly those links servicing industrial, commercial and retailing areas absent from the designated urban road hierarchy, providing access to principal traffic generators, and connecting with economically vibrant local communities.

Urban Transport in the Service of Basic Needs

Basic needs thinking in Indonesia in the context of IUIDP for transport implies priority being simultaneously assigned to the mobility needs of the 'least privileged' of urban communities and to the use of transport to generate economic growth, especially within the local economy. It also seeks the use of transport to enhance/promote access to the community and encourage the better distribution of wealth.

Basic needs thinking of this kind requires differentiation between those 'needs' perceived as important by the various tiers of government ('technically defined needs'), and those seen to be significant by city inhabitants and community residents ('end-user needs'). A related issue is the importance of giving careful attention to the allocation of priorities among declared needs so as appropriately to balance 'need-responses'.

Efforts at basic needs fulfilment will, however, inevitably encounter conflict among the numerous levels of basic need expression, the different aspects of the sub-sector, and other sub-sectors (such as water supply, housing, industry, etc.) for which clear guidelines are required. To be most useful, IUIDP guidelines must not only offer guidance in the resolution of conflicting sub-sectoral demands, but also provide a strategy for cross-sectoral urban infrastructure resource allocation, making simultaneous consistent reference to wider national development objectives and planning frameworks.

To be effective, the application of a basic needs strategy for urban transport within IUIDP requires targeting on particular communities, the disaggregation of these targeted populations, and their territorial identification. The economically weaker section of the community in Indonesia (i.e., those with incomes below US$ 250 per annum) represent on a per capita basis the poorest 40 per cent of the population. Information regarding their basic needs is best arrived at by focusing on selected low-income *kampung* areas where it is known the majority of such persons reside.

Integration of Sub-sector Urban Development Efforts

The concept of integration in the context of IUIDP is directed at the limiting of the duplication of efforts in the provision of urban infrastructure. It is also aimed at the amelioration of adverse side-effects of sectoral developments in a resource constrained environment, as well as arriving at an appropriate balance of investments between the various sub-sectors. An approach of this kind requires efforts at the co-ordination and synchronisation of projects and programmes at the three tiers of government, along inter-sectoral, inter-disciplinary and inter-agency lines, so that resources at all tiers of government may be mobilised towards the achievement of common ends.

If these principles are translated into the urban transport sub-sector of Indonesia, the above implies that the Directorate General of Highways of the Ministry of Public Works would benefit more by improving its collaboration with the Directorate General of Human Settlements in the same ministry, the Directorate General of Public Administration and Regional Autonomy, Ministry of Home Affairs, and the Directorate General of Land Transport of the Ministry of Communications, in the planning, management, maintenance, operation and construction of all levels of the urban road hierarchy. So that, for example, the Directorate General of Highways (through its provincial government representation and in collaboration with its provincial planning agencies) may select urban road projects for development, and pass them on to the Directorate General of Highways, the Ministry of Home Affairs and Ministry of Communications for funding and construction (in association with provincial and local government).

Adoption of Low-cost Solutions

Advocating (as IUIDP does) the pursuance of a low-cost approach to urban transport provision in Indonesia has several origins. The concept is derived in part from the downturn in economic circumstances as a result of declining revenues from the oil and gas sector previously relied upon to finance the bulk of central government transport infrastructure projects. It also has its origin in the realisation that the pace of urbanisation and urban traffic growth in the country is so great that high-cost solutions of the kind commonly adopted by industrialised nations cannot always be afforded nation-wide.

The emphasis placed by IUIDP on the decentralisation of responsibilities and greater participation of local populations in meeting their own needs has gradually encouraged the increased recognition of the value of low-cost approaches to transport infrastructure and service provision. It has, for example, brought to light low-cost and labour-intensive community initiatives in road construction and maintenance that have long been practised but not received the government recognition (or assistance) that they deserve.

Employment of Cost Recovery Principles

In financial terms, the corner-stones of an IUIDP approach to urban transport facility provision are the dual objectives of confining central government investment at the city level to strategic infrastructure that acts as a primer to growth opportunities expected to be taken up by the private sector; and to providing funding to economically viable projects with commitment at a satisfactory level of local government financial participation.

A combination of a change of fortunes in central government resources, and a realisation that local economic resources within urban areas have been inadequately exploited, has led to the opening-up of a host of ideas (very much encouraged by the World Bank) concerning possibilities for the generation of municipal revenues from/for the urban transport sector. Among those most commonly discussed are (TDC S.A., 1988):

1. the imposition of some kind of regional fuel tax, of which a percentage becomes a municipal revenue;
2. the stricter enforcement of parking fee collection, with the expansion of off-road car parks levying appropriate charges;
3. the derivation of a municipal revenue from the enforcement of increased property tax levels;
4. the creation of opportunities for the municipality to participate further in the benefits of 'land value capture' schemes; and
5. the issuing of municipal performance bonds.

Other examples of possible appropriate cost-recovery measures include the issuing of franchises to operators of public transport routes; the imposition of a public transport tax on registered businesses alongside public transport routes that employ more than a set number of people; the increasing of vehicle registration taxes; and the conducting of regular municipal lotteries.

Decentralisation and Municipal Institution Building

The decentralisation of basic responsibilities for implementing IUIDP, together with the concept of integration, is the backbone of IUIDP. This is because it encourages central government to support local government in the formulation, appraisal and programming of their own projects, as well as the operation, maintenance and management of urban facilities and services.

However, as indicated earlier in this chapter, one of the main issues associated with the decentralisation concept is the question of whether local government has the capability and capacity to respond adequately to the initiatives of IUIDP. For the technical and management manpower resources in even the largest provincial cities of Indonesia are insufficient to tackle the current backlog of current transport development needs, let alone anticipated future problems (Dimitriou, 1988). Such deficiencies are expected to be considerably greater in cities of smaller populations, although of course the ensuing problems are likely to be less grave.

In the context of the approach advocated above, it is essential that such specialist training be accompanied by the general dissemination of IUIDP concepts, terminologies and techniques - particularly for senior and middle management staff. This will ensure an effective marriage of sub-sector technical training to the broader IUIDP approach to urban development.

IUIDP SKETCH-PLAN METHODOLOGY FOR TRANSPORT

Methodology Guidelines and Principal Steps

What follows is a summary of a transport sketch-plan methodology, representative of a 'developmental approach' to urban transport planning that incorporates the principles articulated earlier and is capable of application at various levels. The sketch-plan method was formulated in response to a call by the Ministry of Public Works in Indonesia for a quick-response standardised approach to urban transport planning suitable as an input to IUIDP investment development assessment programmes (IDAPs)(5).

The methodology is reliant upon pre-prepared guidelines translated into supporting technical handbooks as inputs to the sketch-planning exercise, regarding (see Figure 12.4) city typologies and associated transport demand characteristics, the

409

relevance of different central and local government settlement policy and planning frameworks, simplified travel demand analysis and forecasting techniques, methods of transport mode performance assessment, priorities in transport plan evaluation and project appraisal, and infrastructure design and cost yard sticks.

Figure 12.4:   The City-Wide Transport Sketch-plan Process and Supporting Guidelines

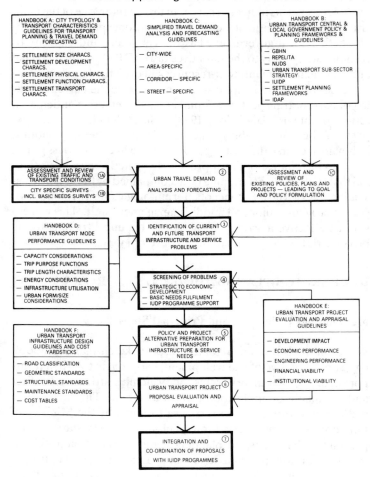

Source: Redrawn from Figure 4.6, TDC S.A., 1988.

The core of the sketch-plan approach comprises the following seven steps (see Figure 12.4):

1. An assessment and review of existing conditions - broken down into information gathering and analysis of existing urban traffic and transport conditions, selected surveys of areas for which critical data is needed, and the assessment and review of existing policies, plans, programmes and projects.

2. The undertaking of urban travel demand analysis and forecasting - by use of tailor-made computer software based upon simplified traffic forecasting techniques, employing O&D survey information, as well as traffic generation and production models with factors derived from land uses from cities in Indonesia of a similar size and kind to those under study.

3. The identification of transport infrastructure and service problems - made on a city-wide and area-specific basis, differentiating among existing and forecast problems, including problems generated by the transport sector as obstacles to the achievement of national development and IUIDP goals, problems of unmet transport needs, and obstacles to the efficient use of urban transport infrastructure and services.

4. The screening of identified problems - involving the categorisation of problems in spatial and temporal terms which impede the strategic creation of economic growth (particularly at the local level), basic needs fulfilment of the least privileged communities and households, the completing of the city's road and public transport hierarchies, and the provision of transport facilities which link IUIDP programmes and projects. These all represent measures of the developmental importance of identified problems.

5. Policy and project alternative preparation - entailing the preparation of responses to screened problems in city-wide, area-specific and project specific terms, in a manner consistent with both IUIDP principles and the transport community hierarchy concept by one or more of the following ways: physically expanding existing transport systems capacity, constructing new systems, improving transport operations through better management and financial assistance, and influencing travel demand patterns through land use control, management and policy.

411

6. Urban transport project evaluation and appraisal - in terms of a project's contribution to development objectives, and as an assessment of the availability of resources to carry out the proposed projects. The former involves an assessment of projects in terms of their environmental impact and their contribution to IUIDP objectives. The latter seeks to ensure the optimum use of resources, involving institutional and financial capability studies of the agencies implementing the projects, and an assessment of the viability of proposals, using traditional project appraisal techniques such as: Net Present Value Methods, Benefit Cost Analysis, Internal Rate of Return Methods and Payback Period Methods (see Chapter 6).

7. Integration and co-ordination of proposals with IUIDP programmes - principally achieved through the budget and the rolling five year programme of projects (IDAP) in which priority is given to transport services and road infrastructure which link areas already in receipt of IUIDP programme support or proposed for IUIDP investment, and along corridors and streets offering a viable basis for future IUIDP investments.

Special Features

The attempt to offer sensitive treatment of travel requirements of cities and communities of different characteristics and sizes, despite the use of a standardised planning methodology, is an important feature of the described 'developmental approach' to urban transport planning. The use of a settlement typology and the storage of associated information in matrix form (see Figures 12. 5 and 12.6) which dilineates characteristics affecting urban transport provision, automatically lends itself to computerised data storage. It offers a critical starting point to the building-up of an urban data bank of essential information for use in future similar low-cost settlement planning exercises.

Supportive of the idea of the use of user-friendly computerised transport planning software by municipal staff is the growing evidence in Third World countries such as Indonesia that with a little more local research and follow-up training, current state of the art personal computer software can accomodate most tasks of the kind advocated by this aspect of the sketch-plan

Figure 12.5: City Data Inventory Frameworks For
Characteristics Affecting Urban Transport
Provision

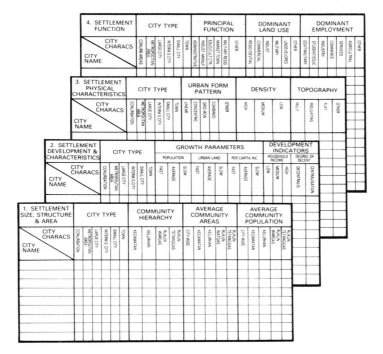

Source: Redrawn from Figure 3.7 TDC S.A., 1988.

methodology (see Harris, 1987). Steps in travel demand modelling which may at first glance seem complicated to the uninitiated,
can now be packaged as 'expert systems' for operation by those
with only the most basic of training in transport planning.

The special emphasis of the recommended approach to
urban transport planning on the appropriate use and performance
of different urban transport technologies, and the attention given
to transport mode integration by the proposed nation-wide use of
technical guidelines seeking to relate on a hierarchical basis trip
purposes and trip lengths generated by communities of different
sizes, provides an important new basis for urban transport policy-
making.

Figure 12.6: City Data Inventory Frameworks for Transport and Travel Characteristics

5. TRANSPORT & TRAVEL CHARACTERISTICS	CITY TYPE						ROAD NETWORK (INFRASTRUCTURE)																						TRANSPORT SYSTEM (SERVICES)													TRAVEL PATTERNS										
							PATTERN					HIERARCHY					CLASSIFICATION						CONDITION						MODE REGISTRATION									MODE GROWTH		TRAFFIC MIX		TRIP PURPOSE					TRIP DISTANCE			TRAFFIC GROWTH		
																													PRIVATE SECTOR				PUBLIC SECTOR																			
CITY CHARACS / CITY NAME	CONURBATION	METROPOLITAN AREA	LARGE CITY	INTERM S CITY	SMALL CITY	TOWN	LINEAR	RADIAL	CONCENTRIC	COMBINED	OTHER	MAJOR ARTERY	SECONDARY ARTERY	MAJOR COLLECTOR	SECONDARY COLLECTOR	LOCAL	CLASS I	CLASS II	CLASS III	CLASS IV	CLASS V	OTHER	GOOD	FAIR	BAD	ASPHALT	DIRT	OTHER	M/CAR	TRUCK	M/WE	CYCLE	INTER C BUS	INTRA C BUS	MINIBUS	OPELET	ETC	MOTORISED	NON MOTORISED	PRIVATE SECTOR	PUBLIC SECTOR	EDUCATIONAL	RECREATIONAL	SHOPPING	WORK	OTHER	SHORT DIST TRAVEL	AVERAGE DIST TRAVEL	LONG DIST TRAVEL	FAST	MEDIUM	SLOW

Source: Redrawn from Figure 4.1 TDC S.A., 1988.

This emphasis led to the development of the concept of 'speed bands' in the aforementioned UNDP/UNCHS study. These are city-wide continuous transport routes designed to accommodating a specific range of travel speeds and transport modes. It also encouraged in the same study the development and proposed use of a new measure of road area utilisation analogous to the passenger car unit (pcu) value that incorporates considerations of the obstruction per passenger carried to other vehicles under different road and traffic conditions, derived from studies conducted in Jakarta (see Cuthbert, 1983).

CONCLUSION

Of all the features of the 'developmental approach' to urban transport planning outlined, the low-cost character of the sketch-plan methodology and the approach's flexibility in application at various scales of urban development are among its main advantages. It is ideally applied as part of a city-wide integrated urban development planning study, utilising common guidelines (as shown in Figure 12.4) which can be employed on:

1.   an area-specific basis (e.g. for CBDs or particular communities);
2.   on a corridor basis (utilising principles of corridor planning as outlined by Gakenheimer and Meyer - see Chapter 10); and
3.   on a street basis (using principles of street management as advocated by Proudlove and Turner - see Chapter 12).

The conclusions of the UNDP/UNCHS funded study suggest however that the rapid changes experienced by urban centres in Indonesia, together with the inherent limitations of sketch-planning itself, make the use of horizon dates of more than fifteen years impractical in such contexts. Sketch-planning is thus more useful for the formulation of five year investment programmes and medium term planning exercises than for the preparation of long-term strategic plan-making.

Another limitation of the sketch-plan method highlighted by this study is the confinement of its recommended use to settlements with populations between 500,000 and 150,000. The same study argues that whilst principles of the 'developmental approach' to urban transport planning apply across the settlement hierarchy, metropolitan and larger cities possess more complicated features than can be accommodated by the proposed sketch-plan method in its present form. In the case of settlements with 150,000 inhabitants and less (especially those which are slow-growing), the same source suggests that the method is too complex for such communities and thus warrants further simplification to arrive at a more appropriate approach.

A 'developmental approach' to urban transport planning of the kind outlined above, has the potential to change radically for the better the way in which urban transport policies, plans and projects are both assessed and implemented. It is anticipated that its use will not only generate a new set of investment priorities within a context of integrated urban development but will also affect the choice of transport technologies. Its use, furthermore, is expected to generate important changes in recommended infrastructure design, particularly with regard to local transport infrastructure needs such as roads, footpaths and mixed use transport routes.

NOTES:

(1)   This part of the chapter is principally drawn from the jointly authored paper 'A Developmental Approach to Urban Transport Planning', by H.T. Dimitriou and M. Safier, first presented at the Universities Transport Study Group Seminar at University College London in 1982.

(2)   This part of the chapter is based on a study conducted for Training and Development Consultants (TDC) S.A., Lausanne, on contract to UNDP/UNCHS and the Ministry of Public Works of the Government of Indonesia between 1987/8. The study report was co-authored by the author as a consultant to TDC S.A. with Professor Budhy Soegijoko of the Institute of Technology, Bandung and Sharif Horthy, Executive Manager of TDC S.A.

(3)   The study utilised data from five settlements in Indonesia, namely: Bandung (1.46 million inhabitants, representing metropolitain sized cities); Solo (502,000 inhabitants, representing large cities); Magelang (123,000 inhabitants, representing intermediate sized cities); Salatiga (85,000 inhabi-

tants, representing small cities); and Bajarnegara (41,000 inhabitants, representing market town type settlements).

(4)   Employing an average exchange rate for 1982 (the time of the conducted survey for the research) of Rp650 to US$1.

(5)   This is a multi-sector, cross-agency five-year infrastructure development investment programme approved by central government, containing projects highlighted in terms of IUIDP priorities.

REFERENCES

Banjo, G.A. and Dimitriou, H.T. (1983) 'Urban Transport Problems of Third World Cities: The Third Generation', **Habitat International**, vol. 7, no. 3/4, Pergamon Press, Oxford.

Bouladon, G. (1967) 'The Transport Gaps', **Science Journal**, April, Associated Iliffe Press Ltd, London.

_____ (1967b) 'Transport', **Science Journal**, October, Associated Iliffe Press Ltd, London.

Colin Buchanan and Partners in association with Pamintori Cipta, TPO Sullivan & Partners, Resource Planning Consultants Ltd. (1983) 'Traffic Management and Road Network Development Study', Final Report, Ministry of Communications, Directorate General of Land Transport, Jakarta.

Cuthbert, R. (1983) 'Assessment of PCU Values', part of 'The Jakarta Traffic Management Study', **Traffic Engineering and Control**, August, Printerhall Ltd, London.

Dimitriou, H.T. (1977) 'A Call for the Effective Integration of Urban Transport Planning in Developing Countries', **Proceedings of PTRC Summer Annual Meeting**, University of Warwick, PTRC Education and Research Services, Ltd., London.

_____ (1988) 'Urban Transport and Manpower Development and Training for Four Asian Cities: A Case Study of Bandurg, Medan, Semarmg, and Surabaya, Indonesia', **Habitat International,** vol.12, no. 3, Pergamon Press, Oxford.

_____ (1989) 'The Urban Transport Planning Process and its Derivatives: An Assessment of their Contribution to the Formulation of Appropriate Guidelines for Third World Cities', Ph.D. Thesis, Department of Town Planning, University of Wales, Cardiff.

Dimitriou, H.T. and Safier, M.S. (1982) 'A Developmental Approach to Urban Trnasport Plannning', Proceedings of Universities Transport Study Group Seminar, University College, London.

Gakenheimer, R., Lennox, L. and Rogers, L. (1984) 'Urban Transportation National Urban Development Strategy', Attachment C NUDS Study, Ministry of Public Works, Government of Indonesia and UNDP/UNCHS, August, Jakarta.

Harris, B. (1987) 'A Software Package for Micro-computer Based Planning for Small Cities in Developing Countries', Unpublished Paper, University of Pennsylvania, Philadelphia.

Kartodirdjo, S. (1981) **The Pedicab in Yogyakarta**, Gajah Mada University Press, Yogyakarta.

Kusbiantoro (1979) 'Bandung: Travel Demand Analysis and its Policy Implications', University of California, Unpublished Masters Thesis, Los Angeles.

Linn, J.F. (1983) **Cities in Developing Countries**, World Bank Research Publication, Oxford University Press, Oxford.

Marler, N.W. (1985). 'Transport and the Urban Poor: A Case Study of Bandung, Indonesia', Paper Presented to Pacific Science Association, Fifth Inter-Congress on Transport and Communication in the Pacific Basin, February, Manila.

Ministry of Home Affairs (1983) 'Highway Operations and Maintenance Study', Jakarta.

Ocampo, R.B. (ed) (1982) **Low-cost Transport in Asia**, International Development Research Centre, Ottawa.

Soegijoko, B.T. (1986) 'The Becaks of Java', **Habitat International**, vol. 10, no. 1/2, Pergamon Press, Oxford.

Sasaki, Y. (1970) 'Concept of a Transport Hierarchy, Unpublished MSc. Thesis, Athens Centre of Ekistics, Athens.

Training and Development Consultants S.A. (1988) 'IUIDP Policy, Planning and Design Guidelines for Urban Road Transport', Final Report to Department of Public Works, Government of Indonesia and UNDP/UNCHS, Jakarta.

UNDP/UNCHS (1985) 'NUDS Final Report', National Urban Development Strategy Project, Directorate of City and Regional Planning, Directorate of Human Settlements, Department of Public Works, Government of Indonesia and ᵀ 'NDP/UNCHS, Jakarta.

World Bank (1985) **World Development Report,** Oxford University Press, Oxford.

Zahavi, Y. (1979) 'The UMOT Project', Prepared for US Department of Transportation and Ministry of Transport of the Federal Republic of Germany, **US Department of Transportation Report,** no. RSPA-DPB-20-79-3, Bonn and Washington DC.

Notes on Contriburtors

George A. Banjo is on the academic staff of the Department of Civil Engineering at the University of Lagos, Nigeria and sometime Director of TDC (UK).

Josef Barat is Secretary of Transportation for the State of Rio de Janeiro and formerly Chairman of the Sao Paulo Metropolitan Transportation Agency, Brazil.

John W. Dickey is professor at the Centre for Public Administration and Policy, and at the College of Architecture and Urban Studies, at Virginia Polytechnic Institute and State University, Blacksburg, Virginia, USA.

Harry T. Dimitriou currently teaches and conducts reasearch at the University of Hong Kong, and is Principal Consultant to TDC SA, Lausanne, Switzerland. He was formerly Director of the Special Programme on Urban Traffic and Transport Planning for Developing Countries at University College, London UK.

Ralph G. Gakenheimer is professor at the Department of Urban Studies and Planning, and the Department of Civil Engineering, Massachusetts Institute of Technology, Cambridge, Massachusetts, USA. He is Director of the Developing Country programmes in the former of the two departments.

Marvin L. Manheim is the W.A. Patterson Distinguished Professor at the Kellog Graduate School of Management, and teaches in the Department of Civil Engineering's Transportation Centre, Northwestern University, Chicago. He was formerly Director of the Centre for Transportation at Massachusetts Institute of Technology, Cambridge, Massachusetts, USA.

Michael D. Meyer is Director of Transportation Planning, Department of Public Works, Commonwealth of Massachusetts. He formerly conducted research at the Department of Urban Studies and Planning at Massachusetts Institute of Technology, Cambridge, Massachusetts, USA.

Alan Proudlove is Professor Emeritus of Transport Studies, Department of Civic Design, University of Liverpool, and formerly a Director of TDC (UK).

M. S. V. Rao is a professor at the Indian Institute of Management, University of Bangalore and formerly Head of the Delhi School of Planning and Architecture, India.

A. K. Sharma is professor at the Delhi School of Planning and Architecture, India.

Alan Turner is Director of Alan Turner and Associates, London, UK.

Peter R. White teaches and conducts research at the Transport Studies Group, Department of Civil Engineering, Polytechnic of Central London, UK.

Luis G. Willumsen is Director of Steer Davies and Gleave Ltd., London, U.K. He was formerly on the academic staff of the Transport Studies Group, Department of Civil Engineering, University College London.

Name index

Subject index